THE HISTORY OF THE ROYAL ACADEMY

1768–1986

Sidney C. Hutchison

Robert Royce Limited

© Sidney C. Hutchison 1968, 1986

First edition published in Great Britain in 1968
by Chapman & Hall Ltd
Second edition published in 1986
by Robert Royce Ltd, 93 Bedwardine Road, London SE19 3AY

British Library Cataloguing in Publication Data
Hutchison, Sidney C.
 The history of the Royal Academy 1768–1986.
 —2nd ed.
 1. Royal Academy of Arts—History
 I. Title
 708.2'132   N1100
 ISBN 0–947728–23–6
Designed by Roger Walker
Phototypeset by Input Typesetting Ltd, London
Printed in Great Britain by
R. J. Acford Ltd, Chichester, Sussex

Dedicated to
MEBMEN

CONTENTS

CONTENTS

PREFACE

by Roger de Grey,
President of the Royal Academy

This book is an enlarged and updated edition of the history of the Royal Academy which was written by Sidney Hutchison and published in 1968 to mark the Academy's bicentenary. Sir Thomas Monnington was the President and, in the Foreword (reprinted here on pages x–xii), he spoke of the author's 'absorbing interest in the subject, throughout almost forty years on the administrative staff, and his great understanding of the many problems'.

By this time Sidney had in fact become Secretary of the Royal Academy and, as such, was in charge of the institution's administration for the next fourteen years, from 1968 to 1982, since when, although officially retired, he has still been on hand as Honorary Archivist. Indeed, having joined the staff in 1929, he has served the Royal Academy for longer than anyone else in its history. The variety of his duties, for a long time in the Registry, then as Librarian for twenty years, coupled with administrative responsibilities for the Loan Exhibitions, and eventually as Secretary, provided him with an unparalleled knowledge of the Academy's workings and activities. This is obvious in the direct style of the narrative and its readability.

So much has happened at the Academy since the original edition was published that it is high time for the developments to be recorded and, moreover, for the relevant changes in which he participated to be seen in their overall context. The last twenty years, while fraught with financial difficulties, have been remarkable for the considerable expansion in the Academy's activities. No institution can ever be perfect of course but, unless it moves with the times and aims at perfection, it is almost certain to become moribund. That the Royal Academy is now more lively and vigorous than it was is unquestioned: it is indeed appropriate that its regeneration should be chronicled by Sidney Hutchison who has contributed so much to it.

FOREWORD TO THE 1968 EDITION

by Sir Thomas Monnington,
President of the Royal Academy, 1966–1976

This work is the outcome of long and penetrating research into the history and pre-history of the Royal Academy by our Librarian, Sidney Hutchison, who, because of his absorbing interest in the subject, throughout almost forty years on the administrative staff, and his great understanding of the many problems, is uniquely qualified to write it. The book is based primarily on the Academy's minutes and other documents but, quite rightly, takes into account the whole range of outside influences.

It examines the early 18th Century background, and the growing recognition of the need for a School to train students in the Fine Arts in this country, and later, the realization that facilities were required for British artists to show examples of their work in public exhibitions. The various efforts that were made to supply these needs, culminating in 1768 in the successful foundation of the Royal Academy under the patronage of George III, are carefully reviewed. The author explains the nature of the foundation and deals in intimate detail with the structure.

The subsequent growth of the Royal Academy is followed in its various homes: first in Pall Mall, then in the old and new Somerset House, later at the National Gallery building in Trafalgar Square and, from the end of 1868, at Burlington House. Throughout these moves, the general policy and the contribution made by Members under the nineteen Presidents up to the present day are fully recorded, providing not only a scholarly review of the Royal Academy's first two hundred years but also a most informative survey of contemporary tastes, interests and developments in the fine arts.

Since very early in its history the Royal Academy has been self-supporting and able to fulfil the two essential purposes for which it was originally created – that is, to provide a School for art and facilities for an Annual Exhibition at which artists could show and sell their work. It is significant that this has been achieved, despite the fact that tuition has always been free and that no commission has ever been charged on sales. Over 6,500 artists have passed through the Academy's schools and more than a quarter of a million works of art have been shown in the exhibitions.

Another of the original intentions, which has also been successfully carried out, is the administration of charitable Trusts for the benefit of distressed artists and their dependants. Other Trusts have made it possible for the Academy to buy contemporary works by British artists, which become, in the case of the Chantrey Bequest, the property of the Nation and, in the case of other Trusts, the property of the Academy or of provincial art galleries.

In addition to these primary functions, the Academy has, since its move to Burlington House, been responsible for the famous Loan Exhibitions, many of which are remembered as events of international importance. These have been of great interest to the general public and the cause of enlightenment and learning to artists and art historians. The catalogues have been a major contribution to art history in the twentieth century.

Until fairly recent times, there were few, if any, alternatives to what the Academy had to offer to students and artists in this country. Now, however, there are alternatives. There are Schools of Art all over the country and, although there is nothing equivalent to the Summer Exhibition, there are other opportunities for artists to exhibit their work. In the charitable sphere, the Artists' General Benevolent Institution does invaluable work for artists and their families who, for one reason or another, have come on hard times.

The question may, therefore, be asked – does the Academy still perform an essential and useful function?

Academies inevitably create opposition. This is good if it is a confirmation of the Newtonian Law that all forces create an equal and opposite reaction. Now, in the 1960s, it is the reaction that, to some at least, seems to have assumed the status of 'official art'. It is, therefore, particularly important that the Royal Academy, which is entirely free from external pressures, should strengthen its support to those artists who wish to remain independent. What is certain – and this emerges from the latter pages of the book – is that the Royal Academy, at its Bicentenary, is still very much alive and that, through its activities, it continues to play an important role in the artistic life of the community.

Finally, I do not think it could be questioned that the Royal Academy Schools, the prime reason for the foundation, still occupy a unique position as a training ground for young artists.

INTRODUCTION

The Royal Academy of Arts in London was founded on 10 December 1768. It is certainly the oldest established society in the British Commonwealth solely devoted to the fine arts and it appears to be unique in the world as a self-supporting, self-governing body of artists which, on its own premises, conducts art schools, holds open exhibitions of the work of living artists and organizes loan exhibitions of the arts of all periods. It was constituted to promote the Arts of Design and, among other things, it serves as a link between the practising artist and the general public.

The Academy's home in Piccadilly, with spacious galleries and private rooms, has the advantage of being in the very centre of London yet withdrawn across a courtyard from its noisy bustle. Its possessions include a considerable collection of pictures, sculpture and other treasures as well as an extensive art library. Its trust funds are numerous and, through them, help and encouragement are regularly given to artists of all ages living in Great Britain.

The first major history of the Royal Academy was written by William Sandby in 1862 and, except for certain publications on specific periods and aspects, as well as a host of magazine articles, this has been superseded only by Sir Walter Lamb's short history which was first produced in 1935 and revised in 1951. Nevertheless there have been many comments on the Academy and its work throughout two centuries in various books, journals, newspapers, speeches and broadcasts. They certainly provide an insight into the institution's significance from generation to generation and show that it has always been considered worthy of notice: sometimes praised, sometimes abused but never ignored. The chief sources of factual information on the Academy, however, are its Minute Books, Annual Reports and other private records which, together with its exhibition catalogues, give a fair idea of its growth and importance.

I am greatly indebted to the President and Council of the Royal Academy for allowing me the privilege of attempting this history, originally to mark the occasion of the Academy's bicentenary in 1968 and now to bring it up to date, and for granting me the use of the Academy's archives. I am also most grateful to all those who have helped me in my task, particularly, in respect of this edition, various members of the current staff, including Piers Rodgers (Secretary), Laurie Bray (Assistant Secretary), Denis Serjeant (Surveyor), Constance-Anne Parker (retired Librarian) and, not least, Helen Valentine. I wish to offer special thanks to Margaret Toms, and, once more, I can but hope that this account may be of interest for some little time and be perhaps of assistance to anyone who may undertake a similar commitment in the future.

S. C. H.

I

HERITAGE

Gentlemen,

An Academy, in which the Polite Arts may be regularly cultivated, is at last opened among us by Royal Munificence. This must appear an event in the highest degree interesting, not only to the Artists, but to the whole nation.[1]

Thus Joshua Reynolds, first President of the Royal Academy, addressed his fellow-members at the opening meeting. This took place less than a month after the Instrument of Foundation had been signed on 10 December 1768 and it is obvious from subsequent remarks in the same discourse that such a project had been under consideration a long time. He spoke of 'numberless and ineffectual consultations' which he had had with many of those present 'to form plans and concert schemes for an Academy'.[2] He also seemed to acknowledge, and this is confirmed by later appreciations of the times, that the early years of the reign of George III were probably more propitious than any previous period in our country's history for forming a society of artists.

The nation was relatively wealthy and certainly the art patrons of the time had no major worries. For at least a decade there was comparative peace and stability. Living conditions continued to improve and there was no lack of good craftsmen. Indeed the houses, furniture and table-ware of the Georgian era are probably the best that Britain has ever produced. If the designers of the time lacked anything, it was the wider outlook which could only be obtained by experience and experiment. Their sole guides were such few textbooks as existed and their scant knowledge of the works of other men. The majority had never had the opportunity of going abroad and, even within their own shores, it was costly and difficult to venture on lengthy journeys. The rich, usually after the grand tour of France and Italy, filled their houses with pictures

I

and sculpture, some good, some bad, but access to them for purposes of study was certainly not readily obtainable. It is true that our great cathedrals and many churches had fine stained glass, statuary and miscellaneous treasures but hardly any possessed good paintings in reasonable condition. Engraved copies, with their severe limitations, were the only pictures available to all but the favoured few. Even the colour and size of the originals had to be guessed and there was no hope of any more subtle appreciation.

Getting about in the mid-eighteenth century, however, was becoming easier provided travellers were prepared to endure discomforts and willing to risk the attacks of highwaymen. The new turnpike roads in England were well used and more gentlemen than ever braved the choppy sea-crossing to the Continent to set out on the long journey southwards from Calais to Italy. Others, such as Reynolds himself, sailed across the Bay of Biscay and through the Mediterranean. The goal was usually the same – Rome, possibly Naples, and a short visit to Florence, Milan or Venice.

Thus an increasing number of people gained first-hand knowledge in a country where works of art could be studied with comparative ease and, in many cases, could hardly be avoided. The town-planning of the ancients could be seen alongside the palaces of the Renaissance. Every major city in Italy had its fountains and open-air statuary. The vast number of churches were treasure-stores of paintings as well as sculpture. Art was taken seriously and the artists' academies were of considerable importance but, above all, there was a tradition of good design which could be traced back to antiquity.

The situation in Great Britain was very different. Except for a few illuminated manuscripts and Anglo-Saxon carvings, there had been little of artistic value prior to the Norman Conquest in 1066. Thereafter architecture became our chief visual heritage but, apart from the evolution of structural form from Norman to late Gothic, it showed little continuity of thought. The change to the Renaissance style, though none too clean a break, was a definite contrast with precedent. Nevertheless there were many fine buildings to be seen dating from the end of the eleventh century onwards, including comparatively recent work by Inigo Jones, Sir Christopher Wren, Sir John Vanbrugh, James Gibbs and others. There was also good carving associated with the architecture despite the destruction of many figures at the time of the Commonwealth. Free-standing sculpture in the open air, however, was extremely rare.

Paintings were confined almost entirely to the stately homes where owners had employed perhaps an Italian or a French artist, such as Antonio Verrio or Louis Laguerre, to decorate the main apartments and where family portraits of solemn dignity stood guard against frivolities. The best were by foreigners who had settled in this country – Holbein, Hans Eworth, Daniel Mytens, Van Dyck, Lely, Kneller and others from the reign of Henry VIII to that of Queen Anne – and, except in portrait miniatures, our own face-painters never attained such consistently high standards. Similarly, to quote but two examples, Wenceslaus Hollar worked here in the seventeenth century as a topographical draughtsman and the Van de Veldes as marine painters but, apart from portraits, the country had only a modest quantity of pictures of high quality compared with the riches of the Continent. The finest collection had been that of Charles I but unfortunately it was dispersed after his execution and many of the best works were never recovered.

It can hardly be disputed that we had no native painter of outstanding importance before the eighteenth century and one may well wonder why this was so. We had certainly not been backward in other walks of life and can boast of famous men of an earlier period in various arts. Literature had had its Chaucer, drama its Shakespeare, music its Purcell and in architecture there had been a procession of good designers though the names of but a few are remembered.

Why had we not produced a Giotto or Raphael? The first possible answer is that there had been no demand for such an artist. Our buildings, at least from the thirteenth to the sixteenth century, left little room for mural paintings as in Italy. For climatic as well as structural and aesthetic reasons, our church walls contained vast areas of glass. Even in our manor houses, where there would have been a certain scope for the decorative painter, tapestries seem to have been preferred and, in later years, the walls were covered with wooden panelling. Probably this was partly due to the technical difficulties of working in fresco in so damp a land. Nevertheless, if our architects had borne pictures in mind when designing interiors, as eventually Inigo Jones did for the double-cube room at Wilton, would there have been a worthy response?

We shall of course never know the answer. There is, however, at least one other circumstance which must be taken into account and that is the lack of facilities for training. Experience and skill in the use of materials could be obtained by working as an assistant to an established painter and the master's style could be studied and copied but there were no art teachers and no art schools on the lines of those we know today. True, the Painter-Stainers' Company of London, in existence since the thirteenth century, had for long laid down rules for apprentices and carried out examinations of their work but these were solely tests of craftsmanship. The Company's main activities were concerned with safeguarding the rights and privileges of its members as journeymen and indeed painting was regarded as a trade, not as a fine art. There was no society of artists or other organization to set standards of design as on the Continent.

Yet in Italy academies had flourished for over two hundred years and they included a number devoted especially to the fine arts. The young Michelangelo was among those who attended Bertoldo's sculpture school in the garden of Lorenzo de' Medici around 1490. At Giorgio Vasari's suggestion and under a code of conduct set out in great detail in forty-seven articles, Cosimo I founded the more formal *Accademia del Disegno* in Florence in 1563. The *Accademia di S. Luca* in Rome came into being thirty years later and was quickly followed by similar institutions in Bologna, Genoa, Milan and other Italian cities. Similarly art academies sprang up in other parts of Europe and exerted considerable influence. The *Académie Royale de Peinture et de Sculpture* in Paris, founded in 1648, acquired almost dictatorial powers. Its principal task was educational but the curriculum was biased to train students in the particular style of drawing and modelling which was favoured by Louis XIV and his court. Only drawing, lectures and analyses were undertaken on the premises. Painting, modelling and carving were carried out in the studio-workshops of the academicians. 'Drawing' was considered superior to 'Colour' and the subjects of paintings were graded in importance, from the highest form, 'History', downwards through 'Portraits' and 'Animals' to 'Landscapes'. Charles Lebrun, one of the founders of the French Royal Academy and its Director from 1663, was even against the inclusion of such 'vulgar beasts' as camels and asses in pictures. The discipline was rigid in the extreme. The students listened to lectures on perspective and anatomy, only the seniors being allowed to attend life classes for two hours a day. Most of the time was spent in copying drawings by the Professors and making drawings from plaster casts.

The whole conception was severely restricted and it is quite understandable that Voltaire for one had no very high opinion of academies. Even Joshua Reynolds admitted, again to quote from his first discourse, that 'these Institutions have so often failed in other nations'.[3] He points out that Raphael 'had not the advantage of studying in an academy; but all Rome, and the works of Michael Angelo in particular, were to him an Academy'.[4] In assessing the need for such a society of artists in England in the eighteenth century, we must surely bear in mind the lack of guidance here at that time compared with the opportunities for study throughout the Continent. Reynolds perhaps sums up the position best in the following sentences:

> How many men of great natural abilities have been lost to the nation, for want of these advantages! They never had an opportunity of seeing those masterly efforts of genius, which at once kindle the whole soul, and force it into sudden and irresistible approbation. . . .[5] One advantage, I will venture to affirm, we shall have in our Academy, which no other nation can boast. We shall have nothing to unlearn.[6]

It is true that the engraver George Vertue (1684–1756) speaks of two academies in London in the seventeenth century but they were limited in scope and certainly not specifically concerned with the fine arts. The first, called the *Museum Minervae*, was held at the house of Sir Francis Kynaston in Covent Garden where there were 'several Proffessors to teach Gentlemen, none but such as could prove themselves such' and the subjects included 'Several Arts and Sciences, Foreign Languages, Mathematicks, Painting Architecture Musick riding. fortification, &c. – antiquity meddals'.[7] It was founded in the reign of Charles I, probably in 1636 when it obtained a patent and issued printed rules, but its activities seem to have come to an end during the Commonwealth. The second was in existence in 1649 at the house of Sir Balthazar Gerbier at Bethnal Green but was destroyed by force on political grounds, the pretext being that it was a hotbed of royalists.

William Sandby in his history of the Royal Academy, published in 1862, alleges that the diarist John Evelyn (1620–1706) produced a plan for an academy but there seems to be no evidence of it today. He says that it is printed in Evelyn's book on engraving called *Sculptura* but it is certainly not in the original edition of 1662; nor does it appear to be in later versions or indeed in any of his other works. It is known of course that Evelyn helped to found the Royal Society and that, in a letter to the Hon. Robert Boyle, he proposed the erection of a college 'in some healthy place, not above twenty-five miles from London' to contain 'a refectory, library, withdrawing-room . . . a pallet-room, a gallery . . . all which should be well and very nobly furnished'[8] where a small membership should be able to study and converse; also that he wrote several booklets on the fine arts but none appears to contain any suggestion for a British art academy. If such a plan had been known in Vertue's time, it is curious that he did not mention it. Yet the scheme quoted by Sandby is in great detail. It proposed the type of building to be used, its contents and its staff, and gave particular rules for the members and students. He could hardly have imagined such a meticulous set of articles and certainly the Royal Academy was eventually brought into being on similar lines.

2

FORERUNNERS: TUITION

London's first academy of drawing and painting from the life was opened in 1711, rather appropriately on St Luke's Day, patron saint of artists, and in a way it can be looked upon as the Royal Academy's elderly spinster aunt. It was held in a large room on the ground floor of a building in Great Queen Street, Lincoln's Inn Fields, near the town house of Sir Godfrey Kneller, who was then the leading portrait painter in Britain. He gave it his active support and was unanimously elected Governor. George Vertue attended the first meeting, when over sixty persons were present and, according to him, twelve Directors were appointed. They included the face-painters Thomas Gibson and Jonathan Richardson, the history painter James Thornhill, the sculptor Francis Bird, the decorative painters Pellegrini from Italy and Laguerre from France and, the latter's compatriot, Nicolas Dorigny the engraver. Three more were *dilettanti* who undertook certain administrative tasks. Among the voters there were, besides Vertue himself, a number of other well-known artists such as the painters J. B. Closterman, Michael Dahl, Peter Tillemans, John Vanderbank and John Wootton, also the architect James Gibbs. The academy was not intended particularly for young students but as a place of study for practising artists and interested amateurs. They paid a subscription of one guinea towards the upkeep of the somewhat dilapidated premises and for the employment of models. Rules were drawn up and are said to have been strictly enforced by the Governor and Directorate.

In the following year twelve new members were admitted including Bartholomew Dandridge, Captain Marcellus Laroon and the essayist Sir Richard Steele. Michael Dahl opted out in disappointment at not being asked to replace Kneller as Director in this second season and Mr Berchet, Senior, excused himself 'being not well, most Tysicky,

7

could not bear the smoke of the lamp'.[1] The fug in the room on a winter's night, perhaps with a peasouper outside, can be imagined.

It should be remembered that the artists were unused to communal discipline and it is therefore not surprising to find that there were dissentient voices even by 1713. Kneller, however, seems to have kept the situation well in hand. He wrote to Thomas Gibson, Director:

> I am very glad to understand the Accademy goes on well, and cannot doubt but ower Laws (which are writ and fram'd) will be continued, for it seems who so ever should make, or will alter, any part of them must be expelld ... for many have contributed to the paying of every thing necessary, and with consent. all which I find mentioned in the Orders which I have now by me to peruse by a Copy, and whear it is agreed to chouse every year a Governor and directors on Monday before St Luke. which is the next week I think, and which I find is expected by all. although sume fiew are out of humour. I cannot doubt but all will be very gentell and just. . . .[2]

He must then have visited the academy immediately and harangued the members as, in a second letter before the election meeting took place, he wrote to Gibson again as follows:

> I would acquaint you that I was at the Accademy Last night, and proposed to the Society (which was above 40 in number) if they would have the Standing Orders as they are now, they all (after I caused them to be read) consented. and holding up their hands as usual. *nemine contradicente.* that their Orders should stand, and that they are to Submit to what you see in the Copy hereby. . . .[3]

Despite these bickerings, the academy had several years of modest but increasing prosperity. The rebels' champion appears to have been James Thornhill who had at one time tried to get an academy founded, under the auspices of the Government, near the King's Mews. He was extremely ambitious and, when this project failed, he attempted to gain control of the Great Queen Street academy. It seems also that he was not above making use of it somewhat artfully to help him in his private work. The story is often told that Kneller was surprised one night to find the model posed in an awkward, crouching attitude. He asked the reason for this and was informed that the position had been suggested by Thornhill who had requested Thomas Gibson to do some drawings of it for him. 'I see, I see,' cried Kneller, 'Mr *Dornhill* is a wise man but, if I was Mr *Dornhill*, I should let Mr Gibson draw all my figures for me.'[4]

However, time was on Thornhill's side and, in 1716, he replaced Kneller as Governor though Vertue tells us that Louis Laguerre, by now a Director, might have been chosen 'had he bin as forward for it'.[5] Although Thornhill had eventually emerged victorious, his management lasted only two or three years and a subsequent academy under his control, opened free in his own house in Covent Garden in 1724, petered out soon afterwards. Edward Edwards asserts that the public of that time were so little conversant with the use of such schools that they were even suspected of being held for immoral purposes.[6] This is despite the fact that by now Thornhill had had honours heaped upon him. He was appointed Sergeant-Painter to the King, knighted and made Master of the Painter-Stainers' Company in 1720 and, two years later, elected a Member of Parliament. When he in turn was deposed in Great Queen Street, Louis Cheron and John Vanderbank took over this academy and moved it to a room in St Martin's Lane. It recommenced there in October 1720, at an increased subscription of two guineas. William Hogarth's name then appears as a member for the first time and afterwards, as is well known, he eloped with Thornhill's daughter. Other subscribers included John Ellis, Joseph Highmore, William Kent, George Knapton, Louis Laguerre and William Cheselden the surgeon. The new proprietors were certainly in office several years and in October 1722 inserted the following advertisement in the newspapers:

> This week the Academy for the Improvement of Painters and Sculptors by drawing from the Naked, open'd in St Martin's Lane, and will continue during the Winter as usual. N.B. The Company have agreed not to draw on Mondays and Saturdays.[7]

The Prince of Wales (afterwards George II) paid a visit a few weeks later and all seemed well till the treasurer embezzled the subscriptions and the landlord, unable to obtain his rent, seized the furniture. This story may be apocryphal but it seems true that the academy somehow became dispossessed of its belongings. Cheron, of whom Vertue speaks very highly, died in 1725 and Vanderbank's management might well have been unreliable. He is known to have led a life of debauchery.

Thornhill died in 1734 and his son-in-law, William Hogarth, using furnishings which he had inherited from the Covent Garden house, reconstituted the academy in Peter Court, St Martin's Lane, in the winter of 1734–35. This may reasonably be looked upon as the younger sister of Kneller's academy and the mother of the Royal Academy. It served as the breeding ground for that body and in it were developed the educational constituents of the later foundation. All participants had equal rights and it flourished until after the opening of the Royal Academy Schools over thirty years later. Hogarth was helped for some years by John Ellis among others. The annual subscription was fixed at two guineas for a member's first season and one and a half guineas thereafter. In 1746 the principal Directors were Hogarth, Ellis, Francis Hayman, George Michael Moser and the Revd James Wills. Moser had run a small society in Salisbury Court (later moved to Greyhound Court, Arundel Street) from about 1735 but this was absorbed into the St Martin's Lane Academy.

At the same time, till his death in 1754, the famous collector Dr Richard Mead allowed copying at his house in Great Ormond Street. This practice was imitated, from 1758, by the Duke of Richmond in his gallery of casts at Whitehall where instruction was given by G. B. Cipriani and Joseph Wilton. In addition, William Shipley held drawing classes at the (Royal) Society of Arts, founded in 1754 for the encouragement of arts, manufactures and commerce, but this was a private venture and the Society itself was not primarily concerned with training. In 1755 it considered a plan for an academy but nothing came of the proposal.

Towards the end of his life, in 1764, Hogarth wrote of his connection with the St Martin's Lane academy as follows:

> I lent to the Society the furniture that had belonged to Sir James Thornhill's Academy; and attributing the failure of the preceding Academies to the leading members having assumed a superiority which their fellow students could not brook, I proposed that every member should contribute an equal sum towards the support of the establishment and have an equal right to vote on every question relative to its affairs. By these regulations the Academy has now existed nearly thirty years, and is for every useful purpose equal to that in France or any other.[8]

It is curious that such a boast should have come from Hogarth. He had spent a large part of his life denying any foreign superiority in the arts, as witness his antagonism to the taste of the 3rd Earl of Burlington and his circle. 'Having never studied,' says Horace Walpole of Hogarth, 'indeed having seen few good pictures of the great Italian masters, he persuaded himself that the praises bestowed . . . are nothing but the effects of prejudice. He talked this language till he believed it . . . and determined to rival the ancients.'[9] Walpole, however, was far from happy with the general level of connoisseurship of his time. He considered that George I was devoid of taste and that his reign was a period 'in which the arts were sunk to the lowest ebb in Britain'.[10] Nor did he think that painting was much better in the time of George II when certainly the country seemed to be a haven for foreign artists. Some, such as Canaletto, were of course of first-rate quality but others were extremely pedestrian in their work. When George II was shown an engraving of Hogarth's *The March to Finchley*, he exclaimed with his Germanic guttural, 'What! a *b*ainter burlesque a soldier? He deserves to be picketed for his insolence! Take his trumpery out of my sight!' and he had already cried 'I hate *b*ainting and *b*oetry too! Neither the one nor the other ever did any good! Does the fellow mean to laugh at my guards?'[11] The last laugh was probably Hogarth's when he subsequently altered the inscription. Instead of to the King of England, he dedicated it to the 'King of Prussia, an encourager of the arts and sciences'. This was Frederick I whose academy Vertue described in detail and much envied.

The patronage of the aristocracy was on the whole more discerning than that of the royal family with the exception of the enlightened judgment of Frederick, Prince of Wales, the son of George II and father of George III. He had many fine paintings in his various residences and discussed with Vertue 'the settlement of an Accademy for drawing and painting'.[12] Unfortunately they did not meet till 1749 when the engraver was rather advanced in age. The Prince died in March 1751. Otherwise the Royal Academy might have been founded earlier and on different lines. During the two years, however, they met quite frequently and it seems that Frederick developed a considerable affection for Vertue. They must have talked of Vertue's quite elaborate scheme for an academy

for the Improvement of the Art of Delineing in this Nation. Being a most certain way, for our Nobility, Gentry and Learned persons to gain knowledge in the Arts of Architecture, Painting, Sculpture, the Drawing of Military Fortifications, Engeneering, Views prospects of Cities Towns houses, with Plans of Ports Bays, both Regular and Irregular &c. whereby they may become as good judges of these Arts.[13]

Vertue proposed that initially three drawing schools should be established – in London, Oxford and Cambridge – under masters appointed by the academy; also that the students be made to copy from specially produced books and casts from the antique. Thereafter they should study anatomy, geometry, architecture and perspective so that

> any tolerable genius, who shall have followed such rules strictly will never after commit as is now constantly done horrid blunders, inconsistent with Nature incoherent, unproportionable figures, joynts ill form'd, muscles, continually erroneous lights & shades wrong placed, or an insipped flatness, either in heads hands or whole bodys it is certain every such person will be correct (& so far well) tho' every one may not arrise to the Sublime. That must be left to providence long study and an excellent genius, of which no doubt this Nation abounds. . . .[14]

He intended that the students should pay for their tuition and that they should, before admission, have a general education in writing, literature and Latin. He had worked out minute details of the expenses and procedures but the exciting and unique feature of the plan was the idea of having such schools in various centres in addition to London. He envisaged preliminary drawing classes at colleges such as Winchester and Eton and altogether his scheme could have formed the nucleus of art education throughout the country under the general supervision of 'an Accademy settled by Publick Authority'.[15] No other plan was so all-embracing.

Some wealthy connoisseurs formed the Society of Dilettanti in the 1730s (probably in December 1732) and, in 1748, one of their members, Robert Dingley, proposed the establishment of an academy but nothing came of it. These gentlemen may have been 'The Grand Clubb for promoting the Arts of Drawing, painting &c.' who, according to Vertue, met one Sunday night in November 1749, at the Bedford Head in Southampton Street, 'to settle the preliminarys for the Establishment of an Accademy – in London'[16] but again nothing materialized.

The artists at the St Martin's Lane academy also had been discussing such matters and, in 1753, called a meeting at the Turk's Head Tavern (then in Greek Street, Soho) to elect a committee of twenty-four to compile a scheme. There appears to have been no immediate result but, two years later, the group was still in being and opened negotiations with the Society of Dilettanti. The artists included Francis Hayman (Chairman), Reynolds, Roubiliac, Thomas Hudson, Gavin Hamilton,

Robert Strange, Samuel Scott and G. M. Moser. Hayman and Francis Milner Newton, who later were to become respectively the first Librarian and the first Secretary of the Royal Academy, submitted the committee's detailed plan to the Society. It is known to have been a printed document and may well be the scheme which Sandby attributed to John Evelyn as, by coincidence, 1755 is the year in which the second edition of *Sculptura* appeared. However, no satisfactory solution evolved and both sides agreed to discontinue the discussions. Briefly the artists wanted the financial and other support from the Dilettanti which these gentlemen were not willing to give without retaining supervisory control. At their general meeting in May 1755 the Society recommended

(1) That the President of the intended Royal Academy be always and annually chosen from the Society of Dilettanti.
(2) That all the members of the Society of Dilettanti be members of the Academy, but that only twelve of the senior members present at the meetings shall have votes.
(3) That any artist may be chosen a member of the Academy, but that only twelve of the artists, to be chosen annually out of the body, shall have votes, and that upon an equality of votes the President shall have a second vote.[17]

Robert Strange, the engraver, who later fell out with his colleagues, was apparently present at the discussions and, in a pamphlet in 1775, said that 'The dilettante finding that they were to be allowed no share in the government of the academy, or in appropriating their own fund, the negotiations ended.'[18] The artists, however, must have been very reluctant to lose such a chance of influential and discerning support. The proposal included a scheme for 'a yearly exhibition of pictures, statues and models, and designs in architecture',[19] and this was very much needed by the practising artists of the time who, mostly, had to go to wealthy patrons cap in hand for commissions.

Strange also mentions that many attempts were made about 1750 to enlarge the plan of the St Martin's Lane academy but they proved abortive. John Gwynn issued a booklet in 1749 which included proposals 'for erecting a Public Academy'[20] and castigates England for being a country where 'Art has been in small Estimation, unless the Artist was foreign'.[21] He talks of enormous outgoings on foreign art and 'the prodigious price which is given for some'.[22] Rouquet, a Swiss miniature painter, in a booklet *L'Etat des Arts en Angleterre*, alleges that

13

English artists had to contend against the interests of the dealers who took care to deprecate their work in order to make more profit on pictures by foreigners and preferably of an earlier period.

Similarly a booklet in 1755 by an anonymous writer (probably the landscape painter Alexander Nesbit) speaks of noblemen 'intirely misled by the Picture-Dealers and Cleaners'[23] who have 'an unintelligible Jargon of their own'[24] and sell pictures 'cleaned of both Dirt and Finishing . . . no better than dead colourings'.[25] He goes so far as to say that 'extravagant Prices are paid to Cleaners for spoiling Collections'[26] and that 'Dealers and Cleaners, and all other ignorant and designing People, will be inveterate Enemies to an Academy'[27] which he advocates not only as a means of improving native artists but also of cultivating taste so that 'our Academy . . . will not only make Virtue amiable, but Vice detestable'.[28] He then writes on 'the Necessity and Form of a Royal Academy for Painting, Sculpture and Architecture'. This was to be on similar lines to those already mentioned but he recommends that the President be 'not a Painter' but 'a Man of Consequence – chosen for life'[29] and that, till we have better artists of our own, 'it will be necessary to procure Professors from some foreign Academy'.[30] With Reynolds already in London, this would seem to have been somewhat of a *faux pas* but it is obvious that the writer looked upon history painting as the highest form of art. Works in this idiom by Benjamin West and others were yet unknown in the capital.

FORERUNNERS: EXHIBITIONS

If the reader will admit that the mother-figure of the future Royal Academy has now been established, it is time to consider the male line, the father and ultimate bread-winner. The elder brother here was the Foundling Hospital, established by Captain Thomas Coram and given a royal charter in 1739. After a short while in temporary premises, it was transferred to a new home in Bloomsbury Fields built in 1742–47. Many people supported this much-needed orphanage. Handel gave performances in aid of it and presented its first organ while Hogarth was largely if not entirely responsible for the important connection between this charity and the visual arts. He became one of the original governors, designed the head-piece for the roll of subscribers and was an active member of its court and general committee. In 1740 he presented his fine full-length portrait *Captain Coram* and this was the first of the Foundling Hospital's considerable collection of pictures. He obtained the co-operation of fellow artists and, in 1746, after fifteen of them had agreed to donate works, Hogarth headed a committee which was to meet every 5 November 'to consider of what further ornaments may be added to this Hospital, without any expense to the Charity'.[1] Thereafter the artists dined there annually on that day and there were one hundred and fifty-seven present at the 'Dilettante, Virtuosi, Feast' in 1757.[2]

Three years later, on 7 December 1760, the artists agreed to appear the following November 'in a suit of Cloths manufactured by the Children of the Hospital at Acworth',[3] a subsidiary establishment in Yorkshire, and it is obvious that the dinner was an annual event of great importance in the artists' calendar. The collection of pictures grew apace; Reynolds, Gainsborough, Allan Ramsay, Richard Wilson and Benjamin West were among the subsequent donors, and many people visited the Hospital for the sake of enjoying the works of art, at the same time leaving something for charity in return for the privilege. The paintings 'being exhibited to the public, drew a daily crowd of spectators in their splendid equipages; and a visit to the Foundling became the most fashionable morning lounge of the reign of George II'.[4] It is somewhat curious that Hogarth thereby introduced unintentionally a feature which was to become an important ingredient of the future Royal Academy – the holding of exhibitions. He was certainly opposed to such an institution on scholastic grounds and in fact died, in 1764, four years before it was founded.

The choice of 5 November for the artists' feasts seems to have had nothing to do with Guy Fawkes Day. It was possibly a commemoration of the landing of William III at Torbay on that date in 1688, an event which was long remembered as a turning-point in the country's history. The Georgian period as a whole was of course still one of antagonism to the Stuart cause, as witness the severe suppression of the rising in 1745.

The annual dinner in 1759 was held as usual among the pictures in the Court Room of the Foundling Hospital. In the flickering candlelight, perhaps with periwigs slightly askew and the red wine from the flagons now but a pink tinge on the cheeks of the diners, silence was called for the singing of an ode in which those present were enjoined 'nobly to think on Hayman's thought'.[5] John Wilkes, the politician who was Hogarth's enemy but held the post of Treasurer of the Hospital, was in the chair and the thought was to found 'a great Museum all our own'.[6] By this was meant an academy wherein works by contemporary British artists could be on public view and the idea was the spark of life for the future Royal Academy. While enthusiasm was still at its height and before the evening was finished, a resolution had been drawn up as follows:

Foundling Hospital, Nov. 5, 1759. At a meeting of the Artists, resolved: That a general meeting of all Artists in the several branches of Painting, Sculpture, Architecture, Engraving, Chasing, Seal-cutting, and Medalling, be held at the Turk's Head Tavern, in Gerrard Street, Soho, on Monday, the 12th inst., at Six in the evening to consider of a proposal for the honour and advancement of the Arts, and that it be advertised in the Public and Daily Advertisers.[7]

It was signed by John Wilkes as President and Francis Milner Newton as Secretary and it will be noted that the Turk's Head Tavern had by now removed from Greek Street where the artists had met in 1753 under the chairmanship of Francis Hayman. This meeting was the moment of conception for the Royal Academy and there followed a gestation period of nine years.

The artists duly considered the position and a decision was made to promote an annual exhibition of contemporary work commencing the following April. This in fact materialized and was the forerunner of the Summer Exhibitions held annually at the Royal Academy from 1769. It was intended to charge an admission fee of one shilling per person but this proposal had to be dropped. The difficulty was to find a building in which such an exhibition could take place and, after further discussions, it was agreed to seek the use of a large room in the Strand owned by the (Royal) Society of Arts. This request was granted by the Society but they would not allow an admission charge. The artists had little option but to accept the situation and the exhibition was duly opened to the public for two weeks from 21 April to 8 May 1760, the year of George III's accession to the throne. Its popularity can be judged from the evidence that 6,582 catalogues were sold at sixpence each and this probably represented a daily attendance of well over a thousand visitors – quite a crowd in one room. There were 130 exhibits including works by Reynolds, Roubiliac, Hayman, Paul Sandby and Richard Wilson. The 1760 exhibition and its successors may be looked upon as the father-figure of the Royal Academy.

Undoubtedly the venture had been a success and £100 Consols were purchased from the profits. At one stroke the means had been found for artists' work to be brought to the notice of the general public and, by profits on catalogues (and, later, charges for admission), a source of revenue had been created other than by self-imposed subscriptions. There had, however, been snags. Edward Edwards, an eager young Londoner at the time, alleges that they were 'consequent to the arrangement of the pictures'[8] and 'occasioned by the following improprieties'[9] in the room of the (Royal) Society of Arts. He says:

> The society, in the same year, had offered premiums for the best painting of history, and landscape; and it was one of the conditions, that the pictures produced by the candidates should remain in their great room for a certain time; consequently they were blended with the rest, and formed part of the exhibition. As it was soon known which performances had obtained the premiums, it was naturally supposed, by such persons who were deficient in judgment, that those pictures were the best in the

room, and consequently deserved the chief attention. This partial, though unmerited selection, gave displeasure to the artists in general. Nor were they pleased with the mode of admitting the spectators, for every member of the society had the discretionary privilege of introducing as many persons as he chose, by means of gratuitous tickets; and consequently the company was far from being select, or suited to the wishes of the exhibitors. These circumstances, together with the interference of the society in the concerns of the exhibition, determined the principal artists to withdraw themselves, which they did in the next year.[10]

The artists had hoped that the 1761 exhibition could be held in June after the pictures submitted for premiums had been removed but this was not to be and indeed the Society ordered that their committee 'have power to examine all such pieces as shall be sent in for the exhibition, with power to reject such as may be deemed improper' and 'that the same Committee may appoint the places where the several productions shall be exhibited'.[11] The first of these restrictions was perhaps understandable from the Society's point of view but the artists felt unable to accept these new conditions and so moved elsewhere.

Nevertheless exhibitions continued for some years in the Strand room though, generally speaking, the exhibitors were of lesser calibre. They formed themselves into the Free Society of Artists in 1762, a misnomer at the time, and they broke away from the Society of Arts in 1765. They then moved first to Maiden Lane, Covent Garden, and afterwards to various addresses until 1783 when they ceased to hold exhibitions. The society certainly deserves to be remembered for its good work in forming a charitable fund which helped artists and their families in need.

Meanwhile the more important artists, with the aid of Reynolds and the architect James Paine, found a large room for their 1761 exhibition in Spring Gardens, Charing Cross, and called themselves 'The Society of Artists of Great Britain'. William Chambers and Joseph Wilton, an architect and a sculptor, signed the contract and the show opened on 9 May with 229 exhibits. The chief participants of the previous year were still represented and were now joined by many others including Gainsborough and Hogarth. The latter designed a frontispiece and a tail-piece for the catalogue which cost one shilling and served as a season ticket for admission. The frontispiece showed a sculptured bust of George III, gazing at Britannia watering three healthy young trees in foliage and marked 'Painting', 'Sculpture' and 'Architecture'. The

1 'King George III', first Patron, Protector and Supporter of the Royal Academy,
by Sir Joshua Reynolds, 1779

2 'Self-portrait', *c.* 1773–80, by Sir Joshua Reynolds, first President of the Royal Academy, in his robes as a Doctor of Civil Law of Oxford University and with a bust of Michelangelo by his side

3 'Sir William Chambers', 1780, by Sir Joshua Reynolds. First Treasurer of the
Royal Academy and architect of Somerset House, London, which is visible at
the left of the portrait.

4 'The Academicians of the Royal Academy' by Johann Zoffany, *c.* 1772. Sir Joshua Reynolds is shown with his ear-trumpet and portraits of Angelica Kauffmann and Mary Moser appear on the right-hand wall (*Reproduced by gracious permission of Her Majesty The Queen*)

5 'Self-portrait' by Thomas Gainsborough, probably painted in 1787

6 'Francis Hayman', first Librarian of the Royal Academy, by Sir
Joshua Reynolds, 1756

7 'The Exhibition of the Royal Academy, 1771' in its room in Pall Mall. Mezzotint by Richard Earlom from a watercolour by Charles Brandoin

9 'John Malin', the Academy's first Porter and Model (died 1769), by Thomas Banks

8 'Self-portrait' attributed to Richard Wilson, 'father of English landscape' (died 1782)

10 'The Conjuror' by Nathaniel Hone. Refused for Royal Academy Exhibition, 1775 (*National Gallery of Ireland, Dublin*)

11 'The Watering Place' by Thomas Gainsborough. Exhibited at Royal Academy, 1777 (*Reproduced by courtesy of the Trustees, The National Gallery, London*)

tail-piece was more waggish and caused considerable comment. In it was a monkey, dressed as a fop, watering three withered stumps marked 'Exoticks' with dates of their deaths as 1502, 1600 and 1604. This was but another example of Hogarth's contempt for the current taste of most of the nobility for works by deceased foreign artists. It is mentioned in a letter published in the *St James's Chronicle* from 'an admirer, but thank God no Encourager, of the Polite Arts'.[12] The point of this can be noted if one remembers that the full title of the (Royal) Society of Arts continues with the words 'for the encouragement of Arts, Manufactures and Commerce'. Undoubtedly there was rivalry between the two exhibitions and this may have done them both good at least as far as attendances were concerned. The free exhibition in the Strand drew a somewhat unruly crowd and constables had to be engaged to keep the peace. The Spring Gardens exhibition appears to have been more orderly but quite merry. Over £50 was spent on illuminating the front on the night of the King's birthday, 4 June, and this included £2 14s 0d for rockets.

At Spring Gardens in 1762, a charge of a shilling for admission was made in addition to the cost of the catalogue. The reasons are given in a somewhat wordy preface which, though anonymous, is thought to have been written by Reynolds, possibly with the help of his friend Samuel Johnson. It claims that 'the purpose of this Exhibition is not to enrich the Artists, but to advance the Art' and says that although 'whoever sets his work to be shown, naturally desires a multitude of spectators' yet 'his desire defeats its own end, when spectators assemble in such numbers as to obstruct one another'. Nevertheless the first serious attempt to sell the exhibits was then made and is explained in this same preface as follows:

Many Artists of great abilities are unable to sell their works for their due price; to remove this inconvenience, an annual sale will be appointed, to which every man may send his works, and send them, if he will without his name. These works will be reviewed by the committee that conduct the Exhibition. A price will be secretly set on every piece, and registered by the Secretary. If the piece exposed is sold for more, the whole price shall be the Artist's, but if the purchaser's value is at less than the committee, the Artist shall be paid the deficiency from the profits of the Exhibition.

This system would seem to have been rather dangerously uneconomic for the promoters of the exhibition but perhaps artists were less demanding and patrons more generous in those days.

In 1765 the Society of Artists obtained a royal charter, as 'The Incorporated Society of Artists of Great Britain' and it had over two hundred members; no limit was set on numbers. They dined together as a body for the first time at the Turk's Head Tavern on St Luke's Day in 1763 and the bill is preserved with the Society's records in the Library of the Royal Academy:

1763. St Luke's Day
Octo^r:18th

	£.	S.	d.
Dinners for 60	9.	o.	o.
56 Tickets each 2/-	5.	12.	o.
45 Tankards Porter		16.	10½
24 Papers of Tobacco		2.	o.
Lemons & Sugar		18.	o.
	£16.	3.	10½
Extra for Hams & 2 Geese	1.	7.	o.
	£17.	10.	10½

It may be noticed that the arithmetic is a little awry. The '56 Tickets each 2/-' were probably for wine.

This function appears to have been the forerunner of the Royal Academy Annual Dinners but there had for long been artists' feasts besides those held at the Foundling Hospital. There was at one time a Society of Virtuosi of St Luke, said to have had its origin in the seventeenth century when Van Dyck developed the practice of inviting artists and connoisseurs to dine at his home. Similar gatherings continued in other painters' houses and, till about 1744, at hostelries such as the Rose and Crown and, later, at the favourite meeting-place of artists for convivial discussions, the Turk's Head Tavern.

It cannot be said that the Society of Artists' exhibitions at Spring Gardens were trouble-free and indeed there is the tale of Richard Wilson's unethical conduct in 1763 to enliven the pictures. He and Benjamin West (the American who by now had settled in this country) were appointed joint hangers and, when their task was done, they were far from satisfied with the result. 'This will never do,' Wilson said. 'We shall lose the little credit we have, for the public will never stand such a shower of chalk and brickdust.' He accordingly sent out for some Indian ink and Spanish liquorice and, dissolving them in water, washed many of the pictures with the solution. 'There,' he cried, 'it's as good as asphaltum, with this advantage that if the artists don't like it they can wash it off when they get the pictures home.'[13] West swallowed hard and had to agree that the end seemed to justify the means.

The other troubles appear to have been caused mostly by the jealousies of those who considered that their pictures should have been hung in better positions. Dissensions broke out in 1767 and there was then a serious attempt to establish a public academy with a wider outlook. This was resisted by the more conservative element. The engraver Robert Strange would have us believe that it fell through because of intrigue on the part of Richard Dalton, the antiquary and George III's librarian who owned a print warehouse in Pall Mall. Strange alleges that, as this business faced financial failure, Dalton approached the King and was able, through his close connection, to induce His Majesty to promise his support in turning it into an academy. This being so the artists dropped their proposal in the hope of better things to come only to discover the folly of wishful thinking. Except that the words *The Royal Academy* were substituted over the door for *Print Warehouse* and some drawing classes were held there even before the foundation of the real Royal Academy in December 1768, nothing else changed. Dalton continued to use the rest of the premises for other activities for three years or so.

Thus the differences within the Incorporated Society became even more strained. George Lambert had become the first President in January 1765, with Hayman as Vice-President, Dalton as Treasurer and F. M. Newton as Secretary. There were also twenty Directors including Wilson, Francis Cotes, Paul Sandby, G. M. Moser and James Paine. Reynolds refused his election as one of them and his place was filled by George Barret. Lambert died a few days later to be succeeded by Hayman with Edward Penny as the new Vice-President. The Directors on the whole did not change over the years and, by 1768, many members clamoured for and obtained a law under which retirements were enforced. Sixteen new Directors were appointed in August and Hayman was turned out as President in favour of Joshua Kirby. This was on 18 October and brought about the resignation three weeks later of the eight remaining original Directors, all artists of standing who were opposed to these sweeping revisions – West, Wilson, Wilton, Penny, Newton, Moser, Sandby and Chambers. The two architects

James Paine and William Chambers, both of whom had schemes for rehousing the Society, were the chief contenders for power and, after the latter's virtual defeat, Paine saw to it that the vacant places were filled by those who supported his opinions. Reynolds again refused a directorship, also Gainsborough. Their letters are dated 25 November and 5 December respectively,[14] only a few days before they became foundation members of the Royal Academy.

The control thereby devolved into the hands of rather lesser men and the situation was aggravated by a relatively unimportant matter which seems to have had little to do with art itself. In this same year, on two days only, 30 September and 3 October 1768, the Incorporated Society held an exhibition to honour a visit to this country by the King of Denmark. It was not open to the ordinary public and admission was by tickets. Those for the first day were to be distributed at the discretion of the Danish Minister but it is alleged that Chambers contrived to get twelve of them for his friends. This incident seems to have been the spark which set inflamed spirits afire. It is not recorded in the Society's minutes but is alleged by Robert Strange in his pamphlet *The Conduct of the Royal Academicians*. Whether it is true or not is now of little account. The Incorporated Society's exhibitions continued till 1791, with James Paine as its ambitious President from 1770, but its influence dwindled in importance with the years and the growth of a tremendously powerful new rival. Indeed the scene was set for the advent of the Royal Academy. The ante-natal period had been a troubled one for all concerned and the pains immediately preceding the birth were considerable.

—4—
BIRTH
1768

The remarkable feature common to the Free Society of Artists, the Incorporated Society of Artists of Great Britain and the St Martin's Lane academy was that they were all conducted by artists entirely without official backing whereas the major plans for an academy in this country had been based on the premise that it should be under the protection of the Crown or the Government. This would have made its organization comparable with examples on the Continent. Such a control might have suppressed or even obviated internal quarrels; it would also have invested it with official authority and this was no doubt in Chambers' mind when he engineered an approach to George III (Plate 1) to support an academy such as had been envisaged off and on over so many years. As Architect of the Works and previously one of the King's tutors, he had means of gaining audience.

James Northcote and John Galt, the early biographers of Reynolds and West respectively, and also Edward Edwards, all state that Chambers, West, G. M. Moser and Francis Cotes presented a petition to the King in order to acquaint him of the situation which had arisen as a result of the recent dissensions in the Incorporated Society. Galt furthermore claims that they ventured to do so following an audience which West had had with the King in which there had been an opportunity to impart the news privately. He says that it was at the American artist's suggestion that the four constituted themselves 'a committee of the dissenting artists, to draw up the plan of an Academy';[1] moreover that George III, who had frequently discussed such a project with West, drafted several of the Laws in his own hand and 'was particularly anxious that the whole design should be kept a profound secret'.[2] Certainly it was a secret from Joshua Kirby who, about this time, as President of the Incorporated Society, assured the membership that the King intended to patronize them and visit their exhibition. The blow for him fell when he was told by the King that West's commissioned picture of *The Departure of Regulus from Rome*[3] was to be shown at the new Royal Academy. Kirby, who had once been a tutor in perspective to George III (as had Chambers in architecture as well as Joseph Goupy and Moser in drawing) and therefore had reasonable access to His Majesty, had fortuitously interrupted when West was handing over the picture to the King. Kirby praised it and hoped that it would be sent to his exhibition but George III said, 'No, it must go to my exhibition – to the Royal Academy.'[4] If this was indeed Kirby's first knowledge of the new rival institution, he must have had a considerable shock. It is reported that 'he bowed with profound humility and instantly retired'.[5] Immediately prior to this he had assured Reynolds that no such scheme was in hand. The King continued favours to the Incorporated Society but, thereafter, the Royal Academy was the art institution to which he gave 'patronage, protection and support'.[6]

Contemporary records are not clear as to the exact dates and sequence of events but many clandestine meetings must have been held shortly before 10 December 1768. On 28 November, the following memorial, signed by twenty-two artists, was presented to George III:

To the King's most Excellent Majesty:
May it please your Majesty, We, your Majesty's most faithful subjects, Painters, Sculptors, and Architects of this metropolis, being desirous of establishing a Society for promoting the Arts of Design, and sensible how ineffectual every establishment of that nature must be without the Royal influence, most humbly beg leave to solicit your Majesty's gracious assistance, patronage, and protection, in carrying this useful plan into execution.

It would be intruding too much upon your Majesty's time to offer a minute detail of our plan. We only beg leave to inform your Majesty, that the two principal objects we have in view are, the establishing a well-regulated School or Academy of Design, for the use of students in the Arts, and an Annual Exhibition, open to all artists of distinguished merit, where they may offer their performances to public inspection, and acquire that degree of reputation and encouragement which they shall be deemed to deserve.

We apprehend that the profits arising from the last of these institutions will fully answer all the expenses of the first; we even flatter ourselves they will be more than necessary for that purpose, and that we shall be enabled annually to distribute somewhat in useful charities.

Your Majesty's avowed patronage and protection is, therefore, all that we at present humbly sue for; but should we be disappointed in our expectations, and find that the profits of the Society are insufficient to defray its expenses, we humbly hope that your Majesty will not deem that expense ill-applied which may be found necessary to support so useful an institution. We are, with the warmest sentiments of duty and respect,

> Your Majesty's
> Most dutiful subjects and servants,

Benjamin West	Richard Yeo
Francesco Zuccharelli	Mary Moser
Nathaniel Dance	Augostino Carlini
Richard Wilson	Francis Cotes
George Michael Moser	William Chambers
Samuel Wale	Edward Penny
G. Baptis. Cipriani	Joseph Wilton
Jeremiah Meyer	George Barret
Angelica Kauffman	Fra. Milner Newton
Charles Catton	Paul Sandby
Francesco Bartolozzi	Francis Hayman.[7]

The words obviously were chosen carefully and were used to present the case very skilfully. Whoever was responsible for the composition certainly did his job well.

George III received the memorial graciously, said that he considered the arts to be a national concern and promised his patronage and assistance in bringing the plan to fruition. He furthermore desired that the artists' intentions might be more fully explained to him in writing as soon as convenient. No time was lost over this. Chambers consulted as many of his confederates as was possible in under ten days and drew up a sketch plan which was submitted to the King on 7 December. This was approved, written in proper form and signed by His Majesty on Saturday, 10 December 1768. It is known as the Instrument of Foundation of the Royal Academy (printed in full as Appendix A).

Following the preamble, there are twenty-six paragraphs defining the membership, giving rules for the election of new members, the appointment of Officers, Professors and servants, the conduct of the Schools, Library and the annual exhibition and the general administration of the institution. It decreed that there should be forty Royal Academicians, 'Painters, Sculptors, or Architects, men of fair moral characters, of high reputation in their several professions; at least five-and-twenty years of age; resident in Great Britain; and not members of any other society of artists established in London'. It will be seen immediately that engravers were not included and this was to be a cause of discontent for many years; also that no opportunity was given for artists to accept the new honour and at the same time retain membership of a rival society. In fact only thirty-six names were mentioned and, of these, two (William Hoare and Johann Zoffany) were added later.

Vacancies were to be filled 'by election from amongst the exhibitors in the Royal Academy' and it was laid down that a new member 'shall not receive his Letter of Admission, till he hath deposited in the Royal Academy, to remain there, a Picture, Bas-relief, or other specimen of his abilities, approved of by the then sitting Council of the Academy'. This Letter of Admission became the Royal Academicians' Diploma, signed by the Sovereign, and the specimens are known as Diploma Works.

The government of the society was to be in the hands of an annually elected President and eight members in succession 'who shall form a Council, which shall have the entire direction and management of the Society'. Members of the Council were to serve for two years but half of them had to retire each year so that there would always be an annual change in its composition. Reynolds (Plates 2, 4 and 18) was unanimously elected as the first President but accepted only after some hesitation. Galt tells us that, on the morning of the day when an evening meeting was to be held at Joseph Wilton's house to consider the institution's Laws, both Edward Penny and G. M. Moser informed Benjamin West that Reynolds did not intend to be present. West then called on Reynolds to find him 'much surprised to hear matters were so far advanced'[8] after the assurance to the contrary which he had received from Joshua Kirby. Following a two-hour talk, Reynolds was at last persuaded to accompany West to the meeting. It was then on the point of breaking up in disappointment but 'on their appearing, a burst of satisfaction manifested the anxiety that had been felt'.[9] The business was dealt with and included the declaration of Reynolds as President, Chambers (Plates 3 and 28) as Treasurer, Newton as Secretary, Moser as Keeper, Penny as Professor of Painting, Samuel Wale as Professor of Perspective and Dr William Hunter as Professor of Anatomy. James Northcote, however, alleges that Reynolds declined to accept the honour till he had consulted his friends Dr Johnson and Edmund Burke and that it was not until a fortnight later that he gave his consent.[10] This probably accounts for the period of time between the presentation of the memorial to the King on 28 November (on which Reynolds' name does not appear) and the date of the Instrument of Foundation of 10 December. The first official General Assembly of the Royal Academicians took place four days later.

Newton, as Secretary, was to deal with minutes, correspondence, etc., and Moser, as Keeper, was to look after the Schools and servants. The only person named in the Instrument was William Chambers as Treasurer in order that His Majesty 'may have a person in whom he places full confidence, in an office where his interest is concerned' – a reasonable precaution in view of possible calls upon the Privy Purse. Although not specifically stated in the case of the President, these four Officers were to be Royal Academicians and approved by the Sovereign.

It was decreed that nine Visitors be elected annually 'to attend the Schools by rotation, each a month, to set the figures, to examine the performances of the Students, to advise and instruct them, to endeavour to form their taste, and turn their attention towards that branch of the Arts for which they shall seem to have the aptest disposition'; also that Professors of Anatomy, Architecture, Painting and Perspective should deliver lectures and that there should be a Library 'open one day in every week' when it was to be supervised by a member of the Council.

Rules were laid down for 'an Annual Exhibition of Paintings, Sculpture, and designs, which shall be open to all Artists of distinguished merit' and there were to be a Porter of the Royal Academy and a Sweeper with salaries of twenty-five and ten pounds a year respectively. The remaining clauses concerned general conduct, the redress of grievances and the means of ratifying new Laws.

According to the Academy's minutes,[11] Chambers was mainly responsible for the content of the Instrument of Foundation. After it was read to the General Assembly on 14 December, those present signed the following Obligation:

His Majesty having been gracious pleased to institute and establish a Society, for promoting the Arts of Design, under the Name and Title of the Royal Academy of Arts in London, and having signified his Royal Intention, that the said Society should be established, under certain Laws and Regulations, contained in the Instrument of the Establishment, signed by His Majesty's own Hand.

We therefore whose Names are hereunto subscribed either Original, or Elected Members, of the said Society, Do promise, each for himself, to observe all the Laws and Regulations contained in the said Instrument, as also, all other Laws, By-Laws, or Regulations, either made, or hereafter to be made, for the better Government of the above mentioned Society, promising furthermore on every Occasion, to employ our utmost Endeavours, to promote the Honour and Interest of the Establishment, so long as we shall continue Members thereof.[12]

Joshua Reynolds was then formally elected President with George Michael Moser as Keeper and Francis Milner Newton as Secretary and the following eight as members of the first Council – George Barret, William Chambers, Francis Cotes, Nathaniel Hone, Jeremiah Meyer, Edward Penny, Paul Sandby and Joseph Wilton. It was a good cross-section of the membership of the time – six painters including Sandby for watercolours and Meyer for miniatures, Wilton as the sculptor and Chambers as the architect. On the same day, nine Visitors were elected – Agostino Carlini, Charles Catton, G. B. Cipriani, Nathaniel Dance, Francis Hayman, Peter Toms, Benjamin West, Richard Wilson and Francesco Zuccarelli.

Thus the names of those who had worked hard to bring about the foundation were all included in the first list as Officers, Council Members or Visitors. Two only are little known to posterity – Charles Catton who was coach-painter to George III and Peter Toms who was a painter of drapery for Reynolds and others.

The remaining original members comprised the painters John Baker, Mason Chamberlin, Thomas Gainsborough (Plate 5), Angelica Kauffmann, Mary Moser, John Richards, Dominic Serres and Samuel Wale, the architects George Dance, John Gwynn, Thomas Sandby and William Tyler, and two engravers, Francesco Bartolozzi and Richard Yeo, though the former was elected as a painter and the latter as a sculptor. It will be noted that there were two women but no others were elected until the 1920s.

On 17 December, the following Professors were officially appointed – Edward Penny for Painting, Thomas Sandby for Architecture, Samuel Wale for Perspective and Dr William Hunter for Anatomy. John Malin (Plate 9) was engaged as Porter and his wife, Elizabeth, as Sweeper.

The first Council Meeting was held on 20 December and three others before the end of the year. It was reported that the King had approved the various appointments and several minor matters were settled. Elizabeth Malin was granted an assistant for whom five pounds a year was allowed; Mr William Bunce was given the privilege of becoming the Printer and Mr William Randall the Stationer. The main business, however, concerned rules and orders and the following is of interest concerning the Schools:

> That those Students who have already paid their Subscription to the Old Academy in Pall Mall, shall be admitted into the Royal Academy to draw this Season, till the Expiration of the Winter Academy, After which Time they shall be subject to the same Regulations as prescribed for the Admission of other Students – Resolved that those Students who have neglected to pay their Subscriptions to the Old Academy, shall not be admitted to draw in the Royal Academy, till they have gone through the usual Forms of Admission.[13]

This would seem to support the contention that Richard Dalton's premises in Pall Mall had become an academy in 1767 and also gives credence to the story that the students there had been induced by Moser to give up their equipment on the promise that it would be available to them in the proposed Royal Academy. Another version is that goods and chattels were wheedled away from the St Martin's Lane academy even earlier by Richard Dalton. Whichever, if either, is true, it would seem that the original Royal Academicians were not above condoning a little sharp practice in laying their hands on these desirable possessions. It must be remembered that, although the new institution was set up under most august patronage and with a discerning code of Laws, it was both roofless and penniless. Indeed it had nothing but the naked body with which it was born. Apart from salaries, the first major expense which it undertook was the employment of four male models at a retaining fee of five shillings a week each plus an additional shilling for each night's work; female models were not to be engaged for the present.

Details for the conduct of the Schools were drawn up and confirmed on 2 January 1769. They are worth quoting in full:

> Rules and Orders, relating to the School of Design.
> The Visitors shall draw lots for the times of Attendance, according as they shall be Annually regulated by the Council, which Regulation, together with the names of the respective Visitors shall be put up in the Academy.
> Each student, who offers himself for Admission into the Royal Schools shall present a Drawing or Model from some Plaister Cast to the Keeper, and if he thinks him properly qualified, he shall be permitted to make a Drawing or Model from some Cast in the Royal Academy, which if

approved of by the Keeper and Visitor for the time being, shall be laid before the Council for their confirmation, which obtained he shall receive his Letter of Admission as a Student in the Royal Academy Where he shall continue to draw after the Plaister, till the Keeper and Visitor for the time being, judge him qualified to draw after the Living Models, when they shall have power to admit him.

The Students shall implicitly observe the Regulations deliver'd to the Keeper by the Council, for preserving Order and Decorum in the Royal Schools.

Any Student that shall deface or damage the Plaister Casts, Models, Books or any other Moveable belonging to the Royal Academy shall be expelled.

No Student shall presume to introduce any Person to see the Royal Academy or any Part thereof, without leave first obtained from the Keeper or Visitor for the time being.

The Winter Academy of Living Models shall begin at Michealmas and end on the ninth day of April following Inclusive.

The Summer Academy of Living Models shall begin on the twenty sixth Day of May and end on the last Day of August.

There shall be three Vacations in the Year.

The First, to commence on Christmass-Eve, and to end on the Epiphani.

The Second, to commence on the tenth Day of April, and to end on the twenty sixth Day of May following.

The Third, to commence on the first Day of September and to end on the Feast of St Micheal.

The Winter Academy shall begin at Six o'clock in the Evening.

The Summer Academy shall begin at Four o'clock in the afternoon, in other respects to be under the same Regulations as the Winter Academy.

Two or more living Models of different Characters shall be provided by the Keeper and Visitors for the time being.

The Model shall be set by the Visitor and continue in the Attitude two Hours (by the Hour-Glass) exclusive of the Time required for resting.

There shall be two different Models, each Week, each Model to sit three Nights.

While the Visitor is setting the Model, the Students shall draw Lots for their Places, of which they shall take Possession so soon as the Visitor hath set the Figure.

During the time the Model is sitting the Students shall remain quiet in their Places.

As soon as any Student, hath done Drawing or Modeling, he shall put out his Candles, and while Drawing or Modeling, he shall be careful to keep them under the Bells.

Rules and Orders for the Plaister Academy.

There shall be Weekly, set out in the Great Room, One or more Plaister Figures by the Keeper, for the Students to draw after, and no Student shall presume to move the said Figures out of the Places where they have been set by the Keeper, without his leave first obtained for that Purpose.

When any Student hath taken possession of a Place in the Plaister Academy, he shall not be removed out of it, till the Week in which he hath taken it is expired.

The Plaister Academy, shall be open every Day (Sundays and Vacation times excepted) from Nine in the Morning till Three in the Afternoon.[14]

On 2 January 1769, Reynolds declared the Academy open in his first discourse, advocating diligence for the students despite 'the impetuosity of youth' being 'disquieted at the slow approaches of a regular siege'.[15] At the same time, however, he warned the Visitors that the diligence must be effectual. 'A Student,' he said, 'is not always advancing because he is employed; he must apply his strength to that part of the art where the real difficulties lie.'[16] He recommended 'an implicit obedience to the Rules of Art'.[17]

The institution was breaking new ground and the first President was showing the way to plough straight furrows and to sow seeds carefully. 'Every opportunity,' he declared, 'should be taken to discountenance that false and vulgar opinion, that rules are the fetters of genius. They are fetters only to men of no genius; as that armour, which upon the strong is an ornament and a defence, upon the weak and mis-shapen becomes a load and cripples the body which it was made to protect.'[18]

A feature of the Royal Academy Schools is that the training was to be free and, until recently, this has always been completely so. Except for the first twelve years, when small deficits were met by the Privy Purse, the provision of tuition and the conduct of the Academy's general administration and its library were paid for during the major part of two centuries from the proceeds of the exhibitions. In addition, mainly through the receipt of a number of trust funds, it has been possible to award certain scholarships and prizes to the students and to carry out other educational and charitable functions which will be discussed in later chapters.

The child was born and the occasion of Reynolds' first discourse may be looked upon as the equivalent of the christening ceremony.

With George III as godfather, it was now the task of the foundation members to foster its growth.

—5—
PALL MALL AND OLD SOMERSET HOUSE
1769–1779

The Academy's meetings for the first eleven years were held in premises on the south side of Pall Mall.[1] They were opposite Market Lane (now Royal Opera Arcade) and on the site of part of the present Institute of Directors (until a few years ago the United Service Club) which stretches eastwards along the street from the corner of Waterloo Place. Previously Aaron Lambe, an auctioneer, had had his business there and then Richard Dalton his print warehouse. The accommodation was modest in size and character and had to be used for all the Academy's activities – administration, meetings, schools and exhibitions. Reynolds' first discourse was delivered there and it was the scene of much daily activity at least until the Schools moved to old Somerset House in the Strand in 1771.

Thirty-six Council Meetings and seven General Assemblies were held on the premises before the end of 1769. More Laws had to be devised. New commitments needed new regulations and the Council's deliberations were lengthy. Much homework was done between meetings and many informal discussions took place. Forfeits were payable for absenteeism and unpunctuality. It was a period of great excitement and rapid development. Reynolds at one stage threatened to resign but the danger was averted and he was given a knighthood on 22 April just before the first exhibition. 'After ten years' forbearance of every fluid except tea and sherbet,' said Dr Johnson, 'I drank a glass of wine to the health of Sir Joshua Reynolds on the evening of the day on which he was knighted.'[2]

In January, agreement was reached that the first exhibition should be held from 26 April to 27 May. In the same month the first gifts were received and the first six students were admitted. It was decided that the lectures by the Professors should commence on the first Monday in October and that they would have to be approved by the

33

Council before being delivered. Those of Dr William Hunter, the Professor of Anatomy, were very popular and he used in his demonstrations both living models and the bodies of hanged criminals. Library rules were drawn up in February and an 'Evening Plaister Academy' was opened. Arrangements were made to provide a female model at the cost of half a guinea a sitting, under conditions designed to deny any complaint of impropriety. It was decreed that 'no Student under the Age of twenty, be admitted to draw after the Female Model, unless he be a married Man'[3] and that 'no Person (the Royal Family excepted) be admitted . . . during the time the Female Model is sitting'.[4]

Seventy-seven students were enrolled by the end of the year – thirty-five in painting, ten in sculpture, three in architecture, four in engraving and twenty-five not specified – and they included Edward Edwards, Biagio Rebecca, William Hamilton, William Parry, Philip Reinagle, John Downman, Joseph Farington, John Bacon, Thomas Banks, Richard Cosway, Thomas Hardwick, John Yenn, John Flaxman, James Gandon, Michael Angelo Rooker, Samuel de Wilde and Francis Wheatley. It was an excellent beginning and, to give the students encouragement, it was decided to award annual premiums. They were to include three gold medals – one for Historical Painting, another for a Sculpture of a Bas-relief and the third for a Composition in Architecture; also 'a number of Silver Medals, not exceeding Nine'.[5] Designs were prepared jointly by G. B. Cipriani and Edward Penny and modelled in relatively high relief by Thomas Pingo, assistant engraver to the Royal Mint. The obverse in each case was the head of George III. The reverse of the gold medal showed Minerva directing a youth to climb a steep and rugged ascent to the temple of fame at the summit, with the inscription 'HAUD FACILEM ESSE VIAM VOLUIT'. That of the silver medal was a torso (based on the Belvedere torso in the Vatican) with the word 'STUDY' above. Both reverses had the inscription 'R · AC · INSTITUTED 1768' at the base. For some reason the prize-winning entries were not to be allowed in the annual exhibition and, for economy, the award of the gold medals was made biennial from 1772.

It was also agreed that every Royal Academician should receive a Diploma (Plate 20) as his 'Letter of Admission'[6] and the Council, Visitors and certain others were invited to submit sketches for the headpiece. The one by Moser was at first chosen but then Cipriani's drawing was modified, accepted and ordered to be engraved by Francesco Bartolozzi. The wording was drafted by Chambers, amended by the King and appeared finally as follows:

George the Third by the Grace of God King of Great Britain France and Ireland defender of the Faith etc. to our trusty and well-beloved ... Esquire greeting.

Whereas we have thought fit to establish in this our City of London a Society for the purposes of cultivating and improving the Arts of Painting, Sculpture & Architecture under the Name and title of the Royal Academy of Arts, and under our own immediate Patronage and Protection.

And whereas we have resolved to intrust the sole management and direction of the said Society under us, unto Forty Academicians the most able and respectable Artists, resident in Great Britain. We therefore in consideration of your great Skill in the Art of ... do by these presents constitute and appoint you to be one of the Forty Academicians of our said Royal Academy, hereby granting unto you all the Honors, Privileges and Emoluments thereof according to the tenor of the Institution given under our Royal sign Manual upon the tenth Day of December 1768 and in the Ninth Year of our Reign. And we are the more readily induced to confer upon you this honorable Distinction as We are firmly persuaded that you will upon every Occasion exert Yourself in support of the Honor, Interest and Dignity of the said Establishment and that you will faithfully and assiduously discharge the Duties of the several Offices to which you shall be nominated. In consequence of this our Gracious Resolution it is our Pleasure that your Name be forthwith invested in the Roll of the Academicians, and that you do subscribe the Obligation in the Form and Manner prescribed.

Given at our Royal Palace of St James's the Sixteenth Day of December in the Ninth Year of our Reign.[7]

Every Royal Academician has received a similar Diploma, signed by the Sovereign, after fulfilling the conditions of his appointment. In the case of all elected Academicians, they have included the deposit of a specimen of their work, duly approved by the Council, as laid down in Clause III of the Instrument of Foundation. This stipulation did not apply to the foundation members nor to William Hoare of Bath and Johann Zoffany who were nominated Royal Academicians by George III towards the end of 1769.

The original members were probably a little conscience-stricken at not having admitted engravers at the foundation and, as early as 19 January 1769, the Council proposed the election of not more than six Associate Engravers. After further thought it was decided to enlarge this idea and include them in a new class, to be called Associates of the Royal Academy and to be chosen from the participants in the annual exhibition, not to exceed twenty in number, not to be apprentices or less than twenty years of age and to comprise Painters, Sculptors, Architects and Engravers. They too were to receive Diplomas, not unlike those of the Academicians but signed by the President and Secretary, and they were also to put their names to an Obligation. The new Associates, however, were not required to deposit Diploma Works. They were allowed no 'Voice in the Deliberations' nor 'any share in the Government of the Academy'[8] but were expected to send a work to the annual exhibition. The first elections to the new class did not take place till 1770 and it was decreed that, thereafter, every subsequent Royal Academician should be chosen from among them.

Under Clause XVII of the Instrument of Foundation, two hundred pounds from the profits of the exhibition had to be given 'to indigent artists, or their families' and applications for 'the Royal Charity'[9] were invited by the Council within two weeks or so of the foundation. The first donations were made in June 1769 and were continued in midsummer for many years. They ranged in value from three to ten guineas and were given to almost thirty artists in need and their dependants, mostly widows and orphans. An interesting and slightly larger item was the payment of eleven guineas for a son of Charles Brooking to be apprenticed to a peruke maker.

John Malin, the Academy's first Porter, who also posed as a model in the Schools, died early in 1769 and his funeral expenses were ordered to be paid in consideration of 'his long and faithful services'.[10] He had in fact been employed at the St Martin's Lane academy for many years previously and was greatly loved by the older Academicians.

At the same time it was agreed that four servants would have to be employed for the annual exhibition, the anticipated means of financing these various commitments. Rules had been drawn up as early as January 1769, as follows:

> That Every Performance once deliver'd, and Admitted in the Royal Exhibition, and printed in the Catalogue shall not be taken away on any pretence, before the Exhibition for that Year ends.
>
> No Picture copied from a Picture or Print, a Drawing from a Drawing; a Medal from a Medal; a Chasing from a Chasing; a Model from a Model, or any other species of Sculpture, or any Copy be admitted in the Exhibition.
>
> The arranging or disposition of the Paintings, Sculptures, Models, Designs in Architecture, &c. for public view to be absolutely left to the Council.

The Council hath Power to reject any performance which may be offered to the Exhibition.

No Picture to be received without a Frame.

No person shall be admitted into the room before the Exhibition opens, the Council and necessary Servants excepted.

Resolved That, The Council shall attend immediately after the Time limited for the reception of the Pictures &c. is expired, to receive or reject the several Performances.

That No Picture &c. &c. shall be received after the time limited for the reception is expired.[11]

These were confirmed by the General Assembly who added that 'All Exhibitors in the Royal Exhibition (tho. they be not Academicians) shall have free admittance during the whole time of the Exhibition'[12] and these regulations form the nucleus of those still in force today. The next move was to publish the following advertisement:

The President and Council give Notice that their Exhibition will open on the 25th April next. Those Artists who intend to exhibit with the Academicians are desired to send their several Works to the Royal Academy in Pall Mall on Thursday the 13th April or before six o'clock in the Evening of Friday the 14th after which time no Performance will be received.

F. M. Newton, Secy.

N.B. – No Copies, Nor any Pictures without Frames will be admitted.[13]

It was then agreed that a committee comprising Edward Penny, Paul Sandby, George Barret, G. M. Moser and F. M. Newton should arrange the exhibits. In other words they were the Academy's first Hanging Committee. Again a similar procedure is followed in our time though the number of those concerned has been increased considerably.

The members were worried lest the exhibition room be overcrowded with people and also perhaps felt that they should make their excuses for charging an entrance fee. They accordingly inserted the following 'Advertisement' as a preface to the catalogue:

As the present Exhibition is a part of the Institution of an Academy supported by Royal Munificence, the Public may naturally expect the liberty of being admitted without any Expence.

The Academicians therefore think it necessary to declare that this was very much their desire but that they have not been able to suggest any other Means than that of receiving Money for Admittance to prevent the Room from being fill'd by improper Persons, to the entire exclusion of those for whom the Exhibition is apparently intended.

There were 136 works in this first exhibition, 129 of which were by professional artists.[14] The remaining seven were by amateurs who are described in the catalogue as 'Honorary' but this term involved no election nor did it convey any particular distinction. It should not be confused with the appointment of Honorary Members from other walks of life. Works marked with an asterisk were for sale and exhibitors were granted a ticket for the following season's lectures. Reynolds showed three portraits and a figure picture and Gainsborough three portraits and a large landscape. There were works by Hayman, Hone, Angelica Kauffmann, G. M. Moser and his daughter Mary, the brothers Paul and Thomas Sandby, Penny, West, Wilton, Chambers and others. The catalogue was not in the order of the exhibition but under the artists' names alphabetically.

There was a visit from the royal family on the 25th and the exhibition closed to the public on 27 May. George Dance did not show a work and therefore had to pay the penalty of five pounds as laid down in Clause XVII of the Instrument.

The year ended with the award of premiums, under an elaborate system of voting in which all the members took part, and the election of Officers, Council and Visitors for 1770. The gold medal for painting was awarded to Mauritius Lowe, for sculpture to John Bacon and for architecture to James Gandon and, in addition, seven students received silver medals. Reynolds delivered his second discourse on the occasion of the distribution of these coveted prizes in words 'which possibly may be more useful ... than barren praise.'[15] 'I could wish,' he said, 'to lead you into such a course of study as may render your future progress answerable to your past improvement; and, whilst I applaud you for what has been done, remind you how much yet remains to attain perfection.'[16] It was the perfect speech to spur both the prize-winners and the less fortunate to greater effort.

The Academy had not, as had been hoped, paid its way in its first year and the deficit of just over £370 was reimbursed from the Privy Purse, a relatively modest sum when one considers how much good work had been started.

An attempt has been made in this chapter to deal with the very early period of the Academy's history in considerable detail but obviously this will not be possible throughout more than two centuries. The succeeding years in Reynolds' Presidency continued on much the same pattern and in the 1770s only a few matters are worthy of special comment. The Schools continued to take in students at an average rate of almost thirty a year. They included Daniel Gardner, John Russell, James Northcote, John Soane, William Beechey, Thomas Rowlandson, Anthony Devis, Thomas Cubitt, Thomas Malton, James Barry, John Hoppner, Thomas Stothard, W. R. Bigg and William Blake.[17]

The exhibitions increased in size and, in 1779, over four hundred works were included. No limit seems to have been set on the numbers submitted by individuals and Reynolds, for instance, frequently showed twelve or more pictures. Many artists changed allegiance from the previous art societies to the new Royal Academy and the room in Pall Mall was crowded out with exhibits. A watercolour by Charles Brandoin of the 1771 exhibition, engraved by Richard Earlom on a larger scale in the following year (Plate 7), shows the walls packed with pictures, making present-day Academy hanging look almost sparse. From 1770 onwards a list of works 'Omitted' was usually printed at the end of the catalogue. They were in fact part of the show and hung with all the other exhibits, the term merely being used to denote that they were late arrivals omitted from the main list as sent to the printer.

Moser and Newton, the Keeper and the Secretary, continued to serve annually on the Exhibition Committee and were joined by three different members duly elected but seemingly taken in rotation. The exhibition was held on comparable dates from year to year and indeed, in 1771, it was laid down that the Annual Dinner should thenceforward take place on St George's Day (23 April) and that the exhibition should open to the public on the following day. The company had in fact adjourned to dine after the opening meeting on 2 January 1769, but the first dinner to coincide with launching the annual exhibition, and held in the Academy's own rooms, took place in 1770. In the following year, twenty-five gentlemen were invited to sit at table with the Academicians and, in 1778, dinner was ordered for a total of sixty-four. As usual, songs composed on the spot added to the gaiety and received great applause. At the dinner in 1774, held at old Somerset House, a salute of twenty-one guns was fired from a small armed ship which had been brought up the Thames for the purpose. The King's birthday each year was celebrated by illuminating the front of the building and in 1771 the fabric was endangered by a mob of people throwing squibs. On the same evening the members used to adjourn to dine at the Free Masons Tavern in Great Queen Street.

The exhibits from 1769 to 1779 included several pictures which have subsequently become famous. West's *The Death of General Wolfe* (Plate 13) was shown in 1771 and, as is well known, Reynolds was very much against the rendering of such an event in contemporary military costume. The picture, however, was a great success and he had to agree that 'West had conquered'. He had the generosity to admit that 'this picture will not only become one of the most popular, but occasion a revolution in the art'.[18] Barry's *Adam and Eve*[19] was in the same exhibition as well as important full-lengths by Mason Chamberlin, Nathaniel Dance, Gainsborough and others. Gainsborough continued to exhibit in 1772 but not again till 1777 when he showed the now famous landscape *The Watering Place* (Plate 11) and the fine full-length portraits *The Duke of Cumberland* and *The Duchess of Cumberland*[20] and *The Hon. Mrs Graham*.[21] Reynolds' contributions were of a consistently high standard and included his *Three Graces adorning a Term of Hymen*[22] in 1774. The daring of M. W. Peters' *Woman in Bed*[23] caused a little stir in 1777 and, from year to year, various pictures attracted particular attention. Gifts continued to come to the Academy and they included casts of the famous doors of the Baptistry at Florence. These were shown in a ground-floor room at the same time as the 1773 exhibition and must have been a revelation to all those who had not seen the originals, particularly sculptors.

Needlework and artificial flowers were apparently allowed in other exhibitions of the time but were specifically excluded from the Academy from 1771 onwards. Models in coloured wax were also not accepted. Works by the members were not above jurisdiction and, in the same year, Nathaniel Hone was made to alter the crucifix in one of his pictures lest it gave offence. This artist was in more serious trouble in 1775 when the Academy refused his picture *The Conjuror* (Plate 10), the content of which imputed plagiarism to Reynolds and included a sketch of a nude female figure (later painted over) which Angelica Kauffmann thought was meant to represent her. She sent the following indignant letter to the President and Council:

Gentlemen,
I have had the honour of a visite from Sir Will Chambers the purpose of which was to reconcile me to submite to the exhibition of a picture which gave me offence, however I may admire the dignity of the

gentlemen who are superior to the malignity of the author, I should have held their conduct much more in admiration, if they had taken into consideration a respect to the sex which it is their glory to support.

If they fear the loss of an academician who pays no respect to that sex – I hope I may enjoy the liberty of leaving to them the pleasure of the academician and withdrawing one object who never willingly deserved his or their ridicule.

I beg leave to present my respects to the Society and hope they will always regard their own honour – I have but one request to make, *to send home my Pictures*. If that is to be exhibited.

I am gentlemen

Your most obedient servant

Angelica Kauffman.[24]

She won the day and Hone's picture was not included. He in fact showed it privately in a room in St Martin's Lane where it attracted many sightseers but no purchaser.

Although it was a rule that intended exhibits should not be received after the appointed time, more and more artists begged leave to send in late for a variety of plausible excuses – Angelica Kauffmann's paintings were not yet dry, George Stubbs was held up for frames and so on. The Council Minutes in 1779 give a list almost two pages long of the many 'craving indulgencies'[25] and the latitude granted must have been a great nuisance to the hangers. There are few things more frustrating than trying to place pictures that have not yet arrived! Nevertheless the shows went on and everything somehow fell into place by opening day.

Brief mention must be made of the plan in 1773 to decorate the interior of St Paul's Cathedral with large historical pictures. Reynolds and Barry were the chief instigators but West, Cipriani, Nathaniel Dance and Angelica Kauffmann were also to produce designs. The King was begged to support the scheme but it failed because of the opposition of the Bishop of London. This prelate's pride was probably hurt as he considered that he was not consulted early enough in the proceedings. Shortly afterwards a similar proposal to decorate the Meeting Room of the (Royal) Society of Arts fell through but this work was subsequently undertaken by James Barry.

The engravers Thomas Major, S. F. Ravenet, P. C. Canot, John Browne and Thomas Chambers, the sculptors Edward Burch and John Bacon, the painters Richard Cosway, Edmund Garvey, William Pars, George James, Elias Martin, Antonio Zucchi and Michael Angelo Rooker, together with the architects Edward Stevens and James Wyatt,

41

were elected the first Associates in 1770 under the Law instituting the class. Of these, Edward Burch and Richard Cosway became Royal Academicians the following year, the former filling the first vacancy on the death of Francis Cotes. The engravers were not considered eligible for promotion to the first rank for many years to come.

Another innovation was the nomination of some Honorary Members in 1770, following Joseph Baretti's appointment as Secretary for Foreign Correspondence at the end of the previous year. Some time earlier, in 1764, Reynolds had founded the Literary Club where regularly he met and talked with some of the great thinkers of the time. Two of these, Samuel Johnson and Oliver Goldsmith, became respectively Professor of Ancient Literature and Professor of Ancient History, while Richard Dalton, the King's Librarian, was given the post of Antiquary. It was a wise move and one may assume that both they and the Academy felt honoured. However, the impecunious Dr Goldsmith is supposed to have commented 'The King has lately been pleased to make me Professor of Ancient History in a Royal Academy of Painting which he has just established, but there is no salary annexed, and I took it rather as a compliment to the institution than any benefit to myself. Honours to one in my situation are something like ruffles to a man that wants a shirt.'[26] At least the Honorary Members had, and still have, a place at table at the Annual Dinner.

Reynolds continued his discourses but, after 1772, they were given biennially. He was annually re-elected President, usually *nemine contradicente*, and he hardly missed a meeting, whereas Gainsborough, who did not settle in London till 1774, seldom visited the Academy and seems never to have been present at the dinners. In 1775 he was the last of the original Academicians to be nominated for the Council, no doubt because it would have been useless to have appointed him earlier, and even so he went through the whole year without putting in an appearance at a single meeting. This did not pass without notice but in the General Assembly Minutes of 11 December 1775 it was resolved that 'Thos. Gainsborough, Esq. continue in the Council'.[27] He did not, however, mend his ways and he made no attendances again in 1776. It had not been intended originally that the Treasurer should be summoned to these meetings but difficulties arose through his not being present and this situation was remedied in 1770. Although Reynolds was President, he once described Chambers as 'the Vice-roy over him'[28] and all the major business with the Sovereign seems to have been done through the Treasurer. George III's approbation was sought even on minor matters.

Another point which is revealed in the minutes is that Angelica Kauffmann and Mary Moser, though full Academicians, were not expected to attend meetings. They voted at the annual award of premiums, for instance, by sending in marked lists. The prize-winners included John Bacon, Thomas Banks, Thomas Rowlandson, John Hoppner and many others equally well known. Mauritius Lowe, the first gold medallist who received an award to travel in Italy, did not fulfil the obligation of sending in a work to the annual exhibition and, with the King's approval, he was replaced by Thomas Banks in 1772. A similar opportunity for study abroad, in Italy or Greece, was afforded by the Society of Dilettanti who invited nominations from the Academy in 1774. One student from the Academy (James Jeffreys) and one other artist (William Pars) duly set out the following year.

The first Librarian was appointed by the King in 1770 at a salary of fifty pounds per annum and the honour went to Francis Hayman (Plate 6) who had tried so hard in the previous years to set an Academy afoot. At sixty-two he was considered at the time to be quite elderly and 'was nominated . . . that he might enjoy its emoluments, small as they were, in consequence of his bodily infirmities which in the evening of his life pressed heavily upon him'.[29] He died in 1776 and his place was taken by Richard Wilson (Plate 8) who was of the same age and even more famous as a character. It is said that the appointment 'happily rescued him from utter starvation'[30] and his Librarianship is mostly remembered for his remark, 'Don't paw the leaves, sirrah . . . have you got eyes in your fingers, boy?'[31]

The administration ran fairly smoothly during these first few years with only a few pin-pricks of trouble. The Keeper of the time, G. M. Moser, was once insulted by a student and the culprit was made to give a public apology. The lamp in the Schools was always causing bother and there was great difficulty in buying a good lay figure. Cipriani, as Visitor, crossed swords with Moser and finally, in 1775, it was 'resolved that the Visitor shall be considered as Master of the Living-Academy; and that neither the Keeper nor any other Academician shall presume to enter the Room whilst the Visitor is setting the Model, nor shall they give any instructions or Orders whatsoever whilst the Visitor is present, nor shall he or any other Academician, except the President, introduce any Friend without first asking leave of the Visitor'.[32]

In the same year, James Barry produced a long motion amounting to a criticism of the hanging in the exhibitions. Basically he suggested that all Academicians should be present to vote on works submitted and that the best places should be allocated by ballot. It would have been an unwieldy process and was wisely turned down in the Council by five votes to two. In 1779 J. H. Mortimer's works were admitted 'he having died within the year'[33] and this seems to be the commencement of a procedure which is still allowable today. Donations continued each year but, in 1775, it was decided that £100 annually be set aside and invested to form a fund for members in distress. Samuel Wale had a paralytic stroke three years later and was the first to benefit. He remained as Professor of Perspective but, in his last days, was allowed to give the lectures at his own house.

Gifts were received from time to time, including the present of the casts of *Truth* and *The Venus of Medici* from HRH The Duke of Gloucester, and in 1777 it was agreed to start a collection of 'the best prints which shall be published in England from this Time forward'.[34] Since 1771 it had been considered 'proper for the present Academicians to give a Picture or some other specimen of their Abilities to remain in the Academy'.[35] This applied of course to the original members and was in addition to the works expected by law from those subsequently elected. It was at the same time permitted to deposit a Diploma Work and change it later if desired.

The last event to be recorded in this chapter is in many ways the most important. It took place on 7 January 1771, and was announced as follows:

> Notice is hereby given to the Members and Students, that the Academy is removed to Somerset House, and will open on Monday next 14th Inst. at 5 o'Clo: in the Afternoon.[36]

This was still old Somerset House and referred to the removal of the schools, library and administration into some apartments there which were put at the disposal of the Academy by George III. Certain royal retainers were made to vacate these rooms and this provided much needed breathing-space for the increasing number of students. The exhibitions, however, continued at the premises in Pall Mall up to and including 1779. Meanwhile plans had been under way for several years for rebuilding old Somerset House and providing therein specially built accommodation for the Royal Academy in all its activities.

6

SOMERSET HOUSE TILL THE DEATH OF REYNOLDS

1780–1792

Sir William Chambers, who had been knighted first in Sweden in 1770 and then allowed to use the title in England, and who since 1756 had held various professional appointments under the Crown, was the architect commissioned to rebuild Somerset House (Plate 16) for the use of the Academy, the Royal Society, the Society of Antiquaries and a number of government departments including the Navy Offices. He thus undertook what was to be one of the greatest examples of English civil architecture, though this involved the destruction of some good work by Inigo Jones which had been built just over a hundred years earlier. Chambers was justifiably proud of the opportunity which was not only important in its own right but which, at the same time, put him on his mettle to design fitting accommodation for the Royal Academy whose welfare he had so much at heart.

Many interests had to be satisfied but the site, with its great vista across the Thames, was an excellent one despite the comparative narrowness of the northern frontage to the Strand. Chambers dealt with the problem sensibly by placing the learned societies on this boundary, where they had immediate access from the street, and disposing them around a beautifully designed central entrance which leads through to the great quadrangle.

The conception as a whole is grand and the terrace front, which looks southwards over the river, is one of London's finest façades even though the water can no longer lap against its massive stonework. There is no doubt, however, that the architect lavished extra attention on the Strand block. His own words prove this:

All the fronts of this structure are decorated with a rustic arcade basement, a Corinthian order of columns and pilasters, enriched windows, balustrades, statues, masks, medallions, and various other ornamental works necessary to distinguish this principal and most conspicuous part of the design; which being in itself trifling when compared with the whole, required not only particular forms and proportions, but likewise some profusion of ornaments to mark its superiority. Decorations, too, have been more freely employed in the vestibule of entrance, and in all the public apartments of this building, than will be necessary in the remainder of the work; because the vestibule, open to the most frequented street in London, is a general passage to every part of the whole design; and the apartments are intended for the reception of useful learning and polite arts, where it is humbly presumed specimens of elegance should at least be attempted.[1]

Chambers, besides being adept in phraseology, recognized to the full the true relationship of sculpture and architecture and, while supervising the whole, examined carefully the smallest details. As he says in *A Treatise on the Decorative Part of Civil Architecture*, the genius of an architect should be 'equally capable of expanding to the noblest and most elevated conceptions or of shrinking to the level of the meanest and minutest enquiries'.[2] The Strand block decoration, mostly designed by Cipriani and carved by Wilton, Carlini, Bacon, Nollekens and Ceracchi, is beautifully balanced, remaining subordinate to the main lines of the design and yet quietly asserting itself as a foil on the lower storeys and developing into a flourish in the surmounting ornamentation.

The Academy's doorway was inside the entrance vestibule on the west side of this compact and stately block. On the Strand front, nine arches of rusticated masonry form a sturdy base comprising the ground and mezzanine floors, and they carry two storeys embraced by Corinthian columns. Above these rises an attic, faced with four figures in senatorial robes, and surmounting it is a group of sculpture by John Bacon (*The Arms of the British Empire* supported by *Fame* and *The Genius of England*). The three central arches lead to the vestibule which runs north and south. It has coupled Doric columns and a splendid coffered vault.

This part of Somerset House was completed in 1780. Both the exterior and the Academy's rooms are described by Joseph Baretti in his *A Guide through the Royal Academy* which was published probably in 1781. The most picturesque views, showing the building in its eighteenth-century surroundings, are the well-known aquatints by Thomas Malton (Plate 16).[3]

A visitor to the Academy's rooms would have passed through the doorway, surmounted by a bust of Michelangelo by Joseph Wilton, and found himself in an entrance hall, only about twenty-five feet square but looking much larger because of the daylight shining from above on to the staircase beyond. It is the subject of an engraving (published in 1810 in Ackermann's *Repository of Arts*, No. 17) which shows it furnished with figures of Apollo, Hercules and the Furietti Centaurs, together with chairs which still exist at Burlington House. George Scharf painted a watercolour of it some years later, in 1836, by which time several more large casts had been added (Plate 17).

On the visitor's right was the Porter's Lodge and the Life School, shown in an illustration by Rowlandson and Pugin dated 1808 (front endpapers).[4] Facing him was a Doric screen and, after passing through this, he would commence a long climb up the elliptical staircase which, says Baretti, 'affords a constant-moving Picture of every gay and brilliant Object which graces the Beau-Monde of this vast Capital, pleasantly contrasted with wise Connoisseurs and sprightly Dilettantes of every size and denomination'.[5] It did not, however, conjure up such a picture of elegance in Thomas Rowlandson's mind. His drawing *A Soirée at the Royal Academy*, sometimes called *The Academy Stare-Case*, c. 1800, is a brilliant caricature (Plate 21). There is, however, the sobering thought that all works submitted for the exhibitions between 1780 and 1836 must have been either carried up this steep, winding ascent, from the entrance hall to the exhibition rooms, or else hauled up the well by ropes. Great full-lengths by Reynolds, Gainsborough, Raeburn and Lawrence, etc., which are now precious treasures, were subjected to this peril. There is proof that the climb was arduous in that a chair used to be placed on each landing when Queen Charlotte visited the exhibitions, in order that she might rest; and also in the fact that, after an illness, Samuel Johnson boasted that he was now so completely recovered that he could run up the whole staircase of the Royal Academy if necessary.

The principal floor contained the Academy of Antiques, the scene of the painting attributed to Zoffany, *The Antique School of the Royal Academy, Somerset House*,[6] also the Assembly or Lecture Room, shown in Henry Singleton's *The Royal Academicians in General Assembly* (Plate 28), dated 1795, and the very fine apartment which was the Library and is still almost unaltered. They were used for their respective purposes except when required for the annual exhibition and, even then, the Assembly Room, called the Council Room in the official catalogues, was mostly hung with the Academy's permanent possessions.

Chambers obviously envisaged the exact position of particular pictures in these private rooms. His scheme for the east wall of the Assembly Room (also used for Council Meetings), which is among the collection of drawings at the Soane Museum, was carried out precisely and is shown in Singleton's painting: the fireplace, by Wilton, surmounted by Carlini's statuette of George III on horseback,[7] with an oval flower picture by Mary Moser on each side,[8] has Benjamin West's *Christ blessing little Children*[9] high up over the centre and Reynolds' full-length portraits *George III* (Plate 1)[10] and *Queen Charlotte*[11] on the left and right. All these works, together with others which can easily be identified in the picture, are still in the Academy's possession at Burlington House. The large ceiling paintings which were in this room will be mentioned again later.[12] They were by Benjamin West and Angelica Kauffmann and were set in a design which also included twelve small circular panels by Biagio Rebecca of great artists of the past.

Reynolds' *Theory* (Plate 12), a female figure seated on a cloud and holding a scroll with the words 'Theory is the knowledge of what is truly Nature', had been painted for the Library in old Somerset House and it was made the centre-piece of the new Library ceiling in Chambers' building. In recent times it has been hung on a wall in Burlington House and naturally its perspective looks somewhat peculiar in such a position. At Somerset House it was surrounded by the work of Cipriani – representations of Nature, History, Allegory and Fable in each of the four coves – and this artist also painted the decorations in chiaroscuro on the staircase.

The would-be visitor to the exhibition was still only half-way up to the Great Room on the next storey and it was eventually reached through an open screen of columns on the top landing and then an ante-room about the same size as the ground-floor hall. The ante-room was furnished with antique busts in niches and with a great deal of painted architectural decoration to simulate in this restricted space a truly grand entrance to the exhibition. Should the elegance of the vestibule and the decorative delights of the long approach not have been sufficient to instil a proper respect in the minds of the pilgrims who had ventured thus far, there was over the final doorway a Greek inscription 'ΟΥΔΕΙΣ ΑΜΟΥΣΟΣ ΕΙΣΙΤΩ' ('Let no Stranger to the Muses enter').

The Great Room lived up to its name. It was 53 feet 3 inches long by 43 feet 6 inches wide and 32 feet high including the lantern, undoubtedly at that date the finest gallery in Britain for displaying pictures. John Henry Ramberg made several drawings of it[13] and they were used by Pietro Antonio Martini for his engraving entitled *The Exhibition of the Royal Academy, 1787* (Plate 18), on which appears the Greek inscription. It shows Sir Joshua Reynolds, equipped with an ear-trumpet, conducting the Prince of Wales, afterwards George IV, round the exhibition. Another by the same artists was published the following year – *Portraits of their Majesties and the Royal Family viewing the Exhibition of the Royal Academy, 1788* – and there is a well-known print of the Great Room by Rowlandson and Pugin – *Exhibition Room, Somerset House* (Plate 19 and back endpapers),[14] dated 1808 – and a lithograph by George Scharf showing it in use for a lecture by Sir Richard Westmacott in 1830. The number of exhibits increased considerably in the new rooms at Somerset House. There were, for instance, 547 in 1781 and 672 in 1791, so that the pictures still had to be hung almost from floor to ceiling and with frames touching one another. It must have been an immense jig-saw puzzle for the Hanging Committee to fit together. The exhibition receipts amounted to £3,069 1s 0d in 1780 and thereafter they grew from year to year so that subsequently the Royal Academy has been able to pay its own way although this has become increasingly difficult in the twentieth century. In 1783 Dr Johnson wrote to his friend Mrs Thrale[15] that, on a certain Monday, £190 was received at the door from 3,800 visitors. Nobody was admitted on Sundays.

Exhibition matters, however, did not run entirely smoothly. Artists still asked for extra time in delivering their works. In 1782 John Downman sought a guarantee that his would be hung in the Great Room but this was refused and, in 1791, Richard Livesay failed in his attempt to dictate how his pictures should be placed. Someone tried to send in two pictures by Angelica Kauffmann without her authority and a Miss Lane wanted to exhibit one made of hair. Others submitted drawings copied from paintings. All were returned. The most famous example of an Academician trying to influence the hanging was when Thomas Gainsborough sent the following letters[16] in April 1783:

To the Council of the Royal Academy.

Mr Gainsborough presents his compliments to the Gentlemen appointed to hang the pictures at the Royal Academy; and begs leave to hint to them, that if the Royal Family, which he has sent for this Exhibition (being smaller than three quarters) are hung above the line along with

full-lengths, he never more, whilst he breaths, will send another picture to the Exhibition. This he swears by God.
Saturday morn.

To F. M. Newton (Secretary of the Royal Academy)
Dear Newton,
   I wd beg to have them hung with the Frames touching each other, in this order. The names are written behind each Picture. God bless you hang my Dogs and my Landskips in the great Room. The sea Piece you may fill the small Room with.

Yrs sincerely in haste,
T. Gainsborough

A sketch was appended and the committee complied with his request. This presumably encouraged him to write again in 1784.[17]

To the Gentlemen of the Hanging Committee of the Royal Academy.
   Mr Gainsborough's Compls to the Gentlemen of the Committee, and begs pardon for giving them so much trouble; but as he has painted the Picture of the Princess, in so tender a light, that notwithstanding he approves very much of the established line for strong Effects, he cannot possibly consent to have it placed higher than five feet & a half, because the likeness & Work of the Picture will not be seen any higher; therefore at a word, he will not trouble the Gentlemen against their Inclination, but will beg the rest of his Pictures back again.
Saturday Evening.

On this occasion the committee refused to be dictated to and replied by return messenger as follows:[18]

Sir,
   In compliance with your request the Council have ordered your Pictures to be taken down to be delivered to your order, whenever send for them.

I am and etc.

Saturday evening 9 o/clo.

Gainsborough never exhibited at the Academy again but, in 1788, wrote to Sir Joshua Reynolds a most touching letter from his death-bed:[19]

Dear Sir Joshua,
   I am just to write what I fear you will not read after lying in a dying state for 6 months. The extreme affection which I am informed by a

Friend which Sir Joshua has expressed induces me to beg a last favour, which is to come once under my Roof and look at my things, my woodman you never saw, if what I ask now is not disagreable to your feeling that I may have the honor to speak to you. I can from a sincere Heart say that I always admired and sincerely loved Sir Joshua Reynolds.

Tho. Gainsborough.

The President duly visited him, inscribed the letter on the back, 'Gainsborough when dying' and saved it for posterity. He also paid him a glowing tribute in his penultimate discourse which was given, as was the custom, on 10 December that year when the premiums were distributed:

> We have lately lost Mr Gainsborough, one of the greatest ornaments of our Academy. It is not our business here, to make panegyricks on the living, or even on the dead who were of our body. The praise of the former might bear the appearance of adulation; and the latter, of untimely justice; perhaps of envy to those whom we have still the happiness to enjoy, by an oblique suggestion of invidious comparisons. In discoursing therefore on the talents of the late Mr Gainsborough, my object is, not so much to praise or to blame him, as to draw from his excellencies and defects matter of instruction to the Students in our Academy. If ever this nation should produce genius sufficient to acquire to us the honourable distinction of an English School, the name of Gainsborough will be transmitted to posterity, in the history of the Art, among the very first of that rising name.[20]

As Gainsborough himself is reputed to have whispered, as his last words, 'We are all going to heaven, and Vandyke is of the party.'[21]

Gainsborough's opinion of Reynolds as an artist was equally high and he had once said of him 'Damn him, how various he is!'[22] The two men, whose names are usually coupled together when speaking of the climax of British painting in the eighteenth century, were very different in their temperaments as well as in their art. Reynolds was born to be a figurehead and leader. His failings were perhaps more obvious than Gainsborough's. He was dignified, sometimes pompous – a man of words as well as deeds. Gainsborough on the other hand was not a literary man. He and his friends loved music and this lyrical streak of warmth and sunshine, usually most delicate but sometimes tinged with a half-mocking cruelty, kept him apart from his artist colleagues. He was content to leave the administrative tasks to others but, egoist as he was, thought little of their efforts. Paradoxically the rivalry of these two men has been far greater since their death than ever it was in their lifetime. In the fashionable world of the eighteenth century their paths seldom crossed; their work differed too much for competition to have had much effect. Their names live today to mark a summit of achievement which would not be so high without the one or the other.

Reynolds' rule was not, however, entirely undisputed particularly in his later period. The Professorship of Perspective had been vacant for three years since the death of Samuel Wale when, in 1789, the President let it be understood that he thought that the members should promote Joseph Bonomi to the rank of Academician and elect him as Professor immediately. The advice was resented and, in particular, the way in which Reynolds had introduced to the Assembly some drawings by the Italian. They were banished from the room by a majority vote and the matter was further complicated by the only other candidate for the Professorship (Edward Edwards) refusing to submit drawings. All this brought about Reynolds' resignation both as President and as an Academician in a letter of 22 February 1790:[23]

> Sir,
>
> I beg you inform the Council, which I understand meet this Evening with my fixed resolution of resigning the Presidency of the Royal Academy, and consequently my seat as Academician, As I can be no longer of any service to the Academy as President, it would be still less in my power, in a subordinate station, I therefore now take my final leave of the Academy with my sincere good wishes for its prosperity, and with all due respect to its members.
>
> I am,
Sir,
Your most humble and most
obedient Servant
Joshua Reynolds.

Chambers took the chair for a meeting or two but the members soon realized that the matter was not important enough to justify the loss of so able and conscientious a President. A face-saving formula for both sides was devised, by a pretence that there had been a misunderstanding, and Reynolds was prevailed upon to continue as the acknowledged leader.

Another pin-prick for Reynolds occurred in 1791 when his advice that £100 should be given towards a memorial to the late Dr Johnson was outmanoeuvred by Chambers. He induced the King to refuse permission on the grounds that the Academy's money was for the purposes of the institution only. In his heart of hearts Reynolds must have acknowledged this. He had in 1787 unsuccessfully tried to excuse the Academy from insuring the Somerset House premises and tried to get the Crown to accept the responsibility.

The Academy was soon to have additional rooms and its finances were sound. The 'Solid Fund', as it was called, amounted to £6,000 in 1785 and the Charity Fund stood at £2,100. The total of donations each year increased, 5s per person was granted for attendance at a General Assembly, half a guinea a day was paid to each member of the Exhibition Committee, the awards to the travelling students were raised from £60 to £100 per annum and a set of engravings by Hogarth was purchased for £105.

Another sign of prosperity was that more guests were invited to the Annual Dinner and, from 1787 onwards, catering was always for a hundred or more. The members paid for themselves at 6s for the main dinner and 1s 6d for dessert. In 1782 the wine was to be 'Claret, Madeira, Port and Carravella' while the servants were to be allowed 'a pot of porter, & a bottle of Port or Lisbon between three'.[24] The Prince of Wales (afterwards George IV) accepted an invitation in 1784 but, though the company waited for him, he had forgotten the appointment and failed to appear. Steps were taken so that the lapse should not recur and he in fact attended regularly from 1785 onwards. The music and jollity at these functions continued and there was the occasion when the usually sober-sided Sir William Chambers vied with James Boswell in composing verses at table.

It has been said that the content of the exhibitions of this period was not of such high standard as in the first ten years and that Reynolds felt bound to bolster them by submitting many of his own works. It was certainly not unusual for him to show between fifteen and twenty pictures at Somerset House. Even so space was still limited and in 1791 it was agreed 'that no single miniature be allowed more than 1″ framing'.[25] Thomas Lawrence first exhibited in 1787 and Reynolds said to him 'In you, Sir, the world will expect to see accomplished what I have failed to achieve.'[26] This was indeed a self-denying tribute to the young man's gifts.

Work in the Schools continued peacefully except that there was a little trouble with James Barry over his lectures. More than two hundred and fifty students were admitted including, besides Lawrence, young J. M. W. Turner and Martin Archer Shee. The studentship was limited to six years but winners of the gold medals were allowed free access for life. Moser died in 1783 and was followed as Keeper by Agostino Carlini and then Joseph Wilton. Edward Penny resigned through ill-health as Professor of Painting and his place was taken by James Barry. John Sheldon followed William Hunter as Professor of Anatomy.

Dr Johnson and Joseph Baretti both died and were replaced respectively by Bennet Langton and James Boswell. To prove his competence as the new Secretary for Foreign Correspondence, Boswell sent in short acknowledgments in French and Italian as well as English.[27] The office of Chaplain was created in 1784 and it was filled by the appointment of the Revd M. W. Peters, RA. There was at one time a suggestion that the Honorary Members might be given Diplomas but George III wished this privilege to be confined to artists.

A major change was caused by the resignation of F. M. Newton as Secretary in 1788. Born in 1720, he had been the Academy's hard-working scribe since the foundation. He was succeeded by John Inigo Richards. The Librarianship passed from Richard Wilson to Samuel Wale, Joseph Wilton and then to Dominic Serres. George Stubbs and Joseph Wright of Derby were the first artists to be elected Royal Academicians but not to complete the necessary formalities. This brought in a new rule imposing a time limit of twelve months and accounts for these artists appearing in the official records as Associates only.

Reynolds reached the age of sixty-six in 1789 and his eyesight began to fail. Although he gave notice that he did not wish to seek re-election as President in December 1791, he was persuaded to carry on but died two months later. His fifteenth discourse in 1790 proved to be his last and he had his desire fulfilled 'that the last words which I should pronounce in this Academy, and from this place, might be the name of – MICHAEL ANGELO'.[28] A joist in the floor-boards cracked and gave way during this speech but Reynolds continued unperturbed.

The Council Minutes in 1792 record 'On the 23rd of Feb^y. 'twixt Eight & Nine in the Evening: Died Our worthy President.'[29] The funeral and burial in St Paul's Cathedral were conducted with great pomp, the body lying the previous night in the Academy's rooms at Somerset House, and so there passed the figurehead of the Academy's first era.

___7___
WEST'S FIRST PERIOD AS PRESIDENT
1792–1805

It was not easy to find a suitable successor to Reynolds but one man seemed to have more attributes than the others. He was the American-born Benjamin West (Plate 26) who had been settled in London since 1763 and was one of the Academy's foundation members. He had before then spent three years in Italy and, as has been noted in previous chapters, he was much favoured by George III. Indeed for many years he received a pension of £1,000 from the King in return for which he painted a large number of historical pictures which are still in the royal collections.

With Sir William Chambers in the chair, Benjamin West was duly elected President by twenty-nine votes to one, cast for Richard Cosway, on 17 March 1792. Throughout his Presidency he wore his hat on all formal occasions at the Academy 'to do honour to the office'[1] and Sir Thomas Lawrence, his successor, continued this practice in the 1820s. West was also instrumental in introducing special gowns for the Academy porters on important occasions. They were in abeyance for a time in the nineteenth century but the custom was revived under Queen Victoria and still flourished on Private View Days up to this decade.

West was not unaware of the difficulty of following a first and successful President. In his opening speech, he said:

> I feel more sensibly the dignity to which you have raised me, as I am placed in succession after so eminent a character, whose exalted professional abilities, and very excellent discourses delivered under this roof, have seemed a lasting honor to this Institution and to the country. . . .[2]

He too gave biennial discourses at the distributions of prizes to the students and it is not belittling to him to suggest that he did his best to carry on the traditions set by Reynolds. He claimed 'it shall be my invariable study to demonstrate my duty to my sovereign, my love for

55

this Institution, and my zeal for the cultivation of genius, and the growth of universal virtue'.[3] On his election, the King was prepared to award a knighthood but West refused. It is evident from his reply that he would have accepted 'a more permanent title'[4] such as a baronetcy if it had been offered but it was not. He vowed that he had no ambition for a title which 'would perish with myself'[5] and we are told that George III was content with the answer.

The Academy's activities under the new President continued much as usual and its finances improved regularly. A profit of £400 per annum was being made and, by 1796, the institution held stocks to the value of £16,000. Chambers had kept the accounts in rather an amateurish fashion and, even before his death that year, steps were being taken to regularize the position. George Dance and William Tyler made a thorough investigation and became the Academy's first Auditors. They recommended among other things that Trustees should be appointed and this system continues today. The President and Treasurer are now automatically Trustees and two other Academicians are elected to serve with them.

The Academy's financial position seemed to be so sound that a pension fund was established for members and their widows though James Barry was against the proposal. As Professor of Painting, he considered that the money would be better employed on acquiring pictures as examples for the students. Joseph Farington (Plate 28), whose diary from 1793 to 1821 is a valuable source of incidental information, 'thought it proper in all respects now to establish the fund proposed, which would contribute to encourage artists to devote some of their time to executing works for reputation, which they would do when relieved from apprehension for themselves and their families'.[6] 'In this,' he writes, 'great service wd. be rendered to the art. – After such provision had been made it would be an object with the Academy to add to their Collections.'[7] Farington was never an Officer of the Royal Academy but was at one time looked upon almost as its dictator. He seems to have been consulted both officially and unofficially on very many subjects and to have exercised a powerful influence on trivial as well as important matters. He served for a long time as one of the Auditors and so would have been familiar with all transactions involving finance.

The number and amounts of donations were considerably increased in this period, Philip Reinagle being awarded the very large sum of £150 to alleviate his distress in 1798, and in that year £500 was voted to the Government 'towards the exigencies of the State'[8] which were brought about by the Napoleonic Wars. The King's birthday dinners had hitherto been subsidized by the two stewards who in turn undertook to run them but, from then on, the Academy agreed to pay any deficiency. More guests than ever were invited to the Annual Dinners which were held immediately prior to the opening of the exhibition. In 1797 the messenger was required to deliver one hundred and sixty-six such invitations and his fee was doubled from one to two guineas for the job. In 1799 the Secretary's salary was raised to £100.

In 1793 there were celebrations to commemorate the Academy's twenty-fifth anniversary. It was agreed for there to be a medal by T. Pingo, examples in gold to be given to the royal family and in silver to the Academicians and Associates but, in that none can be traced today, it may not have materialized. Certainly a loyal address was presented to the King and the President spoke at a special dinner held at Somerset House.

The death of Sir William Chambers in 1796 severed the Academy's closest connection with the Crown and thereafter the institution's other Officers had more standing. John Yenn, Clerk of the Works at various royal palaces, became the new Treasurer but his access to the King was confined to financial matters. The Secretary presented items of business within his own purview and West's audiences with the Sovereign were far more frequent than ever Reynolds' had been. Chambers had even kept the Diploma plates and medal dies under his personal control but these were now housed at the Academy. The institution's petition for more rooms at Somerset House in 1797 was successful and altogether it was a period of fuller development. An abstract of the Laws and regulations was printed and certain laxities were re-examined. The Secretary produced a most useful index to the minutes which survives.[9] In 1797 also a list of members was inserted in the catalogue for the first time, the object being to prevent certain unscrupulous artists from claiming an honour to which they were not entitled. Hitherto the catalogues had always been free but, from 1798, a charge of six-pence was made for them in addition to the price of one shilling for admission.

The Schools continued to function though by 1800 the discipline under the aged Keeper, Joseph Wilton, became extremely slack and some classes were poorly attended. In that year a committee was appointed to look into the matter and stringent reforms were made. A few students in the life class were relegated to draw again from casts and many were threatened with expulsion. More casts were purchased and the Academy received from the Duke of Bedford a set of full-sized copies by Sir James Thornhill of Raphael's cartoons;[10] also, from Miss Margaret Gainsborough, a large landscape[11] by her father. In 1801 a cast of the anatomized body of a murderer (James Legge), fastened to a wooden cross, was obtained for the school.[12] It had been skilfully made by Thomas Banks, under the direction of the surgeon-anatomist Joseph Constantine Carpue, to simulate as nearly as possible a crucified figure. The Council, however, refused the offer to buy Robert Udny's collection of pictures on his death in 1802.

Among the new students there were George Chinnery, George Dawe, Henry Bone, the brothers Richard and Robert Smirke, Augustus Wall Callcott, William Daniell, John Constable, William Mulready, Washington Allston, Benjamin Robert Haydon and David Wilkie. Little is known about many of the others, even among those who won the gold medal. Louis de la Monpeye joined the Schools for 'amusement' and we learn that Thomas Westmacot won a prize and 'dy'd soon after'. What other heartbreaking stories may lie hidden?

In 1792 it was decided that studentships for all those admitted should be for life but that the accompanying privilege of free access to the exhibitions should be for seven years only. This is in strong contrast with today's students who mostly feel confident after only two or three years at an art school. Reynolds had firmly believed in the necessity for sound training although even he accepted that this was but a beginning. 'We can teach you here but very little,' he said, 'you are henceforth to be your own teachers'[13] and most of us will admit that we have learned a great deal in later life which no amount of cramming at school could ever have instilled. In those days, before the common use of India-rubber, it was the custom to rub out with bread and apparently this used to be provided free. On the last day of that year the Council solemnly resolved 'that henceforward, No Bread, be allowed in the Academy for the Students'[14] and the reason for this is gleaned from an entry in Farington's diary of the same date. He records the following circumstances:

Mr Wilton having mentioned to me that the Students in the Plaister Academy continue to behave very rudely; and that they have a practise of throwing the bread, allowed them by the Academy for rubbing out, at each other, so as to waste so much that the Bill for bread sometimes amounts to Sixteen Shillings a week; and this relation of Mr Wilton being corroborated by Mr Richards, I moved that 'in future no bread be allowed the Students'. This was unanimously agreed to. Mr West said independant of every other consideration it would be productive of much good to the Students to deprive them of the use of bread; as they would be induced to pay more atention to their outlines; and would learn to draw more correct, when they had not the perpetual resource of rubbing out.[15]

The students of those days were obviously not all paragons and, in the following year, had to be reminded that loitering and drinking in the entrance hall were forbidden.

The annual 'indulgencies' to artists, permitting them 'to send their performances' late for the exhibition,[16] were becoming a great nuisance and a stop was put on them in 1799. This was indeed only enforcing a regulation which had been in existence on the statute book, though not in fact, since the foundation. In the following year, it was agreed that no one should be allowed to submit more than 'eight pictures and eight drawings'.[17] The size of the exhibitions continued to increase. There were, for instance, 886 exhibits in 1795 and 1,100 in 1800, but the quality was again said to have been not so good. Reynolds' contributions were sorely missed and his standards were long remembered. Lawrence, Beechey and Hoppner were the chief portrait painters (Plates 30–32) and Turner's landscapes attracted considerable attention. Indeed, in 1796, he admitted to Joseph Farington that he had more commissions than he could execute and, in 1804, he opened a large gallery, 70 feet long by 20 feet wide, at his own house. He was elected an Associate of the Royal Academy in 1799 and an Academician only three years later. Raeburn showed two portraits in 1792 but was not represented again until 1798. He was not made an Associate until 1812 but, as was the case with Turner (Plate 23), he had to wait only three years longer before attaining the rank of Academician. James Ward withdrew all his pictures in 1804 following the rejection of a very large one which he had submitted. The exhibitions were frequently abused in the newspapers, particularly by a somewhat scurrilous critic, John Williams, who wrote under the pseudonym of Anthony Pasquin. There was still discontent from year to year on the placing of pictures and rivalries occasionally caused minor explosions.

Twenty-three new Associates were elected between 1792 and 1805 including John Soane, John Flaxman, Martin Archer Shee and, as has been said, J. M. W. Turner, who had only just reached the lower age limit of twenty-four which was imposed in 1796. It is notable that all but four had been Academy students and it must be remembered that the Schools at that time were unique in this country as a source of learning and inspiration in the fine arts. Would Turner and Constable, to name but two, have attained an international repute without such free tuition? Promotion to the rank of Academician was by no means automatic though it was impossible without being first an Associate. Except for the foundation members, this rule has applied throughout the Academy's history but was relaxed from 1981 in respect of artists over seventy-five years of age who then became eligible for direct election as Senior Academicians.

It is sometimes said that the art of writing minutes lies far more in leaving things out than in putting them in and one could wish that the Secretary (John Richards) had not been so proficient at his task. His records are for the most part extremely dry and to the point where one might have hoped for more argumentative information. It is clear, however, that the Council were beginning to be consulted on certain matters outside their normal day-to-day business. They were successful in a plea to the Government for artists returning from Rome to be allowed to import works of art duty-free and undertook the appointment of inspectors to see that the concession was not abused. They advised on coinage as well as on a statue of Lord Cornwallis for Madras and they helped on the question of copyright in sculptured models. At last the country had an organization from which advice could be sought on matters affecting artists. The Academy was gaining considerable influence.

Members were keen to take their turn of service on the Council and, when in 1799 his name had been passed over, Henry Tresham successfully protested that 'the seats in the Council shall go by succession'.[18] 'I wish it here to be clearly understood,' he said, 'that the merits of the gentlemen elected into the Council are unquestionable . . . but the question turns on a point in which superior capacities and attainments have no weight, the Law is clear and explicit.'[19] Tresham was an irascible Irishman who took on the part of chief rebel against West and, in 1804, is thought to have been responsible for some satirical verses which were distributed to the Academicians at the Annual Dinner that year.

A more serious *contretemps* concerned James Barry whose ideas had been at variance with those of his colleagues for many years. Indeed he had not exhibited at the Academy since 1776. As Professor of Painting, he had been a lone wolf in having direct access to the students and imparting views opposed to the opinions of the majority. Matters came to a head in 1799 when the Keeper, Joseph Wilton, sent the following letter to the President and Council:

Had I now the honor of a seat amongst you, I should move, (in consequence of some Transactions, which, with great sorrow, I had heretofore, and have recently witnessed;) that an immediate consideration were had, on a subject, which I conceive, to be of most serious concern, to the Dignity, and permanent Welfare, of our Sovereign's Royal Institution: to its Interests; to the Decorum, necessary to be kept up, and observed, in all the functions of the Academy; to the due reverence for it's Laws and Regulations; and the proper Respect, which ought at all times, to be shewn to the Body of Academicians at Large.

I nevertheless, felt it my particular Duty (from the situation I hold in the Academy) to take this method of representing to the Council, the dangerous tendency of a practice, frequently adopted by the present Professor of Painting; of making long Digressions from the Subject, on which he is bound exclusively to Discourse; in order to utter the most virulent abuse, on the established Laws, the Acts, and Government of the Academy; and calumniating its actual, & even, its deceased Members. And also, hinting to his Auditors, that the Academy's Money was disposed of, in a misterious & secret manner, in Pensions for themselves. And proclaiming to many Strangers then present; particularly to the Students, that the Academy possess'd 16000 pounds; but Alas! Alas! he lamented, & feared, that no part thereof, would ever be employed in the purchase of a few Pictures for their advancement in the Art. Thus encouraging them to Licentiousness and to depreciate the manifest Advantages, which they have long enjoy'd, & continue to receive from the Bounty of this noble Institution.

These, & many other unwarrantable expressions made use of by Mr Barry, at the close of his last, & in the middle of his antecedent Lecture, I hope will induce the Gentlemen of the Council, and the general Body of Academicians, to exert the Power, which the Constitution of the Academy has given them, to put a stop for ever, to such mischievous proceedings; and trusting that I shall not, by this Denunciation incur the displeasure of any Gentleman, as it has proceeded from a meer sense of the Duty, I owe to the Academy, & not from personal ill will, or Enmity to Mr Barry, or any of his Friends, which I most solemnly disclaim. And flattering myself, that I shall ever be regarded (as I sincerely profess myself to be) a well wisher, to the Prosperity, to the Peace, and Dignity of the Royal Academy, I humbly subscribe myself

Mr President and Gentlemen of the Council
Your most obliged
most obedient

Royal Academy   and devoted Servant,
March, 2ᵈ: 1799   Joseph Wilton.[20]

The charges were supported by Dance, Smirke, Daniell and Farington and, on Farington's suggestion, Barry's pamphlet *A Letter to the Dilettanti Society respecting the obtention of certain matters essentially necessary for the improvement of Public Taste, and for accomplishing the original views of the Royal Academy in Great Britain*, dated 25 July 1797, was also taken in evidence against him. Poor Barry was not allowed a copy of the charges but a committee of eleven members (George Dance, Joseph Farington, William Hamilton, James Wyatt, Robert Smirke, Richard Westall, Thomas Banks, John Hoppner, Thomas Stothard, Sir Francis Bourgeois and Thomas Lawrence) was elected to look into the matter and to report. On 15 April 1799, by votes in the General Assembly and with the approval of the Sovereign, James Barry was removed from the post of Professor of Painting and expelled from the the Academy. This has so far been the only expulsion throughout the Academy's history though Ramsay Richard Reinagle was virtually compelled to resign in 1848 following unethical conduct. Fuseli (Plate 22) was elected to the Professorship; he became Keeper on the death of Wilton in 1803 but only after the King had refused the nomination of Robert Smirke. Fuseli, a man of strange habits and strong language, was unpopular at first probably because he was something of a martinet and the cry 'Beware of Fuseli'[21] was often heard in the Schools. Benjamin Robert Haydon, who was one of his early students, called him 'the most grotesque mixture of literature, art, scepticism, indelicacy, profanity, and kindness'.[22] Edward Burch undertook the Librarianship in 1794 and George Dance took Thomas Sandby's place as Professor of Architecture in 1798. Prince Hoare succeeded James Boswell as Secretary for Foreign Correspondence.

Benjamin West managed to keep the ship on an even keel, usually by staying quietly in the background, but he himself was not without his critics, particularly his fellow-American, John Singleton Copley (Plate 28). In 1801 he had suffered some eclipse of his favour with the King and was never thereafter on such intimate terms with him. In

1803 he submitted a picture to the Academy exhibition which was a repainted version of the *Hagar and Ishmael*[23] which he had shown in 1776 and, though he defended himself successfully, his reputation had been tainted. He had wished to resign the Presidency there and then but George III said, 'No, No, all parties concur in wishing you to remain in it, nor can any other be proposed so proper. You have had my friendship & shall continue to have it, and make yourself easy.'[24] West accordingly exhibited the picture in 1804 but, in December that year, he was opposed by a faction who tried to put James Wyatt in the chair. Henry Tresham, the rather disturbing Irishman, suggested that, as West 'had not done his duty as President' and 'had not His Majesty's confidence',[25] it would be highly improper to re-elect him. He therefore proposed Wyatt and was supported by Bourgeois, Beechey, Copley, Cosway and Yenn among others. He then informed the Assembly that Mr Yenn had a message to convey from the King but poor Yenn had no such authority and retreated in agitation. West was duly re-elected by a handsome majority and George III gave his unqualified approval. Matters were not allowed to rest there, however, and there was so much disquiet in the Academy during the ensuing year that West formally resigned the Presidency. James Wyatt was duly elected in his place on 10 December 1805.

One other dispute in 1803 must also be recorded though it was ordered by the King to be expunged from the minutes. It concerned the relative powers of the Council and the General Assembly, a point which has caused differences of opinion again in recent years. The General Assembly had dealt with certain financial matters in a way which was repudiated by the Council, five of whose members were then suspended by the Assembly. They appealed to the King and, on the advice of the Attorney-General, their view was upheld and they were reinstated. Although harmony was in part restored, several discordant notes lingered on and undoubtedly led to the change in the Presidency.

Another matter not recorded in the minutes is the foundation of the (Royal) Society of Painters in Water Colours in 1804. This came about on account of the alleged neglect of these artists and their work in the Academy where only oil painters were considered of sufficient standing for election as members. Watercolours were squeezed into odd corners of the exhibition as a rather inferior class of work and indeed they were often omitted altogether through want of hanging space. This brought into existence, by way of protest, a society which catered especially for works in this medium. Similarly the Academy was almost entirely confined to artists working in London and this caused the Norwich Society to commence their own exhibitions in that same year. These are but the first two examples of new groups which have been formed from time to time since then because of sparse representation in the Academy's exhibitions.

8

THE LAST OF THE FOUNDERS
1806–1820

James Wyatt was President for one year only and even so missed many meetings by being out of town. As the day drew near for his re-election or for the appointment of a successor, various Academicians discussed the possibilities. On 26 November 1806, one of them, Ozias Humphry, wrote as follows to Robert Braun who held a position at the court of George III:

> You may possibly recollect that on account of existing differences among the members of the Royal Academy, Mr Wyatt was chosen President on the 10th of December last, for the ensuing year, with the hope that by affording leisure for consideration some means might be discovered for making arrangements that would improve the Government and render it more tranquil and harmonious in future.
>
> A year has now elapsed without having produced, as it is said, the desired effect.
>
> As the period is now approaching for the annual election of officers in the Academy, I beg leave to ask if you think it is desired by his Majesty that Mr Wyatt should be re-elected, or if there would probably be any objection to Mr West if he should be chosen to the chair, which I believe many of the most respectable members very anxiously desire. I rely upon the favour of hearing from you as soon as you conveniently can.

Humphry kept a copy of the letter and has written on it:

> To this no answer whatever was given. It was therefore concluded that his Majesty was unwilling to supersede Mr Wyatt, or to signify any disapprobation of Mr West. The members of the Royal Academy, thinking themselves at liberty to choose for themselves, exercised their privilege and chose Mr West by a majority of four to one, against Mr De Loutherbourg, Sir William Beechey and Mr Hoppner.[1]

In fact, on 10 December 1806, with James Wyatt absent and George Dance taking his place in the chair, Benjamin West was elected with seventeen votes against four cast for P. J. de Loutherbourg and, at the first ballot, one each for Beechey and Hoppner. West thereafter continued as President, with hardly ever a vote against him, until his death in 1820. It cannot be said that he was as assiduous in his duties as Reynolds had been in his time or that he was an undoubted leader but he was well liked by the majority. Frequently he was late in his attendance at meetings and minor ailments kept him away altogether at times. The Council Minutes of 1 December 1809 open with the words, 'The President in the Gout, Sir William Beechey in the Chair'[2] and it is apparent that he had attacks over long periods. The Secretary (John Richards) became ill in 1810 and died in the following year. Henry Howard first acted as his deputy and afterwards took over the position. Many matters of trifling importance are recorded, including an argument with the Keeper on whether a plate should be fixed over a certain key-hole, and it is obvious that the Council were held down to their task. They even had to forfeit ten shillings if they left a meeting too early.

Joseph Bonomi wrote to West from Rome in November 1807 that Angelica Kauffmann had 'couragiously met the death of the Righteous on Thursday last, 5th inst' and he gave the following account of the illness and funeral:

> During her severe Illness all her numerous Friends, did what they could to restore her and every one was grieved in the apprehension of loosing her; you may easily believe more than I can express how much their grief increased at her Death, I only therefore shall mention that they vied with each other, in endeavouring to perform their last duties in the most decorous obsequies, Celebrated this Morning in the Church of St Andrea delli Frati, conducted by Canova and other virtuosi Friends. The Church was decorated as is customary for Nobles: at 10 o'clock in the morning the Corpse was accompanied to the Church by two very numerous Brotherhoods, Fifty Capuchins and Fifty Priests. The Bier was carried by some of the Brotherhood, but the four Corners of the Pall, by four Young Ladies properly dressed for the occasion, the four Tassels were held by the Four first Gentlemen of the Academy; these were followed by the rest of the Academicians and Virtuosi who carried in Triumph two of her Pictures; and every one with a large Taper lighted.
>
> This Sir is the melancholy account I thought it my duty to transmit to you as President of the Royal Academy.[3]

The other woman foundation member, Mary Moser (by then Mrs Lloyd), lived on till 1819 and in her later years attended a number of the Academy's meetings in person. Paul Sandby died in 1809 and Francesco Bartolozzi in 1815. George Dance was the only one of the original Academicians to survive beyond 1820.

The accommodation at Somerset House which had been occupied as living quarters by the late Secretary was converted on his death in 1811 into exhibition galleries and some newly acquired smaller rooms were brought into use. An innovation for a few years from 1810 was that the Council (or Assembly) Room formed part of the annual exhibition with a display of the Academy's own pictures. They are first listed in the catalogue of 1811. It shows that fifty-nine such works were on view that year, including the full-length portraits *George III* (Plate 1) and *Queen Charlotte* by Reynolds,[4] and it describes the ceiling paintings by Benjamin West (Plate 24a), Angelica Kauffmann (Plate 24b)[5] and G. B. Cipriani.

The interest in the exhibitions continued to increase and the invitations to the Private View were so much in demand that the numbers had to be curtailed. No admission was granted on Sundays except to the Royal Family. David Wilkie's genre pictures were always popular from his first (*Village Politicians*)[6] in 1806. *Blind Man's Buff* (Plate 35) was the picture of the year in 1813. Painted for the Prince Regent, it was hung in the place of honour in the exhibition. Thomas Stothard's only exhibit hung above it and, in a somewhat sorrowful letter to a friend, he wrote:

... Wilkie's *Blind Man's Buff* has ever a crowd round it closely packed; and some of those in the rear, in vain struggling for a view, console themselves for the disappointment by looking upwards at my Shakespeare subject, by which means I get admirers, as one theatre is filled by the overflow of the other. This you will say is but poor consolation, but it is so and I must be content. ... [7]

Turner's exhibits were also appreciated though a small group of diehards, led by Sir George Beaumont, took every opportunity to abuse them. His *Dido building Carthage*[8] and *Crossing the Brook*[9] were both included in the exhibition of 1815 and Thomas Uwins reported that his works 'are said to surpass all his former outdoings'.[10] Yet it seems clear that the appeal of his rather ambitious landscapes was confined to the more discerning and, even at this early date, they were described

67

as 'pictures of nothing and very like'.[11] Some of his later work would no doubt have been quite beyond the comprehension of many people.

The celebrated Antonio Canova visited London in 1815, was entertained to dinner by the Royal Academicians and subsequently sent in three sculptures to the exhibition of 1817. They attracted less attention, however, than Francis Chantrey's Lichfield Cathedral monument. This was in memory of two children and carried the quotation from Milton – 'O fairest flowers, no sooner blown than blasted'. The Battle of Waterloo had been fought in 1815 and, in 1818, Sir Thomas Lawrence exhibited a portrait *The Duke of Wellington* 'in the dress that he wore, and on the horse he rode'.[12] He then set out for Aix-la-Chapelle to commence for the Prince Regent the series of portraits which are now hung in the Waterloo Chamber at Windsor Castle. The Battle of Trafalgar in 1805 was commemorated by many pictures, some of which were in the Academy exhibitions of 1806 and 1807. The Academicians paid their last respects to Lord Nelson from the windows of Somerset House as the funeral procession made its way to St Paul's Cathedral. Subsequently the Academy's advice was sought by the Treasury on suitable monuments for him, for William Pitt and for others.

Meanwhile the British Institution, founded in 1805, held its first exhibition in 1806 'to encourage and reward the talents of the artists of the United Kingdom', and 'to open a PUBLIC EXHIBITION for the sale of the productions of British artists'.[13] It was financed by a large group of subscribers who had sole control of the Institution's affairs including the choice and hanging of the exhibits. In this way it differed from the Academy which was run entirely by artists. The new gallery provided a welcome additional outlet, though portraits were excluded, and many painters both from within and outside the membership of the Academy were eager to take advantage of the facilities. After the first exhibition closed, a collection of Old Masters was assembled there especially for copying and this was a very popular move. Until then artists had had little such opportunity. In 1813 the British Institution held an exhibition of works by Sir Joshua Reynolds and this was the first commemorative exhibition ever to be held in this country. It was followed by other loan exhibitions until 1867 when the Institution came to an end. This facet of its work was soon afterwards continued by the Royal Academy and more will have to be said later on the subject.

The Academy itself was able to help its own members and students to copy Old Masters by an arrangement with Dulwich College. Sir Francis Bourgeois, an Academician, had left to the Governors the pictures[14] collected by Noel Desenfans and they offered to lend examples to the Academy. This was accepted gratefully and, except for a break from 1867 to 1875, the procedure continued for well over a hundred years. The first six pictures were received in 1816, together with some borrowed from other sources, and the Academy opened for the first time a School of Painting. Several writers have assumed from this that painting, as opposed to drawing, had not previously been allowed in the Schools but this is surely not necessarily so. It is true that the word 'draw' was used invariably in the rules but, in the terminology of the period, this could have included the use of the brush. In a drawing by Thomas Rowlandson of the Life School at the Academy,[15] which must presumably have been done when he was a student there in the 1770s, he certainly shows a man with a palette and brushes working at an easel. Also there is the story of William Etty in 1808 or 1809. 'One night in the *Life*,' he records, 'Fuseli was visitor. I threw aside the chalk, took up my palette set with oil-colour, and began to paint the Figure. Ah there, says Fuseli, you seem at home. And so I truly felt.'[16] Direct painting from the model was no doubt unusual in the Schools at the time but does not appear to have been forbidden.

The Academy studentship was lengthened to ten years in 1814 and the Privileged Students (that is those who had won gold medals or certain other prizes) were entitled to continue for life. The complete period allowed, however, was not always used to the full. There were on the other hand frequent applications for extensions of the ten-year term including one from William Etty in 1818. It is said that his continued use of the privilege somewhat embarrassed his fellow Academicians in later years as they thought it rather undignified for an established artist to work alongside young students. Etty, much to his credit, did not allow himself to be browbeaten.

John Opie and Henry Tresham both had two-year periods as Professor of Painting, from 1805 to 1809, when Henry Fuseli again took on the task in addition to his position as Keeper. Sir Anthony Carlisle was Professor of Anatomy from 1808 to 1824 and Sir John Soane was Professor of Architecture from 1806 to 1837. Soane fell foul of the Council in 1810 after including in a lecture some deprecating remarks on the new Covent Garden Theatre by Robert Smirke, Junior. It was then resolved 'that no comments or criticisms on the opinions or productions of living Artists in this Country shou'd be introduced into any of the Lectures delivered in the Royal Academy'.[17] Soane took umbrage at this and refused to give lectures unless the motion were repealed. This the Council declined to do and the quarrel dragged on for three years. The lectures were resumed, however, in 1812 and a complete reconciliation between Smirke and Soane ended the controversy. The latter obviously bore the institution no ill-will and indeed continued his Professorship another twenty-five years till his death. In 1833 he obtained an Act of Parliament for his house and its contents in Lincoln's Inn Fields to become a permanent museum and one of its clauses laid down that the Academy should nominate the Curator.

In 1814 it was agreed that the President should convene a General Assembly 'whenever Five or more Academicians may apply to him in writing for that purpose'.[18] Nowadays twelve signatures of members are required. Another change in the Laws took place in 1810 when the old rule was cancelled that 'Exhibitors who only exhibit Drawings cannot be admitted candidates for being elected Associates. . . .'[19]

An important new regulation was the institution of Varnishing Days for members in 1809. Apparently a great nuisance had been caused by their touching up their exhibits more or less whenever they pleased. The resolution was as follows:

> That whereas great inconvenience and hindrance to the Business for which the Committee of arrangement for the Exhibition are appointed is occasioned by the Members of Council, Painting on their Pictures after being received. He [*Martin Archer Shee*] therefore proposes the following—
> That three days, or more according to the convenience of the arrangement, and the discretion of the Council shall be allowed to all the Members of the Royal Academy for the purpose of varnishing or painting on their Pictures, in the places which have been allotted to them, previous to the day appointed for the annual dinner in the Exhibition Room.

Moved by Mr Shee.   Seconded by Mr Fuseli

and was Unanimous.[20]

Frequently five such days were allowed and Turner, for one, took great advantage of them.

J. M. W. Turner had been appointed Professor of Perspective in 1807 and there are many stories of his mumblings at the rostrum and of his more than once leaving his notes in a hackney-coach. His lectures were more frequently dissertations on the art of landscape painting than on the science of perspective and they were profusely illustrated with beautiful drawings which he had done specially. Thomas Stothard, who replaced Edward Burch as Librarian in 1814, was a regular attender, despite being very deaf, and said, 'There is much to *see* at Mr Turner's lectures – much that I delight in seeing, though I cannot hear him.'[21] According to contemporary reports, Turner was 'almost unintelligible' and 'half of each lecture was addressed to the attendant behind him, who was constantly busied, under his muttered directions, in selecting from a huge portfolio drawings and diagrams to illustrate his teaching'.[22] It is not surprising therefore that the great man, despite his long life, his devotion to the Academy and his tremendous reputation, was never elected to the Presidency.

A Professorship of Sculpture was inaugurated in 1810 and John Flaxman held the post till his death in 1826. George Dance and Joseph Farington continued to serve as Auditors and in 1809 were given presents for their services. They had just completed a comprehensive survey of the Academy's financial position and, as a result, the number of guests at the Annual Dinner was limited to a hundred and forty in order to save expense and the price of catalogues was raised to one shilling.

In this same year J. S. Copley's request for extra time in delivering his portrait *The Prince of Wales*[23] was refused but, on the other hand, in 1816, A. E. Chalon's portrait *H.R.H. Prince Leopold of Saxe-Coburg*,[24] the Prince's son-in-law, was admitted after the allotted time. This was at the express wish of the Prince Regent and was accomplished by rescinding the appropriate Law temporarily and reimposing it immediately thereafter.

The Academy was still strictly governed by the wishes of the Sovereign at this stage but George III had been mentally ill for a long time. In 1812 it had been arranged for the institution's business to be submitted instead to the Prince Regent, afterwards George IV (Plates 18 and 30). This was a wise move and the Prince was very good to the Academy. Besides attending its dinners frequently, he lent the School of Painting more than one of the Raphael cartoons which were then at Hampton Court[25] and made several presentations including collections of casts and, in 1812, a huge bronze lamp for the Great Room at Somerset House. It is said to have weighed about two tons and was so heavy that great difficulty was experienced in suspending it safely. Indeed its rope extended so much that the whole thing collapsed on to a table at the Annual Dinner in 1815. The descent was so gentle, however, that the chandelier itself survived and was still in use for a time in the entrance hall of the Academy's subsequent home in Trafalgar Square. In 1856, when the Council decided to get rid of 'an accumulation of worthless old furniture', 'it was further recommended to dispose of the large bronze Lamp formerly suspended in the Great Room, but now lying useless in the vaults'.[26] Its ultimate fate does not appear to have been recorded. The lamp was designed and made by Vulliamy & Sons of Pall Mall and, according to an aquatint of it by H. Moses and F. C. Lewis, it measured nine feet in diameter and had thirty branches each supporting a light. The whole was decorated with acanthus leaves and female heads in the Neo-Classic style of the time and it was suspended on ten chains which were gathered together in a ring at the apex.

Another matter with which the Prince Regent was involved was a renewed effort to get engravers admitted as Academicians. A direct approach to the Academy by John Landseer had been unsuccessful in 1809 and three years later thirteen other engravers joined him in sending a memorial to His Royal Highness on the subject. This was referred to the Council and the General Assembly and the reply is worth quoting reasonably fully:

The Council beg leave to premise that their Answer to the Memorial presented to them in 1809, alluded to by the Memorialists in their Address to Your Royal Highness, stated 'That the President and Council did not conceive themselves empower'd to act upon propositions involving so essential an alteration in the structure of the Establishment' . . . a reply dictated solely by a regard to the feelings of their Brother Artist. The President and Council could not be ignorant of the power which is vested in the Academy 'to make such new Laws as shall from time to time appear expedient . . .'; but tho' not induced to comply with the wish of the Memorialist, they felt how invidious a task it would be to point out distinctions unfavourable to an Art which they duly esteem, and were desirous to avoid an unpleasant discussion that did not appear absolutely necessary. . . .

The President and Council might not unreasonably represent to Your Royal Highness that in a Society constituted unlike any of the Royal Academies of the Continent, and supported solely by the produce of its Exhibitions, there is a particular necessity for bringing forward *original* Artists, who, alone are capable of supplying sufficient novelty, and interest to excite public attention, without which, the Schools, the charitable Fund, and the Establishment itself must fail.

But the reasons on which the exclusion of Engravers from the first rank of the Academy is grounded are of a more abstract, permanent and immutable nature.

That all the Fine Arts have claims to admiration and encouragement, and honorable distinction, it would be superfluous to urge ... but, that these claims are not all equal has never been denied, and the relative pre-eminence of the Arts has ever been estimated accordingly as they more or less abound in those intellectual qualities of Invention and Composition, which Painting, Sculpture and Architecture so eminently possess, but of which Engraving is wholly devoid; its greatest praise consisting in translating with as little loss as possible the beauties of these original Arts of Design.

With such an important difference in their intellectual pretensions as Artists, it appear'd to the framers of this Society that to admit Engravers into the first class of their Members, would be incompatible with justice and a due regard to the dignity of the Royal Academy. The Council cannot but continue to hold the same sentiments. . . .[27]

The Academicians seemed convinced that engravers should confine their art to copying and did not envisage that they might create their own designs. Thus there remained another dissatisfied faction among the country's artists.

Benjamin Robert Haydon frequently caused trouble and in 1812, when he was particularly disgruntled because Sir George Beaumont had refused to purchase his picture of Macbeth, he made a virulent attack on the Academy. 'Exasperated by the neglect of my family,' he says, 'tormented by the consciousness of debt, cut to the heart by the cruelty of Sir George, fearful of the severity of my landlord and enraged at the insults from the Academy, I became furious. An attack on the Academy and its abominations darted into my head.'[28] Always critical of what he considered to be neglect of history painting within the Royal Academy and unmindful of any debt he may have owed to the institution as a one-time student, he continued this pugnacious attitude throughout his life but received little sympathy or support from his contemporaries. Even after Haydon's suicide, Turner could only mutter again and again, 'He stabbed his mother, he stabbed his mother.'[29]

Under Fuseli's severe Keepership, the Academy Schools gave no worry although, in 1817, the architectural students put in a plea for certain improvements. The newcomers in this period included William

Etty, Andrew Geddes, Cornelius Varley, Philip Hardwick, E. H. Baily, Peter de Wint, Lewis Vulliamy, Charles Lock Eastlake, James Ward, George Bassevi, George Aitchison, Charles and Edwin Landseer, William Wyon, Sydney Smirke and William Tite. Book prizes of Reynolds' discourses and the lectures of Barry, West, Fuseli and Opie were awarded in addition to medals from 1810 and, in 1814, the Law was rescinded which prohibited premium works from being submitted to the annual exhibition. Grants for travel abroad, which had been in abeyance since 1795, were restarted in 1818. New casts and borrowing Old Masters for the School of Painting gave encouragement to the students but the discipline was strict. Remarks at lectures were forbidden and it was decreed that 'no student shall presume to wear his hat in the Schools'.[30]

The library continued to grow and, in 1810, Inspectors were appointed to make biannual surveys of the Academy's books and casts. At the same time the Council had to disclaim responsibility for the safety of works submitted to the annual exhibition. Occasionally an exhibit was damaged accidentally and from time to time one was stolen. A picture was cut from its frame and Richard Cosway's Diploma Work disappeared, both in 1810. In this same year, a clerk was appointed to help promote sales but the venture was not successful and was discontinued in 1813.

John Hoppner had at some time been allowed to borrow his Diploma Work and, on his death in 1810, it could not be traced. The widow replaced it with a self-portrait by the artist. Normally this type of work was not allowed for this purpose, as witness the refusal of a self-portrait by Raeburn in 1815. Other loans of Diploma Works had caused minor embarrassments so that, in 1811, Turner's motion as follows was passed:

> Fearing that many serious inconveniences may occur by allowing Works deposited in the Academy to be removed, The President and Council resolve that no Painting, Sculpture, or Architectural Drawing, shall in future be taken out of this Academy under any pretence whatever.[31]

Meanwhile donations were still given to those in need and it is interesting to note that some of the recipients had no very close connection with the institution. It is understandable that gifts should have been made to members, exhibitors and their dependants but somewhat surprising to find that twenty guineas should have been presented to

Ralph Kirkley in 1817 whose only claim was that he had been a servant of Sir Joshua Reynolds. One reads also that six guineas were paid 'to the widow of an artist, not an exhibitor'[32] and that twenty guineas were paid to a model named Charlotte Birch. The expenses of her funeral, however, were refused though this kind of claim was commonly met at the time.

Many of these items in the minutes (and still more left unrecorded in this narrative) may well seem insignificant individually but, in aggregate, they produce a picture of the institution's day-to-day activities. An event which must have been important was the change to gas for the Academy's lighting. It was tried successfully in the Schools in 1813, then for the Prince Regent's bronze lamp and subsequently for the whole of the building. Its light was soon to shine on a new era. George III, the Academy's first patron, died in January 1820, and Benjamin West in March that year. The President's funeral was on the grand scale. His body lay in state the previous night at Somerset House and he was buried near Sir Joshua Reynolds in the Crypt of St Paul's. His fame as an artist has not stood the test of time and his enormous historical pictures are quite out of fashion in the twentieth century. His *Christ rejected by Caiaphas*,[33] shown on its own in a room in Pall Mall in 1814, measured 16 feet by 34 feet and, even in the artist's lifetime, William Hazlitt wryly remarked that he was 'only great by the acre'.[34]

The fiftieth anniversary of the Academy in 1818 passed almost without celebration except that a loyal address was presented to the Sovereign. There was a proposal that a history should be written to commemorate the event but nothing came of it; also that special medals should be struck but apparently they did not materialize.

Before closing this chapter, it seems appropriate to include some brief account of the Royal Academy Club which was founded in 1813 and still flourishes. Although it has never been one of the Academy's official activities, its membership has always been confined within the institution and its convivial dinners are now held in its rooms. It was started by twenty-one Academicians who agreed to dine together on the first Wednesday in every month from January to July inclusive and Turner was one of the original members. The Club's records are incomplete but they show that its meetings took place for many years at various taverns, that Associates were not eligible for membership until 1853 and that guests have been welcomed at most of its dinners since 1855. In May the members used to assemble at Greenwich and eat whitebait. Later in the summer they invariably had a day's outing in the country to some place of historical and artistic interest. The Club still meets to dine four or five times a year, whitebait is always a feature of the menu at the dinner in the spring and, on every occasion, there is the traditional toast of 'Honour and Glory to the next Exhibition'.

—9—

FINAL PHASE AT SOMERSET HOUSE
1820–1836

George IV, who as Prince Regent had had close connections with the Academy, came to the throne in 1820. His accession involved a change in the preamble to the Diplomas and the substitution of his portrait for that of his father on the obverse of the Schools' medals. The reverse of the gold medal was replaced by a design by Thomas Stothard and is signed 'W. WYON MINT'. It shows three female figures representing Painting, Sculpture and Architecture, with their appropriate emblems and the words 'AEMULA QUAEQUE SORORIS'. The reverse of the silver medal was a new version of the Belvedere torso, in lower relief than that of the former example, and signed 'W. WYON S'. The word 'STUDY' appeared beneath it. Both medals bore the institution's name and date of foundation.

On 30 March, twenty-one votes were cast for Sir Thomas Lawrence (Plate 28) to succeed West as President against one each for John Flaxman and John Jackson. He was re-elected unanimously each year until his death in 1830. Born in Bristol in 1769, he had been admitted a student in the Royal Academy Schools in 1787 and was only twenty-two when elected an Associate in 1791. This was five years before the rule requiring Associates to be at least twenty-four years of age. He was not quite twenty-five when he was made a Royal Academician in 1794. This youthful prowess had been continued throughout his life and he was without doubt the most successful portrait painter in the country. His European reputation, his favour at court and his charm of manner singled him out as the obvious choice for President at the time.

John Yenn resigned the Treasurership in 1820 and Robert Smirke, Junior, who was knighted twelve years later, took his place. On the death of Fuseli in 1825, Henry Thomson became Keeper but resigned owing to ill-health after only two years and was succeeded by William Hilton. George Jones was made Librarian in 1834. His physical resemblance to the Duke of Wellington is supposed to have been quite remarkable but, on being told of this, the Duke commented somewhat drily, 'Dear me. Mistaken for me, is he? That's strange, for no one ever mistakes me for Mr Jones.'[1]

Fuseli's post as Professor of Painting was taken over by Thomas Phillips till 1832, then Henry Howard. Flaxman's death in 1826 made way for (Sir) Richard Westmacott as Professor of Sculpture and John H. Green became Professor of Anatomy on the resignation of Sir Anthony Carlisle in 1825. Soane and Turner continued respectively as Professors of Architecture and Perspective.

It is not proposed to burden the reader with details of all the changes among the Honorary Members but the election of Sir Walter Scott as Antiquary is worthy of note. He held the position from 1827 until his death in 1832.

John Constable was belatedly elected a Royal Academician during Lawrence's Presidency, in 1829, after ten years as an Associate. Unfortunately his wife had recently died and Constable sadly remarked 'it has been delayed until I am solitary, and cannot impart it'.[2] Born in 1776, only a year later than Turner, it took him over a quarter of a century longer to attain the first rank of membership. In his lifetime the landscape painter John Glover, whose works are now relatively unknown, was considered far more important. Constable's paintings were often severely criticized, in particular for his habit of giving them numerous touches of white with a palette-knife. His The Hay-Wain[3] was hardly noticed in the Academy exhibition of 1821 but received due recognition in Paris in 1824. Indeed its influence on nineteenth century French art is now universally recognized. Conversely Géricault's painting The Raft of Medusa[4] was exhibited in London in 1820 and the artist was a guest at the Academy Dinner the following year.

Wilkie's exhibits continued to be popular and a rail had to be erected in 1822 to protect his Chelsea Pensioners receiving the Gazette announcing the Battle of Waterloo[5] from the pressure of the crowds. Lawrence, Turner and Etty frequently attained high standards – Lawrence with his Calmady Children (Plate 31) in 1824 and Master Lambton[6] in 1825, Turner with The Bay of Baiae (Plate 33) in 1823 and Etty with The Combat[7] in 1825. These artists were not, however, without their critics. Turner's Jessica[8] in 1830 was described as 'an incomprehensible daub'[9] and in 1827 someone said that his works were 'worse and worse of yellow fever'.[10] Etty was accused of impropriety with his picture Youth on the Prow and Pleasure at the Helm[11] in 1832. It seems innocuous enough today. Mulready's exhibits attracted attention and praise was forthcoming occasionally for those of Sir William Beechey and Sir Augustus Wall Callcott. Constable's contributions included his *Salisbury Cathedral*[12] in 1823, *The Leaping Horse* (Plate 34) in 1825, *The Cornfield*[13] in 1826 and *The Chain Pier, Brighton*[14] in 1827. He suffered the mortification of having a picture rejected in 1830 and the story reflects credit on the artist. The painting was *Water-meadows near Salisbury*[15] and was one of four sent in by Constable that year. By mistake it was passed before the Council with the outsiders' work and turned down. When the error was realized, they wanted to change the decision but Constable would not allow it. He said, 'It has been properly condemned as a daub. Send it out.'[16]

Without doubt Constable's style was too modern for the taste of his time; his striving for naturalistic effect could not be appreciated. Even in posing a model for the Academy Schools, when he was one of the Visitors there, he introduced foliage as an adjunct so that, instead of a straightforward figure, the students were presented with 'Eve in a Garden of Eden' as a subject. He wrote about it to his friend and biographer C. R. Leslie as follows:

Dear Leslie,

I set my first figure yesterday, and it is much liked; Etty congratulated me upon it; do, dear Leslie, come and see it. I have dressed up a bower of laurel, and I told the students they probably expected a landscape background from me. I am quite popular in the Life; at all events I spare neither pains nor expense to become a good Academician. My garden of Eden cost me ten shillings, and my men were twice stopped coming from Hampstead with the green boughs by the police, who thought (as was the case) they had robbed some gentleman's grounds. ... The fun is, my garden at the Academy was taken for a Christmas decoration, holly and mistletoe.[17]

Constable's attempt to present a subject in a kind of stage setting was followed by Etty who posed several models at once to form a complete scene. The basic idea was sound but allowed to die. Together with Turner's 'vagaries and absurdities',[18] such advanced views were scathingly dismissed. Nevertheless the exhibitions drew large crowds each year and the receipts in 1822, for instance, amounted to almost £6,000.

It was in this year that William Blake's name appeared among the recipients of donations as 'an able Designer and Engraver laboring under great distress'.[19] He was awarded £25 out of a total disbursement of well over £300. At the same time pensions amounting to over £400 were awarded to certain members and their widows.

In the following year the Auditors' Report by John Soane and Richard Westmacott gave an interesting account of the Academy's finances from the foundation in 1768. It showed total receipts of £211,557 11s 9¾d and disbursements of £173,119 14s 2d. The losses incurred until 1780 had amounted to £5,116 1s 1d and had been paid by King George III. Thereafter the Academy was self-supporting. The bank accounts have been with Drummonds (now a branch of the Royal Bank of Scotland) since 13 May 1796, but, even before then, seem to have been held by them, in the name of the Treasurer, Sir William Chambers, from the very beginning. By 1823, £13,500 had been invested in the General Purposes Fund and £20,000 in the Pensions Fund.

Besides the regular charitable donations, special gifts were occasionally made as, for example, two sums of £50 each in 1823 and 1826 to a British Academy which was being founded in Rome. A Clerk was appointed in 1822 at a salary of £30 per annum and, in that same year, a fee of fifty guineas was paid to Monsieur Clias, Professor of Gymnastics from Berne, 'to instruct one of the Models of the Academy in various exercises for the purpose of develloping his form'.[20] The course was to last only six weeks and the payment seems disproportionate compared with the modest sum allotted for the Clerk. He was Thomas Vaughan, who had been part-time assistant to the Secretary for some years, and the Academy possesses a portrait of him in his old age, painted by J. P. Knight. Despite their low wages, the Academy's servants seem to have been loyal, and Charles Cranmer, who retired in 1822, had been a porter from the foundation.

The last surviving original member died in 1825. He was, as has been said, the architect George Dance who had been one of the Academy's Auditors and then a Trustee. He had also been the first Professor of Architecture till 1805 and we are indebted to him for the fine series of profile portraits of his fellow-members which were drawn in the 1790s and were engraved by William Daniell. The Academy possesses fifty-three of them.

In 1820, soon after his accession to the throne, George IV presented a gold medal and chain[21] to Sir Thomas Lawrence to be worn by him and succeeding Presidents on official occasions. The obverse has a portrait of the King and the reverse contains the words 'ACCESSIT XXIX IAN. MDCCCXX' in a wreath of oak leaves with the inscription 'FROM HIS

MAJESTY KING GEORGE IV TO THE PRESIDENT OF THE ROYAL ACADEMY' surrounding it.

Another interesting gift about this time was a very large drawing of *Leda and the Swan*[22] presented by William Lock the younger. The artist is unknown but the influence of Michelangelo is obvious and it is presumably a copy of the design of this subject which is known to have come from his studio. In 1830, however, the Academy received the magnificent present of an original work by the Master – the Carrara marble relief of *The Madonna and Child with the Infant St John* (Plate 37). It was carved in Florence by Michelangelo in 1504–5, soon after he had completed his colossal *David*[23] and just before he was called to Rome to receive instructions for the projected tomb of Pope Pius II. The first owner was a Florentine patron named Taddeo Taddei and the tondo remained in the family house in that city until the early nineteenth century when, in 1812, it was purchased by J. B. J. Wicar, a French collector in Rome. He sold it (apparently for about £1,500) to Sir George Beaumont who, in a letter to Sir Thomas Lawrence in May 1822,[24] wrote excitedly: 'I have been fortunate enough to gain possession of an undoubted work of M. Angelo! ... You may be sure I was made to pay for this, & but for the assistance of our excellent friend Canova probably I should not have succeeded. ...' Unhappily he was not to enjoy his possession over long as he died in 1827. In his will he left the sculpture to his widow with the request that, unless she directed otherwise, it should eventually become the property of the Royal Academy. Lady Beaumont outlived her husband by only three years and the family then duly presented it. The Taddei tondo, as it is often called, was then valued at £600 for legacy duty, which after all was not payable. There is little doubt that, if this treasure were available for sale today, it would command a prodigious price. It is indeed a precious possession.

Another acquisition during this period was a large oil painting (119 × 309 inches),[25] possibly by Marco d'Oggiono, of *The Last Supper* by Leonardo da Vinci. It had at one time been in the possession of the Certosa at Pavia and was brought to this country early in the nineteenth century. The Academy bought it for six hundred guineas in 1821 and, about the same time, paid £600 for a collection of Italian prints made by George Cumberland.[26] It must be remembered that the National Gallery did not then exist, despite many discussions in an attempt to bring it into being, and these accessions provided a means of study that was greatly needed by the artists of the day. The formation of a national collection had been in men's minds a long time and, by the purchase of the late John Julius Angerstein's collection of pictures in 1824, it at last came about. It still had no proper home, however, for a number of years to come.

Meanwhile the daily business of the Academy took into account the smaller things of life. £14 10s 0d was paid for Bow Street Officers to supervise the exhibition of 1820. 'Parasols, umbrellas and sticks' had to be left below stairs.[27] 'No mere transcripts of the objects of natural history' were allowed as exhibits nor 'vignette portraits, nor, generally any drawings without back grounds'.[28] 'Much disorder having arisen at several of the Lectures from an excessive issue of Tickets',[29] it was resolved to limit the admissions. One of the causes of this kind of trouble was that Sir Anthony Carlisle frequently engaged what might be called side-shows for his lectures – prize-fighters, a troupe of Chinese jugglers and, on one occasion, a platoon of Life Guardsmen to show how muscles are exercised in wielding swords. This drew such a crowd that the Bow Street Officers were unable to cope with it and the meeting had to be abandoned. A bill for the lecture tickets at this time shows that they were made of ivory and the Academy still owns one or two examples. The students' admission tickets were similarly ivory discs inscribed with their name and date of entry. This custom survived until very recently and the ivories are colloquially known as 'bones'. They are delightful to handle and have been much prized by generations of students. It is interesting to note that Mr W. Clowes was appointed to print the catalogue in 1824 'on much lower terms than have hitherto been paid'.[30] He founded the firm which in due course was to attain a position as one of Britain's leading printers and which served the Academy well for a century and a half.

The placing of exhibits continuously provoked arguments and, in 1826, an attempt was made to give every member a chance to grade his works in degrees of importance. The following letter was circulated:

Sir,
    I am instructed by the President and Council of the Royal Academy to request that you will number such Works of Art as you propose to send for exhibition, according to the order of preference in which you yourself may regard them, to the end that your wishes and feelings may be attended to as far as a due consideration of the general arrangement may admit.
                            I remain, etc.,
                            H. Howard, R.A. Sec.[31]

12 'Theory' by Sir Joshua Reynolds. Painted in 1779 for the
Library ceiling at Somerset House

13 'The Death of General Wolfe' by Benjamin West. Exhibited at Royal Academy, 1771
(*National Gallery of Canada, Ottawa – Gift of the Duke of Westminster*, 1918)

14 One of a collection of drawings by George Stubbs for his book 'The Anatomy of the Horse', 1766. Bequeathed to the Royal Academy, 1879

15 'The Gods descending to battle.' One of a collection of drawings by John Flaxman for Homer's 'Iliad', 1793; purchased by the Royal Academy, 1880

16 The Strand Front of Somerset House, Aquatint
by Thomas Malton, *c.* 1792

17 'Entrance Hall of the Royal Academy, Somerset House, 1836' by George Scharf,
showing a chair and casts which are still in the Academy's possession (*Reproduced
by courtesy of the Trustees of the British Museum, London*)

18 'The Exhibition of the Royal Academy at Somerset House, 1787', showing Sir Joshua Reynolds escorting the Prince of Wales (afterwards George IV). Engraving by Pietro Martini after J. H. Ramberg

19 'The Exhibition Room, Somerset House'. Engraving
by Thomas Rowlandson and A. C. Pugin, 1808

20 Royal Academician's Diploma issued to Sir Joshua Reynolds; signed by George III, 1768

21 'The Academy Stare-case' by Thomas Rowlandson, c. 1800 (*University College, London*)

23 'J. M. W. 'Turner', Professor of Perspective, 1807–37, by George Dance, 1800

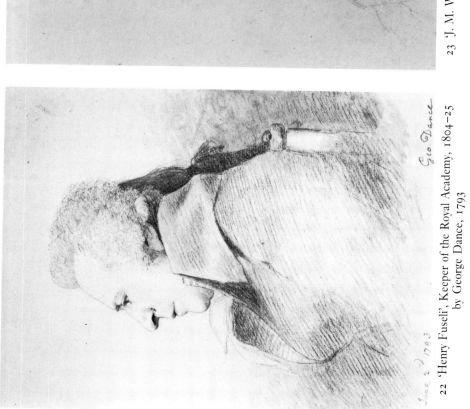

22 'Henry Fuseli', Keeper of the Royal Academy, 1804–25, by George Dance, 1793

Ceiling paintings in the Entrance Hall of the Royal Academy, *c.* 1779:
24a 'The Graces' surrounded by 'Air', 'Earth', 'Fire' and 'Water' by Benjamin West

24b 'Painting' by Angelica Kauffmann

25 'Horses in a Thunderstorm' by Sawrey Gilpin. Diploma Work, 1798

26 'Self-portrait' by Benjamin West, President of the Royal Academy,
with Somerset House in the background, 1793

27 'The Antique School at Somerset House' by E. F. Burney, 1779. The Cartoon of the Virgin and Child by Leonardo da Vinci hangs to the left of the door

28 'The Royal Academicians in General Assembly' by Henry Singleton, 1795, under the Presidency of Benjamin West (wearing hat). The group includes Sir Thomas Lawrence (cross-legged at left), Sir William Chambers (in centre at front), J. S. Copley and Joseph Farington (standing in front of the cast of the Laocoon)

30 'The Prince of Wales' (afterwards George IV) by Sir
William Beechey. Diploma Work, 1798

29 'Boy and Rabbit' by Sir Henry Raeburn.
Diploma Work, 1816

31 'The Calmady Children' by Sir Thomas Lawrence. Exhibited at Royal
Academy, 1824 (*Metropolitan Museum of Art, New York – Bequest of Collis P.
Huntington*, 1900)

32 'A Gipsy Girl' by Sir Thomas Lawrence.
Diploma Work, 1794

33 'The Bay of Baiae with Apollo and the Sibyl' by J. M. W. Turner. Exhibited at Royal Academy, 1823
(*Tate Gallery, London*)

34 'The Leaping Horse' by John Constable. Exhibited at Royal Academy, 1825

35 'Blind Man's Buff' by Sir David Wilkie. Exhibited at Royal Academy, 1813
(*Reproduced by gracious permission of Her Majesty The Queen*)

36 'Sleeping Nymph and Satyrs' by William Etty. Diploma Work, 1828

The scheme certainly seems to have had a quietening effect for a time.

Sir Thomas Lawrence died in January 1830, and was buried in St Paul's Cathedral near to Reynolds and West. His famous collection of drawings was unfortunately dispersed despite strong efforts to retain them for the nation but his architectural casts were bought by the Academy. He was succeeded on 25 January by Martin Archer Shee although there is evidence in letters between Sir Robert Peel and Lord Farnborough that George IV had 'an impression that it would be desirable to alter the constitution of the Royal Academy with a view of placing at its head some distinguished amateur of the arts'.[32] Apparently he toyed with the idea of 'nominating a nobleman to be President of the Academy' but was dissuaded.[33] The appointment of Shee was something of a surprise. David Wilkie seemed to be the favourite candidate but he received only two votes. One each were cast for Augustus Wall Callcott and Thomas Phillips, six for Sir William Beechey and eighteen for Shee. Although he had no particular claims for the honour, his dignified bearing and Irish tongue were great assets and he proved to be an energetic and tenacious President. Haydon called him 'the most impotent painter in the solar system'[34] but Constable spoke of his 'self-devotion and chivalrous sense of honour'.[35] Shee himself said, 'Without a movement on my part, without an attempt to employ the smallest influence, in or out of the Academy, knowing that I have neither wealth nor power, or influence with the great, and that I have never basked in the sunshine of Royal favour ... in spite of all this, they have made me President.'[36] He was knighted in July. Wilkie, it is said, was always shy and awkward but, although he failed to win the Presidency, he duly took Lawrence's place as portrait painter in ordinary to the King. In the year that Shee came into office, George IV died and his brother, William IV, succeeded him on the throne. His head, by William Wyon, then appeared on the Schools' medals but the reverses remained the same.

For many years there had been under discussion the possibility of the Academy's moving from Somerset House. The major reason was that the Government required more room there but the Academy also had outgrown its premises. As early as 1825, a committee had been appointed 'to take into consideration what may be the wants of the Royal Academy in the event of the erection of a new building'[37] and, as the newly formed National Gallery desperately needed a proper home, thoughts turned to housing the two institutions under the same roof. In 1832 the Government commissioned William Wilkins to design a building for this dual purpose on the site of the royal stables, or King's Mews, on the north side of Trafalgar Square. Work commenced in 1833 and was completed four or five years later, the building being the southern range only of the present galleries. Accounts vary as to the amount of money Wilkins was allowed to spend but it seems certain that the Government was not over-generous. The architect was expected to use what materials he could from the previous building (by William Kent) and he was also given some columns from the recently dismantled Carlton House. He was compelled to set his façade back fifty feet from the line originally chosen, so as not to obscure the view of St Martin-in-the-Fields Church from Pall Mall – a laudable proviso but one which meant the sacrifice of his proposed entrance steps direct from the square. An ancient right of way had to be left to some barrack grounds to the north and Wilkins therefore had to devise a clear passage at ground-floor level dividing the eastern part of the building into two sections.

Several contemporary perspectives of the exterior are in existence, especially of the 1840s and 1850s following the final layout of Trafalgar Square and the erection of Nelson's Column. One engraving may be mentioned as typical – by T. Picken after E. Walker, 1852.

The Academy was very much concerned that, in giving up its independence in Somerset House, its rights should not be placed in jeopardy. Shee was a tower of strength in this matter and an agreement was reached under which the National Gallery was to have the western half of the new building and the Royal Academy the eastern half. Some critics of the Academy, however, were against the proposal and, in 1834, the following demand was made by the House of Commons:

> Order'd
>
> That there be laid before this House a statement of the conditions, if any, on which the apartments at Somerset House were originally bestowed on the Royal Academy; and of the period for which they were granted; whether unlimited, or terminable at the pleasure of the Crown, or otherwise.
>
> Order'd
>
> That there be laid before this House a return of the number of Exhibitors at the Royal Academy in each of the last ten years, distinguishing the number of Exhibitors members of the Academy from the number of other Exhibitors.
>
> Order'd
>
> That there be laid before this House a Return of the number of Works

of Art exhibited at the Royal Academy in each of the last ten years; distinguishing for each year the number of historical works, landscapes, portraits, busts, and architectural drawings, respectively, contributed by Members of the Royal Academy, from the historical works, landscapes, portraits, busts and architectural drawings contributed by other artists. Ordered

That there be laid before this House a Return of the number of Professors in the Royal Academy, of the number of Lectures required by the rules of the Academy to be annually delivered by each Professor, and of the number of Lectures which have been annually delivered by each Professor during the last ten years.

J. H. Ley,
Cl. Dom. Com.[38]

The returns were not made out and submitted until the King's sanction had been obtained and the Academy once again had good cause to be thankful for the energy and statesmanship of the President in these negotiations. Had he complied with the demand without the Royal authority, it would have set an awkward precedent in the Academy's relationship with both the Crown and the Government.

A Parliamentary Committee was appointed in 1836 at which the grievances of B. R. Haydon, George Clint, John Martin, George Rennie, George Foggo and others were aired. Evidence in reply was supplied by six members of the Academy – the President (Shee), the Keeper (William Hilton), the Secretary (Henry Howard) and Reinagle, Wilkins and Cockerell. The main substance of the complaints was that academies in general were of no use and that the Royal Academy in particular was unfair to artists who were not numbered in its membership. Many of the questions and answers used in the attack were prejudiced and therefore of little value. Nothing was resolved but it was on the whole a good thing for the Academy to be made aware of the public interest and to have an opportunity to discountenance some rather pernicious and irrelevant criticisms. Shee claimed that the Royal Academy was a much more important institution to the nation than the National Gallery on the grounds that 'a garden is of more consequence than a granary'[39] and the eleventh-hour attempt to prevent its move to the Trafalgar Square building duly failed.

A curious circumstance arose in 1832 as shown in the following record:

85

Resolved that a period of sixty years having elapsed since the election of Elias Martin Associate and no proof of his actual existence having reached the Members of the Royal Academy for many years, or can now be adduced by any individual connected with this Institution, it be recommended to the General Assembly to erase the name of Elias Martin from the list of Associates. And to prevent the recurrence of the inconvenience which has arisen in this case.[40]

It was thereupon decided that

If any Academician, Associate or Associate Engraver shall have wholly neglected during a period of ten years to communicate, personally or by letter, with the Secretary, so as to afford the means of authentic information as to his existence and place of residence he shall be consider'd as having ceased to be a Member of the Royal Academy and his place shall be declared vacant accordingly.[41]

It was subsequently discovered that Elias Martin had in fact died nearly thirty years before in 1804.

New students in the Academy Schools during this period included S. A. Hart, Henry Weekes, James Pennethorne, Daniel Maclise, Augustus Egg, Richard Dadd and W. P. Frith. As they commenced their careers, the institution was in its last days at Somerset House. A farewell dinner was held there on 17 December 1836. The nostalgic atmosphere can be imagined and it reached its climax with a toast given by Sir Francis Chantrey to 'The Old Walls of the Academy'.

10

FIRST PERIOD IN TRAFALGAR SQUARE
1837–1850

The Academy moved into the eastern half of the Trafalgar Square building early in 1837. Except that the central entrance was shared with the National Gallery, its accommodation was quite distinct and consisted basically of a suite of five exhibition rooms, all with glass roofs, on the principal floor with roughly corresponding apartments beneath them at ground-floor level. A short staircase on the right of the main hall led upwards to the North and South Rooms (much later incorporated into the present Gallery XXII) and, through the corridor which divided them, to the larger West, Middle and East Rooms (now numbered XXI, XX and XVIII respectively). The complete range was used for paintings and drawings while sculpture was displayed on the ground floor in a semi-circular room which protruded northwards from the hall. An adjoining Hall of Casts, under the North and South Rooms, reached as far as the passage which had to be retained as a right of way. Although rather a nuisance, the requirement was made to serve the useful purpose of separating the part of the Academy to which the public had access from the Council Room, the Library and the Keeper's quarters, all of which were on its other side.

There was a small octagon for the use of the Secretary adjacent to the East Room though this also was used for exhibition purposes from 1843 onwards. An apartment in the dome completed the Academy's share of the premises and it was to this sanctum that William Etty climbed each evening to continue his studies from the life. According to W. P. Frith's autobiography, it was always known by the students as 'the pepper-box'.[1]

Criticism of the building as a whole was fierce and William IV is alleged to have referred to it as 'a nasty little pokey hole'.[2] Certainly the Academy's private rooms were not as fine as those vacated in Somerset House. The architect, William Wilkins, had done his best, however, within the stipulated budget. A drawing exists[3] which shows his careful arrangement of the Benjamin West paintings set in the ceiling of the Council Room. Angelica Kauffmann's decorations were placed in the Library, also the Michelangelo tondo which was fixed over the fireplace.

There is no doubt that the institution had gained considerably in accommodation. More and more works had been crowded into the exhibitions at Somerset House (for example, 1,278 in 1830) but, in the new premises, the numbers increased again, frequently reaching over 1,400 and, in 1843 and 1846, over 1,500. Even so it was found necessary to insert the following note in the catalogue of 1837 on the occasion of the first exhibition in Trafalgar Square:

> It may be proper to observe that, in consequence of the great number of works sent for exhibition this year, it has been found impossible to assign places to many of those which had been accepted.

Artists were allowed to send in up to eight works 'for the approval or rejection of the Council, whose decision is final, and may be ascertained by application at the Academy, in the week after they have been left there'.[4] Notifications by post were not instituted till 1875. Until then the would-be exhibitors used to queue up to learn their fate. They would timidly whisper their names to the porter on duty who, on occasion, and in a loud voice which reverberated around the hall, would call out 'Mr So-and-So, Eight works – all of 'em chucked'. The poor artist, whose twelve-months' work was thus dismissed and his hopes dashed in an instant, would creep away crestfallen. As the century progressed, there were more artists than ever seeking the opportunity to exhibit their wares and, as was bound to happen, the proportion of rejections to acceptances gradually increased. The situation was alleviated from time to time by the foundation of other societies but the Academy itself was never able to keep up with the constantly growing demand for wall-space.

The Trafalgar Square building provided very little accommodation for the students when the exhibitions were open to the public. During the rest of the year, however, they were able to spread into the galleries with their work. The East Room was used for lectures and the President's discourses; the Annual Dinner also was held there. The close link between the Academy and the National Gallery at this time was good for the students and other connections between the two institutions are worth recalling. Martin Archer Shee and the next President, Charles Lock Eastlake, were both Trustees of the National Gallery. Eastlake was its Keeper (then called Secretary) from 1843 to 1847 and the first Director from 1855 until his death ten years later. He was followed in each office by other Royal Academicians, as Keeper by Thomas Uwins and as Director by William Boxall.

William IV officially opened the new premises on 28 April 1837 and the bells of St Martin-in-the-Fields were rung in jubilation. It was to be, however, the King's last public appearance. He died in June and was succeeded by the young Queen Victoria. Her head, by William Wyon, then adorned the Academy medals but the reverses once again remained unchanged. Sir Martin Archer Shee was granted permission to paint her portrait, full-length, as he had done for William IV, and these two pictures were duly added to the Academy's collection.[5]

There were a number of people who were jealous of the institution at this time, particularly those who had objected to its move to Trafalgar Square. Certain radicals took every opportunity to show their opposition. One of the most active was Joseph Hume who strove to get the Academy exhibition opened free on certain days on the grounds that it was now housed in a public building. Shee fought against this and his reasons are given in a printed letter addressed to Lord John Russell, Principal Secretary of State for the Home Department, published in 1837. He pointed out that the Academy's tenure of the new building was no different from its time-honoured occupation of Somerset House and that 'though rendering important public services, it is not, in any respect, supported or assisted, from any public fund'[6] – in short, that its income from exhibitions was well applied and, through it, as the Academy was able to conduct its art schools and charities without state aid, the institution had 'incurred no new debt or obligation to the public'.[7] His reply was successful and the clamourings were reduced to mere murmurings for a time – but not for long. In 1839 a document was received from the House of Commons demanding yet another Return:

Ordered

That there be laid before this House a Return of the amount of money received for admission, and of the number of persons who visited the Exhibition of the Royal Academy of Arts in each of the years 1836, 1837 & 1838, distinguishing the entrance money from the proceeds by the Sale of Catalogues; together with the amount paid in Salaries and

Perquisites to each person employed in that establishment in each of those years: also, the Miscellaneous Expenses under separate heads in each of these years: and the average number of Students who have attended the Life School, and that of the Antique, in each of these years. In continuation of the account of the President and Secretary of the Royal Academy of Arts in July 1836.

J. H. Ley,
Cl. Dom. Com.[8]

In reply to this the Academy addressed a lengthy Petition to the House asserting its position, integrity and rights and including the following clause:

Yet has the Royal Academy been the object of incessant attacks not only from those who may be supposed to be influenced by feelings of personal or professional disappointment but also from quarters to which they might have reasonably look'd for the exercise of a calm and dispassionate judgment on their proceedings. Even your Honourable House has witnessed a severity of animadversion upon the character and conduct of the Royal Academy which only the most unequivocal and well ascertained evidence of delinquency can be supposed to exite, or justify. But it was in the transfer of the Academy to its present abode that the hostility against it appears to assume a systematic character.

The most strenuous exertions had been used to obstruct the projected removal of the Academy and when the hope of affecting that object failed, the measure which could not be prevented was converted into a new and more effectual engine of molestation.[9]

Thanks to the support of Sir Robert Peel, Lord John Russell, Sir Robert Harry Inglis, Bt., and others, the Petition gained its point and the demand for the Return was rescinded. The Academy maintained that it had nothing to hide or to be ashamed of but, as a private body, it denied that any outsider, including the Government, had authority to enquire into its affairs. Peel said:

I had the greatest satisfaction therefore in bearing my sincere Testimony on a late occasion to the Merits and Public Services of the Royal Academy, and considering the Independence and free Action of the Institution to be essential Instruments of its success, I shall always be disposed to claim for it protection from needless or vexatious Interference.[10]

Hume continued his attacks and they came to a head once again in 1844 when questions were asked in the House. Peel and Lord Palmerston then took up the cudgels on the Academy's behalf and the institution was left in peace for quite a long time.

Its activities were certainly hampered by lack of space but its problems in this respect were no greater than those of its neighbour. The National Gallery already possessed more pictures than it could display and, in 1845, Eastlake recommended either an extension or removal to another site. In 1847 a plan by James Pennethorne to enlarge the premises was put forward but came to nothing for the time being.

The Academy's internal affairs proceeded relatively smoothly. William Wilkins became Professor of Architecture on the death of Soane in 1837 but outlived him by only two years. His place was taken by C. R. Cockerell. William Hilton, the Keeper, died in 1840 and was replaced by George Jones who then resigned as Librarian and, after short periods in this office by William Collins and Charles Lock Eastlake, Thomas Uwins was appointed in 1844. J. M. W. Turner, who had been Professor of Perspective since 1807 but had delivered no lectures for a number of years, resigned from the post in 1837 and J. P. Knight was elected in his place, first of all as Teacher instead of full Professor. Turner's neglect of his duties had been an embarrassment to the Academy for some time but his reputation was such that no one dared to complain to him. Soon after his resignation, however, the following resolution was passed:

> Every Professor shall be allowed two years after his Election, to prepare his Lectures but if he fail to deliver his whole Course within the third year, or if he subsequently omit to deliver them for three years he shall be deemed to have resigned his Office & it shall immediately be declared vacant.[11]

Three very important members of the Academy died about this time – John Constable in 1837 and both Sir Francis Chantrey and Sir David Wilkie in 1841, the last-named while returning from a visit to the Holy Land. His burial at sea is the subject of a stirring picture by Turner.[12] Chantrey left a magnificent bequest for 'the encouragement of British Fine Art in Painting and Sculpture only'.[13] It was to come into effect on the death or second marriage of his widow and under its terms the President and Council of the Royal Academy were empowered to purchase 'Works of Fine Art of the highest merit in painting and sculpture that can be obtained . . . by Artists of any nation' provided that they had been 'entirely executed within the shores of Great Britain'.[14] He expressed 'the confident expectation that . . . the Government or the Country will provide a suitable and proper building or accommodation for their preservation and exhibition as the property of the nation' and directed that 'no part of my residuary and personal estate or of the annual income thereof shall be appropriated in acquiring any depository or receptacle whatever for the aforesaid Works of Art. . . .'[15] At the same time he bequeathed an annuity of £300 to the President and £50 to the Secretary for their services. The bequest did not become available until 1875 and the first purchases were made in 1877. Most of the collection is housed at the Tate Gallery although a few of the acquisitions in recent years have not been accepted by them and therefore have been retained for the time being at the Royal Academy. Some of the works from both institutions are usually on loan elsewhere.

The exhibitions during Shee's Presidency were always well attended. Turner continued to exhibit regularly, particularly views of Venice, and his famous picture *Rain, steam and speed – The Great Western Railway*[16] was in the exhibition of 1844. The works of Etty, Edwin Landseer and Mulready were popular and those of Charles West Cope and Daniel Maclise were quickly gaining favour. E. H. Baily and John Gibson (Plate 40) were two of the busiest sculptors of the time and the architects included Sir Charles Barry and Philip Hardwick. The up-and-coming young painter W. P. Frith first exhibited in 1840 and was elected an Associate in 1845. He tells us of the custom for newly elected members to pay their respects to the Academicians by calling on them one by one. He also gives us a first-hand account of Turner at work on his pictures on the Varnishing Days, often heightening their effects so much that neighbouring paintings paled into insignificance. Most artists were only too thankful to have their works included somewhere in the exhibition but, once having achieved this, quite a few complained that certain pictures, always of course by the particular artist, deserved better places. To be hung 'on the line' was everyone's ambition but only a few people each year could have this distinction. The term, which now merely means roughly at eye-level, had at this time a definite connotation. In the Academy's galleries both at Somerset House and in Trafalgar Square, a narrow wooden ledge projected horizontally from the walls at a certain level. G. D. Leslie says this was eight feet from the ground[17] and he is probably referring to the new height after the line was lowered by eight inches in 1859. A picture was described as hung 'on the line' when the top of its frame came close up to this ledge. Large works, such as full-lengths and half-length portraits and figure subjects, were almost invariably placed 'above the line' and tilted forwards. In 1842, it was resolved that:

> No Picture above the dimensions of a Kitcat, representing a human figure or figures as large as life shall be hung below 'the Line', Portraits of the Sovereign, or the Consort of the Sovereign excepted.[18]

An attempt was made in 1844 to limit exhibitors to six works each but the law was rescinded before coming into effect. Gilt frames were insisted on from 1847 onwards but the rule no longer applies.

A lottery known as the Art Union of London was initiated about this time and continued for many years. The winners received money prizes for the purchase of works of art and special arrangements were made for them to choose Academy exhibits if they so wished. In 1847, for instance, over £10,000 was available and such a large sum provided a most useful market for artists. The promoters also issued engravings and these were extremely popular.

It was in connection with an Art Union prize that R. R. Reinagle, an elderly Academician, was found to have been guilty of improper conduct. A winner in 1848 chose a picture which was exhibited by Reinagle in the Academy that year but another artist, J. W. Yarnold, claimed that it 'was painted by himself about two years ago'.[19] It was proved beyond any reasonable doubt that Yarnold's picture had come into the possession of Reinagle who, though he at one time alleged that he had repainted it, was obviously passing it off as entirely his own work. The Academy set up a committee to investigate the matter and, to save the necessity of expulsion, called for and obtained Reinagle's resignation. He was already in need and drawing a pension from the institution. This of course automatically ceased but, out of kindness of heart and in virtue of his previous services, many donations were subsequently awarded to him in his old age. At one time Reinagle had been quite active in the Academy's affairs. In 1843 he had tried to gain full recognition for engravers as Academicians but once again the attempt had failed.

The new students of this period included John Phillip, James Sant, J. E. Millais, W. Holman Hunt, D. G. Rossetti, Arthur Hughes, Edward Lear, H. H. Armstead, Thomas Woolner, E. M. Barry and Richard

Norman Shaw. Most of them were in their late teens or early twenties but Lear was thirty-seven and Millais only eleven when admitted. Dressed in a long coat, gathered at the waist by a belt, and with a white falling collar on it some four inches wide with goffered edging, he apparently looked even younger. He was nicknamed 'The Child' and was frequently sent on errands to fetch pies and stout for his older colleagues. 'I was told off by the other students,' he tells us, 'to obtain their lunch for them. I had to collect 40 or 50 pence from my companions, and go with that hoard to a neighbouring baker's and purchase the same number of buns. It generally happened that I got a bun myself by way of commission.'[20] He also worked unceasingly and was acknowledged as a youthful genius. He won the Academy's silver medal for a drawing from the antique when he was fourteen and was awarded the gold medal four years later for his historical painting *The Young Men of the Tribe of Benjamin seizing their Brides*.[21]

Millais was still only eighteen years of age when, in 1848, after long discussions with his fellow-students Holman Hunt and Rossetti, the Pre-Raphaelite Brotherhood was formed. Born of the enthusiasm of youth, it was in being for only four years or so but its influence continued into the twentieth century. In 1849 two of the first pictures to be inscribed with the letters 'P.R.B.' were exhibited at the Royal Academy – *Lorenzo and Isabella* (Plate 42) by Millais and *Rienzi*[22] by Holman Hunt. They were hung as pendants in the Middle Room 'in honourable places'[23] and produced considerable comment. The arguments both for and against them were lengthy and fierce. Millais sold his painting to some Bond Street tailors for £150 plus a suit of clothes. Holman Hunt's picture did not find a purchaser until after the exhibition had closed when, with the help of Augustus Egg, it was bought by a well-known collector for £100. The buyer also added £5 for the frame and the artist frankly tells us that 'the purchase of this picture was an act of generosity, for the gentlemen never valued the work, but hid it away in a closet. . . .'[24]

In 1843 some Academy students who were candidates for the annual prizes complained that the Academician E. H. Baily had worked on some of the entries in the class of Models from the Antique. On being questioned about it, he replied 'most solemnly that I have never placed a finger upon the Model of any Student still I must own in passing through the School I gave my advice to one and all . . . no favour can have been shown thereby as all parties enjoyed them equally, or, should it apply, it makes all alike ineligible'. Nevertheless the President and

Council considered his conduct to have been 'an indecorous interference at such a time' and that it was 'calculated to shake the confidence of the Students in the justice of impartiality of the Members' –
rather harsh words to use against a man who was then at the height of his
career.[25] He is reputed, however, to have been a somewhat troublesome
member and he more than once had differences of opinion with
Hanging Committees over the placing of his sculpture in the annual
exhibitions.

The School of Painting seems still to have been mainly concerned
with copying pictures but, in 1847, the Keeper (George Jones) put
forward the following interesting suggestion:

Gentlemen,
　　As we are all solititous for the advancement of Art, and particularly of
the Academic past in which we are concerned, I venture to suggest to
your consideration, whether we could make the Painting School more
useful by introducing the practise of Painting from Nature, in that School
at the same time and in union with the present practise of copying from
the Old Masters.

　　In Foreign Academies, the students paint from nature during the day,
and the model sits draped so far as to expose the head, arms, throat and
chest at the discretion of the Visitor.

　　This might be easily accomplish'd in our painting school, by placing
the model on a small throne near the stove, and students might thus be
employed from nature in the middle of the Room, whilst others were
engaged by the pictures on the walls.

　　This practise might be made useful and effective for Historical Art, by
accustoming the Student to a variety of faces and expressions, and of
diversity of beauty and form, and by this means prevent a similarity of
countenance too frequent in Historical works.

　　Three hours might not be too much, which would leave three hours
for the study of the Old Masters.

　　The Visitor must place the figure at first, after which the Curator or
Senior Student might keep the model in exact position.

　　A few pieces of Drapery would enable the Visitor to aid the character
of the Model, produce contrast, and give an appearance of completeness
in the whole arrangement.

　　I respectfully offer these observations for your consideration and have
the honour to be, Gentlemen, etc., etc.,

30th Oct^r.
　　　　　　　　　　　　　　　　　　　　　　　George Jones
To the Chairman and Council of the Royal Academy.[26]

The proposition was given a trial which was obviously successful as an order was made for it to be continued. In the same year it was laid down that candidates for admission to the Life School must produce 'at least six accurately finished Drawings of Groups or Figures from the Antique . . . accompanied by other drawings as large as nature of a hand and foot'.[27] Having proved their capabilities in dealing with the extremities, they were then allowed to study the whole human form.

It may be noticed that the Keeper's letter was addressed to 'The Chairman and Council', not 'The President and Council'. The reason for this is that Sir Martin Archer Shee had been in poor health for some time and a succession of Senior Members deputized for him at meetings. George Jones himself took the chair at General Assemblies but Turner did so at Council Meetings in 1845 and 1846, followed by Abraham Cooper, Sir Richard Westmacott and Richard Cook. Shee in fact resigned the Presidency in a letter dated 28 May 1845, on the ground of 'advanced age and long protracted illness'[28] but all his colleagues signed an Address to persuade him to change his mind. They called him 'our triumphant champion in the hour of need' and promised to relieve him of certain lesser duties if he would continue in office.[29] He consented and, with the sanction of Queen Victoria, was given a grant of £300 a year. No doubt this was in anticipation of the annuity which eventually would become payable to Presidents of the Royal Academy under the will of Sir Francis Chantrey.

Henry Howard had to give up his active work as Secretary in 1846 and died the following year. He was replaced by J. P. Knight who had been acting as his deputy. The continued illness of Sir Robert Smirke compelled him to resign the Treasurership in 1850 and Philip Hardwick was appointed. Sir Martin Archer Shee died in August that year and George Jones announced his intention of resigning the Keepership at Christmas. Thus, except for Thomas Uwins as Librarian, the latter half of the nineteenth century was to commence under the direction of an entirely new set of Officers.

SECOND PERIOD IN TRAFALGAR SQUARE
1850–1868

It had been learned from the Prime Minister, Lord John Russell, in March 1850, that 'the Apartments now occupied by the Royal Academy would be required for the purposes of the National Gallery'[1] and the following letter was received a month later:

> Downing Street. April 22d. 1850.
>
> Sir,
>
> I have the honor to inform you that in consequence of the want of room in the present National Gallery, for the Pictures belonging to the collection Her Majesty's Government have come to the determination of appropriating the room now used by the Royal Academy to the purpose of the National Gallery.
>
> It is the intention of the Government to propose to Parliament a vote of Twenty Thousand pounds in the present year, and a similar vote in the next year, to enable the Royal Academy to provide themselves with a Building suited for the purposes of Instruction for Students, and for Exhibition of the works of Artists.
>
> Her Majesty will always be desirous to evince to the Royal Academy by Her countenance and protection, Her wish for the success of their endeavours for the promotion and improvement of British Art.
>
> I have the honor to be Sir
> Your most obedt. Sert.
> J. Russell
>
> Geo. Jones Esqr.[2]

The Academy appointed a committee 'to guard the interests of the Institution'[3] in the matter but the Government did not proceed with this particular proposal. They considered instead the removal of the National Gallery but nothing came of it. A Select Committee had in 1848 recommended the Academy's evacuation and another, in 1853, suggested that the nation's pictures should be housed in new premises at Kensington Gore; a third, in 1856–57, was divided in its opinion. Pennethorne's scheme for enlarging the Trafalgar Square building, including an improvement to the Academy's sculpture room, was at last carried out in the winter of 1860–61 but it was by then of little help.

Following the death of Sir Martin Archer Shee, Charles Lock Eastlake (Plate 39) was elected President on 4 November 1850 by an overwhelming majority. He received twenty-four votes against two cast for George Jones and one each for H. W. Pickersgill and Sir Edwin Landseer. It would have been almost impossible at the time to have found anyone more suitably qualified for the post. Eastlake was well-educated, much-travelled and of considerable standing in the art world. He was a painter of historical pictures, portraits and landscapes, a respected connoisseur of the works of the Old Masters and the author of more than one treatise in art history and aesthetics. As has been said, he had been an officer of the National Gallery and, in addition, he was from 1841 the first Secretary of the Fine Arts Commission (for the decoration of the Houses of Parliament) and also one of the Commissioners for the Great Exhibition of 1851 held in Hyde Park. Eastlake was knighted soon after his election and it was decided to allow the President £300 per annum 'until the bequest of the late Sir Francis Chantrey shall come into operation'.[4]

His first year of office coincided with the Great Exhibition and Albert, the Prince Consort, made a point of attending the Academy Dinner 'in order to assist at what may be considered the inauguration festival of your newly elected President – at whose election I have heartily rejoiced, not only on account of my high estimate of his qualities, but also on account of my feelings of regard for him personally'.[5] The usual 'Table of Singers'[6] was restored for the occasion whereas, in 1850, it had been replaced by a military band. The more informal dinner for members only, which had frequently been held at the close of the annual exhibition, was discontinued and it was agreed that 'the Exhibition rooms be lighted and opened one or more Evenings, when the Exhibitors and other persons at the discretion of the Council, might be invited to meet the Members of the Royal Academy'.[7] Refreshments comprising tea and coffee, bread and butter, cakes, ices, etc., were to be provided for 700 and this function appears to be the forerunner of the many Academy Soirées which have taken place in the last hundred years.

George Jones did not after all resign the Keepership at Christmas,

1850, as intended. He was persuaded to continue for a while pending the report of a special committee convened to investigate the duties of this office. Their chief recommendations were that a Visitor instead of the Keeper should have the supervisory control of the Antique School in the evenings, that a Curator should be appointed 'competent to teach Modelling in all its branches including modelling of ornament'[8] and that there should be separate rooms for the study of the Old Masters and for painting from the Living Draped Model; also that the Travelling Students should be excused from having to submit works to the annual exhibition but, instead, should be required to show the results of their labours to the Council at the end of their periods of study. The report was duly adopted and Charles Landseer, the elder brother of Sir Edwin, took over the Keepership in the autumn of 1851. He had in fact been elected to the post six months previously. Thomas Uwins resigned as Librarian in 1855 and was followed by H. W. Pickersgill for eight years and then by S. A. Hart.

The wisdom of admitting engravers to full membership as Academicians was still debated hotly and, in 1852, the matter was again deferred 'until the funded property of the Academy shall have attained such a proportion, as to render the Institution comparatively independent of the annual and fluctuating income'[9] but, in that same year, some 'Historical and Landscape Engravers', including G. T. Doo and J. H. Robinson, sent separate memorials to Queen Victoria and the Prince Consort seeking their support.[10] The documents were forwarded to the Academy and, at long last, in 1853, a new class of members was instituted comprising Academician Engravers and Associate Engravers. There were to be not more than two of the former at one time and not more than four in the class as a whole. The former grade of six Associate Engravers was to be allowed to die out. Samuel Cousins was the first to be elected under the new regulations, as an Associate in November 1854 and an Academician in February 1855.

The exhibitions of this period were well attended and the 'fluctuating income',[11] often around £10,000, frequently enabled the institution to invest about a third of this sum. The exhibitors too had good reason to be grateful. In 1860, for example, 152 works were sold for £7,435 and, as ever, no commission was deducted by the Academy. Of the 2,612 paintings, drawings and pieces of sculpture sent in that year, 1,096 were placed in the exhibition. This number is considerably less than the average of the previous twenty years and for a time there seems to have been an attempt to be more selective. Even so the chances of success for non-members were some three or four times higher than they have become in the twentieth century. The system of selection was for about two-fifths of the submissions to be 'Accepted' but not necessarily hung, two-fifths to be 'Crossed' or 'Rejected' and the remaining one-fifth to be called 'Doubtful'.

J. M. W. Turner, who as student, member and Professor had been a staunch supporter of the Academy for over sixty years and was, with little doubt, its most brilliant star, died in 1851. His works had been a regular feature of the exhibitions and his pictures were sorely missed by the more perceptive visitors. Edwin Landseer was probably the best-known artist of the time to the ordinary public and he was very much in the favour of Queen Victoria. He was given a knighthood in 1850 and this was the year in which he showed his painting, *A Dialogue at Waterloo*.[12] One of his most famous pictures of a stag, now called *The Monarch of the Glen*,[13] was shown in the following year. The literary subjects painted by C. R. Leslie and others were well received but even more acceptable to the majority of people were the genre scenes by such artists as Thomas Webster and Richard Redgrave. Most pictures told a story and none were more popular than those by W. P. Frith depicting 'modern life'.[14] His *Ramsgate Sands*[15] (then called *Life at the seaside*) was exhibited in 1854 and *The Derby Day*[16] in 1858. The latter attracted such crowds that the picture was in danger of being damaged by the crush until a protecting rail was erected in front of it. Frith records: 'Couldn't help going to see the rail, and there it was sure enough; and loads of people.'[17] Subsequently the painting 'left this country for its travels abroad, first to the Antipodes, then to America, and amongst other places to Vienna. . . .'[18]

It will be remembered that Turner was a keen supporter of the Varnishing Days but that, since they were instituted in 1809, they had been for members only. In November 1851, however, with the grand old man out of action through illness and within a month of his death, this privilege was rescinded and, instead, it was agreed that both members and non-members should only be allowed to retouch pictures which might require such treatment 'in consequence of accident'.[19] The decision was unanimous but obviously made somewhat reluctantly. The new rule was not to come into effect till 1853 and even then the Council had to point out that 'the chilling or the want of varnish does not constitute an accident'.[20] C. R. Leslie is reported to have said '. . . had the varnishing days been abolished while Turner lived, it would almost have broken his heart'.[21] He records that when such a measure was hinted, Turner remarked, 'Then you will do away with the only social meeting we have, the only occasion on which we all come together in an easy, unrestrained manner. When we have no varnishing days, we shall not know one another.'[22] The social aspect, however, was not the only loss. In 1855 it had to be admitted that there was 'injury to the general appearance of the exhibition caused by many pictures requiring the aid of varnish'.[23] Finally, in 1862, it was resolved that the members should be allowed two days and the non-members one day 'to varnish and retouch their pictures'[24] and this is the principle still in force today.

The Academy has good reason to remember J. M. W. Turner quite apart from his long and dedicated service to the institution. His will was so complicated that several years elapsed before a settlement could be reached but, in 1856, by an order of the Court of Chancery, the sum of £20,000 was received and invested as a separate trust fund. The income is used to provide annuities and gifts, to 'Artists of reputation, not Members of the Academy',[25] a biennially awarded gold medal and scholarship and an annual contribution towards the support of the Royal Academy Schools. Turner's bequest was the first such benefaction to be placed at the disposal of the President and Council but the example has happily been followed by many others. The sculptor E. H. Baily was invited to design the gold medal but both his first and second attempts failed to please the Council. A sketch by Daniel Maclise was eventually chosen and the medal, executed by L. C. Wyon, was first awarded in 1857. The obverse had Turner's head surrounded by an inscription giving his full name and dates of birth and death. The reverse showed a long-haired youth reclining with a palette and brush ready for use whilst, watched over by three muses in the heavens, he contemplates various tokens of landscape. The medal was minted regularly until the death of George V in 1936.

In 1865 the Art Union of London complained that their prizewinners had difficulty in selecting works from the Royal Academy exhibitions as there was nothing to indicate whether or not they were still for sale. As a result of this it was decided to place a red star on the frames of all works as 'from day to day' had been purchased as well as on all works 'not for sale'.[26] A note to this effect was to be inserted in the catalogue. It duly appeared and was afterwards repeated regularly but referred only to works actually sold. Those not for sale presumably had no distinguishing mark attached to them.

Another notation in the catalogue that year invited 'Exhibitors of this or last year' to become candidates for Associateship 'by inscribing their names, or communicating by letter to the Secretary during the Month of May'.[27] This was then normal procedure but never appears to have been advertised like this again; a notice was pinned up every year.

As early as 1851 a suggestion had been made that the exhibition might be open in the evening but nothing came of it. Ten years later, however, a memorial 'signed by several Ministers of State, Noblemen and Gentlemen' was submitted advocating such a course 'on certain Evenings during the season for the admission of the working classes'.[28] Doubts were expressed on the practicability of carrying out such a proposal in view of the possible dangers both of overcrowding and of the use of gaslight but it was agreed that, 'with the experience and care of the Officers and attendants of the Royal Academy, added to the vigilance of the police, no bad consequences are to be apprehended'.[29] Beginning in June 1862, the exhibition was opened on Monday, Tuesday and Wednesday evenings from 7 to 10 p.m. at the reduced prices of sixpence for admission and sixpence for a special smaller catalogue. Closing time was enforced 'by gradually lowering the gas' and the employment of police officers to clear the rooms.[30]

E. J. Poynter, W. B. Richmond, Albert Moore, W. L. Wyllie, Thomas Brock and Ernest George were among the students admitted into the Academy Schools during the period 1850–68 and some consternation was caused in 1860 when it was discovered that 'one of the probationers recently admitted to the Antique School is a young woman'.[31] She was Laura Anne Herford, aged 29, and apparently, as she had put her initials only on the drawings which she submitted, it was not suspected that she was a female. There had in fact never been any regulation prohibiting the entry of women into the Schools but it would seem that, until then, none had ever applied. Young ladies indeed by this time had their own 'Government School of Art for Females'[32] in Gower Street and the Academy more than once made contributions to its upkeep. This may have been the reason or excuse for the limit which appears to have been imposed unofficially on the admission of women into the Academy Schools over the next few years. However, one of them, Louisa Starr (later Madame Canziani), soon proved her worth. She gained a silver medal in 1865 and trounced the men by capturing the coveted gold medal for painting in 1867.

The Council no doubt felt the weight of their responsibility in matters of moral welfare. It was resolved 'that young women students be placed in communication with the Housekeeper and be especially recommended to her' and 'that the strictest propriety be observed in the Antique School with reference to such students'.[33] There was a suggestion that the Law preventing unmarried students under twenty from studying the female model might be repealed but this was quickly quashed. Sir Edwin Landseer asked the Council to consider 'the adoption of some means of rendering the study of the nude model in the Life School, less offensive to decency and morality'.[34] The subject was debated at length and it was finally decided:

> That as a general principle it is desirable that the model in the Life School should be undraped, and that any partial concealment for considerations of decency would rather tend to attract attention to what might otherwise pass unnoticed. It appears to the Council that the particular objection suggested by a needless fidelity sometimes observable in drawings, is a question rather of taste than of morals, and they are therefore of opinion that the objection should be met by recommending and requiring the Visitors to dissuade Students from bestowing unnecessary attention on unimportant parts, especially when decency suggests their being passed over.[35]

J. C. Horsley had just been elected an Academician and it is tempting to speculate on his influence, if any, at the time. His puritanical advocacy of draped figures in pictures earned him in later years the nickname of 'Clothes-Hors(e)ley'. Such attitudes of mind over the admission of females and the study of the human form were, of course, characteristic of Victorian codes of conduct.

The length of the studentship in the Academy Schools was shortened from ten to seven years in 1853 and, twelve months later, the period of the travelling studentships was reduced from three to two years. Associates were still considered to be very inferior to Academicians and, when one was given permission to give a lecture to the students in 1857, this was called 'a dangerous innovation'.[36] By 1868, however, they were allowed to take their turn as Visitors.

Ten years earlier it had been agreed that Academicians over 65 years of age could apply to be classed as 'Honorary Retired Members'. There were, however, to be no more than four at one time and admission to this rank was to be regarded as 'a Privilege, and not a Right'.[37] E. H. Baily and C. R. Cockerell were the first to have their applications approved, in 1862. They retained the letters 'RA' after their names but were no longer allowed to hold any office or to attend meetings and were limited to the submission of one work to the annual exhibition.

In 1855 another Return was requested by the House of Commons requiring details of attendances at the exhibitions and of the profits on catalogues. It was successfully resisted again but this was by no means the end of the matter. A Royal Commission was appointed in 1863 'to inquire into the present position of the Royal Academy in relation to the Fine Arts, and into the circumstances and conditions under which it occupies a portion of the National Gallery, and to suggest such Measures as may be required to render it more useful in promoting Art and in improving and developing public taste'.[38] The evidence took five months to collect and was published in 557 closely printed pages. The President, Sir Charles Lock Eastlake, had to bear the brunt of the questioning but there were 45 other witnesses besides him. They included artists of varied ages such as William Mulready, Sir Edwin Landseer, George Gilbert Scott, Holman Hunt and J. E. Millais, as well as three Members of Parliament and some well-known art critics, for example Tom Taylor and John Ruskin.

The resulting report was very much in the Academy's favour as an institution 'of great service to the country, in assisting to keep up and to cultivate a taste for Art'[39] but it made certain suggestions for possible improvements. It recommended that more architects and sculptors should be elected to bring the total number of Academicians to fifty and that there should be an additional ten members 'not being artists';[40] also that the number of Associates should be increased to fifty (or even more in due course) and that they should have equal rights with Academicians in running the Academy's affairs. It advocated a class of Honorary Foreign Members and one of Art-workmen, the latter to comprise 'workmen of great excellence in metal, stone, wood, and other materials'.[41] Another suggestion was that there should be two Vice-Presidents selected from the categories of art to which the President might not belong. In other words, if he happened to be a painter, then the triumvirate should be completed by the election of a sculptor and an architect.

Various ideas were put forward in connection with the exhibitions and the Schools and the report stressed more than once the urgent need for additional space. It was the opinion of the Commissioners that this should be provided by the Government but that the Academy should be reconstituted under a Royal Charter 'on a wider and more liberal basis'[42] and form 'a valuable permanent Council of advice and reference in all matters relating to the Fine Arts, public monuments, and buildings'.[43] If this had come about, the Royal Academy would have become virtually a government-sponsored organization with attendant advantages and disadvantages.

In the event, certain recommendations were adopted in 1866 but no great change was made and the Academy retained its independence. The number of Academicians remained as before and that of Associates became indefinite but with a minimum of twenty. Both classes in future were allowed to nominate and elect new members, age limits were discontinued and the ban was lifted on concurrent membership of other art societies. The succeeding years brought no appreciable increase in total numbers, however, and nothing came of the proposal regarding Art-workmen. An order of Honorary Foreign Academicians was instituted in 1868, to consist of 'distinguished Foreign Artists not resident in the United Kingdom'.[44] Six were elected in 1869 (Louis Gallait, Claude Guillaume, Eugène Viollet-le-Duc, Louis Henriquel-Dupont, Jean Louis Meissonier and Jean Léon Gérôme) and, though no limit was set, this number was never exceeded or indeed equalled for well over a hundred years. Quite a few British artists had by this time been similarly honoured in other lands and it was high time for some reciprocal arrangement. The word 'Foreign' was dropped from the title in 1933 in order to be able to include artists of British nationality resident abroad.

The Commissioners had recommended that the Academy should issue an Annual Report but this procedure had in fact already commenced in 1860. It has been continued ever since as an internal document from the Council to the General Assembly and it provides year by year concise summaries of the institution's activities. The first report gave a general abstract of the finances from 1769 to 1859. It shows, among other things, that the Academy had made profits amounting to £267,000 on its exhibitions throughout the period, had spent £218,000 on its Schools and administration and paid out £61,000 as pensions and donations to artists and their families. Its books were balanced by the receipt of dividends on investments and its financial assets then amounted to a little over £100,000. It was currently making a profit of about £3,000 a year but its continued prosperity depended very much upon the enjoyment of adequate accommodation. The Prince Consort died in 1861 and the Academy made a contribution of £500 to the Albert Memorial Fund. Philip Hardwick gave up the Treasurership that same year and was succeeded by another architect, Sydney Smirke, who had not long taken over as Professor of Architecture from

C. R. Cockerell. The Clerk (Henry Eyre) was given the title of Registrar from 1862 onwards.

Some considerable time previously, in 1851, a memorial had been addressed to Queen Victoria praying for more space if the National Gallery should move and, in 1856, there was a suggestion of buying the whole of the Trafalgar Square building which was then in danger of being demolished to make way for a large hotel. In 1858 the Prime Minister (Lord Derby) agreed that the Royal Academy had 'a moral claim, should the Public Service require their removal from their present locality, to have provided for them equally convenient accommodation elsewhere'[45] and, in 1859, the Chancellor of the Exchequer (Benjamin Disraeli) made an offer for the Academy to choose a freehold site at Burlington House in Piccadilly and for the Government to erect premises there for its use. As this would be at the public cost, he could not, however, promise 'that the Acad'. would be free from the interference of Parliament or of future Governments' but was ready to offer the same site for the Academy to build on out of its own funds and, in these circumstances, 'the independence of the Institution could be guaranteed'.[46] A Building Committee was appointed and Sir Charles Barry was elected as the architect but he died in the following year. The situation was then complicated by proposals to house the National Gallery in premises on the gardens to the north of Burlington House. They were defeated but probably led to the Government's original offer being limited in 1865 to a choice between the Piccadilly and Burlington Gardens frontages, both very restricted in depth and on a mere ninety-nine-year lease.

This was the position when Eastlake, the President, died at the end of that year and there was some difficulty in nominating his successor. Sir Edwin Landseer was elected by an overwhelming majority but declined the office on the plea of bad health. A second election then took place, on 1 February 1866, and resulted in twenty-three votes for Francis Grant, three for Richard Westmacott, two for J. R. Herbert and one each for C. W. Cope, J. P Knight and J. E. Millais. Born of wealthy parents in Perthshire in 1803, Grant (Plates 41 and 51) became a well-known figure in mid-Victorian society on both sides of the border, not only for his portraits and sporting pictures but as the owner of a hunting establishment at Melton Mowbray in Leicestershire. His first exhibit at the Royal Academy was indeed *The Melton Breakfast*[47] in 1834. He subsequently painted portraits more than once of Queen Victoria and the Prime Minister, Lord Melbourne, and both his artistic talents and somewhat extravagant way of life, coupled with aristocratic connections by marriage, brought him into contact with many influential people of the time.

The new President was knighted before the end of 1866 and, in this same year, the Academy was offered a substantial amount of ground on the new Kensington Gore estate. The Queen was known to be in favour of this scheme and Grant had to proceed very delicately. There was still a faint possibility of the whole of the Trafalgar Square building becoming available for the Academy's use but, when this hope finally vanished, the President used all his endeavours to get accepted a new plan devised by Sydney Smirke. This was for the existing Burlington House to be made available for the Academy's administrative purposes and for its exhibition galleries and Schools to be built immediately adjacent to it on the northern gardens. The current offers were refused and Grant's persuasive powers were able to convince all concerned that Smirke's ideas were both sensible and imaginative. The original house would be preserved and there was no need to spend much on the exteriors of the new buildings as they would be hidden from sight. In August 1866 the Government agreed to grant a 999-year lease at a nominal rent of £1 per annum on the understanding that the Academy would, at its own expense, build galleries and Schools as suggested, make any necessary alterations to the house without spoiling the main, southern façade and add a third storey. This last provision, an expensive item, was to raise the height of old Burlington House to conform with new buildings which the Government instructed R. R. Banks and C. Barry to erect on the Piccadilly frontage and its flanks and thus complete a rectangular courtyard. The Academy's lease was finally signed on 6 March 1867, to date from Christmas 1866, and the institution's indebtedness to Sir Francis Grant was duly acknowledged in a vote of thanks for his 'skill and untiring energy'[48] in bringing the negotiations to such a satisfactory conclusion and, later, by commissioning him to paint a self-portrait (Plate 41).

Sydney Smirke had by this time been appointed as the Academy's architect and he estimated that his new buildings, apart from the additional storey to the original house, would cost about £70,000. This figure was eventually exceeded by over £11,000 and another £34,000 was spent on the alterations to the existing mansion. The latter expense, however, was met by a bequest of over £40,000 from John Gibson who died in 1866 and also left the Academy a large collection of plaster casts of his sculptures.

Work began in April 1867 and, by May 1868, the new building on the gardens was said to be nearly completed. It comprised the present Galleries I to XI (though then numbered differently), together with the Lecture Room, a domed Central Hall of octagonal plan and a Vestibule, all very lofty with glass roofs and set at first-floor level with storage accommodation below. The Schools were built alongside the northern face of the galleries. They consist basically of two ranges of studios stretching the whole length of the building plus a large room on the east, originally for the School of Architecture and concealed from the courtyard by an annexe. This was added later to the old house as living quarters for the Keeper.

A meeting was convened in the new building on 24 November 1868 and it was available for occupation immediately afterwards, one hundred years from the Academy's foundation. The annual distribution of premiums was held on 10 December as usual and, to mark the centenary, the members then adjourned to supper at Willis's Rooms, in the apartment normally used by the Society of Dilettanti and hung with their fine paintings by Reynolds. The next minutes were proudly headed 'Being the first meeting of Council in the Second Century'.[49]

12

FIRST DECADE AT BURLINGTON HOUSE
1869–1878

It seems only right that this chronicle should contain a brief record of the previous history of Burlington House (Plates 46, 48 and 55).[1] Samuel Pepys noted in his diary that it was being built in 1664 and that he paid a visit there in 1668. It was certainly begun by Sir John Denham, who was Surveyor-General to Charles II, but it was sold before completion to Richard Boyle, first Earl of Burlington and second Earl of Cork. Hence the nomenclature of some of the nearby roads; the name 'Burlington' is said to be a variant of Bridlington, in Yorkshire, where Boyle owned a vast tract of land.

The mansion was of two main storeys, together with a basement and an attic, and two rooms in depth from front to back. It was built of plain brickwork and stone quoins, with walls over four feet in thickness and a hipped roof. There were wings at both ends, projecting some ten feet to the south, and the centre of this main façade, comprising the doorway with two windows on each side, was slightly recessed. The whole treatment was very simple, the only non-structural features being a balcony over the door and a small triangular pediment in the centre of the cornice above it. The house itself stood well back from Piccadilly (then called Portugal Street), with single-storeyed buildings on the east and west sides of an intervening courtyard and screens linking them to the main gate in a very high street wall. It is all clearly shown, together with the gardens and open country to the north, in a bird's-eye view which was drawn by Leonard Knyff about 1698 and published as an engraving by Jan Kip in 1707 (Plate 46). The interior was neatly divided into fair-sized rooms which led one into the other and the rather narrow stairs were placed to the east of the main entrance.

The 3rd Earl of Burlington, later to become a celebrated dilettante and patron of the arts, came into possession of Burlington House in 1704 when he was only ten years of age. Alterations seem to have been started about 1712, including remodelling the staircase, and were probably under the direction of James Gibbs, but obviously they were too modest for the young earl's taste after his first visit to Italy in 1714–15. He then employed Colin Campbell who, in Volume III of his *Vitruvius Britannicus*, published in 1725, makes the following claim and illustrates it with designs made in 1717:

> The Front of the House, the Conjunction from thence to the Offices, the Great Gate and Street Wall were all designed and executed by me. In the double Plate you have the principal Front, where a bold rustic basement supports a regular Ionick Collonade of ¾ Columns 2 Feet Diameter. The Line is closed with Two Towers, adorned with Two Venetian Windows in Front, and Two Niches in Flank. . . . In the next Plate you have the great Gate, adorned with 4 ¾ Columns of the Dorick Order, 2 feet Diameter, agreeable to the Colonade in the Court. . . .[2]

Perhaps spurred on by Campbell's Palladian style, Lord Burlington went to Italy a second time, in 1719, to study in particular the works of Andrea Palladio in Vicenza and Venice but by then the new southern façade, faced with stone, must have been all but complete. He brought back with him to London his 'proper priest',[3] William Kent, who thereafter lived in the house until his death in 1748. It is known that he made 'a sketch in Collers for the Great Roome in the front'[4] (now the Saloon) and the rest of the ornaments, 'al Italiano',[5] were probably by Giovanni Battista Guelphi who, according to Vertue, had been encouraged to settle in England and 'was much employed for many years by Ld. Burlington in his house in London'.[6] The top of the staircase was decorated by another Italian, Sebastiano Ricci, with four large paintings (Plate 62) which are still in good condition at the Royal Academy. Horace Walpole records that the 'staircase is painted by Sebastian Ricci in his best manner; the cielings by Kent in his worst'.[7] The latter judgment is a little hard in relation to the roundel over the central staircase today. This is very similar in content to the frontispiece in Kent's book *The Designs of Inigo Jones*[8] and is almost certainly by him.

The aim of all these alterations was to transform a rather uninspiring house into a palatial, Italianate mansion and it certainly succeeded although Denham's north front remained for another hundred years. By doing away with the attic storey and the southern hipped roof, Campbell was able to convert the front of the first floor into a *piano nobile* and the house was made into a fitting meeting-place for Lord Burlington's circle. Besides the artists already mentioned, Handel stayed there and it was the resort of men of letters, among them Pope, Swift and also John Gay, who wrote in his *Trivia*:

> Yet Burlington's fair palace still remains;
> Beauty within, without proportion reigns,
> Beneath his eye declining art revives,
> The wall with animated picture lives;
> There Handel strikes the strings, the melting strain
> Transports the soul and thrills through every vein,
> There oft I enter (but with cleaner shoes)
> For Burlington's belov'd by Ev'ry Muse.[9]

Nevertheless, His Lordship had his critics. 'The Great Gate',[10] designed by Colin Campbell, is featured in two satirical engravings by Hogarth. The word 'TASTE' is inscribed over it in one and 'ACCADEMY OF ARTS' in the other (Plate 47), a curiously prophetic idea. Both plates were gibes at Lord Burlington's patronage and William Kent is shown standing high above the reclining figures of Raphael and Michelangelo.

It is noticeable that Campbell barely mentions the once famous colonnade in the courtyard and it seems likely that it was designed by James Gibbs. It was so beautiful, and of course exceptional in London, that Horace Walpole said, 'It seemed one of those artifices in fairy tales that are raised by genii in a night's time.'[11] Unfortunately it had to be demolished in 1867, together with the gateway and the forecourt buildings, to make way for the new work by Banks and Barry.

The 3rd Earl of Burlington died in 1753 and, on the death of his widow, the property passed to their grandson William Cavendish, Marquis of Hartington and subsequently 5th Duke of Devonshire. It was then tenanted in turn by two kinsmen, the 3rd Duke of Portland and Lord George Cavendish, and the latter bought it from his nephew, the 6th Duke of Devonshire, in 1815. The new owner (afterwards Earl of Burlington in a re-creation of the title) employed Samuel Ware, between 1815 and 1818, to construct a great central staircase and convert the previous one into rooms, to refashion the north front in stone, to build a block for guests on the east side of the courtyard and generally to bring the property into the state in which the Government purchased it from his descendants, in 1854, for £140,000. The subsequent major alterations were not begun until after the Royal

Academy had built its new galleries and James Pennethorne had erected, in 1869, premises for the University of London on the northern boundary of the gardens.

The first exhibition at Burlington House was held in 1869 from 3 May to 31 July. It was preceded by the Annual Dinner on Saturday, 1 May, but the Soirée, instead of taking place as previously at the end of the season, was brought forward to 24 June. This pattern has, generally speaking, been followed ever since but the Soirée, occasionally omitted in recent years for reasons of economy, is no longer a regular feature. Over 4,500 works were submitted and 1,320 of them formed the exhibition. This was not a tremendous increase on the numbers shown during the previous few years in the much smaller space in the Trafalgar Square building but, in the new galleries, it had been decided that 'every picture should be more or less separated by intervening wall space' and that 'no picture should be hung with its base line higher than 12 feet from the ground'.[12] The intention was good but had to be reluctantly abandoned beyond the first four rooms in order to accommodate all the 1,284 works which had been 'Accepted' during the selection.

The exhibition was a great success. There were 315,000 visitors and a profit of almost £15,000. In addition, a total of £14,905 7s 4d was reached for the sale of 189 works and thus more artists than usual reaped direct financial benefit. Oil paintings were hung in Galleries I to V and in four galleries on the eastern side, now numbered VII, VIII, X and XI. Architectural drawings, engravings and miniatures were shown in the Lecture Room and the watercolours were in the small adjoining gallery, now numbered IX. This left the whole of the central axis for sculpture – the Vestibule, Central Hall and the present Gallery VI – and it does not appear to have been mixed with the pictures at all. The majority of the galleries measure about 40 feet by 32 feet and the really large gallery, still called No. III (Plates 50 and 51), is over 82 feet by 42 feet. The amount of display space in the new building was therefore more than double the area which had hitherto been available. In order to 'preserve the gilded ceiling from the deleterious influence of smoke arising from the large amount of gas required to light the galleries',[13] the evening exhibition was no longer held but an extra week was added at the end of the season at half-price charges of sixpence for admission and sixpence for a catalogue.

A refreshment room was provided but it is not clear where this could have been. In 1873 access was made from Gallery II to the dining-room (now called the General Assembly Room) of old Burlington

House for this purpose but, until then, the original mansion was still used by the Royal, Linnean and Chemical Societies who had moved there some sixteen years previously. The new courtyard buildings were ready for their occupation in 1873–74 and the Society of Antiquaries, together with the Geological and (Royal) Astronomical Societies, joined them as neighbours. By then, Smirke had already built his third storey as agreed with the Government. Its recessed central portion is dressed with Corinthian columns and, in between them, viewed from west to east, are the statues *Leonardo da Vinci* (by Edward Stephens), *John Flaxman* and *Raphael* (both by Henry Weekes), *Michelangelo* in the middle and *Titian* on its left (both by W. Calder Marshall) and *Sir Joshua Reynolds* and *Sir Christopher Wren* (also both by Edward Stephens). There are also busts of these seven artists high up in the octagonal Central Hall, together with an eighth whose identity seems not to have been recorded and remains a mystery. Two other statues, *Phidias* and *William of Wykeham* (both by Joseph Durham), look towards one another from the flanks of the wings, whose southern fronts have loggias which follow the style of the Venetian windows at first-floor level. The new storey contained the Gibson Gallery on the east and three galleries intended for the display of Diploma Works. The former was opened to the public in 1876 and two of the others in 1878 but the North Gallery was not built until 1885.

Meanwhile the plans for the interior of the old house had been slightly modified by G. E. Street as a measure of economy and Smirke's idea of a domed, marble staircase to the main galleries did not materialize. The Keeper was provided with living accommodation on the ground floor of the eastern wing and in a newly erected, three-storey annexe adjoining it. These alterations were completed by 1874 when Smirke, then over seventy-five, resigned as Treasurer and gave up active work. He was succeeded by yet another architect, E. M. Barry, who, in 1876, was responsible for the rather fine staircase as we know it today. The library, which until this date had still been in Trafalgar Square, was then moved into the ballroom (now the Reynolds Room) on the first floor of the eastern wing.

The long series of exhibitions of works by living artists and also of Old Masters, which had been held by the British Institution for well over half a century, unfortunately came to an end in 1867 when the lease of its building was about to expire. The funds were transferred to the Charity Commission in 1885 and a Board of Trustees was subsequently formed for the award of scholarships and prizes to art students. The Secretary of the Academy has so far always acted as its Secretary and it consists of representatives appointed by the Department of Education and Science, the Royal Academy, the Royal Scottish and Hibernian Academies, the Royal Institute of Painters in Water Colours, and the Universities of Oxford, Cambridge and London.

The cessation of the Old Masters' Exhibitions was a serious blow to art lovers and students and, in 1869, the Burlington Fine Arts Club (which, despite its name, had no connection with Burlington House or the Royal Academy) asked whether they might use the Academy's new galleries for such a purpose in the winter months. The request was considered sympathetically but some doubts were expressed as to whether a purely private society would be able to obtain the loan of works of sufficiently high standard. The Academy thereupon 'undertook the duty solely in the interest of Art ... and to guard against the supposition that the Institution in its action was influenced by the prospect of pecuniary gain, it was determined that should any profit accrue after the payment of expenses, the surplus ... should be disposed of in objects of charity and for the benefit of Art'.[14] A committee of seven Academicians was appointed to carry the resolution into effect and an exhibition of 235 works, mainly by two British artists who had recently died (C. R. Leslie and W. Clarkson Stanfield) but also including some Old Masters, was opened to the public on 2 January 1870 and continued for eight weeks. It was reasonably successful but the total receipts were only about £3,000 as opposed to well over £17,000 for the 'Exhibition of the Works of Living Artists' that year. There were, however, a considerable number of free admissions including the artist exhibitors of the previous year. This privilege was continued up to 1919 but then unfortunately had to be stopped as such exhibitions became more and more expensive to organize. The first one had cost only £1,300 and the profit was duly divided between three artists' charities.

These exhibitions were entirely composed of works from collections in the British Isles and usually filled about half the galleries. They continued annually on much the same lines until 1913 except that, occasionally, a single artist was represented, such as Sir Edwin Landseer in 1874 and, in later years, Leighton, Millais, Rembrandt, Van Dyck and Alma-Tadema. The Landseer exhibition drew 105,000 visitors, exclusive of free admissions, and over 30,000 catalogues were sold. The receipts (nearly £6,000) were well in advance of any former year and, as the expenses were no more than usual, there was a good surplus

37 'The Madonna and Child with the Infant St
John' by Michelangelo, 1504–5. Presented to the
Royal Academy, 1830

39 'Sir Charles Lock Eastlake', President of the Royal
Academy, by J. P. Knight, 1857

38 'Torso of a Girl' attributed to Timotheus, *c.* 375–350
B.C. Presented to the Royal Academy, 1855

41 'Self-portrait' by Sir Francis Grant, 1876. President of the Royal Academy.

40 'John Gibson', sculptor and benefactor to the Royal Academy, by Sir Edwin Landseer, c. 1850

42 'Lorenzo and Isabella' by Sir J. E. Millais, Bt. Exhibited at Royal Academy, 1849
(*Walker Art Gallery, Liverpool*)

43 'A Visit to Aesculapius' by Sir Edward J. Poynter, Bt. Chantrey Bequest Purchase,
1880 (*Tate Gallery, London*)

44 'The Ball on Shipboard' by James Tissot. Exhibited at Royal Academy, 1874.
Chantrey Bequest Purchase, 1937 (*Tate Gallery, London*)

45 'An Interior in Venice' (the drawing-room of the Palazzo Barbaro) by J. S. Sargent.
Diploma Work, 1899

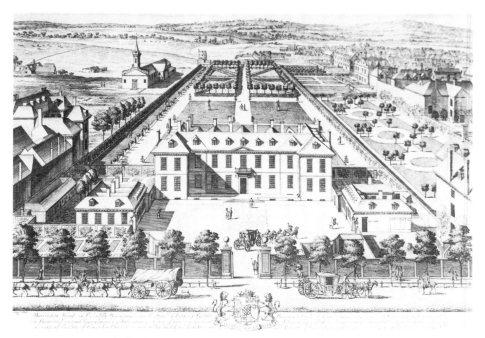

46 'Burlington House in Pickadilly'. Engraving Jan Kip
after Leonard Knyff, 1707

MASQUERADES AND OPERAS. BURLINGTON GATE.

47 'Masquerades and Operas' with the words 'Accademy of Arts' on the Gateway of
Burlington House. Engraving by William Hogarth, 1724

48 'South Front, Burlington House' by J. W. Archer, 1855 (*Reproduced by courtesy of the Trustees of the British Museum, London*)

49 Lord Leighton lying in state in the Central Hall of the Royal Academy, 1896

50 'The Private View of the Royal Academy, 1881' by W. P. Frith. In the centre, Lord Leighton (bare-headed) talks to Lady Lonsdale with the Archbishop of York and Lily Langtry nearby. W. E. Gladstone (with high collar) is on the left and Oscar Wilde (with flower in button-hole) on the right (*C.J.R. Pope, Esq.*)

for distribution. Owners of works of art seem to have lent very readily in those days but the demands on them were of course far less frequent. The Academy's Winter Exhibitions soon gained an enviable reputation for their content but it was not till 1877 that any kind of scholarly or descriptive notes were attempted in the catalogue. The main problem for the organizers was that of transport and it is quite amazing to remember that, apart from a few things dispatched by rail, most of the exhibits had to be collected and returned by horse and van.

The annual 'Exhibition of the Works of Living Artists' had, for obvious reasons, begun to be known by the early 1870s as the Summer Exhibition. A special day for the Press View was instituted in 1871 and, following an Act of Parliament that year making the first Monday in August a Bank Holiday, it was decided that, from 1872, the exhibition should be extended to include this as the last day. Opening on the first Monday in May and continuing until the first Monday in August became standard practice till 1912. These Summer Exhibitions during the period 1869–78 had average attendances of around 300,000 visitors. One need only remember such paintings as *The Boyhood of Raleigh*[15] by Millais in 1870 or *When did you last see your father?*[16] by W. F. Yeames in 1878 as instances of pictures which attracted the public but the exhibits of G. F. Watts, John Pettie, Lawrence Alma-Tadema and Briton Riviere, to name but a few, were equally popular. Whistler showed the famous *Arrangement in Grey and Black: Portrait of the Painter's mother*[17] in 1872 but this was his last painting in the Academy. Five years later he won a lawsuit against John Ruskin who had described one of his pictures as 'flinging a pot of paint in the public's face'[18] but, as is well known, he was awarded only one farthing in damages. Ruskin's pungent criticisms were feared by many artists and the following mock lament was sometimes all too true:

> I paints and paints,
> Hears no complaints,
>   And sells before I'm dry;
> Till savage Ruskin
> Sticks his tusk in
>   And nobody will buy.[19]

W. B. Richmond frequently protested that exhibitors should be allowed to have glass on their oil paintings but the proposal was always defeated. In 1876, an attempt was made to share more equitably the best hanging places and it was resolved that no artist should have more than four pictures 'on the line'.

The occupation of the new premises at Burlington House, with the resultant growth in the Academy's activities, involved more work for all concerned. From 1871 the Council was increased to twelve members (though curtailed to ten from 1878) and the committee for arranging the Summer Exhibition was enlarged to consist of five painters (including engravers), one sculptor and one architect; three Academicians were elected annually as Auditors to act as a finance committee and four as Inspectors of Property. The Secretary, J. P. Knight, had been in poor health for some time and his resignation was accepted in 1873 when it was decided that the post should be held by a layman. Frederick Eaton (Plate 51) was then appointed at a salary of £500 per annum and, subject to his authority, the responsibility of all household supervision devolved upon the Registrar. Until then it had been undertaken by the Keeper but, as the Schools were now fully active throughout the academic year, he had less time to spare for extraneous duties. F. R. Pickersgill took over the post from Charles Landseer and E. M. Barry was elected Professor of Architecture. Barry, as has been said, became Treasurer also in the following year. This position had, since the days of Sir William Chambers, entitled the holder to attend Council Meetings and a similar privilege was now extended to the Keeper as well.

In 1874 a reform was introduced in the method of procedure at elections. Hitherto, after the first voting, the two candidates who had obtained the highest number were put to a ballot straightaway. Thereafter, it was agreed as follows:

> ... all those candidates who have no scratches, or who have less than four, be eliminated from the List, and those who have obtained more than three scratches be again scratched for preliminary to the final ballot of the two highest in number from the second scratched List.[20]

The proposers might well have found a happier phraseology but at least the sense is clear and, basically, the same procedure is still used today.

Although the Royal Commission in 1863 had strongly recommended a substantial increase in the number of Associates and, in 1866, the Academy had decided that their maximum should be indefinite, no action had been taken to alter the situation. This negligence provoked many arguments in 1875 and resulted in a definite proposal that twelve new Associates be added immediately. This was rejected but, in the following year, it was agreed to elect 'a first instalment of four . . . with a view to raising the number of Associates to thirty within two years'[21] and, indeed, such an acceleration is noticeable in the records. Honorary Members were appointed as usual when vacancies occurred and W. E. Gladstone (Plate 50) became Professor of Ancient History that year.

There were, as ever, a few dissatisfied artists, particularly among those whose works had not been placed in the exhibitions. An infamous pamphlet in doggerel, said to have been written by a painter named John E. Soden, was published privately in 1875 under the title *A Rap at the R.A.*[22] It is perhaps best forgotten but the following lines from it cannot fail to elicit some sympathy:

> The toil of months, experience of years,
> Before the dreaded Council now appears:-
> It's left their view almost as soon as in it. –
> They damm them at the rate of three a minute. –
> Scarce time for even faults to be detected,
> The cross is chalked:- 'tis fling aside 'REJECTED'.
> ....
> Shame! that they, Artists, should such pain have given
> To those who struggle as themselves have striven.[23]

The majority of artists, however, recognized that the opportunities in the new building were better than they had ever been. Though understandably never quite content, they readily accepted the challenge of keen competition. The chances of success were fewer as the number of submissions grew steadily from year to year and it became even more of a distinction 'to be hung in the Academy'.

The increased accommodation for the Schools at Burlington House, together with the fact that their work could now be conducted continuously without interruption on account of exhibitions, brought about a number of reforms. Probationership was limited to a term of three months, a preliminary class was established to study the practice of oil painting and another class to encourage mural painting. Teachers of sculpture and architecture were appointed in addition to the Professors and a Schools' Committee (disbanded in 1874) was given the task of supervising the many changes. A Professorship of Chemistry was instituted in 1871, to which F. S. Barff was duly elected, and, besides the regular courses of lectures, single talks were given on such subjects as 'Beauty' and 'Light'.

It was no longer necessary to impose an arbitrary limit on the admission of female students but they were still not allowed in the Life School. A request from them for facilities for such study separate from the men was, in 1872, 'declared inexpedient, and unanimously refused'[24] but, in the following year, they were permitted to attend the lectures on anatomy 'subject to the condition that two of the six Lectures shall be reserved for Male Students only'.[25] The sexes were segregated even for painting from the draped model and modelling from the head. Frank Dicksee, J. Seymour Lucas, Stanhope Forbes, Hamo Thornycroft and Alfred Gilbert were among those admitted during the first decade in the new buildings.

In 1877 Edward Armitage presented £1,000 to form a trust fund through which prizes could be given, in an annual competition among the students, for a sketch in monochrome of a set subject from scripture, ancient history or mythology. In accordance with the donor's wishes, it was for many years conducted on the lines of an examination. The subject would be announced at the commencement of the first day and candidates were not allowed out of the room until they had completed a preliminary drawing. This design had to be deposited with the Keeper and three days in all were allowed for it to be carried out in a finished sketch, 12 × 18 inches in size. Cash prizes have always been awarded to the winners and runners-up and, from 1882, special medals (with the Sovereign's head on the obverse and the words 'ARMITAGE MEDAL' in a laurel wreath on the reverse) were added. The rules have, however, been considerably relaxed in recent years and the medals now issued are of the same pattern as those for all the other competitions.

The income from the Chantrey Bequest began to be received by the Academy soon after Lady Chantrey's death in 1875 and, as has been said, the first purchases were made in 1877. They included the large painting *Amy Robsart*[26] by W. F. Yeames for £1,000, *Harmony*[27] by Frank Dicksee for 350 guineas and the bronze group, *An Athlete struggling with a Python*[28], by Frederic (later Lord) Leighton for £2,000. The Government did not, however, as had been hoped, see their way to providing special accommodation for these newly acquired works and, in the following year, they were sent to the South Kensington Museum for 'temporary exhibition'.[29] There, with subsequent purchases, they remained till 1897 except for quite frequent loans to the provinces.

The health of the President, Sir Francis Grant, had been declining for some time when, in 1878, he found himself unable, for the fourth year in succession, to wait upon the Queen with the annual record of the institution's business and he died in October. The election for the new President took place on 13 November and it is noteworthy that all the Royal Academicians were present. There were no absentees. Frederic Leighton received thirty-one votes, against five for J. C. Horsley, two each for Sir John Gilbert and George Richmond, and one each for W. P. Frith and J. E. Millais. Leighton was received by Her Majesty twelve days later and knighted.

13

THE PALMY DAYS
1879–1896

Sir Frederic(k) Leighton (Plates 50 and 51), whose Christian name seems to have been spelt without the final 'k' from about 1891 onwards, was born at Scarborough in 1830, the son and grandson of well-known doctors. He spent most of his youth in Florence, Rome, Berlin and Frankfurt, with shorter periods in Brussels, Paris and other continental cities. By the age of twelve he was a fluent linguist and, by fourteen, a young expert on anatomy with his mind made up to be an artist. 'Shall I make him a painter?' his father asked rather reluctantly and Hiram Powers, the American sculptor, replied, 'Sir, you cannot help yourself; nature has made him one already. . . . Let him aim at the highest, he will be certain to get there.'[1]

This was about the time when Millais, just six months older, was a student in the Academy Schools and, less than a decade later, W. M. Thackeray warned him, 'Millais, my boy, you must look to your laurels. I have met a wonderfully gifted young artist in Rome, about your own age, who some day will be the President of the Royal Academy before you.'[2] Leighton worked in Rome from 1852 and, in 1855, he had his first exhibit in the Academy. The picture, $87\frac{1}{2} \times 205$ inches, entitled *Cimabue's celebrated Madonna is carried in procession through the streets of Florence*,[3] was bought by Queen Victoria and his reputation was made. He did not, however, settle in London till 1860 and this is the probable explanation of his not being elected an Associate until 1864, by which time Millais was already an Academician.

He built himself a magnificent house in Holland Park Road in 1865–66 but still continued to travel, particularly in Spain, Algiers and Egypt, though with frequent visits elsewhere over the years and never neglecting his beloved Italy. No doubt his wide knowledge of foreign works of art led him to be a firm supporter of the Academy's promotion of Loan Exhibitions from 1870 and he served regularly on the organizing committees. He was also devoted to the Artists' Volunteer Corps which he joined when it was formed in 1860. He soon took full charge and became its Lieutenant-Colonel Commandant in 1876. Nowadays known as the 21st SAS Regiment (Artists) TA, it has for many years provided a Guard of Honour on the occasion of the Academy's Annual Dinner.

Leighton had taken his turn more than once as a Visitor in the Academy Schools and Hamo Thornycroft, for one, spoke of him as 'an *inspiring* master'.[4] He was a sculptor as well as painter and, according to his contemporaries, he was of commanding presence, an eloquent speaker, punctual to a degree in his appointments, absolutely fair in all his dealings, vital in thought and action, catholic in his tastes and masterly in his judgments. It is therefore not surprising that he should have been chosen as President and that he was annually re-elected unanimously until his death in 1896. His period of office marked a peak in the Royal Academy's relationships with the general public and, largely due to him, its standing was impregnable.

There was a slight difference of opinion in the Academy in 1879 as to whether the Treasurer should be allowed almost automatically to act as the Academy's architect, as hitherto seems to have been so, and the decision was in the negative. It was agreed, however, that he should continue to hold a watching-brief over the buildings and a Surveyor (R. Phené Spiers) was then appointed to report to him and to supervise any duly authorized work. E. M. Barry died in 1880 (as he rose to speak at the Council table) and thereafter the Treasurer, instead of being appointed for life directly by the Sovereign, has been elected and approved for a limited term of years as in the case of the Keeper and, until 1920, the Librarian. G. E. Street became Treasurer but lived only another year. He was followed by J. C. Horsley after R. Norman Shaw had refused the post and this was the first time that it had not been held by an architect.

The Librarian, S. A. Hart, died in 1881 and was succeeded by J. E. Hodgson. The Registrar, Henry Eyre, retired in 1884 after thirty-five years' service and was replaced by Charles McLean. No one was found to take over the Professorship of Architecture on the death of G. E. Street until George Aitchison was appointed in 1887 and there was even greater difficulty in filling the vacancy of Professor of Sculpture. After the resignation of Henry Weekes in 1876, Thomas Woolner took over the title but did not fulfil the responsibilities and there was no occupant of the post from 1878 to 1900. Arrangements were made, however, for lectures to be given by various members and others during these periods. Arthur Herbert Church was appointed Professor of Chemistry in 1879.

In this same year, the question of the admission of women members was seriously considered after Elizabeth Butler had just been narrowly defeated and, despite the inclusion of Angelica Kauffmann and Mary Moser in the original foundation, the Council made the rather surprising pronouncement that, in their opinion, by the letter of the law, the Instrument did not provide for the election of females. In specifying eligibility for membership, it uses the phrase 'men of fair moral characters . . .'[5] and, in their opinion, this had to be interpreted as not including women. Nevertheless, at the request of the General Assembly, they framed a resolution to make them eligible but limited their 'privileges'.[6] The matter then seems to have been forgotten as no women were elected till Annie Swynnerton and Laura Knight in the 1920s.

The number of Associates had reached thirty by 1879 and it was then decided that this should be the minimum number. No immediate, or indeed subsequent, increase took place but this is probably accounted for at the time by the number of gaps caused by deaths over the next two or three years. It certainly brought about a new rule, in 1881, whereby such vacancies could be filled in any month from November to July whereas, previously, an Academician could only be elected in June or December and an Associate in January. In 1884, it was resolved that Associates could apply to be retired under the same terms as Academicians.

The first Summer Exhibition under Leighton's Presidency, in 1879, was a huge success. It attracted the greatest number of paying visitors (391,197) ever recorded in the long series of these shows and 2,878 season tickets (first introduced in 1876) were issued. The holders of these would have had to use them at least five times to make their purchase worthwhile so that, with free admissions for the exhibitors and others, the total attendance must have reached well over 400,000. More than 115,000 catalogues were sold and the excess of receipts over expenditure on the exhibition amounted to £20,814 0s 4d. The largest number of paying visitors on a single day was 7,643 and the smallest 2,589. True, this was an exceptional season but the average total attendance over the next eighteen years was about 355,000.

These exhibitions used to reopen in the evenings during the last week at 7.30 p.m. and, on the final day, August Monday, they were available continuously from 8 a.m. to 10.30 p.m. On these occasions, the admission charge was reduced to half-price (6d) and, in 1881 for example, 17,286 visitors took advantage of this, of whom 8,290 attended as their Bank Holiday treat. The Sunday Society more than once pressed for the exhibition to be open on one or two Sundays but this was never allowed. The sales of works were not tremendous in comparison with present-day standards. Usually about 170 were sold for around £15,000 though there was an exception to this in 1888 when, for some reason, the total reached 284 for £21,594 17s 6d.

There was an enormous increase in the number of works sent in (6,415 in 1879, 8,686 in 1887 and 12,408 in 1896) and, several times, there were over 2,000 exhibits. An attempt was made in 1883 to limit members to six submissions and others to three, followed by a similar effort in 1887 to cut down everyone to four (instead of eight), but both failed. The sending-in days were changed in 1885 from Monday, Tuesday and Wednesday to Friday, Saturday, Monday and Tuesday, and this sufficed for almost a century. From 1891 to 1895, the 'Doubtful' oil paintings were subdivided into two categories – one marked 'o' and the other with the figure '1'. The latter included 'all those from which the Hanging Committee should select for exhibition' and the former 'all those which, though not bad enough to cross, were not considered good enough for the exhibition'.[7] Paintings on pottery were admitted from 1879 provided they were framed though it appears to have been forgotten that George Stubbs had, so it seems, exhibited enamel work on Wedgwood plaques in the eighteenth century. In the following year, gilt mounts or close gilt frames were insisted on for watercolours but this regulation was rescinded in 1884. From 1881, except for the years 1885 and 1886, members were allowed three Varnishing Days and non-members one and this practice continued until recently.

C. W. Cope's painting *The Council of the Royal Academy selecting Pictures for the Exhibition* (Plate 51), dated 1876, and Paul Renouard's drawings in 1887, for *The Graphic*,[8] provide an interesting record of the methods of receiving and handling the vast number of submissions, while W. P. Frith's *The Private View, 1881* (Plate 50) portrays a galaxy of notables which such an occasion produced, resplendent in morning dress with top-hats and long elegant gowns. Leighton talks to Lady Lonsdale with the Archbishop of York, Lord Coleridge and Lily Langtry nearby. To the left are various clusters including Anthony Trollope, John Bright, W. E. Gladstone, Thomas Huxley and Robert

Browning. On the other side, Oscar Wilde holds court in front of a small group comprising Ellen Terry and others, with Henry Irving and Millais a little to the right.

The Annual Dinner continued to take place on the Saturday prior to the opening day and the Prince of Wales (afterwards Edward VII) almost invariably attended with other members of the royal family and, in 1882, the King of the Netherlands. The table of singers was permanently supplanted from 1891 by the Royal Artillery Band who played the national anthem after the loyal toast and subsequently a programme of music in the Lecture Room. This procedure was followed for upwards of a century. In addition a Soirée was held each year about eight or nine weeks later, always with a plentiful supply of strawberries and cream.

The most popular pictures were frequently those bought for the nation through the Chantrey Bequest. Among them, in the chronological order of their purchase, were *A Visit to Aesculapius* (Plate 43) by E. J. Poynter, *Napoleon on board H.M.S. Bellerophon* by W. Q. Orchardson, *The Last Voyage of Henry Hudson* by John Collier, *The Vigil* by John Pettie, *Carnation, Lily, Lily, Rose* by J. S. Sargent, *St Martin-in-the-Fields* by William Logsdail, *A Hopeless Dawn* by Frank Bramley, *The Bath of Psyche* by Leighton, *Love Locked Out* by Anna Lea Merritt, *Between Two Fires* by F. D. Millet, *August Blue* by H. S. Tuke and *'Speak, Speak!'* by Millais, as well as such sculptures as *A Moment of Peril* by Thomas Brock and *Teucer* by Hamo Thornycroft.[9] The genre scenes by W. P. Frith, Marcus Stone and Luke Fildes, together with historical subjects by Alma-Tadema and Lady (Elizabeth) Butler and the portraits of well-known people by W. W. Ouless and G. F. Watts, all attracted attention.

It was quite often necessary to place a railing in front of a particular picture in order to prevent possible injury from the crowds of people and, in 1885, one was put up as a relatively permanent fixture all round the galleries except in the new South Rooms and Architectural Room where the pictures themselves, watercolours and drawings, were protected by glass. In 1896, one exhibit, a full-sized model of an equestrian statue *Lord Roberts*[10] by Harry Bates, was placed in the courtyard.

There was one failure during this period of Summer Exhibitions when, in 1886, a large illustrated catalogue was produced. Two photographers were sent over from Paris to take the necessary negatives of the exhibits. This was done in the open air, again in the courtyard, where a shed was erected in which they could be developed. They were then sent to the French capital for copper plates to be made in typogravure but the Academy's printers in London were responsible for the production of the album at one guinea a copy. It took so long to prepare under this complicated procedure that it was not ready for sale until mid-July and the experiment, which was not repeated, resulted in a considerable financial loss. Cassell & Co Ltd produced annually from 1888 to 1915 an illustrated volume called *Royal Academy Pictures*. It was in the form of a souvenir of each exhibition and not a complete catalogue. From 1875, Henry Blackburn used to edit each year a publication under the title *Academy Notes*. It gave an abstract in catalogue order of the exhibits and included many small engravings. From 1883, the same author produced *Academy Sketches* annually and this was an illustrated souvenir of various art shows in London. At about the same time, there were occasionally other booklets on the Academy's exhibitions and, from 1855, John Ruskin of course had published his *Notes on some of the Principal Pictures exhibited in the Rooms of the Royal Academy*.

The Old Masters' Exhibition of 1879 was conceived on a much larger scale than its forerunners and occupied nine galleries. It comprised 258 oil paintings, many miniatures and 477 drawings, including the Holbeins from Windsor Castle. Nevertheless, the attendance was the smallest on record to that date – 34,932 paying visitors. The special feature of the 1880 exhibition was a collection of paintings by Holbein and his followers and, in 1881 and 1884, there were extensive loans respectively from Panshanger and Bowood. Selected displays of Turner's watercolours were included in 1886, 1887 and 1889, and a number of drawings and models by Alfred Stevens in 1890. In 1895 and 1896, there were many precious objects illustrating 'the sculptor-goldsmith's art'. Even with such attractions it was difficult to make these exhibitions pay their way and frequently the receipts did not cover expenses. The Private View in 1888 is shown in a painting by H. Jamyn Brooks.[11]

Minor alterations were made to the Vestibule and the Sculpture Gallery (now No. VI) in 1881 and, in this same year, a report was considered from a specially appointed Building Committee proposing the erection of a refreshment room, with gallery accommodation above it and a connecting staircase, on the vacant ground to the west of old Burlington House, as well as other alterations including an additional Diploma Gallery. R. Norman Shaw was appointed as architect and the bulk of the work, which cost over £47,000 was completed by 1885.

Besides the present South Rooms (the large one for watercolours and the small one for works in black and white), together with the Restaurant and its rather fine staircase, he built the Architectural Room at the south-east corner of the galleries and the North Diploma Gallery. At the same time, he converted the most westerly room of the original mansion into the General Assembly Room (though intended as the Council Room) and two rooms beneath it as offices. He also made desirable alterations in the Schools, including improvements to the roof lights and the addition of rooms at the east end of the corridor for the Professors of Anatomy and Chemistry. The parquet flooring in Galleries I and II was already completely worn through and was replaced by oak blocks on concrete.

After an experiment in the Lecture Room on the night of the Soirée in 1881, the Old Masters' Exhibition and the Annual Dinner in the following year were both lit with 'Swan's incandescent lamps'. The Annual Report states that 'nothing could exceed the beauty of the light, and the atmosphere remained comparatively cool and pleasant' but 'only thirteen persons on an average passed through the turnstiles after dark'.[12] This probably caused the postponement of any major conversion but when, in 1891, the Saloon was redecorated by J. D. Crace 'in accordance with the intentions of Kent' and the Reynolds Room ceiling was cleaned from its 'filthy state . . . the combined effect of gas and fog',[13] electric lights were installed in all five of the main apartments at the front of the old house. The change was made in the galleries after their redecoration in 1893 and, in the next year, it was recorded that 'no gas is now used for lighting purposes in any part of the building'.[14]

Many important gifts and bequests were received by the Academy in the period under review. Charles Landseer, the ex-Keeper, died in 1879 and bequeathed not only a fine collection of drawings by George Stubbs for his book *The Anatomy of the Horse* (Plate 14) but also £10,000 to found scholarships for art students. In 1883, Samuel Cousins gave £15,000 to be invested and its income devoted to providing annuities for artists, other than members, in need of such assistance. Fifteen oil sketches by John Constable[15] were presented in 1888 and his large painting *The Leaping Horse* (Plate 34) in 1889. Other bequests included smaller funds for prizes in the Schools, for donations to poor artists and their widows and for scientific investigation into the nature of pigments and varnishes.

Work in the Academy Schools continued smoothly but with certain modifications. The length of studentship was reduced in 1881 from seven to six years, divided into two terms of three years each in a Lower School and an Upper School. At the same time, it was decided that the travelling studentships should be coupled with the gold medal awards and offered biennially. Since the foundation they had been available only to those who had already won the medals and they had been granted rather irregularly. Indeed there had been no travelling student in painting since 1868 but, in architecture, suitable candidates had been found almost every year from 1867 to 1878. Additions to the list of premiums included a scholarship of £50 in conjunction with the Turner medal, a prize for sculptors for a model of a design (on the lines of the recently inaugurated Armitage prizes for painters) and a substantial one for mural painting. From 1882, any Associate who had served as a Visitor was allowed to join the Academicians in the ballot for the awards and the winners of money prizes were also given a printed document as evidence. All Associates were considered eligible for Professorships from 1885. The maximum age limit for students was fixed at 23 in 1889 but raised to 25 for sculptors and architects in 1893. In the former year, the length of studentships was again reduced, this time to five years, the second term in the Upper School being shortened to two. The Royal Academy Students' Club, for past and present students, was formed in 1889 and seems to have lasted about ten years. George Frampton, William Goscombe John, Francis Derwent Wood, Reginald Blomfield, Banister Fletcher, W. Curtis Green and Charles Sims were among the new students. Sims, who in the years ahead was to become Keeper, was expelled for misconduct. With others, he had been involved in tearing down a notice prohibiting smoking in the Schools following some previous infringement of the rule against it.

The problems of co-education in the Victorian age still bothered the members and, in 1881, it was sternly resolved 'that the Male and Female Students work in different Painting Schools'.[16] The women, however, were far from satisfied with their lot and at last gained some support for their plea to be allowed a nude, male model. It was granted finally in 1893 but with carefully stipulated precautions to comply with standards of decency. The decision was announced in the following words:

It shall be optional for Visitors in the Painting School to set the male model undraped, except about the loins, to the class of Female Students. The drapery to be worn by the model to consist of ordinary bathing drawers, and a cloth of light material 9 feet long by 3 feet wide, which shall be wound round the loins over the drawers, passed between the legs and tucked in over the waist-band; and finally a thin leather strap shall be fastened round the loins in order to insure that the cloth keep its place.[17]

Never was there such a diaper but painting of course is an inventive art. 'I very much doubt,' said Sir Joshua Reynolds in his first discourse, 'whether a habit of drawing correctly what we see, will not give a proportionable power of drawing correctly what we imagine.'[18]

F. R. Pickersgill resigned the Keepership in 1887 and P. H. Calderon took his place. The Librarian, J. E. Hodgson, had increased the scope of the library by adding a considerable number of reference books of general interest such as Chambers' Encyclopaedia, the works of Browning, Byron, Carlyle, Goethe, Hazlitt, Macaulay, Tennyson and others, but he died in 1895 and was succeeded by W. F. Yeames in the following year. Robert Browning, who had been a friend of Leighton since their early days in Italy, was appointed Secretary for Foreign Correspondence in 1886.

Edward Burne-Jones was elected an Associate in 1885 and, in a letter to him, the President wrote: 'I am not aware that any other case exists of an Artist being elected, who has never exhibited, nay has pointedly abstained from exhibiting on our walls. It is a pure tribute to your genius and therefore a true rejoicing to your affectionate old friend Fred Leighton.'[19] The event came as a great surprise to Burne-Jones and he accepted only after considerable heart-searching. 'For many reasons,' he replied, 'I cannot forsake the Grosvenor Gallery; they gave me an assured place of distinction from the first . . . much that I do would look strange and without reason on the Academy walls. . . . I do want this clear, that there may be no after-difficulties.'[20] He thereafter continued to exhibit at the 'greenery-yallery, Grosvenor Gallery' and sent only one painting in to the Academy, in 1886. He resigned his membership in the following letter, dated 10 February 1893:

Gentlemen,
    It is now nearly eight years since you did me the unlooked for honour of voluntarily electing me an Associate of your body – an honour which I accepted with cordiality as a sign of sympathy from brother artists which it was impossible to reject.
    But you on your part have never asked me to enter further than the threshold which you invited me to cross, and I, on mine, have found that

it was too late to change the direction of my life and work, so as to be able to carry on the traditions of a school in which I did not grow up.

Today I am no longer a young man – too old a man certainly to spend time in competition which I neither sought nor desired, and which is deeply distasteful to me; yet for the past eight years I have found myself involuntarily forced into competition at each successive election for the final admission which you have denied me.

These facts have gradually brought me to the conclusion that it would be a relief to both of us, if without reproach from either side our formal connexion is brought to an end.

This I beg respectfully to do now by resigning my Associateship, in the hope that some one else may be elected in my place to whom its conditions will be helpful and inspiring.[21]

His obvious pique at not having reached the degree of Academician by this date was quite unjustified. No other painter had overtaken him and he was almost at the top of the list in seniority. Certainly his aloofness had not encouraged any special dispensation in his case. He wrote a personal letter to Leighton who, in his reply, said, 'I have seen only too plainly for a long time, ever since that first year when I was filled with hope, that an unbridgeable difference divides our several views about your attitude towards what was till yesterday your Academy. It has been a constant sorrow and a deep disappointment to me, and the one dark spot in the term of my Presidency, as your election was the brightest.'[22] Burne-Jones at the same time sent a long note to Alma-Tadema and the following sentences probably reach the root of the matter:

You see, dear friend, I am particularly made by nature not to like Academies. I went to one when I was a little boy, and didn't like it then, and thought I was free for ever when I grew up, when suddenly one day I had to go to an Academy again – and now I've run away.[23]

He bore the institution no ill-will and exhibited two drawings in 1894, the year he was created a baronet.

In 1887 a special committee of nine members was appointed to consider some suggested reforms and, in 1889, after twenty-nine meetings, a very long report was issued embracing fifty-eight resolutions under the headings '(1) The Composition and Government of the Royal Academy; (2) The Schools of the Royal Academy; (3) The Summer Exhibition of the Royal Academy.'[24] Thirty-eight were accepted by the

General Assembly. Several of these have already been mentioned and the most important of the others included:

1. That in the Class of Engravers all Artists be eligible who produce Works of Art by any form of Engraving, either as original productions, or from the designs of other Artists.

2. That in order to provide for the presence on the Council of at least one Sculptor and one Architect, the following proviso be added to the Rule by which seats on the Council go by succession to all the Academicians: 'But in the cases of Sculptor and Architect members the succession shall be accelerated or retarded as may be necessary for providing that the Council shall always contain one member from each of those classes, or for preventing more than one member of each of those classes being nominated to the Council in a single year.'

6. That in the event of there being no Candidate for any Professorship the tenure of which is limited to Members of the Royal Academy, it shall be in the power of the Council to appoint a Lecturer or Lecturers in that branch of art the chair of which is vacant.

23. That a Day School of Modelling be established, for Male and Female Students. . . .

24. That the Evening School of Modelling be open for Male Students only. . . .

38. That none of the Works done by the Students in the Schools be eligible for the Exhibition.[25]

The vast majority of the remaining clauses laid down in great detail the tests for the admission of probationers and students, the courses of study and the conditions for various awards. The recommendations concerning the Summer Exhibition were not approved and item 2 was amended in 1892 so as not to interfere with the jealously guarded privilege of strict rotation on the Council. It was then agreed to elect a sculptor or an architect to serve if these classes were not represented in any particular year but only as additional members and in a limited capacity. They were to be allowed to give their opinions but have no vote.

Leighton had been made a baronet in 1886 and, in the New Year Honours of 1896, he was awarded a barony. He thus became the first British artist to be raised to the peerage and, on 24 January, the day before his death, he assumed the title of Lord Leighton of Stretton, a village in Shropshire where his ancestors had lived. The funeral took place with great pomp. His body lay in state (Plate 49) in the Central Hall at the Royal Academy with the coffin covered in rich embroidery and raised on a bier, surrounded with innumerable wreaths and palms, on a dark coloured floor-covering. A bronze bust of the artist, decorated with the President's gold medal and chain, was set at the head on a white marble pedestal draped in black crepe. His palette and brushes[26] were placed on the pall-cloth at the foot of the coffin and his many orders and medals were displayed on crimson velvet cushions. In the centre of this profuse array, the plain laurel wreath from his colleagues stood in simple dignity. The funeral procession left Burlington House at 11 a.m. on 3 February and arrived at St Paul's Cathedral 'as the hour of noon struck'. 'So,' records the Annual Report, 'thus in death as in life, our President was punctual to his last appointment.'[27]

His two sisters subsequently paid over to the Academy, 'to carry out the wishes of their brother',[28] the sum of £10,000, the interest on which is used 'for the purpose of acquiring or commissioning works of Decorative Painting, Sculpture and Architecture'[29] for the adornment of public places. The artist's home and studio, Leighton House, was opened for concerts and lectures in 1898 and, a few years later, as an arts centre and museum.

On 20 February 1896, Sir John Everett Millais, Bt. (Plate 51), was elected President by thirty-three votes to one for P. H. Calderon and, on hearing the news, Edward Lear is said to have remarked, 'Ah! Now the Millais-nium has come!'[30] As a child prodigy, a founder-member of the Pre-Raphaelites and later the painter of many pictures which had immense popular appeal, Millais had been under consideration for the post for many years and, indeed, had acted as Leighton's deputy in the chair at the Annual Dinner of the previous year. Unfortunately his period in office was all too brief. Trouble with his throat proved to be a malignant cancer and his last appearance at the Academy was on the next Private View Day, 1 May. His devotion to the institution was heart-warming. 'I love everything belonging to it,' he said, '– the casts I have drawn from as a boy, the books I have consulted in the Library, the very benches I have sat on – I love them all.'[31] He died on 13 August and he also was buried in St Paul's Cathedral. Thus the Academy lost in little over six months its two most distinguished members. No dinner was held, the attendance at the Summer Exhibition fell to under 300,000 for the first time in years and the whole atmosphere was one of deep mourning.

14

INTO THE TWENTIETH CENTURY
1896–1914

Having been deprived of two Presidents in so short a time, the members appeared to be greatly divided in their views on the most suitable successor. The election took place on 4 November 1896 and, at the first marking, Briton Riviere received twelve votes, E. J. Poynter eleven, Frank Dicksee five, P. H. Calderon two and there were one each for Luke Fildes, J. C. Horsley, W. Q. Orchardson, Valentine Prinsep, W. B. Richmond and Marcus Stone. Those who had obtained four or more were then considered a second time when Frank Dicksee's support remained as before. Riviere and Poynter increased theirs to sixteen and fifteen respectively but, at the final ballot between them, E. J. Poynter (Plate 52) emerged as victor with nineteen votes while Riviere stayed at his previous figure.

The new President, born in 1836, had at one time been a student in the Academy Schools and had spent a good deal of his younger life in Paris. He had exhibited at the Academy since 1861, been elected an Associate in 1869 and an Academician in 1877. He became the first Slade Professor of Fine Art at University College, London, in 1871 and, later, Principal of the National Art Training School (now the Royal College of Art) and Director for Art of the South Kensington Museum (now the Victoria and Albert and the Science Museums). In 1894, he was appointed Director of the National Gallery and thus, on his election as President in 1896, he held at one and the same time two of the most important positions in the field of art in this country. He was received by the Queen on 25 November and knighted. His wide culture, with a distinctly French bias, and his considerable experience of art teaching made him a suitable choice and he soon commanded the respect of his colleagues and the outside world – so much so that he was re-elected each year, with no votes ever recorded against him, until his resignation in December 1918, a few months before his death.

J. C. Horsley resigned as Treasurer in 1897 and was succeeded by Alfred Waterhouse but he held the position for only a short while and Thomas Graham Jackson took up the post in 1901. P. H. Calderon died in 1898 and Ernest Crofts was then elected Keeper in his place. The long-vacant Professorship of Sculpture was filled by the appointment of Alfred Gilbert in 1899 and Arthur Thomson became Professor of Anatomy.

The Winter Exhibition of 1897 comprised 293 oil paintings, 107 drawings and 13 sculptures, all by Lord Leighton. It attracted over 50,000 visitors and was followed, in 1898, by one devoted to the works of Millais. This proved even more popular and drew over 80,000. In 1899 and 1900, two rather more ambitious projects were undertaken – exhibitions of the art of Rembrandt and Van Dyck – both inspired by recent displays in Amsterdam and Antwerp respectively. Hardly any foreign owners could be persuaded to part with their treasures but there was scarcely a work left in this country by either artist which was not included. Even so the Rembrandt exhibition was attended by only a few more people than had visited the Leighton exhibition and the numbers at the Van Dyck exhibition fell to 35,000. This was about the level reached for most of the Loan Exhibitions since 1870 and was only a tenth of the crowds who flocked to the annual summer show by living artists. This is somewhat surprising when one remembers that the public collections at the time were not nearly so numerous or rich in content as they are today and that this was long before the days of stately homes being on show.

In 1901 an experiment was tried of confining the Winter Exhibition to the works of British artists who had died in the previous fifty years but it was a failure in more ways than one. First, it was difficult to trace the whereabouts of the pictures suggested; secondly, the owners were reluctant to lend as it would have deprived their homes of modern decorations and there were constant requests for this type of work for many exhibitions. The content was therefore below the standard that had been envisaged. The total attendance was under 17,000 and, in a second such exhibition in 1911, it slumped to below 12,000. From 1902 these exhibitions, generally speaking, reverted to a combination of Old Masters' works with occasional representations of those recently deceased artists whom it was desired to honour in this way. G. F. Watts was commemorated in 1905 (over 60,000 visitors) and 1906, and E. A. Abbey in 1912 (18,000 visitors). The exhibition of 1913 was entirely devoted to the works of the late Sir Lawrence Alma-Tadema but, despite the artist's fame in his lifetime, it attracted a mere 17,000.

There were only 250,000 people at the Summer Exhibition in 1897 but this seems to have been entirely due to the gloom which had descended on the institution following the deaths of Leighton and Millais. The Queen's diamond jubilee was celebrated on 22 June by hoisting the royal standard over the building and illuminating the front but the whole of the Academy's activities were closed for the day. The attendances were reduced to about 200,000 in the period between the death of Edward VII in 1910 and the outbreak of the Great War in 1914 but, even so, the average over the eighteen seasons from 1897 exceeded 280,000.

Each year produced about 12,000 submissions (though in 1902 the figure reached 14,243) and the number of exhibits varied between 1,800 and 2,000 (but amounted to 2,245 in 1914). Several attempts were made to reduce the quantity of works for selection and two special committees, in 1899 and 1901, were appointed to consider this and other relevant matters. The latter recommended that both members and candidates for membership should be allowed to contribute six works and other artists two but this proposal was not accepted. In 1902 a memorial from the outsiders suggested a limit of two or three submissions from anyone and, finally, in 1903, a decision was made to restrict members to six and non-members to three, instead of eight each as hitherto, and this rule is still in force today. Analyses for the previous ten years up to 1898 had shown that each person had sent in on the average slightly under three works and therefore no hardship was anticipated under the new regulations. About 5,000 artists were involved from year to year so that, at the most, only two-fifths of them could be represented in the galleries. In fact, there were usually about 800 to 1,000 exhibitors as is still the case in the 1980s.

In 1908 it was resolved that, for the two following years, 'Oil Pictures, not more than 6 ft sight measurement in their greatest dimensions, obtaining a place on the line in the Summer Exhibition, may have glass put over them if so desired by their authors, on an appointed day before the opening of the Exhibition'.[1] The experiment, long desired by W. B. Richmond and others, was evidently successful and was continued. The regulation was modified in 1912 by altering the allowable size to 'not exceeding 30 square feet'[2] and remains so today. The composition of the Selection Committee was changed, also in 1908, but suggestions two years later that Associates and outsiders should be represented on it were firmly refused. Charles Sims proposed that the Summer Exhibition should consist of oil paintings only and the Winter Exhibition of works in all other media but he found no supporters. In 1914 it was resolved that 'no work which has not been executed within the preceding ten years is admissible'.[3]

There was no great change in the style of the popular pictures of this period compared with those of the previous twenty years or so. W. P. Frith, G. F. Watts and James Sant, all very elderly, were still at work at the turn of the century. Lawrence Alma-Tadema, Luke Fildes and Hubert von Herkomer were names to conjure with and there were attractive painters among the slightly younger men, such as John Singer Sargent with his brilliant portraits. The painting called *Boulter's Lock – Sunday afternoon*[4] by E. J. Gregory was 'the picture of the year' in 1897 and *Diana of the Uplands*[5] by C. W. Furse, in 1904, became familiar to thousands through reproductions. There was a cult for what came to be known as 'problem pictures', such as *The Sentence of Death*[6] in 1908 and *A Fallen Idol*[7] in 1913, both by the Hon. John Collier. They were large-sized subject-paintings, not very different from such pictures of the nineteenth century but with the added interest of presenting the spectator with an exercise in psychological detection.

The Chantrey purchases included *Colt-hunting in the New Forest* by Lucy Kemp-Welch, *London River* by C. Napier Hemy, *The Return from the Ride* by C. W. Furse, *A Favourite Custom* by Alma-Tadema and *Lucretia Borgia reigns at the Vatican* by F. Cadogan Cowper.[8] The President and Council also purchased works on behalf of the National Galleries of New South Wales and Victoria.

All the paintings and sculpture so far acquired under the terms of the Chantrey Bequest were transferred to the newly erected Tate Gallery in 1897. The Government agreed that they should be displayed there as a separate collection and that, although they would be vested in the Trustees and Director, no power of selection or elimination was claimed. In 1904, however, some criticisms came to a head and a Select Committee of the House of Lords was appointed to enquire into the administration of the trust. It was alleged that the collection was incomplete and unrepresentative and the resultant report went so far as to express the opinion 'that the constitution of the purchasing body, as appointed by the testator, is inherently defective.'[9] It recommended instead the nomination of a committee of three to undertake all purchases. The Academy quickly pointed out that this would be a contravention of the will and that it was 'unlikely that such a Committee would be broader in their views than the whole Council of ten, or more impartial in the exercise of them'.[10] The President justifiably objected to having been required to state a case for the Academy 'at least until they should have heard what their assailants had to say'[11] and he added that 'the evidence . . . resolves itself . . . into an expression of an opinion on the merits of the Collection, a point on which a body of artists like the Royal Academy have at least as good a right to an opinion as any one else. . . .'[12] The one good thing which emerged from the discussions was the setting-up of two separate subcommittees of three painters and three sculptors to 'report on and recommend such works as are in their opinion proper to be purchased'[13] but, quite rightly, this was not to diminish the clear authority of the President and Council to purchase or not as they might decide.

A more comprehensive and bitter attack had been made on the Academy in 1898 by an elderly landscape painter named W. J. Laidlay. He produced it in the form of a book entitled *The Royal Academy – its uses and abuses* and included the following indictment:

1. That Academicians neglect their duties and grossly abuse their powers and privileges.
2. That Academicians, while professing a concern for national art, and claiming that the Royal Academy is a national concern, really manage the affairs of the Academy for their own interest and advancement, to the neglect and discouragement of national art.
3. That Academicians, by neglecting to adapt their rules to the altered state of art production, are responsible for the vast quantity and tentative nature of the work submitted to the selecting jury.
4. That Academicians do not discharge their administrative or judicial functions with any degree of care or impartiality, and in no way consult the convenience of the outside artists, who support their exhibitions.
5. That Academicians are responsible for (a) the inefficient and unpopular state of our art schools, and the fact that our art students have to seek tuition abroad; (b) for the loss of the American art market; (c) for the gradual destruction of that spirit of independence among artists which relies on merit and despises toadyism; and for (d) that feeling of discontent and uncertainty which beyond all doubt exists.
6. That not only is the hanging of the pictures at the Royal Academy Exhibitions unfairly done, but the general tendency of Academicians, as trustees of a popular show, is to receive and reward popular rather

than artistic work, and to foster a mercantile rather than an artistic spirit.

7. That Academicians, by their unfairness to foreign artists, restrict the interest and educational worth of their annual exhibitions.

8. That the Royal Academy is conducted so as to discourage landscape painting.

9. That Academicians fail to show ordinary courtesy and consideration to those who exhibit at their galleries; and

10. That the Academy, being nationally subsidised, Academicians have no right to withhold from the public a full statement of their affairs – that is, of the Academy's income, expenditure, pensions, and charities.[14]

His premises were frequently incorrect and, although he was a barrister-at-law, his arguments were poorly constructed. The whole amounted to little more than the rantings of a sea-lawyer and, not surprisingly, it enlisted no supporters. To the Academy, the attack was a mere flea-bite which, though irritating, did nothing to hinder the institution's activities.

The first proposal for a commission through the Leighton Fund was to erect a memorial to Van Dyck in St Paul's Cathedral. The idea arose at the time of the Winter Exhibition of his works early in 1900 and the suggested monument was to replace the original one which had perished with the old cathedral in the Great Fire of London in 1666. A sketch model by Thomas Brock was approved but the new memorial never materialized in this form or by this artist. The next project was for a bronze lamp-post, by S. Nicholson Babb, which was duly placed at the end of Downing Street, by the side of the Horse Guards Parade, in London, in 1908, and this was followed by a mural painting, by A. C. Gow, in St Stephen's Hall, Westminster, in 1912.

In 1899 the Entrance Hall of the Academy was redesigned by T. G. Jackson and the floor was repaved 'with black and white marble slabs after the pattern of the old pavement in the Hall of Burlington House, as seen in the entrance passage of the Keeper's House'.[15] At the same time, the paintings by Angelica Kauffmann and Benjamin West, which had originally been presented to decorate the Academy's home at Somerset House, were inserted in the ceiling. Those by West are in the centre – a roundel of *The Graces unveiling Nature*, surrounded by *Air*, *Earth*, *Fire* and *Water* (Plate 24a). Two of the circular paintings by Angelica Kauffmann – *Composition* and *Design* – are at the west end of the hall and the other two – *Painting* (or *Colouring*) (Plate 24b) and *Genius* (or *Invention*) are at the east end.

Another small alteration was the provision of two basement entrances for tradesmen on the southern frontage and, in 1905, the courtyard, which until then had been 'all dust in summer and all mud in winter',[16] was paved with 'creosoted fir'.[17] The Academy had, in 1899, tried to get the offer of the first refusal on the University of London building in Burlington Gardens (later the Civil Service Commission and now the Museum of Mankind) but was unsuccessful. This was indeed a great pity. Such additional space was already highly desirable and would have been of incalculable value in subsequent years.

Queen Victoria died in January 1901 and was succeeded by her son, Edward VII. No Annual Dinner was held that year. The Schools' medals were redesigned by Thomas Brock with the head of the King on the obverse and Poynter painted a full-length portrait of him for the Academy's collection. The reverse of the gold medal was to comprise three figures representing Painting, Sculpture and Architecture. It eventually materialized but not till 1910, by which time Edward VII had just died and George V had come to the throne. His head, also by Brock, then adorned the medals until his death in 1936. The reverse of the silver and bronze medals during both these reigns was a new version of the Belvedere torso with the word 'STUDY' on the left and the inscription 'THE ROYAL ACADEMY OF ARTS INSTITUTED MDCCLXVIII' on the right.

Brief mention should perhaps be made of the Royal Drawing Society, which was incorporated in 1902. Its annual exhibition became known colloquially as 'The Children's Royal Academy' but it had no official connection with the subject of this book.

Some important new regulations were made in 1903 concerning the Schools. It was decided to abolish the age limits for admission and also all preliminary teaching, to establish a class of drawing from the life for females and to allow all other classes to be mixed. Other minor alterations were made and certain new prizes were instituted. In 1904 it was agreed to admit without examination all 'Colonial Students in Painting and Sculpture, who had been awarded Travelling Studentships to study Art in Europe'.[18] In the following year, a Japanese student entered the Schools. C. de Gruchy replaced R. Phené Spiers as the Master of the Architecture School and, thereafter, it was open five instead of three evenings a week. He also became the Academy's Surveyor in 1913. The Lower School of Painting and Drawing was re-established in 1909 and its students had to pass an entrance examination into the Upper School. There was also an Advanced School of Decorative Art. The conditions of the Landseer Scholarships were changed to be tenable for two years and, in 1910, a Curator was appointed 'to assist the Keeper in teaching in the Lower School of Painting and Drawing, and in maintaining discipline throughout the Schools'.[19] It was originally intended to call him an Assistant Master and this terminology would of course have been more accurate.

Sir Hubert von Herkomer, W. R. Colton and Reginald Blomfield became Professors of Painting, Sculpture and Architecture respectively in 1907 but in 1911 it was decided that, when these positions should next fall vacant, they should not be filled. The three posts were in fact all empty by the end of that year. At the same time an annual examination was insisted on for painting and sculpture students and failure to pass it almost invariably involved dismissal from the Schools. The new students of this period included Frank Cadogan Cowper, Gerald Brockhurst, Ivon Hitchens, Gilbert Ledward, E. Vincent Harris and Louis de Soissons.

In 1905 moves were made by the Art Union of London drawing attention 'to the decay of the art of Engraving in England'[20] and urging the establishment of a school of instruction in the subject at the Royal Academy and another at South Kensington. The Academy replied sympathetically though no immediate action was taken on these particular lines but, in 1906, two engravers (Frank Short and William Strang) were made members and these were the first such elections since 1883. At the same time, it was resolved that 'in order to be eligible for election as an Associate, a Painter must obtain five signatures to his nomination, a Sculptor three, an Architect three, and an Engraver three',[21] all of course from existing members. In 1907 it was decided to hold an annual conference 'for the purpose of making suggestions with regard to the Schools and the Summer Exhibition'[22] and, in 1914, it was agreed that 'all Elections of Associates be held on one of the Members' Varnishing Days in the month of April'.[23]

The Academy's Annual Dinner was held on a Thursday in 1908 and a Friday in 1909 but reverted to Saturday evenings from 1910. In the first of these years, there were no speeches 'in accordance with the express desire of H.M. The King and of H.R.H. The Prince of Wales'[24] but the move was very unpopular and was not repeated.

Charles McLean, the Registrar, retired in 1905 'owing to his age and health'[25] and thereafter proceeded to draw a pension for longer than he had been employed at the Academy. He was replaced by E. F. Dixon. The Rt Hon. John Morley (afterwards Viscount Morley of Blackburn) had been appointed Professor of Ancient Literature in 1903 and, in 1909, a class of Honorary Foreign Corresponding Members was instituted. The first to be elected were Il Commendatore Giacomo Boni, Director of the Excavations in the Forum at Rome, and Osman Hamdy Bey, Director of the Museum at Constantinople. From 1911, the Presidents of the Royal Scottish Academy and the Royal Hibernian Academy had been *ex-officio* Honorary Members and, in 1930, it was resolved that they should 'retain their Honorary Membership during life if they have retired from their office'.[26]

Towards the end of 1905, the Council's attention was drawn to Alfred Gilbert's conduct 'in respect to commissions entrusted to him, for which it was asserted he had received full payment, and had done nothing in return'.[27] The matter was in fact not new to the Academy. For many years past, the sculptor had accumulated more work and enquiries than he could handle. His talent was in great demand and his ideas were boundless but, in striving for perfection, he was for ever discarding and postponing. His financial affairs became impossible to manage and, after being declared bankrupt in 1901, he eventually settled in Bruges. The tomb for the Duke of Clarence,[28] commissioned in 1892, was still unfinished and indeed remained so till 1928. Gilbert was attacked in the Press in 1906 and 1908 for failing to carry out other work for which he had received payments in advance and he took no notice of many letters of a friendly and helpful nature which the Academy sent him over a long period. Finally, in 1908, the Council felt bound 'to suggest to him the advisability of his resigning his membership of the Royal Academy'[29] and this he did in a letter dated 24 November. In 1926 he returned quietly to London, was received at Buckingham Palace, proceeded to complete the Clarence tomb and then designed the Queen Alexandra Memorial. This, set in the wall of the garden of Marlborough House opposite St James's Palace, was unveiled in 1932 and was the sculptor's last major work. On 31 May, he was readmitted into membership of the Academy and, a few days later, he was knighted.

In 1907 an Act of Parliament gave the Metropolitan Water Board power to charge for water at the rate of five per cent on the rateable value of all premises which they served and the Academy was faced with a bill of over £300 as opposed to the average annual cost of £40 by meter readings. An artesian well was then sunk but it is doubtful whether it proved to be a great saving. It cost £1,250 to install and a payment still had to be met for emergency supplies. Grit in the water continually fouled the pumps and its operation was abandoned in 1919.

This item arose at a time when the Academy was becoming increasingly worried about its financial affairs. Owing to higher costs and reduced attendances at the exhibitions, the margin between receipts and expenditure had been diminishing for a number of years and had developed into annual deficits from 1908. A special committee was appointed to investigate the situation and, in 1911, it was decided to employ a professional Auditor, to form the existing Auditors into a Finance Committee and to carry out certain stringencies. All fees to members were abolished except when acting as Visitors or serving on the Exhibition Committees and various minor cuts in expenditure were made. It will be remembered also that this was the year when certain Professorships were terminated, again an economy. The Summer Exhibition was extended a fortnight in length from 1912 and kept open until 10 p.m. on all Thursdays. The new Auditor soon earned his money by discovering that the Academy had been paying income tax on its trust funds unnecessarily and some of it was reclaimed.

More such charitable funds had been acquired during this period – the Sandby Gift, in memory of Thomas and Paul Sandby; the Sparkes Fund for female artists; the Redgrave and Aitchison Funds; and, not least, Bird's Charity 'for or towards the maintenance, support, or benefit of poor and deserving young artists of either sex, who are of good character, of British nationality, and under 33 years of age, and possessed of reasonable diligence and ability. . . .'[30]

Ernest Crofts, the Keeper, died and W. F. Yeames, the Librarian, resigned in 1911 and both posts were then filled by A. C. Gow, yet another reduction in running costs. Sir Thomas G. Jackson gave up the Treasurership and was replaced in the following year by Sir Aston Webb. A. P. Laurie took over as Professor of Chemistry from Sir Arthur Church at the same time. The Secretary, F. A. Eaton, who had been knighted in 1911, died in 1913 and was succeeded by W. R. M. Lamb (Plates 60 and 71). It is worth recording that this appears to be the first year in which Winston Churchill was one of the speakers at the Royal Academy Dinner. He replied to the toast to the Government and he undertook precisely the same task again forty years later, in 1953 and 1954 (Plate 63), as Prime Minister.

There was talk in 1913 of the formation of a Ministry of Fine Arts but it came to nothing. It was also the period of trouble with suffragettes. An abortive attempt was made to start a fire in the ladies' lavatory and to hold a public meeting in the galleries while, in 1914, a woman made three slashes with a chopper through the glass and canvas of the portrait *Henry James*[31] by J. S. Sargent. Another female slightly damaged Sir Hubert von Herkomer's portrait *The Duke of Wellington*[32] and a third caused serious injury to the painting *Primavera*[33] by George Clausen. The iron railings around the galleries were then set further from the walls and additional detectives were employed but the Academy did not in fact close its doors as did certain important permanent collections at the time.

Such troubles quickly ceased, however, at the outbreak of the Great War in August 1914. The use of the galleries was immediately offered for any military purpose and, from October,the eastern half was occupied for a few months by the United Arts Force. Their rifles were stored in the Refreshment Room and drills were carried out vigorously in the courtyard. The building was insured against damage by hostile aircraft for £120,000 and the Academy's possessions for £80,000. The highest individual valuation (£3,500) was placed on each of the following items – the Michelangelo tondo (Plate 37), the Leonardo da Vinci cartoon (Plate 79),[34] the painting *Temperance* (then considered to be by Giorgione and later attributed to Palma Vecchio), *Theory* (Plate 12) by Reynolds, his *Self-portrait* (Plate 2) and his full-length paintings *George III* (Plate 1) and *Queen Charlotte*. Forty of the Academy's chief treasures were stored in a specially adapted 'safe chamber'[35] in the basement together with sixteen pictures from Sir John Soane's Museum.

15

THE GREAT WAR AND ITS
EFFECTS
1914–1928

As the war got into its stride, the majority of the male students enlisted in the armed forces. The Architecture School and the Day Modelling School had to be closed in 1915 followed by all the Evening Schools in 1916. There were no male classes for the duration and all prizes were suspended. The Diploma and Gibson Galleries were closed and no Annual Dinners or Soirées were held. The Winter Exhibition of 1915, called the War Relief Exhibition, took the form of a collection of works by living artists contributed by invitation. The exhibitors received one-third only of the proceeds of sales and the remaining two-thirds, together with the profits on running the exhibition, were divided between the Artists' General Benevolent Institution, the British Red Cross and St John Ambulance Association and a fund for the relief of Belgian artists. Towards the end of the year, the galleries in the eastern half of the building were used as ladies' work-rooms for 'sewing shirts for soldiers' and similar purposes.

The Summer Exhibition took place as usual except that the attendance dropped from about 170,000 in the previous year to 130,000. Soldiers and sailors in uniform were admitted free in the last three weeks. Arrangements were made with Walter Judd Ltd to publish *The Royal Academy Illustrated*, from half-tone blocks, and the volume continued annually in their hands from 1916 to 1940.

The deficit in the year's accounts amounted to over £2,000 and the Academy's financial position was in a precarious state for a considerable time. The situation could not, however, be blamed entirely on the war as there had been losses every year but one since 1908. Various economies were adopted but suggestions for charging fees for exhibited works and a commission on sales were not approved. Artists were having a very thin time and it seemed hardly fair to impose fresh burdens on them. Indeed, a Benefactors' Fund was formed 'for the relief of distress

143

among artists of reputation, whether Members of the Royal Academy or not, or the Widows of such artists'.[1] In 1916 the practice of claiming a pension by retired members 'as a matter of right'[2] was abolished and the question of letting the galleries to kindred societies was considered favourably. The attendances at the Summer Exhibitions fell again that year and still further in the tragic months of 1917. Thereafter they rose and levelled at about 160,000 a season throughout the period under review, with one or two peaks of over 200,000. It appeared at first that the Academy's exhibitions might be subject to the new Entertainments Tax which was introduced in 1916 and, in fact, it was levied on admission to the Winter Exhibition of Graphic Art in 1917, but exemption was granted in time for the Summer Exhibition that year. A bomb fell on Gallery IX and, in view of the greater dangers to be feared from the latest high explosives, the Academy's chief treasures were removed in the following year to a specially prepared chamber in the underground railway beneath the General Post Office.

The number of submissions declined to about 8,000 from 1916 to 1919 but increased again to 10,000 or so in the early 1920s and the total of works exhibited varied between 1,250 and 1,950. Many of the pictures depicted the grimness of war, such as, all in 1916, *Youth mourning*[3] by George Clausen, *Defeat of the Prussian Guard*[4] by W. B. Wollen and *A Fight to the Last*[5] by W. L. Wyllie, while others in the same year, such as *Sunny Morning*[6] by Alfred Parsons and *A Spring Revel*[7] by R. Anning Bell, seemed to be specially designed to keep at bay the horrors of the time. William Orpen and R. G. Eves were busy painting portraits of serving officers while heroes and heroines, such as Nurse Cavell, were always popular subjects. Incidents in the great battles of Ypres, Verdun, the Dardanelles, Jutland and many others were seized upon, followed by scenes of the armistice and the signing of treaties. Eventually, there was a spate of war memorials and the Academy set up a special committee in 1918 to advise on them.

The Chantrey purchases included *The Poulterer's Shop* by Frank Brangwyn, *Forward, the Guns!* by Lucy Kemp-Welch, *King Cophetua and the Beggar Maid* by Burne-Jones, *Epsom Downs: City and Suburban Day* by A. J. Munnings, *Hammersmith Bridge on Boat-race Day* by Walter Greaves, *Mrs Raynes* by P. Wilson Steer and a bronze statuette *Eros* by Alfred Gilbert.[8]

All was not well, however, with the workings of this bequest. In 1917 a Board of Trustees was established for the Tate Gallery and soon complained of 'what they considered to be the anomalous position they found themselves in as regards the housing, purchase, loan, and arrangement of the Chantrey pictures'.[9] The Academy Council then agreed to consult the Tate Board on works proposed for purchase by the subcommittees, the Board claiming no veto, and to consider suggestions from them of particular items which they would like to acquire. At the same time, the Royal Academy and other art societies, through the Imperial Arts League, sent a memorial to the Treasury regarding 'with gravest misgiving' the absence on the Board 'of Members directly and adequately representing the artists of this country'.[10] In 1920 the Government appointed three such professional artists and, in 1922, two representatives from the Tate Board were added to each of the recommending committees.

The Schools, with female students only, just about kept going during the war but used only two studios. Others were occupied by the British Red Cross Society and, from 1917, five rooms were allocated to the Admiralty for experimental work in the camouflage of ships at sea. When not required for the annual Summer Exhibition, the main galleries were occasionally lent to other art societies and, in the winter of 1919–20, an exhibition was held under the auspices of the Imperial War Museum of the nation's war paintings and various records.

The armistice was signed on 11 November 1918 and it was not long before the Academy's permanent possessions were once more on display. A memorial tablet, to commemorate those students who had lost their lives, was placed under the portico at the western end and this was matched by a similar memorial for the Artists' Rifles at the eastern end. Young war veterans such as Cosmo Clark and L. M. Glasson entered the Schools and a special committee was appointed to revise the curriculum and the whole character of the training. It was hoped that there might emerge 'The Royal Academy State School of Art',[11] as had been mooted in 1915, but, with the country in such an unsettled state and its finances at such low ebb, the Government was unable to proceed with the scheme. Various reforms were, however, carried out and can be summed up by saying that a real attempt was made to streamline the organization and raise the standards.

Meanwhile, the Academy's overall constitution had been under consideration. In 1917 it was decided that there should not be less than six Sculptor Academicians and five Sculptor Associates in the membership and not less than four Architect Academicians and four Architect Associates. Similar regulations regarding Engravers and Draughtsmen were not approved. In 1918 a Constitution Committee was formed to study and report on a memorandum from Reginald Blomfield. By the end of the year they had recommended and it had been resolved that:

> Academicians and Associates on reaching the age of 75 years shall cease to be Acting Academicians and Acting Associates. They shall thereupon become Senior Academicians and Senior Associates, and their promotion shall create in each case a vacancy in the Class of Acting Academicians or Acting Associates.[12]

Thus, for the first time, a means was devised of getting in new blood other than through death, expulsion, resignation or retirement. By a stroke of irony, when Blomfield himself reached the age limit, he was still as lively as a two year old and he lived on in complete possession of all his faculties for another eleven years.

Other recommendations included the institution of a class of Artist-Craftsmen, which was not approved, and Standing Committees for the Academy Schools and for Public Policy. The constitution of the Council was amended to ensure proportionate representation of the classes of membership and arrangements were made for regular meetings of the painting, sculpture, architecture and engraving sections of the Academy. Unfortunately, not all of these businesslike proposals have been continued. Blomfield was an architect in more senses than one and would have made an excellent Managing Director of the institution if there had ever been such a position.

Sir Edward Poynter was over eighty and in poor health when these reforms were carried out and he resigned the Presidency in December 1918. A special toast was drunk to him at the next Annual Dinner (the first after the war and resplendent with Admirals and Generals) and he died in July 1919. The election of Sir Aston Webb (Plate 53) had taken place on 21 January when he received twenty-four votes against two for Sir George Frampton and one each for Reginald Blomfield, Sir Arthur Cope, Frank Dicksee, Sir Frank Short and Henry Woods. Except for the makeshift appointment of James Wyatt in 1805, when Benjamin West was temporarily out of favour, Webb was the first architect to be made President. He was already in his seventieth year and the election was the culminating point of his busy career. He had been President of the Architectural Association as early as 1884 and of the Royal Institute of British Architects in 1902. In 1905 he received the latter's royal gold medal and, in the following year, was the first

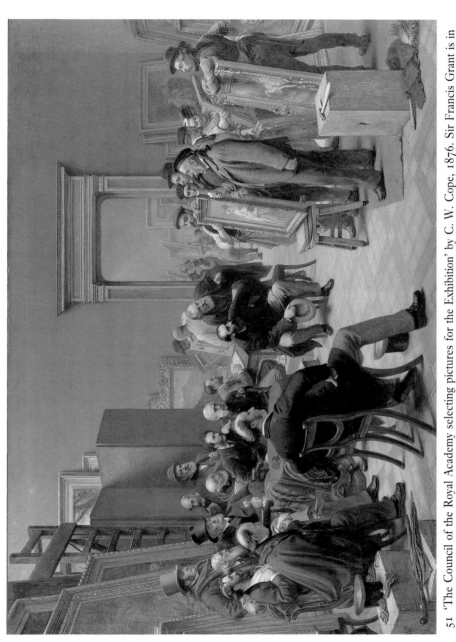

51 'The Council of the Royal Academy selecting pictures for the Exhibition' by C. W. Cope, 1876. Sir Francis Grant is in the President's chair with Lord Leighton seated next but one on his right and Sir J. E. Millais, Bt, in the foreground. The Secretary, Sir Frederick Eaton, is writing at the desk.

53 'Sir Aston Webb', President of the Royal Academy, by
Sir William Llewellyn, 1921 Diploma Work

52 'Sir Edward J. Poynter, Bt.', President of the Royal
Academy, by Sir Arthur S. Cope. Diploma, 1911

54 'Spring' by Dame Laura Knight, 1916–20 Chantrey Bequest Purchase, 1935
(*Tate Gallery, London*)

55 South Front of Burlington House in 1935

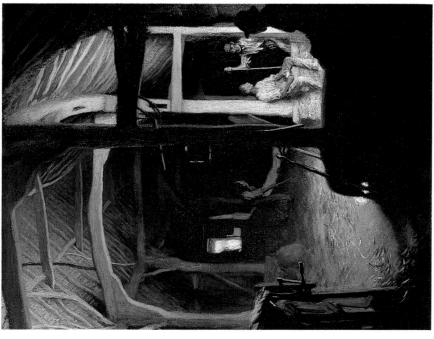

57 'Interior of an Old Barn' by Sir George Clausen.
Diploma Work, 1908.

56 'On Strike' by Sir Hubert von Herkomer, 1891.
Diploma Work

59 'W. B. Yeats', c. 1907, by Augustus John. Chantrey Bequest Purchase, 1940 (*Tate Gallery, London*)

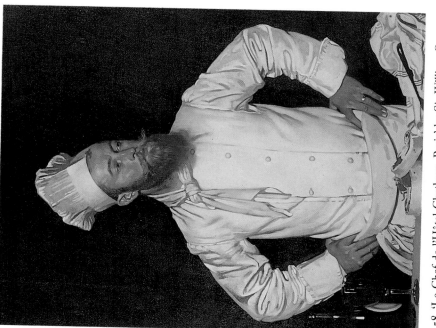

58 'Le Chef de l'Hôtel Chatham, Paris' by Sir William Orpen. Diploma Work, 1921

60 The Selection Committee, 1943. *Left to right:* Sir Walter Lamb (Secretary), R. O. Dunlop, S. J. Lamorna Birch, Sir Henry Rushbury, Sir William Russell Flint, L. Campbell Taylor, Sir Edwin Lutyens (President), Sir Gerald Kelly, Stanley Anderson, W. Curtis Green, Gilbert Ledward, Sir William Reid Dick and A. F. Hardiman

61 Pictures 'crowded out' from the Summer Exhibition, 1949

62 Ceiling painting in the Council Room of the Royal Academy,
by Sebastiano Ricci, *c.* 1715

63 Sir Winston Churchill speaking at the Royal Academy Dinner, 1954

64 'The Farm Gate' by Sir Stanley Spencer, 1950. Diploma Work

recipient of one awarded by the American Institute of Architects. He designed Imperial College and the Victoria and Albert Museum at South Kensington in 1891 and, in 1913, was responsible for the Admiralty Arch, the Mall and the existing front of Buckingham Palace, giving the layout a simple dignity which forms a suitable setting for the pomp and glitter of processions on ceremonial occasions.

Webb's place as Treasurer was filled by the appointment of Sir Frank Short and, when A. C. Gow died in the following year, Charles Sims was elected Keeper. A layman, E. E. V. Wright, who had been on the staff since 1905, was then given the title of Librarian and he held the post till 1948. The Visitorships in the Sculpture School were abandoned in 1921 when Henry Poole was made Master and the various Curators were replaced by senior students who were called Prefects and paid modest fees to be responsible for law and order.

The galleries were lent in the winter of 1920–21 for an exhibition of Spanish art and this was the first occasion on which any appreciable number of works from abroad had been gathered together at the Academy for a Loan Exhibition. Compared with later efforts, it was a very small affair but, followed by the Australian exhibition of 1923 and the Swedish exhibition of 1924, it led the way to the large-scale international shows from 1927 onwards. The other Winter Exhibitions, such as that of decorative art in 1923, drew only meagre attendances.

The Summer Exhibitions continued with little change. In 1919 it had been agreed that small photographs, if not more than half-plate size, could be allowed in the architectural section 'but only in connection with working drawings and included in the same frame'.[13] In 1920 a sale was held of unclaimed works to 1913 but the collection was of no great consequence. There were ninety items in all and they fetched £266 5s 6d. After the deduction of £20 for expenses, the remainder was presented to the Artists' General Benevolent Institution. The exhibits of H. H. La Thangue, Philip Connard and Sir John Lavery were among the most popular of the period.

In 1920 the Academy headed a protest against the demolition of nineteen churches and expressed concern over the cleaning of certain pictures in the National Gallery. Dissensions on the former matter continued for several years but the latter was clarified immediately. In 1922 a conference was called and several meetings held to press the Government for a (Royal) Fine Arts Commission and this materialized in the following year as a body from which advice could be sought on siting and design in public places. In this same year, there commenced and met regularly for quite a while a committee to investigate the qualities of artists' materials and the various methods of cleaning old pictures. The artistic potentialities of the British Empire exhibition, held at Wembley in 1924, were discussed, also the preservation of Flatford Mill as a memorial to John Constable and the possibility of saving Waterloo Bridge. Altogether it was a period of great activity in matters outside the Academy's jurisdiction but well within its sphere of interest. More trust funds were received – in memory of William Hilton and others – and the advice and support of the Council were frequently sought on a variety of problems.

Internally, the period was one of comparative peace. The President gave fancy dress dances annually for the students and their contemporaries from other art schools, the bicentenary of Reynolds' birth was duly celebrated in 1923 and, in the autumn of that year, an exhibition of British primitive painting and sculpture was held. A month or two later, 'acting on expert advice',[14] the Council decided to reduce the stock of 1887 port and it was offered to the members at £9 a dozen bottles. For many years, until the Second World War, the Academy's wine-cellar was quite renowned and a special snuff, still in use, was always available at meetings.

Unfortunately Sir Aston Webb was seriously injured in a motor accident in 1924 when returning home from the Annual Dinner with Melton Fisher, Sir Luke Fildes and Sir William Llewellyn. He was out of action until almost the end of the year, by which time he had to resign the Presidency on becoming a Senior Academician. The election for his successor took place on 10 December and, in the first ballot, ten votes were cast for Sir Reginald Blomfield, seventeen for Frank Dicksee, four for Sir George Frampton and one for Charles Sims. The names of the first two were then put to the ballot again and Dicksee was elected by seventeen votes against thirteen. He was knighted in the New Year.

It was rather a shame for Blomfield that he was thus narrowly defeated as, from several points of view, he was better equipped than Dicksee to take up the position. He was both scholarly and forthright. He had been for many years an indefatigable worker on the Academy's behalf and had done more than anyone else to bring its workings up to date. If he had been a painter, there is little doubt that he would have been elected but, at the time, there was a large consensus of opinion against having another architect to follow Webb. The new President was a truly professional painter who had spent little of his time on outside activities but he was courteous, warm-hearted and courageous in his convictions. He was born in 1853 and it will be remembered that his painting *Harmony*[15] was one of the first Chantrey purchases in 1877. From that period, he had worked unceasingly towards his ideals, hardly deflected by any current events but striving again and again to attain perfection in his particular but versatile style of romantic art.

Hitherto unaccustomed to cope with the difficulties of business or diplomacy, Dicksee soon had a very ticklish problem on his hands. Charles Sims had been granted sittings in 1922 for his portrait *George V*. It was shown in the Academy exhibition of 1924 and a reproduction of it forms the front page of *The Royal Academy Illustrated* of that year. The King, however, informed Dicksee of his dissatisfaction with the finished picture, which, although a splendidly flamboyant composition, was somewhat whimsical. The legs might have belonged to a ballet dancer. Sims duly received his fee (250 guineas) and it was agreed that the picture should be destroyed but he subsequently exhibited it in New York in the autumn of 1925 and had arrangements in hand to show it in Canada. This put the President and the Academy in a very embarrassing position and, on payment of a further 750 guineas, they took possession of it 'unreservedly'.[16] The official records are silent as to its ultimate fate but rumour has it that the head was cut from the rest of the canvas and retained for a short while though both pieces were eventually burned to ashes in the boiler-house at the Academy under the supervision of the Treasurer and the Secretary. Meanwhile the Council arranged for a new portrait by Sir Arthur S. Cope. This was duly approved and Queen Mary always considered it to be the best likeness of George V.[17]

J. S. Sargent died suddenly in April 1925 and the next Winter Exhibition was devoted to his paintings, the first one-man memorial show of a member's work since that of Alma-Tadema in 1913. There were 631 exhibits, a special illustrated souvenir was produced and 108,022 visitors paid for admission. It was followed in 1927 by an important exhibition of Flemish and Belgian art from 1300 to 1900 and, in 1928, by a mixed exhibition including the Iveagh Bequest pictures before they were placed on permanent view to the public at Kenwood. E. F. Dixon, the Registrar, died in 1925 and was replaced by the promotion of the Clerk, C. W. Tanner.

Dicksee continued the dances for the students and, as a good many members and their wives used to attend, there was a happy liaison between the artists of standing and the younger generation on these cheerful occasions. Work in the Schools was carried on in a very free and easy manner under Charles Sims as Keeper and a report of the Schools Committee in January 1926, with Sir Reginald Blomfield as chairman, complained that the direction was too casual and that 'Students are allowed too much freedom in their methods of study'.[18] There is no doubt that the discipline had become very lax and matters were brought to a head when Sims disappeared to America later that year and was not back when the Schools reopened after the summer vacation. On 2 November the Council sent him a telegram 'expressing their anxiety'[19] and the reply was an offer of his resignation from the Keepership which was accepted at once. He had for some considerable time been in a disturbed mental state and in 1928, at the age of fifty-four, he ended his own life.

There had been serious disorder in the Schools at the time of his resignation particularly when, in his absence, a number of students had been failed in an examination of their work. George Clausen was then made Director of the Schools and Master of the Painting School and, after a few months, he submitted a lucid report from which the following paragraphs are extracts:

The old system, which came to an end with the war, was perfect of its kind. Attendance was enforced, lectures were regularly given, models were engaged by the Visitors; each School – painting, drawing, sculpture, architecture – had its Curator – four in all; and if some of these were of little use as teachers, they maintained order. The Schools were, if anything, over-staffed and the system was too rigid. But it worked without much difficulty, because of the prestige of the Academy, and because at that time its teaching had not been seriously challenged or questioned.

Contrast this with what now exists – not so much a School, as a rather freely-run life class. The attendance is somewhat casual – this is due to some extent to the necessity of earning money – and the Students work, to a great extent, as they please. I have no fault to find with them – they are well-behaved, orderly and, on the whole, steady at their work. But they are impatient of control; and it must be recognised that the younger generation no longer accepts the old ideals: a different spirit exists and must be reckoned with. It must be remembered too, that Students enter our Schools after some years' attendance at other schools, and their habits are formed. Their average age on admission is, men 22, women 23. They are naturally anxious to begin earning, and not to begin their studies all over again. It would be desirable, perhaps, to limit the age at entry to 22, instead of 30 as at present, in the Painting School.

The administration has been practically left to the School porter. . . . There is at present no other provision for carrying out the routine or maintaining order: the prefects hardly count, and should be discontinued. . . .[20]

George Harcourt (Plate 71) followed Clausen for a term and then a new Keeper, W. W. Russell (Plate 71), was elected to commence his duties in October 1927. He was of quiet disposition but a man with whom no one could take liberties. He was strict but fair. The system of Prefects was brought to an end and a Curator, Charles Genge, was appointed 'for the maintenance of discipline and order among the Students. . . .'[21] The age limits for admission were fixed at 21 for painters, 25 for sculptors and 30 for architects, with possibilities of their being slightly exceeded in exceptional circumstances.

It was resolved that the Keeper should no longer reside in the Academy and the main part of the ground-floor of the Keeper's House was made into one large apartment to house the library (Plate 74). This work was carried out by W. Curtis Green (Plate 60). A donation of £1,000 from Sir Aston Webb was used at the same time to adapt the adjoining section as an annexe 'for the proper keeping and study of prints'.[22] The first-floor accommodation which hitherto had been used for the library (that is, the old ballroom of Burlington House) was then furnished with pictures and called the Reynolds Room. For many years it was then used for meetings, lectures and occasional dinners.

Although there had been Honorary Members of the Royal Academy since 1769 when Joseph Baretti was made Secretary for Foreign Correspondence, George III had not wished them to receive Diplomas and they had never done so until George V gave his permission in 1926. Wording was then agreed as follows;

His Most Gracious Majesty King George V
Patron of the Royal Academy of Arts, London,
Founded by his royal ancestor King George III, A.D. 1768

Having been pleased to approve and confirm the Constitution and Laws of the said Royal Academy of Arts, whereby it is provided that there shall be a class of Members to be called Honorary Members of the Royal Academy of Arts, to consist of men of distinguished reputation nominated by the President with the approval of the Council and the sanction of the General Assembly, We, the President and Academicians of the Royal Academy of Arts, have had the honour to appoint you

....

to be ....

as by rules set forth and enacted.[23]

As is the case with Associates and Honorary Academicians, these Diplomas are signed by the President and Secretary. The Very Revd William Foxley Norris, Dean of Westminster, was appointed Chaplain that year and he instituted an annual service for artists to take place in Westminster Abbey. This was in abeyance throughout the Second World War but, for some years now, has been held at twelve noon on non-members' Varnishing Day in St James's Parish Church, Piccadilly.

At long last, in 1928, the engravers were placed on complete equality with other members of the Academy and the Laws were changed to provide that 'among the forty Academicians not less than two shall be engravers, and that there shall not be less than two Associate Engravers. . . .'[24] Thus a struggle which had gone on since the earliest days of the institution was finally resolved.

Troubles over the Chantrey Bequest broke out again in 1927 and 1928 and, because of disagreements with the Tate Gallery, no purchases were made in either of these years. The President and Council declined to buy certain works which had been recommended from the exhibition of the New English Art Club and the Tate Gallery representatives stayed away from the usual meeting for the consideration of possible purchases from the Summer Exhibition. The situation worsened when, even after the suggestion had been made by their chairman, the Tate Gallery Board refused to attend a proposed conference between them, the Academy and the Chantrey Trustees. They insisted on (a) a discussion in cases of any disagreements over recommendations and (b) sole responsibility for accepting and exhibiting purchases. In reply the Council 'offered to agree that the President would be willing to explain to the Board the Council's reasons for rejecting any recommendation'[25] but this concession was not acceptable. There the situation stood at the end of 1928, despite some mutual sympathy when twenty-one Chantrey pictures were damaged by the flooding of the Thames that year, but Sir Frank Dicksee died in October and hopes were pinned on being able to reopen negotiations after the appointment of a new President.

The election took place on 10 December 1928 and Sir Reginald Blomfield, then seventy-two years of age, was once again in the running. He polled seven votes, as opposed to eight for Sir William Orpen and seventeen for Sir William Llewellyn. At the second ballot, six more were added to Orpen's score but, although Llewellyn's remained the same, he duly won the day.

16

UNCERTAIN PEACE

1929–1939

It was thought at the time that the new President was then sixty-five years of age and, even in his obituary notices thirteen years later, his date of birth was given as 1863. Some years after his death, however, it was found that Llewellyn had been born in Cirencester in 1858 and, as he was re-elected unanimously each year till 1938, he in fact served for five years beyond the age limit. He died early in 1941.

Llewellyn (Plate 71), a good-looking Welshman, who always retained the upright bearing of a distinguished courtier, had at one time been a student under Sir Edward Poynter at the National Art Training School and also studied in Paris. He began exhibiting regularly at the Royal Academy in 1884 and soon turned to portrait painting as a profession, one of his most successful works being the state portrait of Queen Mary[1] in 1910. He seldom expressed personal opinions but was skilful in summing up at meetings and, when he did speak, it was with an autocratic finality. His manner was pleasant but full of the dignity of his office. His soft, rather twisted smile was inscrutable and his demeanour imperturbable.

The Chantrey troubles were soon allayed. The new President reviewed the whole position with the Director of the Tate Gallery and, on the latter's assurance that his Board did not question the legal right of the Academy to reject works put forward by the recommending committees, the Council agreed to discuss the grounds on which they had declined to purchase particular items 'without further dispute as to the rights of the Board as exhibitors of the works purchased'.[2] A stone group, *The Little Apple*[3] by Henry Poole, was bought immediately and, before the end of the year 1929, twelve other works had been added to the collection.

The most important feature of Llewellyn's Presidency was the series of international Loan Exhibitions. That of Dutch art, 1450–1900, which was open from January to March 1929, was especially strong in works by Rembrandt and Vermeer and that of Italian art, 1200–1900, in the following year, was absolutely staggering in its content of world-famous masterpieces. There were about 1,000 exhibits and they included *The Birth of Venus*[4] by Botticelli, *The Dead Christ*[5] by Mantegna, *The Crucifixion*[6] by Masaccio, *La Donna Velata*[7] by Raphael, *The Tempest*[8] by Giorgione and *Paul III*[9] by Titian, as well as fine sculpture, drawings and *objets d'art*. It would be impossible nowadays to assemble in one place such a treasure-store. There were seventy-eight loans from the Uffizi Gallery in Florence, twenty-two from the Brera in Milan and twenty-one from the Accademia in Venice as well as numerous contributions from Bergamo, Berlin, Budapest, Naples, Paris, Rome and elsewhere. The loans from Italy were brought about by the personal intervention of Mussolini and they were transported to and from this country in an Italian vessel which was renamed *Leonardo da Vinci* especially for the purpose. There was sudden alarm when she temporarily went aground on the return journey, perhaps through the sheer weight of her responsibility, but, regaining composure, she sailed home safely.

The attendances at the exhibition were enormous. Nearly 540,000 persons paid for single admissions and, with the sale of almost 10,000 season tickets, this brought the total number of visits to about 600,000, far more than had ever been recorded for an exhibition at the Academy. The period was extended until 20 March and the crowds of visitors in the last few weeks were so great that queues of people formed across the coutryard until it became safe to allow a few more at a time to enter the galleries. The Academy received 17½ per cent of the profits – over £6,000.

This Italian exhibition was followed by one of Persian art in 1931 and, although most people had no previous knowledge of individual exhibits, the magnificent array of carpets, jewellery, miniatures and various *objets d'art* captured people's imagination. Many pieces had started their journey from the Middle East by primitive transport and some had been packed in camel dung, as was only too evident when the cases were opened at Burlington House many months later. A platform was built in Gallery VIII for the display of a fine collection of the Shah's jewels. This was protected by an invisible ray alarm system, its first use for such a purpose, but news of it soon became known and otherwise well-behaved visitors could not resist the temptation of leaning over the rope to set the bell ringing. On the walls were silk, gold and silver carpets and the whole effect was reminiscent of the

Arabian Nights. The expenses of the exhibition were so heavy that, despite about 300,000 visitors, no profit was made.

The exhibition of French art, 1200–1900, in 1932, was more usual and palatable to European taste. It contained some splendid works of art by François Clouet, Poussin, Watteau, Chardin, Ingres and others too numerous to mention and, for the first time in the Academy's long series of Loan Exhibitions, a really important representation of the Impressionists and Post-Impressionists. The attendance amounted to nearly 350,000 but again, owing to the fall in value of the pound sterling, there was hardly any profit. This was the first of these international exhibitions for which the Academy undertook complete administrative responsibility in this country and this came about by doubt having been expressed as to whether the institution was in order in allowing outside authorities to sponsor such activities on its premises. A new system of electric lighting, with large reflectors, was installed on this occasion and served for many years.

The commemorative exhibition of works by late members (Dicksee, Orpen and twelve others), in 1933, was modest by comparison but over 40,000 people attended. This was followed in 1934 by a gigantic exhibition of British art, c. 1000–1860. There were over 1,600 exhibits and special exhibitions in connection with it were held concurrently at the National Gallery, the British Museum and the Victoria and Albert Museum. Besides about 600 oil paintings and over 200 watercolours, there were large and choice displays of miniatures, drawings, manuscripts, alabasters, ivories, silver, porcelain and sculpture as well as tapestries, armour and furniture.

A conference had been held in 1929 to discuss 'the training of British artists in Design for Manufactures'[10] and, in his speech at the Royal Academy Dinner in 1932, Prince George (afterwards Duke of Kent) spoke at some length on the possibilities of improving the attractiveness of British manufactured goods. 'Between artists and manufacturers,' he said, 'there has been in the past, perhaps, some lack of mutual understanding and an absence of co-operation. The manufacturer has not sufficiently appreciated the artist, and has not, therefore, taken full advantage of his services; perhaps the artist for his part has too often felt that industry was a wheel to which he did not care to put his shoulder.'[11] The President also took up the same theme and the outcome was the exhibition of British art in industry held at the Royal Academy three years later in collaboration with the Royal Society of Arts. The intervening period was used to good effect to bring together artists and manufacturers and the final exhibits were selected by panels of experts in various sections – ceramics, glassware, leatherware, silver, jewellery, furniture, carpets, fabrics, printing and so on. The task of organization was tremendous but an exhibition of over 2,200 items was opened as planned in January 1935. The appearance of the galleries was completely transformed by the building of various erections for display purposes and by the extensive use of artificial lighting. The attendance was reasonable, over 100,000 visitors, but the expenses were enormous and there was a financial loss of about £10,000 which was met by guarantors. A torch had been lit, however, and there were important outcomes, not least the institution of Royal Designers for Industry in 1936 and, some years later, the formation of the Council of Industrial Design (now the Design Council).

The next great international exhibition was that of Chinese art in the winter of 1935–36 (Plate 66). It comprised over 3,000 exhibits from the earliest times to about AD 1800. The Chinese Government contributed more than 800 items and other examples were procured from almost every major country in the world. A colossal marble statue of a Buddha,[12] over 20 feet high and weighing 14 tons, dominated the Central Hall and the gallery walls and fitments were covered throughout with a hand-made Chinese canvas. It was only about 17 inches in width and originally cost not much more than an old penny a yard. A battery of machinists stitched it together and it formed a most effective wall-covering for many years.

The exhibition contained paintings, calligraphy, sculpture, porcelain, pottery, lacquer, glass, embroidery, fans and carpets. The bronzes and jades were of superlative quality and the Architectural Room, fitted as a Chinese interior, was delightful. Well over 400,000 people came to the show and, on the last Thursday, there were almost 20,000 visitors in the one day. The cult for *chinoiserie* took London by storm and aspects of it were reflected in fashions and furnishings for some time to come.

The exhibition of seventeenth century art in Europe, held in 1938, was both scholarly and attractive but had no wide appeal, while the exhibition of British architecture in 1937 drew fewer than 9,000 visitors in a period of eight weeks. The last Loan Exhibition before the Second World War, in 1939, was that of Scottish art. Schemes for exhibitions of American, Japanese, German and Indian art were under way but all had to be abandoned as Adolf Hitler destroyed the peace of Europe and eventually the world. An era was at an end and once again the Academy had to restrict its activities.

Meanwhile the Summer Exhibitions had continued steadily. Between 10,000 and 12,000 works were submitted each year and approximately 1,500 were placed on show. They included certain 'pictures of the year' such as *Were you there when they crucified my Lord?*[13] by Mark Symons in 1930, *The Young Rower*[14] by L. M. Glasson in 1932, the poignant portrait *Delius*[15] by James Gunn in 1933, *I dreamt that I dwelt in marble halls*[16] by George Belcher and *The Harpist*[17] by L. Campbell Taylor, both in 1936, and *Why War?*[18] by Charles Spencelagh in 1939. There were some fine portraits by Augustus John, such as *W. B. Yeats*[19] in 1931, and the paintings by Stanhope Forbes, Laura Knight (Plate 54), Gerald Brockhurst and W. Russell Flint were always popular. In 1934 Sir Edwin Lutyens exhibited a large model of the proposed Metropolitan Cathedral of Liverpool but, unfortunately, this project never materialized. The exhibitions were criticized every year as they always have been but the annual attendance seldom fell below 130,000 and, in 1939, for the first time in the Academy's history, a television programme was broadcast from the galleries on non-members' Varnishing Day. An appreciable number of artists, it is true, had no wish to be associated with such large, mixed exhibitions and, in 1937, a suggestion was made that particular works might be invited specially each season but, for practical reasons, it received very little support

Among the Chantrey purchases were *The Chess Players* by Sir John Lavery, *The Green Dress* by Walter Greaves, *The Jester* (W. Somerset Maugham) by Gerald Kelly, the bronze heads *Einstein* by Jacob Epstein and *Paderewski* by Sir Alfred Gilbert, *Lord David Cecil* by Augustus John, *The Ball on Shipboard* (Plate 44) by James J. Tissot, *Their Majesties' Return from Ascot, 1925* (Plate 70) by Alfred J. Munnings, *Bird-nesting, Ludlow, 1898* by P. Wilson Steer and *Fresh Air Stubbs* by R. G. Brundrit.[20]

Sir Aston Webb died in 1930 but Sir Reginald Blomfield was still active in the Academy's affairs. In the following year, he produced a plan for extending Gallery VI northwards to form a large Sculpture Gallery but the Government would not allow it; he also acted as one of the two directors of the Persian exhibition. His position was not unlike that of Joseph Farington at the turn of the eighteenth century. Neither was ever elected an Officer of the institution but both were influential in many matters of domestic policy. As an architect, Blomfield was overshadowed by the brilliance of Sir Edwin Lutyens but, as a dogged and scholarly champion of the Academy he had no equal.

As far back as 1914, the question of a statue of Sir Joshua Reynolds had been discussed and a commission for it was given to Alfred Drury in 1917 through the Leighton Fund. The final model was approved in 1929 and the finished figure, in bronze, was erected in the courtyard in 1931 (Plate 55). Two years later, a pair of wrought-iron lamp standards, designed by Sir Edwin Lutyens and Sir William Reid Dick, were paid for through this same fund to stand in front of the west entrance of St Paul's Cathedral and, in 1937 and 1939, the bronze statues *J. M. W. Turner* by William McMillan and *Thomas Gainsborough* by Sir Thomas Brock were placed in niches at the top of the main staircase in Burlington House.

Sir David Murray made a present in 1930 of a stained glass window (which was designed by G. Kruger Gray) for the Diploma Gallery staircase and, after his death in 1933, it was learned that he had left the Academy a large sum of money (about £38,000) to be used for encouraging the study of landscape painting. He had in mind the foundation of 'an out-of-door residence where students could live and receive in the neighbourhood . . . direct training from landscape visitors of the Members and Associates of the Royal Academy'.[21] It was not considered practicable to carry this out precisely but, by a judgment of the High Court, a scheme was evolved under which 'David Murray Students' are duly elected each year and awarded maintenance allowances. They are required to reside for specified periods in localities suitable for the study of landscape painting and are visited by a member of the Royal Academy, who must be a landscape painter, to advise them in their work.

In 1932 the trustees of the first Viscount Leverhulme instituted an annual gift, originally of £500, to be used for the award of scholarships 'to those students who, on completing their studies in the Royal Academy Schools, are considered . . . to be most deserving of assistance in commencing their work as professional artists'.[22] This has been of immense value in the difficult period of transition from studentship to having to earn a livelihood. Other funds were received in the next few years from different sources for the provision of lectures and other purposes.

The largest and perhaps the most important bequest was the sum of almost £50,000 from Mary Gertrude Abbey, to form 'The Edwin Austin Abbey Memorial Trust Fund for Mural Painting in Great Britain'. Ned

Abbey, as he was known to all his friends, was born in Philadelphia in 1852 but he spent most of his life in London. He was a history painter and an illustrator of such periodicals as *Harper's Weekly* and various editions of Dickens and Shakespeare. Three times in his career he was given commissions for mural paintings – in the then new Boston Public Library in Massachusetts, in the State Capitol of Harrisburg, Pennsylvania, and in the Royal Exchange in London – but none was well paid. It was in fact only by carrying on with his black and white work at the same time that he could afford to undertake such tasks and he longed to be able to devote all his energies to painting on the grand scale. This frustration was undoubtedly in his mind when he discussed the possibility of founding a mural painting fund and, on his death in 1911, it was left to his widow to carry out his ideals. She died in 1931 and, after some legal arguments on both sides of the Atlantic, the money became available shortly before the outbreak of the Second World War. This catastrophe caused yet more delay in the operation of the fund and the first commission was not awarded until 1950.

Work in the Academy Schools was considerably regularized during the Keepership of W. W. Russell. Visitors were largely replaced by permanent teachers, William McMillan becoming Master of the Sculpture School in 1929 and W. T. Monnington taking up the position of Assistant Teacher of Painting two years later. There had been a Schools Committee again since 1919 but this was disbanded in 1930. The Council took over responsibility for the award of premiums in 1931, thus bringing to an end the rather cumbersome procedure of voting by all members of the Academy. A scheme for the interchange of students between the principal art schools in London was started in 1933 but came to an end some twenty-five years later. Professor A. P. Laurie ran a practical class in chemistry in addition to his lectures and, though it was restricted to about ten students, it had a marked influence on the interest in good craftsmanship. Walter Bayes gave regular lessons in perspective and H. Chalton Bradshaw conducted annually a course in architecture for painting and sculpture students. They learned the rudiments of construction, studied shapes and proportions and, according to their tutor, showed 'a remarkable aptitude for architectural drawing'.[23] The period was notable for the integration of various studies and the family atmosphere in the Schools.

The Academy frequently undertook commitments beyond its domestic activities. The President attended the ceremonies to celebrate the opening of new buildings for the American Academy of Arts and

Letters in New York in 1930 and, in the following two years, confer-
ences were held in connection with the Town Planning Act, the import
duty on works of art, the preservation of old pictures and on higher art
teaching in general. Even the proposal to erect new Law Courts at
Athens did not escape the Council's notice and a successful protest
was made against the suggested tower on the grounds that it was likely
to spoil the existing aspect of the Acropolis.

In 1931 it was decided that new candidates for Associateship should
require a certain minimum of nominations before they could be
included in the official list – 'five signatures, of which three shall be of
Painter Members, in the case of a Painter, and three, of which two
shall be of Sculptor, Architect or Engraver Members respectively, in
the case of a Sculptor, an Architect or an Engraver'.[24] Furthermore, it
was resolved that, even after a candidate had polled the highest number
of votes, his name should again be put to the ballot to decide whether
or not he be elected. In 1937 another hurdle was imposed by the
requirement of a two-thirds majority in the final ballot but it caused a
stalemate in a number of elections and was rescinded in 1952. Dame
Laura Knight was elected a Royal Academician in 1936 (the first woman
since the foundation members) and a special Law was passed to make
Women Academicians eligible for service on the Council. She duly
took her place in the following two years. Her husband, Harold Knight
(Plate 71), was elected an Associate and then an Academician one year
later than Laura in each case, in 1928 and 1937, and they were the
first married couple to be members. Sir Frank Short became a Senior
Academician at the end of 1932 and was replaced as Treasurer by
Sydney Lee (Plate 71). H. J. Plenderleith took over the Professorship
of Chemistry from A. P. Laurie in 1936.

Two members of the Royal Academy resigned in 1935 and, whatever
were the rights and wrongs in each case, the effects on outside artists
were greatly to be deplored. The first was Stanley Spencer who did so
in protest at having two of his pictures that year – *The Lovers* (sometimes
called *The Dustman*)[25] and *St Francis and the Birds*[26] – turned down by
the Council at the request of the Hanging Committee of the Summer
Exhibition. He was informed by letter and wrote back immediately as
follows:

Dear Mr. Lamb.
　　Please do not hang *any* of the pictures I have sent.
....

Weather good or bad it is very unlikely I shall ever paint any differently from what I do now, so please accept my resignation, and let it be done as quietly as possible.

Yours sincerely,
Stanley Spencer.

P.S. – I am sorry for any inconvenience but if *any* of my pictures are hung they are to be withdrawn at once.[27]

The Secretary replied that the three works included would have to remain until the close of the exhibition and the contretemps received considerable publicity as Stanley Spencer himself seems to have notified the press. His point of argument was that the Academy should automatically hang pictures submitted by a member and, in a subsequent letter, he explained:

> . . . I thought that being a member meant one was entitled to exhibit six pictures every year. This was the chief reason of my accepting membership. There was no question in my mind of sending less than six and the more room my pictures could take up and the less room there was for other Academy artists (with a few exceptions) the better pleased I should be. I also had in mind that if six of my works were present at one of your exhibitions, there would be sufficient 'atmosphere' to make my pictures feel at home. . . .[28]

Unfortunately in an effort to placate the artist, the Secretary (W. R. M. Lamb) had inadvertently caused him yet more annoyance by telling him that a large work by an Academician had been omitted at the same time and that the latter had written expressing his entire approval of the Council's action. 'What other Academicians do or how they behave is no concern or business of mine,' was the heated reply, '& I have no wish to have their behaviour held up to me as an example.'[29] The whole episode was unpleasant but the wound was healed in time and, thanks to the efforts of Sir Gerald Kelly when he became President, Stanley Spencer accepted re-election in 1950.

The Academician referred to was W. R. Sickert and the large work was his portrait *Lord Beaverbrook.*[30] 'You know me well enough,' he wrote, 'to know that I should never think of complaining of any action of a Hanging Committee nor any decision of the President and Council.'[31] Only a month had elapsed, however, before he himself resigned his membership of the institution and this was the result of a misunderstanding of events. Apparently the President, Sir William

Llewellyn, had been asked to sign a petition for the preservation of the statues by Jacob Epstein on a building in the Strand which had recently been acquired by the Rhodesian Government from the British Medical Association. He had been asked to sign in his personal capacity 'but felt unable to do so without seeming to commit the Academy as a whole to its support'[32] and there had been no meeting to consider the matter. Nevertheless, the refusal was broadcast and reported in certain newspapers as from the Academy itself and, in his letter of resignation,[33] Sickert commented, 'If the R.A. cannot throw its shield over a great sculptor, what is the Royal Academy for?' He was very apt to act impulsively and, on one occasion, travelled all the way to London from Thanet by taxi merely to obtain entry forms for a young friend to submit works to the Academy exhibition – incidentally, then walking off happily but forgetting all about the taxi and leaving it unpaid at the back entrance. He died in 1942 and, in his last days, the Academy organized a fund to assist him financially.

There was yet a third resignation in 1938 after the Academy had rejected a portrait of T. S. Eliot[34] by Wyndham Lewis. It came from Augustus John who wrote: 'After the crowning ineptitude of the rejection of Wyndham Lewis's picture I feel it is impossible for me to remain longer a member of the R.A. . . .'[35] He refused to change his mind at the time but, not long afterwards, it was learned that he might be willing to resume his membership and, with the Sovereign's permission, he was reinstated early in 1940.

George V died in January 1936 and no Dinner or Soirée was held that year. His successor, Edward VIII, did not wish his head to appear on any medals except 'King's Medals' and the Academy thereupon commissioned E. G. Gillick to produce a design with the head of its founder sovereign, George III. He did so, showing the King in a tricorn hat surrounded by the inscription 'KING GEORGE III – PATRON PROTECTOR SUPPORTER'. The reverse had the words 'BENE MERENTI' separated horizontally by a spray of laurel and surrounded by the inscription 'ROYAL ACADEMY OF ARTS – FOUNDED MDCCLXVIII'. This design has been used for all Academy Schools' medals since that date, in gold, silver and bronze, and whether or not paid for through any trust fund. The abdication of Edward VIII took place in December 1936 and his brother, George VI, then came to the throne. To mark the coronation in the following year, the Academy's royal portraits were hung together in the Central Hall as a feature of the Summer Exhibition.

Gifts continued to be received over the years and one of the most important came from Arthur Acland Allen who, in 1938, presented a great treasure-store of Turner's *Liber Studiorum* prints.[36] He had gathered together over a long period 'as complete a representation as possible of the various stages through which each plate passed'[37] and it may fairly be claimed that the collection is unrivalled.

This was Llewellyn's last year as President and the election for a successor took place on 10 December. The first voting was well scattered – fourteen for Sydney Lee, ten for Sir Edwin Lutyens, six for A. J. Munnings, three for Harold Knight, two each for Francis Dodd, George Harcourt and Gerald Kelly and one each for Philip Connard and W. Russell Flint (Plates 60 and 71). Munnings was eliminated at the second ballot and Lutyens finally defeated Sydney Lee by the narrow majority of twenty to eighteen.

Sir Edwin Landseer Lutyens (Plate 60), born in London in 1869, was best known to the public as the designer of the Cenotaph in Whitehall and the most prolific architect of his time but, to the initiated, his name meant much more. It stood for fertility of invention and elegance of style in his work at New Delhi, his civic buildings in this country and his variety of country houses. He was a lovable man, full of fun, and the owner of many tiny pipes which had to be collected and returned to him wherever he had been. His wit was crisp and unbounding. 'Doctors are luckier than architects,' he said, 'they can bury their failures'[38] and he used to tease the Secretary (W. R. M. Lamb) by calling him his 'pet lamb'. Lutyens was for ever drawing on whatever paper came to hand, on menu cards particularly and even on the tablecloth but, behind the boyish spirits, there was a brilliant brain and a great kindness of heart. He had been knighted in 1918, made a KCIE in 1930 and, in 1942, was awarded the Order of Merit. His Presidency came to an end with his death on New Year's Day in 1944 and, unfortunately, his period of office was hampered by the exigencies of the Second World War.

Mankind had been plunged into devastation on a scale which had never before been known and the Academy's first task was to protect its inheritance. Arrangements were made for the chief treasures to be stored safely and precautions against air-raids were put in hand at Burlington House. In the event, the building escaped with only minor damage but the threat of disaster was ever present.

17

THE SECOND WORLD WAR AND
ITS EFFECTS
1939–1954

The war had begun in September 1939 and the arrangements for an exhibition that winter of the art of Greater India, which were well advanced, had to be abandoned. A conference of representatives of seventeen art societies was held at the Academy on 5 October when it was agreed to promote instead a United Artists' exhibition on similar lines to the War Relief exhibition of 1915. Eight other art societies subsequently joined in and, in fact, no serious artist in the country, whether a member of any society or not, was debarred from participating. All were allowed to contribute up to three works, but not more than two of them in any one medium, and the Committee undertook to show the utmost liberality in placing them, even to the extent of an advance promise to include at least one by each artist or to invite a substitute should they be unacceptable. Almost twelve hundred artists were represented in the exhibition and there were 2,219 exhibits. Despite the uncertainties of the time, 201 items were sold for over £4,000. The artists retained half the selling price while the other half was divided between the Lord Mayor's Red Cross and St John Fund and the Artists' General Benevolent Institution.

Plans were then put in hand for a similar exhibition in the following year but they had to be set aside when the Academy's glass roofs suffered severe damage from nearby bomb explosions in September and November 1940. Such shows, however, were again held in 1942 and 1943 and were even more welcome as by then many other societies had no usable premises. Owing to the ever increasing risk of destruction by air attacks, no major Loan Exhibition could be held but there were small ones of Greek art in 1942, Yugoslav art in 1944, Soviet graphic art in 1945 and Greek art again in 1946. Other art societies, all homeless, were allowed the use of certain galleries whenever possible and the Academy can claim to have kept its doors wide open throughout the period of the war.

Perhaps the greatest triumph was to have continued the series of Summer Exhibitions, dating from 1769, without a break. With so many artists on war service, it is understandable that the number of submissions fell but most surprising that the total in any one year was never less than five and a half thousand. In 1944 and 1945, members were allowed to send in seven works and non-members four but the figures reverted to the usual six and three in 1946. Galleries IV to VII were unfit for use from 1941 to 1943 inclusive but as many works as possible were shown in the other rooms. The attendances slumped to below 50,000 in 1940 and 1941 but reached almost 150,000 again from 1943 and over 200,000 in 1945. With all the major permanent collections closed, the public was starved of art and, after an initial period of hibernation, was willing to face even flying-bombs to visit the Academy's exhibitions. Union Jacks were raised along the Piccadilly frontage of Burlington House during the exhibition in 1944 (and indeed for each major exhibition subsequently) and this reflected the determination of all concerned to keep spirits high. The Academy's influence also extended into the provinces as, for several years from 1942, the newly formed Council for the Encouragement of Music and the Arts (known as CEMA and later to become the Arts Council of Great Britain) ran a series of touring exhibitions of a selection of works from each Summer Exhibition.

It was nevertheless a period of austerity as well as of danger and initiative. Even picture frames and tubes of paint were in short supply. Neither the Dinner nor the Soirée was held throughout the war. *The Royal Academy Illustrated* could not be published after 1940 owing chiefly to the scarcity of suitable paper and, unimportant as it may now seem, both top-hats and tail-coats disappeared as the accepted dress of the majority for Private View Days. The exhibits, perhaps rightly, provided the only colour during these grim years. Occasionally there emerged a 'picture of the year', such as *Pauline in the Yellow Dress*[1] by James Gunn in 1944, but the exhibitions are best remembered for their unobtrusive but consistent standards of craftsmanship. Living from hour to hour was beset with more excitements, frequently terrible and shocking, than were required. Most artists seemed instinctively to shun the sensational and, instead, to work steadily and purposefully on more normal subjects. This is far from saying that they were not affected by the horrors of war but rather that they turned to their art as a means of maintaining sanity in a mad world. Some of course recorded events and personalities of the time and others worked on camouflage but they were almost as few in number as the Battle of Britain pilots. The majority of artists had to set aside their profession and channel their minds in other directions. The Academy Schools closed down at the end of the summer term in 1940. No lectures and none of the prize competitions were held until after the cessation of hostilities. Owing to damage to their own buildings, the Governors of Dulwich College were given permission to hold their meetings in the Council Room at Burlington House and this practice still continues.

The succession of Officers of the Academy proceeded as usual. Sydney Lee resigned as Treasurer in 1940 and was replaced by Sir Edwin Cooper (Plate 71) but he died two years later and E. Vincent Harris was then elected. Sir Walter Russell retired from the Keepership in 1942 and, although the Schools were not then in operation, Gerald Kelly took on the post temporarily and without salary. It was agreed that the minimum number of Associates should be raised from thirty to forty but, in 1946 when there were discussions on enlarging their role in the Academy's affairs, this was modified to there being 'not less than thirty and not more than thirty-five'.[2] Draughtsmen were included in the membership from 1942 and Edward Bawden was the first, admitted in 1946. In 1943 a painter candidate for Associateship, (Sir) William Coldstream, was duly elected but asked that his name be removed. He had accepted nomination three years earlier but, on reconsidering the matter, felt that his election was inappropriate as he had never exhibited at the Academy.

The financial situation brought about by the war was quite serious and, during the years 1940 to 1943, the Pilgrim Trust came to the Academy's aid with grants totalling £8,000. The position was in fact to become much more acute before very long but all hopes at the time were pinned on a return to normal conditions after hostilities had ceased. The devastation in London had become enormous and in 1941, under the chairmanship of Sir Edwin Lutyens, the Royal Academy Planning Committee was formed 'to draw attention to the advantages that may be obtained by replanning on imaginative lines, and to initiate a long-term policy of public benefit'.[3] Illustrated booklets were issued in 1942 and 1944, entitled *London Replanned* and *Road, Rail and River in London*, and they at least stirred up some public awareness of the problems of rebuilding which had to be faced.

Unfortunately Lutyens, who had been ill for a long period in 1943, died on the following New Year's Day before any of this work could be undertaken but the ground had been prepared. The election for a new President took place on 14 March and, at the first ballot, seventeen votes were cast for A. J. Munnings, eight for Augustus John, three for Gerald Kelly, two each for Philip Connard and Harold Knight, and one each for Sir William Reid Dick (Plate 60), Meredith Frampton, Dame Laura Knight and Sir Giles Gilbert Scott. At the second ballot, Munnings beat John by twenty-four votes to seventeen and he was knighted in June that year.

Sir Alfred James Munnings (Plate 75) had been born in 1878 in East Anglia and, from 1920, lived at Dedham in the heart of the Constable country. From his early youth, he had painted landscapes with gypsies, cattle and ponies and, from the days of the 1914–18 War, he had more and more chosen horses and their surroundings as his favourite subjects. He scarcely ever missed an important race meeting, though he never placed bets, and eventually he had a studio provided for him at Newmarket. Despite the loss of the sight of his right eye by an unfortunate accident at the age of twenty-one, he was the keenest observer of the effects of light. He was a born countryman, addicted to pepper-and-salt suits, and notoriously forthright in his speech – the very opposite of Sir William Llewellyn. He was bluff and honest, often to the extent of causing embarrassment, and prone to wave his arms wildly to emphasize a point of argument. He saw no place in art for abstractions and 'isms' and had a very low opinion of their adherents.

'A. J.', as he was so often known, became President at a time when the financial tide was beginning to turn temporarily in the Academy's favour. Germany surrendered in May 1945 and that year brought over 200,000 people to the Summer Exhibition. Arrangements were made for the Painting and Sculpture Schools to reopen in 1946, with Philip Connard as Keeper, and there was talk of resuming the large Loan Exhibitions. A. E. Richardson became Professor of Architecture (the first revival of this post since 1911) and also Director of the Architecture School which commenced, in 1947, a new but comparatively short-lived era as a postgraduate course of one year's duration. Marshall Sisson was appointed Master, and at the same time Surveyor of the Royal Academy, both in the place of C. de Gruchy who had recently died. Meanwhile the sums available in certain trust funds had been mounting up and several new ones had been presented, the largest being the Alma-Tadema Fund of some £37,000. The value of money had, however, decreased enormously and this was to bring great difficulties in the general runnng of the institution.

The problem was held at bay for a time by the tremendous success of the first post-war Loan Exhibition which took place in the winter of 1946–47 and was entitled *The King's Pictures*. Over five hundred paintings were assembled from the various Royal Palaces and they included masterpieces from the collection of Charles I, Dutch and Venetian pictures acquired by George III and George IV, early Italian works collected by the Prince Consort in the nineteenth century and an unrivalled series of portraits by Holbein, Van Dyck, Reynolds, Gainsborough, Lawrence and others. Such an exhibition would have been bound to attract a large public at any time but, coming as it did immediately after the deprivations of war, people flocked to it and the total number of admissions exceeded 366,000.

The pre-war project for an exhibition of Indian art materialized in 1947–48 although India and Pakistan had by then become separate countries. It was a show rich in sculpture, paintings and textiles but the costs of mounting it were extremely heavy and, with only a modest attendance of about 118,000 visitors, it resulted in a serious financial loss. Unfortunately a dispute arose between the two countries concerning the ultimate disposal of certain of the exhibits and, when it was finally resolved about eighteen months later, some necklaces and other items, originally found in the North West of the continent but for many years housed at New Delhi, were cut in two and shared. The result was not quite so bad as the effect of Solomon's judgment as each half could still be shown against a mirror to produce a complete impression but it was sad to witness.

There were also further arguments between the Tate Gallery and the Royal Academy over purchases under the terms of the Chantrey Bequest but this situation was improved following the display of the whole collection at the Academy in 1949. Many of the works had not been on view for a long time and some of the pictures evoked nostalgic memories particularly for the older generation. The President, Sir Alfred Munnings, was a great champion of this show and he received considerable support for his strongly held views on modern art. There was much talk at one stage of a separate Chantrey Gallery under the control of the Academy Council but nothing came of it. The exhibition gave both sides ample opportunity to place their views before the public and, while still disagreeing over the merits of the collection as a whole, a serious attempt was made to obviate differences of opinion in the future. The Tate Gallery was granted equal representation with the Academy on the recommending committees, three members from each institution, and works were not to be purchased unless the Tate Trustees gave an assurance that they would be acceptable.

In 1948 the Rt Hon. Winston S. Churchill was appointed Honorary Academician Extraordinary by the unanimous vote of the General Assembly. This was the first time in the Academy's history that there had been such a title and it may well be that it will never be repeated. Churchill had been an enthusiastic and accomplished amateur painter (Plate 72) for over thirty years and had first had his works shown in the Royal Academy Summer Exhibition in 1947. They were sent in under the pseudonym of 'David Winter' and it was not till they had been duly approved by the Selection Committee that Munnings, who had been entrusted with the secret and could hardly contain himself, waved his arms and exploded, 'Good job you passed them – they're Churchill's.' Thereafter the great statesman's pictures were represented in the Summer Exhibition every year until his death in 1965 and a retrospective exhibition of his works was held in the Diploma Galleries in 1959.

The Royal Academy Illustrated commenced publication again in 1948 and from that date has been completely under the Academy's direction. John Merton exhibited his triple portrait *Mrs Daphne Wall*[4] that year and it created quite a sensation. The picture was at first hung in the Small South Room but, owing to the crowds always around it, was moved on to an easel in Gallery III where it could be seen more easily. It is significant that the attendance at this exhibition reached almost 240,000. The Librarian, E. E. V. Wright, retired in December and was replaced by the author, Sidney C. Hutchison (Plates 74 and 83), who had been on the general staff since 1929. Philip Connard gave up the Keepership at midsummer 1949 and this post was taken over by Henry Rushbury (Plate 60).

An important change in the constitution took place that year when it was decided that two Associates be appointed to the Council each year 'from those who have been Members for at least three years. . . .'[5] It was anticipated that the Academy 'would benefit both by their new ideas and suggestions, and by an increase of understanding and unity among the Members'.[6] The former certainly proved to be so, not least in the selection and hanging of the following year's Summer Exhibition, and the Associates' influence was soon to become even more marked.

Sir Alfred Munnings was one of 'the boys of the Old Brigade' and indeed he secretly contrived to get the band to play this song at the

Academy Dinner in 1949. This was the first time since before the war for the function to be held, though the Soirées had been resumed in 1947. Everyone stood up and joined in the refrain and it was with such a background that he struck his last blow as President. In his main speech he criticized the work of, among others, Matisse and this brought forth some good-humoured protests from fellow-members. 'I am President,' he cried, 'and I have the right to speak. I shall not be here next year, thank God.'[7] He had in fact previously announced that he intended to resign from the post and he did not stand for re-election at the end of the year. The voting took place on 8 December when, at the first ballot, eleven votes were cast for R. G. Brundrit, ten for Sir Gerald Kelly, five for Charles Wheeler, two each for Stephen Gooden (Plate 71) and Henry Rushbury, and one each for Stanley Anderson (Plate 60), E. Vincent Harris, Edward Maufe, A. E. Richardson and Sir G. G. Scott. Wheeler was eliminated in the second ballot and Sir Gerald Kelly emerged as the victor over R. G. Brundrit by twenty votes to thirteen.

Kelly (Plates 60, 68 and 75), one of the best known portrait painters of his time, was then seventy but still full of drive. In temperament and methods he was not unlike the famous actor-managers of his youth. He had many friends and acquaintances in high places and, through a number of successful broadcasts on television, he became very popular with a large public. His conversation and speeches were always entertaining and his personal style in letter-writing most persuasive. He gathered around him, from outside the Academy, important groups of advisers on finance and the assembling of Loan Exhibitions but, in judgments on art, he would accept no interference with his own intuition and experience.

His Presidency was chiefly noteworthy for a succession of very attractive Loan Exhibitions, greatly enhanced by his personal choice of many of the pictures. *Holbein and other Masters, L'Ecole de Paris, 1900–50, The First Hundred Years of the Royal Academy, Dutch Pictures, Flemish Art* and *European Masters of the Eighteenth Century* were held in the main galleries but he also initiated a series of exhibitions in the Diploma Galleries. These rooms, damaged in the war, had been out of action ever since but no major repairs could be undertaken without a government licence and this had not been forthcoming. Art galleries were understandably low in the list of priorities but at last, in 1951, the rooms were made weatherproof again and redecorated. A lift from the main entrance hall was installed and the *Leonardo da Vinci Quincentenary*

Exhibition opened in March 1952. In content it covered the great range of the artist's creative genius and it attracted a much wider public than usual. Indeed the exhibition had to be extended till September to accommodate, in such a relatively confined display area, a total of more than 200,000 visitors. It showed a handsome profit out of which the Academy was able to pay for much needed improvements in the building's heating system. Air-conditioning was also considered but had to be turned down on the grounds of expense. This exhibition was followed immediately by others including a retrospective display of the work of Sir Frank Brangwyn, the first time that a living artist had had the honour of a one-man show at the Academy. The new policy meant that these galleries could not be employed for their original purpose of housing the Diploma Works permanently but it was an economic necessity at the time to earn some money from their use and the post-war demand for good exhibitions was still at its height.

In 1951, as an economy, neither music nor refreshments were provided at the Soirée and this sparked off an argument on the Council's conduct of affairs and on its constitutional powers. The Academy's Laws are not sufficiently categorical in the matter and have more than once led to misunderstandings. One says that 'the government of the Society is vested in a President and Council, and the General Assembly of Academicians'[8] and another that 'the Council ... shall have the entire direction and management of all the business of the Society'.[9] On this particular occasion, it was at least agreed 'that the General Assembly should be fully consulted on important matters, in particular with regard to the finances of the Academy'.[10] Expenses were steadily increasing and the value of money depreciating. In 1952 the Dinner was not held owing to the death of George VI but, even so, investments to the value of £10,000 had to be sold in order to reduce the overdraft at the bank.

The Summer Exhibitions continued as usual, with average attendances of about 150,000, and the following pictures attracted considerable attention: *The Little Concert*[11] by Augustus John and a *Resurrection* series[12] by Stanley Spencer in 1950, *The Revolt in the Desert*[13] by William Roberts in 1952, a fine portrait *Ralph Vaughan Williams*[14] by Sir Gerald Kelly and a portrait group *The Teaching Staff of the Painting School, Royal College of Art*[15] by Rodrigo Moynihan, both in 1953, and *Girl in a blue Armchair*[16] by Edward Le Bas and *Queen of the Sea*[17] by Richard Eurich in 1954

The Chantrey purchases throughout the period 1939–54 included

Pelicans by Philip Connard, *The Surrey Canal, Camberwell* by Algernon Newton, *Blue Cineraria* by Augustus John, *The Doctor* by James Pryde, *The Artist's Mother* by Harold Gilman, a statue *Aphrodite* by Charles Wheeler, *Hearts are Trumps* by Millais, *The Resurrection* by Stanley Spencer, *Signals* by Edward Wadsworth, *Mr Hollingbery's Canary* by Ruskin Spear, *The Pool of London* by André Derain, *Nude: Fitzroy Street, No. 1* by Matthew Smith and *Frying Tonight* by James Fitton.[18] The Leighton Fund had commissioned Gilbert Ledward (Plates 60 and 71) to design a fountain for the centre of Sloane Square and this project was completed in 1953.

Sandra Blow, Anthony Caro and Bryan Kneale were among the new students and Maurice Lambert took over as Master of the Sculpture School in 1950. A Students' Society was formed in 1949 and it was followed, in 1951, by the foundation of the Reynolds Club, an association of past students of the Royal Academy Schools. Both are still active. In 1954 it was agreed that the period of attendance in the Schools to enable a student to qualify for the Royal Academy Schools' Certificate should be reduced from five years to four. In the previous year, a bequest from the widow of the late Sydney Lee was received and the income from the resulting fund has since been used for the library. It has proved to be of immense value in providing new books and better services.

The Secretary of the Academy, Sir Walter Lamb, retired at the end of 1951, after having held the post since 1913, and he was replaced by Humphrey Brooke (Plate 81). There had thus so far been only three laymen in this particular Office from the appointment of Frederick Eaton in 1873. Two other Officers had to give up in December 1954, on reaching the age limit of seventy-five. One was the President himself, Sir Gerald Kelly, and the other was the Treasurer, E. Vincent Harris, the latter being succeeded by another architect, Sir Edward Maufe, pronounced 'Morfe'. There is a tale that this extremely polite gentleman, on arriving a little late for a dinner, took his vacant chair quietly and, as he did so, turned to his neighbour and said, 'Good evening, I'm Maufe.' The reply, with raised eyebrows, was 'But you've only just arrived.'

The election for a new President took place on 7 December 1954 and, in the first ballot, twenty-one votes were cast for A. E. Richardson, nine each for Charles Wheeler and James Fitton, two for Henry Lamb and one each for Stephen Gooden, Edward Le Bas, W. T. Monnington, Rodrigo Moynihan and A. R. Middleton Todd. In the second ballot,

Richardson received a clear majority of twenty-eight votes against ten for Fitton and eight for Wheeler. Accordingly, an architect once again took up this important position.

18
TOWARDS THE BICENTENARY
1955–1968

Albert Edward Richardson (Plate 75) was probably the most genial President of all time. Even his heart-felt denunciations of modern architecture were delivered good-humouredly, with such epithets as 'bungalitis'[1] for the bungalows and semi-detached houses of suburbia and 'breeding-boxes'[2] for the later developments of multi-storeyed blocks of flats. He looked upon the majority of modern buildings as little more than 'maggotries full of pale and squirming people'.[3] His ideal was to recreate the style of living of the well-to-do classes of Georgian times and his own home at Ampthill, lit with candles and oil-lamps, was overflowing with furniture, books, costumes and *objets d'art* of the period. As an architect, his work was refined and, as Professor of Architecture at London University for over twenty-five years and later at the Royal Academy, he exhorted his students to design on the grand scale in a scholarly manner. His lectures, all impromptu and illustrated with freehand drawings, were a delight. He was, however, already seventy-four years of age when elected to the Presidency and he should by the Laws have had only one year in office. With the permission of the Queen, Elizabeth II, who had succeeded her father on the throne in 1952, Richardson was nevertheless re-elected for a second year and he was knighted in January 1956.

Even with this extension he had little time to effect any marked changes and, indeed, showed no desire to do so except to re-emphasize the Academy's role as a training ground for young artists. Her Majesty inspected the Schools and the Library on the afternoon of 24 March 1955, the first such visit by the Sovereign in all the years of the Academy's existence and, in 1956, Sir Albert was instrumental in promoting the first of the services which have been held annually since then, on non-members' Varnishing Day, in St James's Parish Church, Piccadilly. In the winter following his election, two Loan Exhibitions

175

took place almost simultaneously in the main galleries. One was *Portuguese Art, 800–1800* and was undoubtedly the most comprehensive display of the arts of that country ever to have been assembled under one roof. The famous Belem Monstrance[4] was included, also the great polyptych of *The Veneration of St Vincent*[5] by Nuno Gonçalves, the State Coach of Queen Maria Francisca[6] and a large gathering of carvings, tiles, furniture, carpets, silver and other paintings. The other exhibition was on a subject very dear to the President – *English Taste in the Eighteenth Century* – and it contained a magnificent collection of treasures illustrating the changing fashions of taste from the Baroque of William Kent to the Neo-Classic of Robert Adam.

The Summer Exhibition of 1955 was extremely successful, owing mostly to the inclusion of the portrait *Her Majesty the Queen* (Plate 65) by Pietro Annigoni. The painting, which received immense publicity, had a great popular appeal and the attendances throughout the fifteen weeks reached a total of almost 300,000, the highest for over fifty years. The sales figures of 740 works for £31,212 surpassed all previous records and A. R. Thomson painted that year a group portrait of the Selection Committee[7] at their task of examining the vast quantity of works submitted.

The arrangements between the Royal Academy and the Tate Gallery for the purchase and display of Chantrey Bequest works were still unsatisfactory and, in 1956, the effective power of veto, which had been held by the Tate Board for some years, was amended as being contrary to Sir Francis Chantrey's will. Thereafter the Tate Gallery Trustees were to receive only those works which they were willing to accept and any other purchases were to be offered by the Academy on loan elsewhere. This agreement in fact followed the Academy's decision to purchase a bronze statue *Margot Fonteyn* by Maurice Lambert despite its refusal by the Tate. The statue has ever since been on loan to the Royal Ballet School at White Lodge, Richmond.

Just before the President's term of office came to an end, the Academy opened a comprehensive exhibition of British portraits and this marked very fittingly the centenary of the National Portrait Gallery. The election for a new President took place on 11 December 1956, when Charles Wheeler, with twenty-four votes, emerged with a clear majority over James Fitton with thirteen, W. T. Monnington with four and Henry Lamb, Edward Le Bas and Rodrigo Moynihan with one each. This then was the first time that a sculptor had attained the highest office in the establishment though Lord Leighton, basically a painter and elected to the Academy as such, had produced several statues of importance. Wheeler (Plate 75), born in the village of Codsall in Staffordshire in 1892, had been trained first at the art school at Wolverhampton and then under Professor Edouard Lanteri, whom he greatly admired, at the Royal College of Art. His whole working life had been spent in London and his work can be seen on many public buildings, for example the Bank of England.

He was re-elected President for ten successive years and, during this time, he attended and frequently spoke at many City Livery dinners and elsewhere, not only as the head of the Academy but as the representative of fine tradition in the arts generally. Within the institution he was continually advocating tolerance and a broadminded approach to all forms of design and there was considerable evidence of this in the Summer Exhibitions during this period. Whereas previously most of the experimental work had been placed in Gallery VIII, it was now spread throughout the galleries and was often given the traditional positions of honour. This certainly enlivened the walls but some critics complained that there followed inevitably a certain lack of serenity in favour of 'a new look' which at times brought restlessness in its wake. Exhibition attendances in galleries throughout the country fell during this period and the Academy's regular public similarly diminished in numbers, averaging about 100,000 and, in 1966, falling to just under 60,000. Sales figures, however, increased and in 1963 reached a record of 769 works for £49,089.

Strained finances haunted the Academy throughout this decade, mainly due to increased costs in all activities and especially because of the very heavy expenses involved in maintaining so venerable a building, in running the Schools and in organizing exhibitions. In 1957 a handling fee of ten shillings per person had to be levied on all non-members submitting work for the Summer Exhibitions, the first time that such a charge had had to be made, and this was raised to £1 in 1962 and to £1 10s 0d in 1966. Members at the same time made voluntary contributions but a proposal for annual subscriptions was defeated. Admission rates for the public also had to be increased and this no doubt adversely affected attendances to some extent. The Soirées were quite frequently omitted and the last was held in 1964. Other economies were made but, despite additional revenue from the sale of publications and the proceeds of hiring catalogues from 1956 onwards, the financial situation rapidly deteriorated and something drastic had to be done. One or two Loan Exhibitions made handsome profits but the necessity for some regular increase in income was only too apparent. Over £100,000 had had to be spent on the building in the ten years ending in 1958 and, even so, this left much undone which should have been done.

By 1962, following a substantial loss on the *Primitives to Picasso* exhibition, the overdraft at the bank had risen considerably and it seemed certain that it would become even greater year by year. The Academy's work was in danger of being brought to a standstill or at least severely curtailed by lack of funds and, if financial independence were to be maintained, it seemed that some major possession would have to be sacrificed. The decision was then made, most reluctantly, to sell the cartoon *The Virgin and Child with St Anne and St John the Baptist* by Leonardo da Vinci (Plate 79).[8] Legally, of course, the Academy could dispose of any of its assets for the purposes of furthering the objects of its foundation but, as there were no records of the acquisition of this particular work of art, there were likewise no personal associations to be taken into consideration. The cartoon appears in a drawing made by a student, E. F. Burney, in 1779 of the Antique School at Somerset House (Plate 27) and may well have been purchased originally for study in the Schools. There is no record of it in the very early minutes of the institution until 1792 and its rarity was presumably not then appreciated.

The decision having been made in Council and General Assembly, the next consideration was how best to dispose of the cartoon bearing in mind the members' desire that it might be retained in Great Britain. Valuations from three leading firms were then obtained which averaged about £750,000 and it was offered to the Government in a letter dated 20 February 1962 to the Prime Minister, Harold Macmillan, ending as follows:

> ... The Members have also decided that in spite of the reasons which compel a sale, and their obvious duty only to part with the Cartoon on substantial terms, yet some gesture should be made to meet Her Majesty's Government's known policy that works of art in the highest category, should not be dispersed. I am accordingly authorised to let you know that if the Government wishes to acquire the Cartoon for the nation a price of £675,000, which is substantially below what is expected at auction, would be accepted.
>
> Charles Wheeler,
> President.[9]

65 'Her Majesty The Queen' by Pietro Annigoni. Exhibited at Royal Academy, 1955
(Worshipful Company of Fishmongers, London)

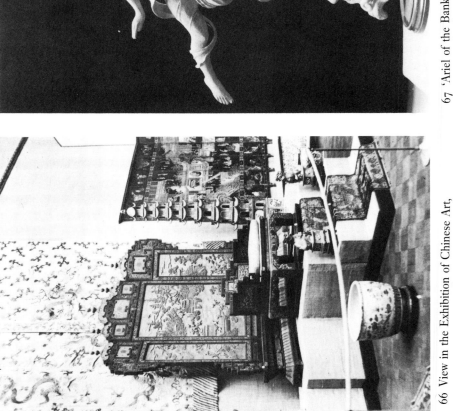

67 'Ariel of the Bank' by Sir Charles Wheeler. Diploma Work, 1940

66 View in the Exhibition of Chinese Art, 1935–6

69 'Coventry Cathedral: the Nave looking towards the Altar' by Sir Basil Spence, 1953.
Diploma Work

68 'Sir Gerald Kelly', President of the Royal Academy,
by Maurice Lambert, 1954

70 'Their Majesties Return from Ascot, 1925' by Sir Alfred
Munnings. Chantrey Bequest Purchase, 1937 (*Tate Gallery, London*)

71 'The Royal Academy Selection and Hanging Committees, 1938', by F. W. Elwell.
Left to right: F. W. Elwell, Sir Edwin Cooper, Sir William Russell Flint, Sydney Lee,
Sir William Llewellyn (President), Sir Walter Lamb (Secretary). Oliver Hall, George
Harcourt, Sir Walter Russell, James Woodford, Stephen Gooden, Gilbert Ledward,
S. J. Lamorna Birch and Harold Knight

72 'Cap d'Ail, Alpes Maritimes' by Sir Winston Churchill, 1952.
Diploma Work

73 'French People talking and drinking' by Cosmo Clark, 1953.
Diploma Work.

74 The Royal Academy Library, 1953, with the Librarian, Sidney C. Hutchison, standing at left

75 Sir Alfred Munnings, Sir Gerald Kelly and Sir Albert Richardson (all Past-Presidents) toasting the new President, Sir Charles Wheeler, 11 December 1956

76 Selection of Silver and Relics belonging to the Royal Academy,
in the Exhibition of Treasures of the Royal Academy, 1963

77 View in the Exhibition of Treasures of the Royal Academy, 1963.
The Sitters' Chair of Sir Joshua Reynolds is shown in the foreground

78 'Station Approach' by L. S. Lowry, 1962. Diploma Work

The offer was declined with an expression of appreciation of the Academy's gesture and subsequently the opportunity of further time for consideration was also not accepted. Arrangements were then made for the cartoon to be sold at auction in June. The announcement of this on 10 March created a sensation and there was immediately a suggestion in *The Times* that a national appeal might be launched for the purchase of the cartoon. This quickly gained support and, at the request of the Prime Minister, the auction was postponed to enable such an appeal to be made by the National Art-Collections Fund in order that the work could be acquired for the National Gallery. His letter said that 'it would be important to know at what price the Academy would be willing to sell the Cartoon in these circumstances'[10] and, in view of new evidence which had come to light since the original estimates had been made, this was a most difficult question to settle. It now seemed definite that the cartoon would fetch at least one million pounds at auction and in due course it was revealed that two American galleries had made initial bids of one and a half million pounds and that a third gallery had funds of two and a half million pounds available for the purchase. Conversely, the National Art-Collections Fund hoped that the Academy would still be willing to part with the cartoon at the figure originally suggested to the Government. Counsel's opinion, broadly speaking, was that the cartoon could be sold at a price less than its estimated market value if such action would itself be 'promoting the Arts of Design' and 'would increase public goodwill towards the Academy' so that 'such goodwill facilitates and promotes the activities of the Academy'.[11] It added that the sum decided upon should not 'give grounds for a contention that it has been fixed in an arbitrary and ill-considered manner, without reference to the furtherance of the Academy's object and to its own financial needs for that purpose' and suggested that 'such a contention could not seriously be raised in relation to a figure of £800,000 or upwards ... as the sale price to the nation'.[12] The figure was then fixed at this hypothetical minimum though this was to cause much misunderstanding. On the other hand, if the original valuations had proved to be too high, the Government and the National Art-Collections Fund would surely have expected a comparable reduction.

The cartoon was taken to the National Gallery for display and the appeal opened on 30 March. In the event of its failure, it was agreed that the auction should take place in the autumn. For a time all went well but, except for one or two large contributions initially, the amounts received in the ensuing weeks were modest and soon the Academy, which had been praised in the press in March with such headings as 'Three cheers for the self-help Academy', was being accused of avarice and of having deliberately concealed the cartoon for years. The first charge was quite without foundation and the second was ridiculous. The cartoon had been on permanent public view free of charge in the Diploma Galleries from the 1870s to 1939 and, since the Second World War, besides being available to anyone who would take the trouble of asking to see it, had been in several major exhibitions at the Academy. Elaborate security precautions were mounted at the National Gallery for its display but, even so, a crazy trouble-maker hurled an ink-bottle which penetrated the perspex shield of the cartoon. Mercifully, no major damage was caused.

In July, the possibility of reducing the price and extending the period of the appeal were both considered by the General Assembly but rejected on the grounds that 'the Academy had already made too substantial a concession and that the prospect of earning goodwill from this or any other gesture was already illusory'.[13] On the last day of the appeal, 31 July, the fund stood at just over £400,000 and, with an added contribution of £350,000 from the Government, the National Art-Collections Fund undertook to make up the necessary balance. Thus the nation obtained the picture and the Academy the much-needed cash but the final phase of the appeal had been marred by a variety of misrepresentations over the issues involved. True, the errors of fact were withdrawn one by one but, as usual, the apologies were given less publicity than the original damaging statements. As the controversy died down, the Academy emerged with its finances strengthened but with little recognition of its sacrifice in agreeing to put off the auction and to accept substantially less than the full market price for the cartoon. Old antagonisms had been stirred up and the unnecessary battle had produced more wounds than medals.

The Academy's first action was to pay off its overdraft at the bank and then to invest the remainder of the purchase price. The Entrance Hall and main staircase were extensively refurbished in the winter of 1962–63 under the direction of Raymond Erith and the paintings by Sebastiano Ricci, William Kent, Benjamin West and Angelica Kauffmann were all cleaned. Two handsome chandeliers were purchased and, less spectacular though more necessary, considerable renovations were carried out to the stonework of the exterior of the building. New oil-fired boilers were installed shortly afterwards and various repairs and redecorations were undertaken in the galleries and elsewhere. All this maintenance work was long overdue but had had to be postponed again and again through lack of funds.

The Academy's work had of course continued throughout the lean period despite the difficulties and, if every penny of expenditure had not been taken into consideration, the debt by 1962 would have been even greater. Twenty Loan Exhibitions were held during the first part of Sir Charles Wheeler's Presidency (he was knighted in 1958) and fifteen more before he retired at the end of 1966. They included one-man shows of the work of Sir Gerald Kelly, Sir Matthew Smith, Sir William Russell Flint, Dame Laura Knight and Pierre Bonnard, reappraisals of Wilkie, Landseer, Lawrence and Allan Ramsay, private collections such as those of Paul Oppé, Edward Le Bas, E. Assheton-Bennett and Mr and Mrs Paul Mellon, and large assemblies such as *The Age of Louis XIV, Italian Art and Britain, The Age of Charles II, Primitives to Picasso* and *Goya and his times*. The Goya exhibition, in 1963–64, was the most popular and the vast expenditure on it, fully justified by the results, was only made possible by having available by then the income from the Leonardo Endowment. Such a financial risk could not have been undertaken without this additional revenue. There was a total attendance of almost 350,000 visitors and a handsome profit but no charge was then made against such accounts for the general staffing and services of the institution.

Goya is represented very inadequately in public collections in this country and there had never before arisen the opportunity of a large-scale exhibition of his work in London. Loans were collected together from thirteen different countries but naturally the most important contribution came from Spain. The Prado lent about a dozen paintings including the famous *Maja Vestida*[14] and *Maja Desnuda*[15] and the project had the full support of the Spanish Government. At their request, very special security arrangements were made, including surveillance by their own plain-clothes guards, and the works were transported from Madrid under conditions of strict secrecy. They in fact travelled in special railway vans attached to a train used for bringing tomatoes to the London market as this was the fastest service.

The exhibition of Russian painting in 1959 could have been equally successful but, unfortunately, its content was disappointing. There was a fine group of icons and a strong representation of the work of artists of the last thirty years but examples of the art of the eighteenth and nineteenth centuries were sparse and, for the most part, small in size. The project had received immense publicity as the first such arrangement for an exchange of exhibitions between the USSR and Great Britain but the Soviet authorities could not be persuaded to send more pictures. The attendance at first was high but dwindled swiftly when the limitations of the display became known.

Sixty-two paintings by Sir Winston Churchill were shown in the Diploma Galleries from March to August that year and drew large crowds of people. The majority of course were admirers of the great statesman in whatever activity he might have undertaken and the few critics who were a little too ready to doubt his prowess as an artist had to admit that he had a deep feeling for colour and form. 'There are things here,' said a well-known painter, 'that only an amateur would let out of his studio but there are at least a dozen of these pictures which any professional would have given his ears to have painted'.[16] This was no doubt very true.

In 1961 one volume of *The Book of Kells*, on view outside Ireland for the first time in its history, formed the chief feature of an exhibition in aid of Trinity College, Dublin, and, in 1963, the Academy showed some of its own possessions under the title *Treasures of the Royal Academy* (Plates 76 and 77). Both shows were well received. In 1966 a major exhibition of the work of Rembrandt was planned but had to be abandoned, not least owing to the understandable reluctance of certain owners and custodians abroad to lend works of the highest importance. Other deterrents were the enormous sum which would have been involved in insurance premiums and a warning that the world insurance market would be unlikely to cover so great a risk under one roof. Transport costs too would have been even heavier than usual and, sadly, it was agreed that no such temporary exhibition could possibly be made to pay its way unless it contained absolutely world-famous masterpieces from places difficult of access to the general public.

For some years the Academy had had counsel on its programme of Loan Exhibitions from an advisory committee comprising Sir Kenneth (Lord) Clark, (Sir) Ellis Waterhouse, (Sir) Trenchard Cox, (Sir) Francis Watson and Sir Anthony Blunt (whose knighthood was later rescinded). They dined periodically with the President (together with the Secretary and the author who, since 1955, had dealt with the detailed correspondence involved with such projects) and their expertise was of inestimable value. This committee was enlarged in 1965 to some twenty people, including six members of the Academy, and, although each newcomer to it brought added specialized knowledge, the number was too unwieldy to be really effective.

Meanwhile the day-to-day business of the Academy had its ups and downs whilst always in the background there was the constant battle against rising costs. Sir Edward Maufe, who had to give up the Treasurership on becoming a Senior Academician in 1958, generously paid personally for the private rooms on the first floor of Burlington House to be redecorated. He was replaced by Louis de Soissons who died suddenly in 1962, to be followed in office by Sir Basil Spence (Plate 81), Sir James Gunn and Donald McMorran in quick succession and then by Marshall Sisson (Plate 81). Sir Henry Rushbury retired as Keeper in 1964 and his place was taken by Peter Greenham. The Registrarship also changed hands that year when, after fifty-two years on the staff, C. W. Tanner was succeeded by his son, K. J. Tanner. Peter Foster was appointed Surveyor in 1966.

Rodrigo Moynihan gave up his membership in 1957 on moving to France but he was reinstated in 1979. F. E. McWilliam, elected in 1959, opted out in 1963 from both the Academy and the London Group as he did not intend in future to take part in large mixed exhibitions. Both these resignations were regrettable but more disturbing were the circumstances of Keith Vaughan and Edward Burra declining membership after election though both had previously consented to be candidates. There have of course always been artists who preferred not to belong to societies and, although this tendency has developed to some extent in recent years, it is probably now no greater in proportion to the total number of people involved than ever it was. As the number of artists has increased, so have more societies come into being and the lone wolves are still in the minority. The one comparatively new feature is that of working for dealers under contract.

It has been mentioned before that, although Associates were elected as early as 1770, they had little power within the Academy until recent years. In 1949 it was agreed that two should serve on the Council and, in 1965, this number was increased to three but, far more important, all Associates were then given the right to attend General Assemblies although, until 1967, they were not entitled to vote on resolutions until three years after their election. The first such meeting was held in June 1965 when the point at issue was whether the Michelangelo tondo (Plate 37) should be allowed to leave the building on loan. The Council had already decided on such a course but there had been considerable opinion against it, from outside as well as within the Academy, culminating in a negative vote by the General Assembly of Academicians. This brought up once again the question of the Council's powers and, on legal advice, it was accepted that the General Assembly had no right of veto over them. The enlarged Assembly, that is with the Associates for the first time, was overwhelmingly in favour of the loan policy and, in 1966, the tondo was displayed at the Victoria and Albert Museum for a few weeks. The proposal that it be sent subsequently to Moscow, Leningrad and perhaps Amsterdam, was not proceeded with at the time as it was partly involved in the hope of reciprocal loans for the Rembrandt exhibition.

The E.A. Abbey Fund for mural painting had begun active work in 1950 and by 1960 there had been seven commissions. From this date onwards, the tempo increased considerably and seventeen more projects were completed in the following six years. The buildings decorated so far through this fund have included churches, hospitals, a theatre, civic halls and universities, and they are spread over a wide area from Brighton to Glenrothes and Weston-super-Mare to Kingston-upon-Hull. They range in date from the Russell Chantry in Lincoln Cathedral and the Chapter House Doorway of Manchester Cathedral to the new Charing Cross and Whittington Hospitals in London, Wolfson College at Cambridge and the operational headquarters of the Open University at Milton Keynes. The paintings vary in style from figurative to abstract, the criterion in each case being their suitability in all aspects of their setting. The Leighton Fund similarly paid for a mural painting, *An Artist's Progress*[17] by Gilbert Spencer, and this was installed in the Restaurant at the Royal Academy in 1959.

The Academy Schools during the period under review produced several students who quickly gained recognition in competition with their contemporaries when they set out on their own. Arnold Machin replaced Maurice Lambert as Master of the Sculpture School at the end of 1958 and Walter Woodington was appointed Curator in 1961. Also in that year, Sir Basil Spence took over the Professorship of Architecture on the retirement of Sir Albert Richardson. The Architecture School, which had been dormant since 1957, then reopened as an evening school with a panel of distinguished Visitors but even this failed to attract sufficient students of postgraduate status. It closed again in 1964 and, until 1967, annual series of lectures by eminent architects were organized by the Professor particularly for the painting and sculpture students. Spence's successor, E. Maxwell Fry, gave the lectures himself but, when interest in them dwindled, they were discontinued. Uli Nimptsch succeeded Arnold Machin as Master of the Sculpture School in the winter of 1966–67. Meanwhile major alterations in the general running of the Schools were the reduction of the normal course of study from four years to three years from 1960 onwards and the gradual progression towards postgraduate training. The curriculum at the same time was widened to include training in carving and in engraving, lithography and other graphic arts.

In November 1966, following the disastrous flooding in Italy which caused serious damage to many works of art, particularly in Florence, the Italian Art and Archives Rescue Fund was set up and held its meetings in the General Assembly Room. A donation of £1,000 was made from the Sydney Lee Fund and over £1,300 was contributed by Academy exhibitors.

Sir Charles Wheeler resigned the Presidency at the end of 1966 and, on 6 December, W. T. Monnington (Plate 81) was elected as his successor after one of the closest contests in the history of the Academy. At the first ballot, Carel Weight (Plate 81) obtained fifteen votes, Monnington fourteen, James Fitton thirteen and there were two votes for Peter Greenham and one each for Richard Eurich, Marshall Sisson and Ruskin Spear. At the second ballot, between the three with four or more votes, Fitton was narrowly eliminated and, finally, Monnington just beat Weight by twenty-five votes to twenty-three.

The new President, then aged sixty-four, had been an Associate since 1931 and an Academician since 1938, one of the youngest members in each class in recent times. In his youth he had won the coveted Rome Scholarship and, when only twenty-four, he had painted one of the historical scenes in St Stephen's Hall at the Houses of Parliament. He followed this with mural paintings in the Governor's Parlour of the Bank of England and, as has been said, he became the first Assistant Teacher of Painting in the Royal Academy Schools in 1931. During the Second World War he worked on camouflage and this undoubtedly strengthened his interest in a scientific approach to the arts. From then on his sympathies were drawn to geometric painting as seen in his huge ceiling decoration in the Council Chamber of the Civic Centre at Bristol (also commissioned through the E. A. Abbey Mural Painting Fund) and other post-war works. He enjoyed working with young people throughout his career and, in later years, his chairmanship of the Faculty of Painting of the British School at Rome was but one of his many commitments on various advisory committees. He was knighted in 1967.

It was obvious from the commencement of his Presidency that his taste was catholic and that there were no cobwebs in his thoughts. He took steps immediately to begin discussions with the Arts Council, the

Institute of Contemporary Arts and other bodies on matters of mutual concern. 'I do not believe,' he said in his speech at the Annual Dinner in 1967, 'that the Academy's function is to maintain a status quo or to further the acceptance of the acceptable. . . . Surely, any development in art derives from perception free from preconception.' This was the occasion on which, for the first time in the Academy's long history, a few distinguished ladies were invited to be present. Dame Laura Knight and other women members at last took their rightful places at table and the toast of the Royal Academy was proposed with superb wit by Baroness Asquith of Yarnbury.

In the autumn there was a retrospective exhibition of the work of John Nash and, overlapping it, one on André Derain which was organized by the Arts Council. The principal Winter Exhibition, from January to early March 1968, and on the theme of *France in the Eighteenth Century*, occupied all the main galleries. It was a splendid display, accompanied by a large, scholarly, illustrated catalogue, but, despite a good attendance, it resulted in a considerable financial loss.

By this time the arrangements for celebrating the Academy's Bicentenary were well under way. The author's first edition of this book, under the title *The History of the Royal Academy, 1768–1968*, was duly published in May and, as it transpired, he had a very busy time ahead, not only as Librarian and dealing with the administration of a special Bicentenary Exhibition planned for the following winter, but through soon being required to take on other duties. The Secretary, Humphrey Brooke, burdened with personal troubles for some time, resigned in mid-July and the author, Sidney C. Hutchison, who had been his deputy since 1965, was asked to take over as Acting Secretary and, following the necessary procedure required by the Laws for the appointment, was unanimously elected Secretary on 1 October.[18]

The Annual Dinner had taken place on Wednesday, 1 May, with HRH Princess Alexandra as the Guest of Honour, and the Summer Exhibition of 1968, the two hundredth in an unbroken series since 1769, was open to the public from 4 May until 4 August. Eight paintings from it, all modest in price and by non-members, were purchased through the General Fund as a bicentenary gesture and subsequently presented to the Towner Art Gallery at Eastbourne.[19] A buffet lunch was given to the exhibitors on non-members' Varnishing Day and this popular event has been continued ever since.

Obviously something had to be done about the Academy's financial situation which had worsened alarmingly in the previous few months.

As a first step the Financial Advisory Committee was reconstituted[20] and a proposal from Professor Carel Weight that a special committee should be set up 'to thrash out what the function of the Royal Academy in the future should be' led to the formation of a Policy Advisory Committee.[21] Neither of course could hope to solve the many problems overnight, if ever, yet the day-to-day business had to continue somehow.

In October, Gilbert Spencer, who by then was a Senior Academician, resigned from membership, as had his brother Stanley way back in 1935. His main reason appeared to be that his picture *Mrs Christopher Gardner*, which had been in the Summer Exhibition of 1962, could not be found when he came for it in 1968 (maybe because it had been collected years earlier as, indeed, it should have been). He also renewed long-standing grievances which he harboured concerning the E. A. Abbey Mural Painting Fund.[22] Both complaints were dubious. Nevertheless when, three years later, he asked to withdraw his resignation, he was reinstated. Yet again family history was repeating itself.

Archbishop Lord Fisher of Lambeth retired from the Chaplaincy of the Royal Academy, an office which he had held since 1939 when he was Bishop of London, and it was decided that he be replaced by the Very Revd W. P. Baddeley, Rector of St James's Church, Piccadilly. It is the Academy's parish church and, in that services connected with the institution's membership and activities had almost invariably been held there for many years, the choice was very fitting.

Peter Greenham, in his Keeper's Report for 1968,[23] neatly summarized the conditions for entry into the Schools and the qualifications obtainable, as follows:

> . . . anybody under the age of 25 can apply, though we can make exceptions to that age limit. Candidates who have the Dip. A.D. or a university degree are given the Royal Academy Schools Post Graduate Certificate at the end of three years if they satisfy a panel appointed by the Keeper; others are given the Royal Academy Schools Certificate; but the Department of Education and Science states that the Royal Academy Schools Certificate will not confer the 'qualified status' of a teacher unless it is supported by 5 'O' levels.

and he added:

> As for the policy of the School, it is to give the help of appropriate teachers to students of every inclination, whether abstract or figurative. But all probationers spend the first term drawing from life in the drawing

school, with a day a week in the second month on still-life or life-painting. There are also life models for second and third year students if they wish to use them, in the sculpture school. There is another life model and a head model between 4.30 and 6.30 four evenings a week. All students in their second year do one day a week, in rotation, at lithography, etching, wood-engraving or graphics under instructors; we are lucky to have Gertrude Hermes as one of them.

Earlier in the year it had been decided that in future (a) the admission of probationers and (b) the admission of students be settled by a committee under the Keeper but that their decisions be subject to the approval of the President and Council; that (c) the annual examinations and (d) the final examinations be conducted by a committee under the Keeper but that any failures should be submitted to the President and Council who should have the opportunity of seeing all works sent in; and that (e) the prize competitions should be judged by a committee under the Keeper but that their recommendations should be subject to the approval of the President and Council.[24] Thus a means was devised of enabling the teachers concerned, with their closer experience, to participate in the decisions while at the same time the Council were released from these time-consuming tasks without relinquishing their ultimate authority in such matters.

Some redecoration of the first-floor rooms of old Burlington House was undertaken during this same year and, even more necessary, a start was made in fixing new lead to the roofs of the main galleries, several of which had been leaking water whenever there was heavy rain or rapid thawing of snow. Almost a century had elapsed since they were built and time was taking its toll. Also the Restaurant was divided into two parts (one for the public and the other for the students) and, by modifying the Registry, additional access was made to it, direct from the Entrance Hall, through a new bar at the foot of its staircase from the galleries. Until then the Restaurant had always been in the hands of outside caterers but, henceforth, the Academy assumed full financial responsibility and retained executive control although, for some years to come, such a firm was still employed to provide and manage the service.[25]

The last exhibition within 1968, from 21 September, was a survey of the activities of the Bauhaus and it was highly successful. Sponsored and considerably subsidized by the Federal Republic of Germany, this was its first showing in a tour which included major cities in Holland,

France, the United States of America and Japan. Dr Walter Gropius, founder of the Bauhaus and an Honorary Member of the Academy, was present at the opening ceremonies and there were over 75,000 visitors during its short run of five weeks. Unfortunately the showing could not be extended owing to the necessary preparations for the Academy's Bicentenary Exhibition and the exhibition's own schedule. In fact it had to be closed, for security reasons, on Saturday, 26 October, one day earlier than planned, as there were threats of trouble connected with some demonstrations in London. Most national museums and galleries were already shut and remained so throughout that weekend.

19

UPWARD STILL AND ONWARD
1968–1975

Her Majesty the Queen attended the Bicentenary Dinner which was held in Gallery III on Tuesday, 10 December 1968, being the anniversary of the Academy's foundation. It was the first time that the reigning Sovereign had dined officially in the institution (although Her Majesty and the Duke of Edinburgh, in 1953, had honoured the then President, Sir Gerald Kelly, and his wife at a private dinner party which, by chance, was the Queen's first engagement in her coronation year). All Members, Honorary Members, Professors, the Loan Exhibitions Advisory Committee, the Bicentenary Exhibition Committee, certain senior members of the staff and members of the Royal Household, together with their wives, were invited and formed a great family party. There were no formal speeches but, after the loyal toasts and the time-honoured special toast of 'Honour and Glory to the next Exhibition', the President, Sir Thomas Monnington, expressed the Academy's humble duty and gratitude to Her Majesty who afterwards toured the Bicentenary Exhibition.

This opened to the public on 14 December and continued until 2 March. It was on a vast scale and occupied not only all seventeen of the main galleries but also the General Assembly Room, the Reynolds Room and three of the Diploma Galleries (the fourth not being available). The main problem in the choice of works was how best to illustrate activities which had spanned two centuries yet produce a coherent display and touch on the current scene. Obviously there had to be drastic pruning and, sadly, there was no room to represent the Loan Exhibitions since 1870 which, being so varied in content, would have needed many areas for even a token display; nor could the work undertaken through the trust funds be adequately demonstrated. Therefore the exhibition was concentrated on examples from the annual Summer Exhibitions (shown in the main galleries), a selection of the

Academy's possessions (in the General Assembly Room and the Reynolds Room) and works by living and recently deceased members, together with a few by some students in the twentieth century (in the Diploma Galleries). Reynolds, Gainsborough, Turner and Constable were rightly well represented and, in all, there were 1,037 exhibits. Unfortunately the attendance was disappointing, numbering just over 75,000 in eleven weeks (the Bauhaus exhibition had reached that figure in five) and at first this was thought to be due to the Christmas shopping season. Despite additional advertising and other attempts from early January to engender greater interest, it was not until after a special press conference a month later that the situation improved. As 'a failure' the exhibition then attracted further newspaper comment and the attendances more than doubled in the last two weeks, but this was too late to make any appreciable difference to yet another large financial deficit.

The discovery of dry rot in parts of the basement and the necessity for new electrical wiring in the Schools were unwelcome additions to the running expenses and, except for the introduction of some wood-working machines for the students, in an area which until recently had been their canteen, and the essential provision of a new telephone exchange, all other improvements, including the installation of direly needed additional lavatories, were either abandoned or postponed owing to the lack of cash. Moreover, it was learned that further major expenditure would shortly have to be undertaken in respect of the wiring in all other parts of the building and in renewing the floors of the main galleries.[1] One thing was abundantly clear. The Bicentenary had not only marked the end of an era but was the starting post for the next stage which, haunted by general inflation, already gave every indication of being a yet steeper uphill struggle.

Later in the summer of 1969 the Secretary submitted a memorandum[2] on the Academy's finances, setting out suggestions which had been made in recent years for increasing annual income and commenting on their desirability (or otherwise), their practicability and, if adopted, their possible effects; also, although much more controversial, listing some proposals which would involve curtailing or changing the institution's activities. These suggestions are perhaps worth recording here since, in fact, the majority of them were eventually brought into operation. They were to:

(a) ask for government aid for the whole or part of the Academy's activities

(b) seek financial support from cultural trusts, industry, etc.

(c) sell possessions

(d) re-invest in stocks and shares of greater yield and forego appreciations in market value

(e) introduce classes of fee-paying membership and association with the Academy

(f) charge fees to all or a proportion of the students in the Schools

(g) increase the handling fees for would-be exhibitors

(h) institute hanging fees for exhibitors

(i) charge commission on sales

(j) develop the Publications Department and/or the Restaurant

(k) open the Private Rooms and perhaps the Diploma Galleries as a quasi-permanent exhibition and/or let parts of the premises for suitable functions

(l) seek government permission to rebuild the galleries and Schools in such a way that income could thereafter be derived by letting to suitable occupants, the whole project to be financed by developers.

Hardly any of these suggestions were given serious consideration at the time, no doubt because they all in some way seemed to threaten independence or because they involved charges on artists, both being unpalatable remedies. Only a few of the items were aired at General Assembly, resulting in a large majority vote in favour of charging fees in the Schools, a narrow vote against charging a commission on sales in the Summer Exhibition and a substantial vote against annual subscriptions for members (although such a levy, which at the most could only have been a drop in the ocean, had never been envisaged).

These recommendations and other points arising from the memorandum were then referred to the Policy Advisory Committee. The suggestion that consideration be given to rebuilding the premises (which, in fact, had been proposed by a leading property developer and would have involved demolishing much of the existing buildings) was understandably and rightly dismissed immediately, but the arguments for and against all the other ideas seemed to go on almost interminably. Even the firm recommendation to charge fees in the Schools was not brought into effect for another eight years. Instead, but only of minimal revenue, an administration fee was imposed on applicants for entry as probationary students, while a more lucrative source of new income, from 1970, was through the occasional hire of some galleries and the Private Rooms, for approved purposes within the terms of 'promoting the arts of design'.[3] Much time was spent on the vexed question of whether to sell possessions. Such a course was strongly advocated by various financial advisers but was considered far too heart-rending and unethical. Only the sale of the most precious treasures could have made sufficient monetary impact and the culling of lesser works might have become a dangerous slippery slope. Also there were poignant memories of the disposal of the Leonardo da Vinci cartoon in 1962.

The Secretary pinned his hopes on government subvention, preferably by direct grants but on the lines of the subsidies made through the Arts Council for drama, opera, ballet and orchestral music. His contentions were that the fine arts were equally deserving of support, that the Royal Academy was the body in that field comparable with those being assisted in the other arts and that, while some administrative investigations might have to be accepted, there was no reason to anticipate a consequent loss of control in aesthetic matters. At the time, the Royal Opera House, Covent Garden, for instance, was receiving over £1,250,000 a year whereas the Academy's problems could have been solved by a fifth of such a sum. Even so there was much misgiving within the Academy on the wisdom of making any such request, although a new Treasurer, Lord Holford (who succeeded Marshall Sisson in 1970), certainly favoured the idea. The President and Secretary had a meeting with Viscount Eccles, who was then Paymaster-General and Minister with special responsibility for the Arts, to explain the institution's financial difficulties but his immediate reaction was more encouraging than actually helpful. He thought that there should be no dramatic break in function, that the Academy should not sell possessions or discontinue Loan Exhibitions and that advice should be sought from an eminent financier with an interest in the arts.[4] This was done but nothing came of it. Many outside opinions were sought but all tended to confirm that the promotion of the fine arts could not be expected to be financially viable.

The Librarianship, left vacant for a while when the author became Secretary, was filled by the appointment of Philip James in July 1969. He was a veteran in the art world, having at one time been in charge of the Library at the Victoria and Albert Museum, then seconded to the Council for the Encouragement of Music and the Arts during the Second World War and, on its being transformed into the Arts Council, becoming their first Director of Art until his retirement. In 1970 he also took over the duties of Exhibitions Secretary but his health deteriorated and he died in 1974. Although he was with the Academy only a comparatively short time, his experience was most useful and, during his period in office, the Royal Commission on Historical Manuscripts started work on listing and indexing the Academy's considerable collection of manuscript material, a publisher agreed to produce in book form a continuation series of Royal Academy Exhibitors from 1905 to 1970 and the North Kent group of NADFAS (National Association of Decorative and Fine Art Societies) undertook first of all to treat the many leather bindings which were in a sorry state and, subsequently, to make a complete shelf-list of the library. Indeed their invaluable assistance still continues. Also, in 1969, Willi Soukop succeeded Uli Nimptsch as Master of the Sculpture School.

Some years earlier, the architect E. Vincent Harris had generously donated his own office premises and studio on the understanding that they be leased to him and that he would pay the Academy a rent which would be available to defray various expenses of the School of Architecture. When this School as such ceased to function, he did not take kindly to the money being used in connection with lectures on architecture to the painting and sculpture students and, in 1967, expressed a wish that it be allocated to 'the mural painting School on the lines of the E. A. Abbey Trust'. It was then agreed that the income arising from the eventual sale of the property 'should be applied as to one half for the purpose of Mural Decoration and the other half for the Royal Academy Schools generally . . .'.[5] In the following year he ceased to occupy the premises and they were sold by auction in 1969. The Schools have subsequently benefited from half the income and, in 1970, it was decided that the other half, henceforth used to form the E. Vincent Harris Fund for Mural Decoration, be administered by the same committee as for the E. A. Abbey Memorial Fund for Mural Painting. This was a sensible move and, although these two funds must perforce be treated separately under their individual terms, they neatly complement one another.[6]

A comprehensive exhibition of Polish art was held in the main galleries early in 1970 and it proved to be particularly nostalgic for the many émigré Poles who visited it time and time again. Tape-recordings of their national music were played softly as a background in the Central Hall and daily the nearby seats were filled with moist-eyed patriots. The Spode Bicentenary exhibition took place in the autumn, followed in November by the 21st Anniversary Show of the Young Contemporaries whose evening preview coincided with Guy Fawkes Night and, unfortunately, came in the middle of a prolonged dustmen's strike. There was warning on the day of the intention of some of the young participants to stage demonstrations and, despite vigilance, a few slipped in with bags of rubbish from the streets, strewed them on the floor and proceeded to let off fireworks in the galleries and hurl abuse against the establishment in general as well as against the Royal Academy and the student organizers of the exhibition in particular. Arrangements had been made to have the police in readiness and, at one stage, they had to be called to the courtyard. It was all highly dangerous on account of the risk of fires but, after the ring-leaders had shouted themselves hoarse, the assembled company left quietly. Charlotte Halliday commemorated the fracas in an amusing drawing, inscribed with the following verse:

> We'll always remember
> This 5th of November:
>   Demos and Rubbish and Rot.
> There seems every reason,
> Next Gunpowder Season,
>   To have them all lined up and shot.

All three of these exhibitions, as well as some smaller ones, were subsidized and it was obvious that the Academy would have to rely on this means for such shows in the foreseeable future.

From the Bicentenary onwards there had been a marked increase in the number of Loan Exhibitions held, of which the most notable in the following five years were *Vienna Secession* and *Ensor to Permeke* in 1971, *British Sculptors, Victorian and Edwardian Decorative Art (Handley-Read Collection)* and *The Age of Neo-Classicism* (organized by the Arts Council for the Council of Europe) in 1972, *Rossetti, Futurismo* and *The Genius of China* (fraught with problems of national ideology) in 1973 and *Impressionism* early in 1974. There was also an attractive exhibition of paintings and drawings from the collection of Dr Armand Hammer, the American businessman and philanthropist, who paid all the major costs of the project and, in addition, made an extremely generous gift of £50,000 to be paid in annual instalments over five years. This and the sum of £30,000 received from the sale of some calotypes to the National Portrait Gallery, together with reasonable financial results from most of the recent exhibitions, enabled the Academy to pay off half of its bank overdraft and provided encouragement to embark on some urgently needed repairs and improvements, despite the adverse effects on exhibition receipts of the newly imposed Value Added Tax.

Meanwhile the Diploma Gallery roofs had been completely renewed and, aided by a donation for the purpose, the front of old Burlington House had been dry-cleaned by sand blasting. This latter, a choking experience during its progress, was a most striking and enlivening revelation.[7] There was also a welcome addition to the Academy's furniture by gifts from individual members of thirty Regency-type chairs, inscribed with the names of the donors and presented as an alternative to the traditional silver.

From 1 June 1972, the number of Academicians was increased from forty to fifty (with a minimum of eight sculptors, six architects and four engravers or draughtsmen) but, conversely, the Associates were reduced to twenty-five (with proportionate allocations in category), thus keeping the membership to the same maximum total of seventy-five.[8] Lord Pearce succeeded Viscount Simonds as Professor of Law and, on the death of the Marquess of Salisbury, Lord Butler of Saffron Walden was elected in his place as Secretary for Foreign Correspondence. Arrangements were made through the Privy Purse Office that the Audience of the President and Secretary with Her Majesty the Queen should be biennial instead of every year but Her Majesty confirmed that she would be pleased to grant an audience at any time should matters of importance arise.[9] The business, however, was to be, and still is, submitted annually for the royal approbation.

The Policy Advisory Committee was very active at this time, not only meeting frequently as a whole but in subdivisions of four study groups on Membership, Buildings, Schools and Exhibitions. In 1973 they put forward nineteen recommendations (together with the Secretary's minority report on some of them).[10] All were the result of long deliberations and worthy of careful consideration. Some, but not all, were approved by Council in principle or at least to be pursued and these will be referred to as they materialized. The chief thing which happened almost immediately was the removal of the temporary dividing wall which had been erected in the Restaurant only a few years earlier and the restoration of the room to its original Norman Shaw design but with its basement converted into a students' common room where, among other uses, meals could be served.[11] This was an excellent improvement, not only giving more space again to the general public but in creating a better meeting-pace for the Schools and providing increased facilities for exhibitions of the work of selected past students (the first of which had been held in 1972). It would have been of even greater advantage if a suite of lavatories could have been included in the scheme. This was, and still is, physically possible but was considered too expensive. Another improvement carried out was the rehousing of the students' etching and lithography rooms in part of the old Architectural School.

In 1972, and for the first time, a series of evening concerts was given in the Summer Exhibition by the Philomusica Orchestra who thereafter continued to do so for several years. AIR and SPACE (the newly formed Art Information Registry and its offshoot for Studio Provision and Cultural Education) were allowed the use of three rooms in the basement of the Keeper's House during their formative years and, in 1973, sixty-four Diploma Works by current Academicians were lent for a special exhibition in the University Art Gallery at Nottingham. The Academy was certainly broadening its horizons.

Since the Second World War (except for a few weeks in 1966 when it had been on show at the Victoria and Albert Museum), the Michelangelo tondo (Plate 37) had been affixed to the wall over the fireplace in the General Assembly Room, not the happiest of positions visually and not readily accessible to the general public. True, there was a notice in the Entrance Hall inviting people to ask to see it but few took the trouble and, if the room was in use for a meeting, even fewer came back later to try again. The President, Sir Thomas Monnington, was most anxious to remedy the situation, also to make some of the Private Rooms, hung with a changing selection of the Academy's other possessions, available for viewing and thus, as far as possible, replace the original use of the Diploma Galleries. There was still a small vacant space, L-shaped and twelve feet wide, beyond the north end of the Reynolds Room between old Burlington House and the south wall of the nineteenth-century main galleries. Moreover this wall was so thick that a niche, two feet deep, could be scooped from it without seriously detracting from its strength and this could be made into a very suitable setting for the tondo. By converting a blocked-up window, near the north end of the east wall of the Reynolds Room, into a doorway, access could be gained to such an annexe which would also form a most desirable additional link between the two buildings, incidentally revealing, for the first time in over a hundred years, the exterior of the rather fine north window of the room. The necessary work, designed by Robin Wade, was carried out in 1974 and, in March of the following year, the Saloon, Council Room and Reynolds Room, with the tondo annexe, were opened to the public until October and, as soon as the Summer Exhibition closed, there was added a display of nineteenth-century Diploma Works in the now adjoining Architectural Room.

Meanwhile, Lord Clark of Saltwood had been elected as the Academy's first Professor of the History of Art and Dr Armand Hammer as an Honorary Corresponding Member, also Constance-Anne Parker, who had been on the Library staff since 1958, was made Librarian (the first woman in the post) and Robert Hunt succeeded Peter Foster as Surveyor. The administrative year of the institution, including service on Council, was changed from being a calendar year to an academic year, namely from 1 October to 30 September,[12] and thus was brought into line with the financial accounts. However, the tradition of electing the President on, or as near as possible to, 10 December was maintained. Also the quorums for General and Election Assemblies were adjusted, somewhat belatedly, to take into reckoning the inclusion of Associates at these meetings since 1965.[13]

The rewiring of the main galleries was undertaken, making it possible to install a lighting track of varying potential and a sufficiency of sockets at low level. Gone were the days when one relied on daylight supplemented occasionally by strong, but somewhat yellow, artificial lighting with little thought given to any harmful effect on the exhibits. Several of the major shows in these years (for example *The Age of Neo-Classicism* and *The Genius of China*) had been in elaborate installations dependent on good, man-made lighting, at times with a standby generator at hand for emergencies, but there was always the fear of a breakdown in the supply of electricity, either through power-cuts or by overloading. The new capability of modifying the sources, intensity and colour of light had become an important ingredient in the display of some exhibitions and was a great asset.

It was certainly used to good effect in the exhibition marking the bicentenary of J. M. W. Turner which, organized jointly by the Royal Academy and the Tate Gallery, occupied all the main galleries from 16 November 1974 to 2 March 1975. There were over 650 paintings, drawings and sketchbooks by the artist himself, together with some 150 other items associated with his life and times. Because the watercolours had to be shown in weak light, several galleries were blacked out and their electric lighting was of course strictly controlled. In the fifteen weeks there were over 400,000 visitors and the exhibition attracted more attention and praise than any other previous exhibition of work by a British painter. At an Academy Club Dinner, held on 19 February to honour Turner (who, himself, had once been a member of the club), he was likened to Shakespeare in accomplishment and, following the inception of the Turner Society, there was a strong feeling that his work belonging to the nation should be housed together as he had wished.

Several mural paintings were commissioned through the E. A. Abbey Fund (for example, *Holy Week* by John Ward surrounding the chancel arch of St Mary's Church, Chesham, in 1970; a series on the theme of *Pilgrim's Progress* by Norman Adams throughout St Anselm's Church, Kennington Cross, in 1972; and *Earthly Paradise* by David McClure in the University of St Andrews Students' Union, in 1975). Through the Vincent Harris Mural Decoration Fund a sculptured panel was commissioned from John Skelton for the Lister Hospital at Stevenage in 1972, and three bas-reliefs from Henry and Joyce Collins for the exterior of Gwent House, Cwmbran (a new town in Wales), in 1973.

The position in regard to purchases for and the housing of the Chantrey collection had not improved and, in 1970, the Tate Gallery withdrew from attending joint meetings of the recommending committees. Shortly afterwards it became apparent that they had ceased to appoint representatives for this purpose, although they continued to claim first refusal of any works acquired. By this time there were upwards of fifty items not accepted by them and soon this figure was to be doubled. Some were sent out on loan to appropriate institutions but this still left too many in store at the Academy. The trustees of the bequest, very worried about the situation, concluded that it would be more desirable and in conformity with Chantrey's will for the whole collection to be administered, and if possible housed, by one authority. It was realized that the withdrawal of works from the Tate would create difficult gaps there but this could no doubt be obviated by long-term loans to them of whatever they might require. Investigations were made over the next ten years on the possibilities of using the Strand front of Somerset House or, failing that, a National Trust property or other stately home being made available for the collection but, alas, to no avail.

The Summer Exhibitions proceeded steadily, comprising works by living artists of all ages and styles, including veteran painters born in the final years of the nineteenth century, such as R. O. Dunlop (Plate 60), Allan Gwynne-Jones (Plate 81), William Roberts and James Fitton, and their successors of later generations, such as Norman Blamey, (Sir) Robin Philipson, David Tindle, Olwyn Bowey and Anthony Green, who were all elected to membership of the Royal Academy during this period. The annual attendances averaged some 65,000 visitors, but overall expenditure increased so that the handling fees had to be raised (and were applicable to members as well as non-members from 1975), also the admission charges (to 60p) and the prices of the catalogue (to 30p) and of *The Royal Academy Illustrated* (to £1). In June 1974, the Council recommended the introduction of a 10 per cent commission on sales in the Summer Exhibition but the proposal was defeated at the General Assembly in October.[14]

There were also suggested amendments to the Laws concerning the Presidency. Many felt that election, or re-election, for one year, as had been the case since the foundation, was too uncertain a tenure, that the initial appointment should be for three or perhaps five years, to give the holder a fair time in which to promote possible changes, and that some limit should be imposed on the length of service other than by age. The final proposal was for the first election to be for three years, with eligibility for two more such periods, thus restricting the total term of office to nine years. It was approved by the General Assembly but not subsequently confirmed by the necessary two-thirds majority. Council then decided not to pursue the matter.[15]

In 1975 there were considerable changes in the Professorships, those newly appointed being H. T. Cadbury-Brown in Architecture, Dr Gerald Libby in Anatomy, S. Rees Jones in Chemistry and B. A. R. Carter in Perspective (a reinstatement of the post after a lapse of thirty-six years).

Regrettably the health of the President, Sir Thomas Monnington, was failing and, although he was re-elected in the December of 1974 and again in 1975, he died suddenly but peacefully at his home in the early hours of 7 January 1976. He had thus been in office just over nine years. Much had been accomplished during this period but all against a background of financial stress. No magic formula had been found to alleviate the situation but seeds of goodwill had been sown. Largely due to his integrity and appreciation of other people's problems, there was no longer virulent opposition to the establishment. He was always at pains to help fellow artists, particularly the younger ones, and the great feature of his Presidency was surely the quiet evaporation of an antagonism, some latent and some spiteful, from quite a few painters and sculptors, which had lasted far too long. Tom, as he was affectionately known by so many, agonized over the necessity to make massive changes in running the Academy but he certainly paved the way for his successor to do so.

The Treasurer, Lord Holford, had died only a month or two earlier and was replaced by Sir Hugh Casson who, however, had only been in the post a few weeks before being required for another role.

20

TRY AND TRY AGAIN
1976–1982

The election of the new President took place on 17 February 1976, when thirty-seven votes were cast for Sir Hugh Casson, seven for Frederick Gore, three for Sir Frederick Gibberd and one each for Norman Adams, Raymond Cowern, Richard Eurich and Kyffin Williams. There being a clear majority for Sir Hugh, the Secretary, by previous arrangement, telephoned the result to Buckingham Palace and, within minutes, received a message that the Queen had delightedly approved the appointment. Her Majesty subsequently, on visiting the exhibition *The Golden Age of Spanish Painting* on 19 February, invested Sir Hugh with the Presidential Gold Medal and Chain.[1]

Born in 1910, Hugh Casson (Plate 90) had been in private practice as an architect since 1937 but this was but one of his many activities. As Director of Architecture for the Festival of Britain from 1948 to 1951 and, in that capacity, Chairman of the Design Committee, his enlivening spirit had played an important part in counteracting the austerity of the war years and, as he said a good deal later, 'You see, everything and everybody had got to look shabby and fatigued. What we needed was a party'.[2] He was knighted in 1952 and, from 1953 to 1975, was the Professor of Environmental Design at the Royal College of Art. His architectural partnership was responsible for a number of award-winning buildings, including the Elephant House at the London Zoo, and he produced designs for city festivals, for performances at Covent Garden and Glyndebourne, also for interiors at Windsor, Sandringham, in the Royal Yacht and the Royal Train, yet he still found time to write books on architectural subjects, to illustrate others, to serve on the Royal Fine Art Commission and many other committees and, not least, to draw and to paint an abundance of watercolours.

On his own admission he was by nature impulsive but the resulting momentum was much needed at the Academy when he took over the

Presidency. A Ways and Means Committee was already in being but its members, the Council and, above all, the General Assembly hesitated to go ahead with various reasonable proposals in the fear that independence might thereby be forfeited. Sir Hugh immediately pointed out that there was no independence in bankruptcy and, in the next few months, meetings were held with the Chairman of the Arts Council (Lord Gibson), the Chancellor of the Duchy of Lancaster (Harold Lever, later to become Lord Lever of Manchester, who had been commissioned by the then Prime Minister, (Sir) Harold Wilson (now Lord Wilson of Rievaulx), to report on sponsorship for the Arts) and the newly appointed Minister for the Arts (Lord Donaldson of Kingsbridge). Much time was spent in producing financial statements and budgets requested by the Arts Council but to no avail. Indeed, there was no official reply whatsoever to these approaches and it was obvious, not least to Roger de Grey who had become Treasurer in April 1976, that something else must be tried.

The first major step was to launch the Friends of the Royal Academy on 1 January 1977, an organization through which its members, by paying an annual subscription, would be entitled to free and immediate admission to all exhibitions held by the Royal Academy (not only for themselves but accompanied by husband or wife and their children under sixteen years of age, or some other guest), to invitations for the Friend and a guest to a Private or Special View of such exhibitions (including, of course, the annual Summer Exhibition), to obtain the exhibition catalogues at reduced prices and to have access to the Academy's Library and Archives. In addition it was proposed to organize lectures and other events especially for the Friends and a room on the premises (the Aston Webb Room) was allocated for their use as a resting-place where coffee could be obtained (Plate 86). The facility for immediate admission was particularly attractive, avoiding the frustration of having to join the long queues in the courtyard for the more popular exhibitions.

Four categories were instituted – the main body of Friends contributing £10 annually (but with concessions for pensioners, young people aged sixteen to twenty-five, the staffs of museums, public galleries and teachers in accredited educational institutions), Artist Subscribers at £17.50 (to include the submission of their work for the Summer Exhibition without the usual handling fee and the opportunity to purchase artists' materials at a discount) and, with certain other privileges, Corporate and Individual Sponsors at £500 and £100 respectively and

Benefactors on a single payment of £1,000 or over. These amounts have subsequently had to be increased over the years but so have the activities. The principle of gathering together an association of Friends greatly benefited the institution, not only financially but, by word of mouth, the issue of news-letters and, now, the publication of a magazine, the various endeavours of the Academy and other items of interest to art-lovers have become more widely known and appreciated. Within a few months more than 8,000 Friends had enrolled and, by the end of 1980, there were over 25,000. Not all the income was profit of course. Additional administrative expenses were involved and it had to be borne in mind that many of the Friends would normally have paid individual admission charges for some of the exhibitions. However, there could be no doubt that, overall, the enterprise was a huge success.

At the same time a 15 per cent commission on sales was introduced, commencing with the Summer Exhibition in 1977, and soon there were increased profits from the Publications Department and the Restaurant due to larger attendances. Also, from September, fees were charged in the Schools (mostly paid by the Department of Education and Science and by local education authorities for those students in receipt of maintenance grants) but up to six places a year, i.e. a maximum of eighteen at one time in the three-year course, were retained in order to continue as far as possible the tradition of free training being available at the Academy.[3]

The number of exhibitions each year multiplied dramatically. There were five in 1976 but around a dozen or more in subsequent years, together with shows in the Students' Common Room during the vacation periods (of the work of past students) and occasional varied displays in the Entrance Hall. The programme involved not only dividing the main galleries into sections, which was usually not too difficult to arrange, but having displays in the Diploma Galleries and making use of most of the Private Rooms for temporary exhibitions. Sadly this left hardly any good spaces for the Academy's permanent possessions, although as many as possible were placed in offices and on staircases. In addition, the increased work-load brought about by the many exhibitions, the development of the Friends' organization and other projects necessitated a larger staff and they too had to be housed. Not an inch of space was left unoccupied and the institution's Inspectors of Property reported that the building was 'being used beyond its capacity and beyond that of the Academy's staff'.[4] By then the Bursary had already been moved to the basement, the Housekeeper's Flat had been taken over, basically for the Exhibitions and Press Departments, and, at last, some more adequate staff lavatories had been provided. The wear and tear on the Private Rooms of constantly changing exhibitions was considerable, especially as so many of the shows seemed to need structural installations. Built in the seventeenth century as apartments in a stately home, they had never been intended to accommodate large numbers of people tramping through them daily. The Academy's activities had certainly been expanded but not without cost and the accumulation of new problems.

Obviously it is impossible in a narrative of this length to describe so many exhibitions but they are listed in Appendix E. A few, however, warrant a sentence or two as perhaps being outstanding in importance or exceptional in some way. The scene was set for the L. S. Lowry exhibition in 1976 (organized before his death in February that year) by a brass band playing in the courtyard on Private View Day. His work had become very popular and he may be the only artist to have had it recorded in song. *Matchstalk Men and Matchstalk Cats and Dogs*, with words and music by Michael Coleman and Brian Burke, was published in the following year. It has pertinent verses about his painting 'Salford's smokey tops' and wearing an 'old flat cap', followed by a catchy refrain:

And he painted matchstalk men and matchstalk cats and dogs:
He painted kids on the corner of the street that were sparking clogs.
Now he takes his brush and he waits outside them factory gates,
To paint his matchstalk men and matchstalk cats and dogs.[5]

The first exhibition (other than displays of the Academy's own possessions) to be held in the Private Rooms was open throughout the summer of 1977. Entitled *This Brilliant Year*, it was a commemoration of Queen Victoria's Golden Jubilee of 1887 but used to echo the celebrations of the Silver Jubilee of Her Majesty Queen Elizabeth II which were then in full flow. A Loyal Address was presented and, later, a collection of drawings (one by each current member of the Royal Academy), mounted and placed in three perspex boxes suitably engraved, was graciously accepted by Her Majesty on 24 November when the members and their wives were present and the Queen attended lunch with the President. A special Jubilee Prize of £1,000 was offered in connection with the Summer Exhibition and it was won by Leonard McComb for his watercolour *Portrait of a Lady*, while Anthony Green's *Hall of Mirrors* was voted Exhibit of the Year by the public, also winning £1,000. Subsequently the Academy was awarded a Jubilee Tourism Award by the British Tourist Authority.

The institution could not afford to continue such prizes in future years but nevertheless was enabled to do so by certain sponsorships, including a generous offer from Charles Wollaston, retired Principal Lecturer in Art at Bognor Regis College of Education, to finance the setting up of a trust fund from which an award could be made for the most distinguished exhibit in each year's Summer Exhibition. The first recipient, in 1978, was Peter Greenham for his portrait of Lady (Charlotte) Bonham-Carter, followed by Roger de Grey in 1979 for *Marenne Estuary* and in 1980 by Anthony Gross for *Les Causses*, all three happening to be oil paintings. Other prizes were donated and, by public vote, Sydney Harpley was the winner two years running, in 1978 and 1979, for versions of his sculpture *Girl on a Swing*. A lottery, with tickets at 25p each, was held in connection with these exhibitions but was later superseded by one based on the purchase of a catalogue and sponsored by the *Daily Mirror*. However, an open-air Book Fair, started in the summer of 1978 and held in the West Yard, has continued on its original lines for some years now – yet another example of utilizing an odd corner and giving it a little life. Various evening events were encouraged, including a Midsummer Ball that year, and they developed to such an extent that, ever since, the building has more often than not been buzzing with activity from dawn until the small hours of next morning. A most welcome innovation, under the auspices of Youth and Music, has been the series of Cushion Concerts (Plate 87), so called because the audience, all under twenty-five years of age, sit on cushions on the floor, surrounded by the Summer Exhibition. This neatly avoids the problems of hiring, setting out, clearing away and storing chairs, makes unnecessary the erection of a high platform for the musicians and, above all, engenders a suitably informal atmosphere.

The main Winter Exhibition of 1976–77 had been *Pompeii AD 79*.[6] This was largely organized by a consortium from outside the Academy and it comprised frescoes, mosaics, sculptures, jewellery and many household objects (particularly in bronze and silver) which were arranged in sections to depict the life prior to the volcanic disaster. There were specially made models of the town plan, of a garden peristyle and of the House of Menander, together with full-size reproductions of the paintings in a reconstruction of the Hall of the Mysteries and of a wall in the newly excavated Villa at Oplontis, all incorporated in a most effective lay-out designed by Alan Irvine. Scheduled to close at the end of February, it was extended for a further two weeks because of its popularity, but its organization and financial arrangements, over which the Academy had little control, were not so satisfactory. True, a weekly 'rent' was received but only 25 per cent of the profits. The net result to the institution was a surplus of £58,000, not a negligible sum but, during the period of occupation, it had cost the Academy some £150,000 to exist. Steps had to be taken to secure more advantageous terms in any future sponsorship and to ensure that the Academy should always be master in its own house.

On the day following its closure and despite there being other exhibitions in the Private Rooms and Diploma Galleries and, moreover, the bulk of the main galleries being in use during its dismantling and subsequent preparations for the forthcoming Summer Exhibition, yet another show was squeezed into the programme. The South Rooms were completely blacked out to house *Light Fantastic*, an exhibition of laser beams and holography – three-dimensional images in space – whose novelty captured the attention of a large, mainly young, audience, many of whom had perhaps never before entered an art gallery. It was extremely popular and another version of it, on a larger scale, was held in the following year. Meanwhile, in December, there had been yet another first-time event, namely *The Burlington International Fine Art Fair* in which thirty-six leading British and Continental art dealers participated. Later, under the title *The Burlington House Fair*, this became a regular feature in the Academy's wider programme.

There were in fact fifteen exhibitions during 1978, not least in importance being *Gustave Courbet, 1819–1877*, *Thomas Rowlandson Drawings* from the Paul Mellon Collection and *Alvar Aalto, 1898–1976* (Plate 84), subtitled 'The Finnish Master of Architecture and Design'. The main Loan Exhibition of 1978–79 was *The Gold of El Dorado*, which included many items from the Museo del Oro in Bogota, and, in the following winter, *Post-Impressionism*, which was a highly successful enterprise, but, in between, *The Horses of San Marco* (Plate 85) was surely the most noteworthy and imaginatively designed, again by Alan Irvine. It was made possible by the opportunity of borrowing one of the four bronze horses which had overlooked St Mark's Square, Venice, for 800 years from their position on the Basilica and by obtaining other sculptures of comparable date together with a rich variety of supporting material by, among others, Leonardo, Canaletto, Rubens, Canova, Turner and Sickert. Administratively it was an example of true sponsorship, thanks to the efforts and financing by British Olivetti, who later received an award from ABSA (Association for Business Sponsorship of the Arts), as did IBM (UK) Ltd for their participation in the Post-Impressionism exhibition. Thus two out of the three such recognitions 'for the best single sponsored event' that year were won in respect of exhibitions held by the Royal Academy. In addition, the Academy itself received from National Heritage a Museum of the Year award for its year's exhibition programme from 1 July 1979.

Other ventures included the establishment early in 1978 of a trading company, Business Art Galleries Ltd, in partnership with Curwen Prints Ltd, for the distribution of contemporary works of art, viz. original prints, paintings and sculptures, especially with a view to encouraging business firms of all types and sizes to make purchases for their premises. It was housed in the North Diploma Gallery (which became known as the Upstairs Gallery) and the Academy had a 52 per cent share in the enterprise.[7] Eight years later, the holding was transferred to Curwen largely because, by then, the Academy sorely needed the space in connection with scheduled improvements to that part of the building. Another undertaking was the formation of a Framing Department in 1979–80. Initially on a small scale, it was not fully developed until its reorganization in 1985.

Despite all these new and increased activities, the Academy's parlous financial situation continued to cause grave concern, especially as, by the autumn of 1977, the bank overdraft had reached about £500,000 and was soon to exceed this figure. Once again certain advisers strongly recommended the disposal of possessions, in fact advocating the sale of the Michelangelo tondo rather than the gradual erosion of works of art of historical as well as aesthetic value to the Academy. It was of course the only single item which, if sold, could not only have wiped out existing debts but, if the balance had been invested, provided a substantial income for the foreseeable future. Such a move was a tempting solution in the circumstances but it was firmly resisted and, following yet more meetings with Lord Goodman, Lord Donaldson and the new Chairman of the Arts Council, The Rt Hon. (Sir) Kenneth Robinson, it was decided to apply officially to the Arts Council for subvention. Requests had already been made to Westminster City Council for complete relief from rates and to the Department of the Environment for financial help in maintaining the Academy's premises but both were refused. Therefore, on 25 September 1978, an application was made to the Arts Council for an annual subsidy but, twelve months later, a reply regretted that there were no funds available for overall subvention to the Academy in the current year.[8] Nevertheless the matter was pursued and sympathetic consideration was then promised of up to £300,000 per annum but eventually, in February 1981, a letter was received from them saying that it had proved quite impossible to take on any new commitments of a substantial nature.[9] This was a great blow. Meanwhile, of course, their support to various performing arts had increased considerably, as no doubt was needed (e.g. £7 million a year to the Royal Opera House, Covent Garden, almost £5 million each to the English National Opera and to the National Theatre and over £2 million to the Royal Shakespeare Theatre) but no explanation was ever forthcoming as to why a fresh applicant, who had hitherto always been self-supporting, should not be permitted a modest slice of the cake. Indeed, the amount so desperately required by the Academy would, by comparison, have been but a few crumbs.

At about the same time, the Royal Academy was invited to submit a memorandum and to appear before the House of Commons Education, Science and Arts Committee in respect of investigations being made by them on 'Public and Private Funding of the Arts'. The memorandum, dated 20 March 1981, was duly sent in and the President and Secretary were the Academy's chief witnesses to give evidence in the matter on 1 April (amusingly enough, April Fool's Day, but the deputation was received most courteously, given full opportunity to put its case and encouraged to submit a supplementary memorandum, dated 13 April).[10] Concurrently new personnel had been appointed to the institution's Financial Advisory Committee and the accounting system had been revised to apportion to individual departments (such as the Schools, Restaurant and Publications) and to each exhibition a share of the ever-mounting overhead costs. Largely owing to inflation, the expenses of merely maintaining and staffing the building, to the degree necessary to enable relevant activities to be undertaken, had become a factor which could no longer be ignored.

It was with this background that the Royal Academy Trust, referred to in the minutes of evidence, had been formed, under the chairmanship of Lord Lever of Manchester, and this was announced by the President at the Annual Dinner on 11 May 1981. Under its auspices, an appeal for £6 million was launched in the following year, one of the first major contributions being the promise of £250,000 from the Government, to be used for repairs to Burlington House.

Understandably some considerable time elapsed before the House of Commons Committee was able to produce its report but, when it did so in October 1982, it was found to be wholeheartedly in favour of support for the Royal Academy, as shown by the following two paragraphs:

> We were impressed by the evidence from the Royal Academy illustrating their long history of achievements in the fields of education, and the mounting of great exhibitions, as well as their record of self-help, supplemented by recent success with respect to business sponsorship and in developing the Friends of the Royal Academy. We welcome the Minister's recent announcement that the government is to give £250,000 to the Royal Academy Appeal. We are, however, concerned that an institution of such distinction should have been refused public funding on a number of previous occasions and that they were forced in the past to resort to the desperate measure of selling a treasured asset, the Leonardo Cartoon, in order to survive. By the same token, the Michelangelo Tondo, which is beautifully displayed and constantly on view to the public at the Royal Academy, is a work of such supreme importance that no export licence for it could possibly be granted and yet the recurrent expense of its display is borne by the Academy.
>
> We accept the evidence that the 'main cause for grave concern is . . . the cost of maintaining the building and staffing it, to the degree necessary to be able to undertake activities for the benefit of artists and the general public', and we note that the PSA [Property Services Agency] already maintains the rest of Burlington House. It is inappropriate that the Royal Academy, as one of the country's major postgraduate schools, should carry the loss on its Schools, especially bearing in mind that the tutors who are members of the Royal Academy, and other distinguished artists, accept half the daily rate which is paid in other art colleges in the country. We believe that the Minister will wish to keep in close touch with the Royal Academy over forms of help for its exhibition programme. Accordingly, *we recommend that in keeping with its standing as a national institution the Royal Academy should receive some current public funding for its exhibitions and for the Royal Academy Schools and the Property Services Agency should take responsibility for the maintenance of the buildings.*[11]

Perhaps this may yet come about one day. The report, which was an impressively comprehensive document, revealed tremendous growth in the attendances at the Academy's exhibitions, being runner-up in 1980 in the list of art galleries to only the National Gallery and the Tate Gallery in having more than a million visitors and far in excess of any others. It did not comment directly on the curious fact that exhibition activities in the fine arts are organized by the Arts Council whereas, in

79 'The Virgin and Child with St Anne and St John the Baptist', cartoon by Leonardo da Vinci, *c.* 1495. (*Reproduced by courtesy of the Trustees, The National Gallery, London*)

80 Mural painting by Sir Thomas Monnington, 1964. Commissioned
through the E. A. Abbey Mural Painting Fund for the University of
London Union

81 Approving the Summer Exhibition, 1967. *Left to right*: David McFall, Humphrey Brooke
(Secretary), Sir Thomas Monnington (President), Carel Weight, Sir Basil Spence,
George Tuck (Foreman), Frederick Gore, Andrew Freeth, John Ward,
Allan Gwynne-Jones, Marshall Sisson and Maurice de Sausmarez

82 Entrance Hall of the Royal Academy, 1971

83 'Sidney C. Hutchison', Secretary of the Royal Academy, 1968–82, by Walter Woodington, 1975 (*The author*)

84 View in the Alvar Aalto Exhibition, 1978

85 View in The Horses of San Marco Exhibition, 1979

86 The Aston Webb Room, when in use for the Friends of the
Royal Academy from 1977–8 to 1986

87 HRH The Prince of Wales at a Youth & Music Concert, July, 1980;
Sir Robert Mayer and the Choirboys of King's College Chapel, Cambridge,
in the background

88 View in The Great Japan Exhibition, 1981–2

89 View in The Genius of Venice Exhibition, 1983–4

90 Sir Hugh Casson, President of the Royal Academy, 1976–84, and his successor, Roger de Grey

91 View in the Elisabeth Frink Exhibition, 1985

92 'Spring and the Student' by Norman Blamey. Diploma Work, 1975

the performing arts, the programmes of events are initiated and run by the particular professional bodies concerned, albeit subsidized, but it did recommend that it 'should transfer its promotional activities and its responsibility for initiating exhibitions and concerts to the appropriate national and regional performing organisations, museums and galleries'.

The sentence about the Michelangelo tondo referred to the Academy's having agreed in principle, sometime in 1977–78, to lend it to the Metropolitan Museum of Art in New York, and possibly to other prestigious museums in the USA, for temporary exhibitions. It transpired that it was necessary to apply for an export licence but this was refused on the grounds that the risks of travel were too high for a work of art of such national importance.[12] The decision was taken at ministerial level on the recommendation of the Advisory Council on the Export of Works of Art, although it seems doubtful whether it was ever intended that their purview, designed to prevent permanent removals from the country, should extend to temporary loans. Despite representations from the Academy that there was no question of sale and that, being a compact object in marble, the tondo was certainly not fragile (compared with paintings or ceramics) and need not be removed from a specially constructed case, the refusal was repeated more than once, much to the disappointment of the Soviet Union, Italy and Japan who all hoped that one day it might be made available to them for short periods. The Academy was in the invidious position of, on the one hand, requesting works of the highest quality from other countries for its exhibitions, yet being forbidden to reciprocate with its own most precious possession. Certain 'Treasures of the Royal Academy', which had been on show in three cities in Japan (Tokyo, Sapporo and Sendai), were diverted to the Soviet Union on their return journey and exhibited at the Pushkin Museum, Moscow, and the Hermitage Museum, Leningrad, while more and more individual works, and sometimes substantial groups of them, were lent for specialized exhibitions in Great Britain and abroad.

The financial year which had ended on 30 September 1981 had been particularly disastrous for the Academy, resulting in a deficit of around £350,000 on its exhibitions (compared with a surplus of £379,000 in the previous year) although all but the Summer Exhibition and one other had been partially sponsored to varying extents; also it was by this stage frequently possible to obtain a government indemnity against loss of, or damage to, works borrowed for the Loan Exhibitions (not, be it said, likely occurrences but risks which are expensive to cover through commercial insurance). There was, for instance, a huge deficit on *A New Spirit in Painting* and considerable short-falls on *Stanley Spencer RA*, *British Art Now*, *Some Chantrey Favourites* and even *Leonardo da Vinci (Codex Hammer and Drawings from Nature)*, also on the Summer Exhibitions of both 1981 and 1982. It was clear that, without a substantial injection of funds from external sources, the Academy would be faced with the unpalatable prospect of being forced to reduce the scope of its activities (even to the extent of closing Burlington House for part of the year) or disposing of some of its possessions, or both.[13] Mercifully however, by September 1982, £2¼ million had been collected from, or promised by, donors to the Royal Academy Trust, and the Friends organization, which in 1981 had added 'Country Friends' to its categories, continued to flourish.

Much time was taken up over these financial worries but other matters demanded attention, not least certain revisions in regard to the Academy's membership. In 1978 the procedure for nominations was changed, thereafter requiring for each candidate the signatures of seven members, namely a proposer and six seconders (the proposer and at least half of the seconders to be of the category of the candidate), 'Print-makers' were added to the category of 'Engravers and Draughtsmen' (with, from 1982, only the proposer and one seconder needing to be of the category of the candidate), the class of 'Corresponding Members' (hitherto limited to a total of four) was made available to an unlimited number provided that not more than two a year were elected to it and a new class of 'Honorary Fellows' was initiated to consist of 'persons of distinguished reputation but not practising artists of the categories of the Membership'. There were to be up to six on the inauguration of the class but, subsequently, not more than two additional in any one year.[14] The first, elected in 1981, were Lord Charteris of Amisfield, Sir Trenchard Cox, (Sir) Brinsley Ford, Baroness Lee of Asheridge and Lord Lever of Manchester, all having very close connections with the art world. In 1980, the requirement for candidates for Associateship to be 'resident in the United Kingdom' was changed to being 'professionally active' therein, the regulations were amended to allow artists over 75 years of age to be elected direct to Senior Academicianship and the hitherto complicated procedure of appointing the Selection and Hanging Committees for each year's Summer Exhibition was replaced by the simple formula of making the Council automatically 'the Committee for the Summer Exhibition (co-opting other Members as and when necessary)'.[15] In that, under the

Academy's Laws, the Council comprises a suitable representation of the various categories of the membership by rotation, including a system whereby newly elected Academicians and Associates are given priority, this was a welcome simplification.

There was, at the same time and over a period of years, much discussion on whether the total membership should be considerably increased in number and, above all, whether the current Academicians and Associates should be amalgamated into one class of Academicians and, if so, whether a new class of Associates, by this or any other name, should then be formed. The potential membership was in fact marginally increased by five, in the class of Associates, in 1982[16] but there was never any agreement on the more radical proposals. Basically, those in favour of such changes argued that the current total of some eighty-five to ninety members (viz. 50 Academicians, 25 Associates and perhaps 10 to 15 Senior Members) was insufficient to reflect the tremendous growth in the number of practising artists since the eighteenth century, that, by age and status, those now elected to Associateship should be Academicians and that, in any case, there had for some time been little difference in the rights of these classes within the institution. Conversely, those against contended that a large increase in the membership would weaken its distinction, that it was correct for such a body to be an élite and that the majority of artists had no objection to being elected first as Associates as had been the case throughout the Academy's history. The arguments on each side were quite fierce and, at times, somewhat heated but it was obvious that there was little likelihood in the foreseeable future of there being the necessary two-thirds majority to bring about such changes in the constitution. A definite proposal 'that the class of Associate Members should be abolished and that all Members should be elected direct to Academicianship' was later placed before General Assembly in December 1983, but was defeated by a narrow majority (seventeen votes in favour and twenty against).[17]

Meanwhile Balthus, Chagall, S. W. Hayter, Manzù, Miró and Sert had been elected as Honorary Academicians, Lord Carrington had become Secretary for Foreign Correspondence and, among the new Associates, there were (Sir) Lawrence Gowing, William Scott, Philip Sutton, Gillian Ayres, Philip King, (Sir) Philip Dowson and Richard Rogers.

A great deal of work on the building had to be done during this period. The Surveyor, Robert Hunt, retired in 1980 and was replaced by Denis Serjeant who then took over a number of crucial maintenance operations, such as the renewal of the main drains (whose earthenware had begun to disintegrate) and of lead on the roofs (which again were leaking), and the insertion of a steel frame to carry the floor of the Saloon (being one of the original rooms of Burlington House which, weakened by structural alterations in years gone by and now used as an exhibition area, could not withstand the new stresses to which it had been subjected). There was never a shortage of lesser jobs essential for keeping the building in reasonable order and, soon, various necessary improvements were put in hand, for instance the conversion of Gallery XI into a shop (designed by Leonard Manasseh), making a new strong room (as required by the insurers) and revising the lay-out of, as well as refurnishing, the Restaurant. One overriding difficulty, besides that of keeping the Academy in full operation while the work was going on, was the lack of space within the building for all the increased activities. The Inspectors of Property reported that 'the only solution would appear to be the acquisition of additional accommodation either in other premises or, if feasible, by embarking on structural alterations within the present building'[18] but nothing on these lines was possible for some time. The Library had been particularly hard hit, having to give up space to the Friends' organization and perforce becoming little more than a corridor to and from the rest-room set aside for them – and this when its services were being called upon more and more and it had taken on several new administrative commitments. At one stage there was hope of moving the Library to premises next door in the courtyard, recently vacated by the British Academy, and of gaining a meeting room there, but it was not to be. Throughout the building, the impossibility of squeezing a quart into a pint pot had become only too apparent.

The Annual Reports of the Keeper, Peter Greenham, were always amusing as well as being percipient and it was undoubtedly his personal qualities which had helped to keep the Academy Schools trouble-free when most other art schools in London had suffered from student unrest. He seemed at times to err on the side of *laissez-faire*, but in fact this was not so, although he was strongly opposed to regimentation. He spoke lovingly of the plaster casts, the old studios, the modest equipment and the bare amenities available at the Academy and his poor opinion of certain modern developments elsewhere is clearly seen in this extract:

Nor do the fees, the degrees, even the affiliation of the students' society with the National Union of Students, make any difference to our artistic aims though it seems to me a pity that art schools should have been pushed into thinking that they acquire virtue by taking these terms from universities, which have nothing to do with art and generally show themselves ignorant of it. Under the panoply of BAs and postgraduate diplomas and tutorials and seminars and theses, the standard of drawing has declined to such an extent that the student who has not been to an art school at all may well draw better than the postgraduate. The first term of compulsory life drawing in the Academy is barely enough to put them on the right path.[19]

Nevertheless, the Academy Schools had to come into line, at least administratively. A Schools' Committee, the first since 1930, was reformed in 1977–78 and, as already mentioned, fees were introduced. It was agreed to take in up to eight students a year fresh from a foundation course and this involved more attention being paid to art history and the writing of essays. The Keeper reported that:

The student of today – or at any rate the student straight from a foundation course – expects an even greater degree of attention, one which might have been resisted twenty years ago. He wants a course on which he can summon a group of teachers at any moment to review a group of paintings; perhaps other students are brought into the discussion; there are references to politics and philosophy. And since far more students go to art schools than can become good artists, it is important that there should be this other form of teaching, which substitutes general discussion for demonstration, a philosophy for painting, and makes more of the process than the product. . . . So teaching of two kinds is wanted though both may be invested in the same teacher: the inspiration, the extension of horizons, the grand references to history; and also the patient sojourn among knuckles and elbows and other points of articulation.[20]

At the same time many students, particularly those not in receipt of official grants, were faced with financial worries although in a number of such cases the Academy was able to provide aid through its trust funds, through help supplied by the Leverhulme Trust, through benefactions from Sir James Walker and, from September 1981, with bursaries kindly donated by Jack Goldhill through his charitable trust. The situation for those setting out on their careers was usually far worse, although perhaps no more daunting than for most young artists in the past. Indeed, for the few, there were chances of fellowships at several of the newer universities and, through a fund presented to the Academy by (Sir) Brinsley Ford (in memory of his ancestor, Richard Ford), awards for visits to Spain for the purpose of studying paintings, particularly in the Museo del Prado, Madrid.

The E. Vincent Harris Fund for Mural Decoration was able to help several students who took up outdoor mural painting, for example Desmond Rochfort and David Binnington under the fly-over at Paddington and David Bratby in London's East End, while the E. A. Abbey Fund, which may only employ artists 'who have proved themselves draughtsmen, designers and Mural Painters of a very high order', commissioned, among other works, a painting *High Summer* by Sir Robin Philipson for Dundee College of Education, an abstract work by Andrew Yates for Manchester Polytechnic, a group of three paintings by David Tindle for the Coffee Room of the Open University at Milton Keynes, a painting entitled *British Infantry since 1945* by Colin Hayes for the School of Infantry at Warminster and *The Founding of Wolfson College* by Gordon Davies for that new building in Cambridge.

The Centre for Advanced Studies in Architecture, comprising about a dozen students, was, with difficulty, housed at the Academy from October 1976 for an experimental period of two years. Its request for permanency and integration within the institution's structure was carefully considered but refused owing to lack of space and because the course appeared to be designed more for theorists than for practising architects. They were, however, provided with accommodation for one more year.[21]

All sections of the Academy had become overloaded with work and the pressures were tremendous, always a race against time, but there was considerable satisfaction in increasing activities despite financial stringencies and the restricted space available. It was a challenge which had to be met and mastered. Attempts were made to rationalize procedures: for instance, in 1979 a General Purposes Committee was formed in order to vet major proposals before they were placed before Council, but all was dependent on the team spirit of the enlarged staff. By then, Kenneth Tanner had been promoted to a new post as Comptroller, being replaced as Registrar by Laurie Bray who, in turn, made way for his assistant, Trevor Clark, to become Bursar and take charge of all the financial transactions, while Norman Rosenthal had been appointed to deal with the administration of the Loan Exhibitions and serve a newly constituted Exhibitions Committee.

The Secretary, who had joined the staff in 1929, had been the

Academy's Librarian (in addition to working on exhibitions) from 1949 to 1968 and its Secretary since 1968, gave notice that he would have completed fifty years' service by 1979 and suggested that it might be best for him then to relinquish the Secretaryship on pension but thereafter continue 'Emeritus' with reduced duties, perhaps as archivist or consultant. Council agreed this in principle although there was a feeling that the change-over might be postponed a little longer. When the time came, he was showered with gifts, Members attended a Royal Academy Club Dinner in his honour on 31 October and, on the following evening, there was a party of over three hundred people, including the staff, past and present, some Members again, Honorary Members and Professors, the Advisory Committees and other guests, together with their wives – certainly occasions to be remembered. By then it had been decided that he should continue in office for a while, particularly to carry on his chairmanship of the Executive Committee of *The Great Japan Exhibition (Art of the Edo Period, 1600–1868)* which was being negotiated for the winter of 1981–82, but that a Secretary-Elect should be appointed as from 1 October 1981, with a view to taking over the post in 1982. Following a public advertisement and the composition of a frightening schedule of duties, seventy-two applications were received and examined by a committee comprising the President, Keeper, Treasurer, Secretary and Bryan Kneale. They interviewed ten candidates and, of these, recommended the appointment of (Andrew) Piers (Wingate) Rodgers, aged 36, who had previously been Director of the International Council on Monuments and Sites, in Paris. This was approved by Council and confirmed by General Assembly. He joined the staff as planned and one of his first tasks was to serve an Academy committee formed to look into the proposed reform of copyright law and to prepare a report for submission to the Government and to the British Copyright Council.[22]

The Great Japan Exhibition (Plate 88), which was the result of several years of complicated negotiations, occupied the main galleries from 29 October 1981 to 21 February 1982, while the Private Rooms were used for ancillary services and a succession of evening events. It was certainly the most comprehensive display ever devoted to the Edo Period, even in Japan itself, and it was held in two parts: the first closed on 20 December and the second opened a week later. This was due to the nature of the works, especially those on paper and in lacquer which were only allowed to be shown for a limited number of days and hours. Over four-fifths of the exhibits had to be exchanged for similar pieces of comparable quality at the end of the first session and, throughout, everything was displayed in specially built show-cases in which the levels of light, temperature and humidity were strictly controlled. The exhibition was a feast of paintings, including some spectacular screens by the most famous Japanese artists of the time, astonishing textiles and a variety of lacquer, ceramics, metalwork, sculpture and small items such as *netsuke* and *inrō*.

A handsome illustrated catalogue, edited by William Watson, was produced and the exhibition, designed by the Japanese architect, Kishō Kurokawa, in association with Alan Irvine, was the most expensive the Royal Academy had ever organized. Installation alone accounted for over £400,000 and the total costs were around £3 million but a third of this, largely in kind, was met by the Japanese side. Despite the misfortunes of snow and of transport strikes, which made it difficult for some people to reach Piccadilly, the attendances were good, amounting to more than 523,000 visitors. The result was that the exhibition not only covered its costs, including a substantial reimbursement of the institution's overhead expenses, but made a small surplus of £18,000, while the sales of catalogues and associated merchandise realized almost £1 million. There was unfailing support from a group of British sponsors who provided guarantees against loss of up to £625,000 but, happily, in the event, they were not called upon and it was fitting that the prime sponsors, the Midland Bank, were later given an award by the Association for Business Sponsorship of the Arts.

The author retired from the Secretaryship on 31 March 1982, but, on pension, has maintained his association with the Academy by becoming Honorary Archivist, continuing certain activities (particularly his connection with the E. A. Abbey and E. Vincent Harris Mural Funds) and taking on some other commitments. The new Secretary, Piers Rodgers, commenced his duties as such on the following day.

21

PRESENT AND FUTURE
1982–1986 and beyond

The Royal Academy Trust had set up an Appeal Committee early in 1982, with Robin Leigh-Pemberton as its chairman, and, to aid its work, a film on the Academy's activities was made by James Archibald. A member of the staff, Griselda Hamilton-Baillie, was appointed Director of the Appeal and it was launched to commerce and industry on 15 April, announced to the public on 22 June and, by 30 September, nearly £2¼ million had been donated or promised.[1] The opening events had considerable panache. HRH The Duke of Edinburgh gave a Reception in the Picture Gallery at Buckingham Palace on 18 May and there was a Midsummer Eve Celebration in the Academy's main galleries, with dancing of course and Elizabeth Welch providing cabaret, followed in the early hours of the morning by a champagne breakfast. Unfortunately this event necessitated the Summer Exhibition being closed to the public for three days, but it was possible to make use of the first of these for free visits by disabled people and mothers with children under five. The entrance to the galleries was via the goods lift (thus avoiding the difficulties of the main staircase) and special facilities, including a food service, were available.[2] Those who paid £35 per head (£60 for a double ticket) for the celebration no doubt enjoyed themselves but so did those less fortunate for whom the day-time outing was even more eventful.

There was certainly an atmosphere of renewed hope at the time. The success of *The Great Japan Exhibition* had helped to relieve the financial situation but the anticipated assistance through the Royal Academy Trust was nevertheless eagerly awaited as most exhibitions continued to be in deficit, not least due to disappointing attendances. This was particularly so with the Summer Exhibition of 1982 and, despite partial sponsorships, with *Painting in Naples*, *Treasures of Ancient Nigeria* and *Murillo* that winter, followed by *The Hague School* in the spring. It was of little comfort to discover that all London galleries had suffered some 20 per cent decline in their numbers of visitors.

The Academy's programme had been so arranged that there were two, and sometime three, exhibitions open at any one time.[3] This seldom pays, even though each may be of the highest distinction. The costs are thereby increased considerably and concurrent shows rob one another of attendances. Indeed, except for occasional overlapping for the sake of a few people from far afield, such a procedure is too extravagant and should be avoided. Conversely, it is important always to have some exhibition in being so that the would-be visitor (particularly a paid-up member of the Friends), after crossing the courtyard, is not disappointed. Once again there was a heavy deficit on the year's activities.

It was obvious that good husbandry was always likely to be a key factor in aiding financial recovery and, to help towards this, the Academy's trading activities (the Shop, Restaurant, Gift Catalogue and Framing Department) were incorporated into a subsidiary company, R A Enterprises Ltd, on 1 October 1982.[4] The Summer Exhibition of 1983 had a good attendance and, for the first time, this annual exhibition enjoyed sponsorship, namely a generous but limited guarantee against loss by IBM (UK) Ltd. These two factors, together with the handling fees and the commission on sales, enabled its income and expenditure to be reconciled.

In November 1982, the Prime Minister, Margaret Thatcher, had given a dinner at 10 Downing Street in aid of the Appeal and the Trust set up a tax-exempt corporation in the USA entitled 'American Associates of the Royal Academy Trust, Inc.' To help this promotion, an exhibition *Paintings from the Royal Academy*, comprising forty-one important works from the institution's collection, was sent across the Atlantic on an extensive tour of eight American cities (Palm Beach, Cincinnati, New York, Seattle, New Orleans, San Antonio, Richmond and Wilmington) from January 1983 until April 1984, and on its return was shown in the Private Rooms at Burlington House. At the same time an increasing number of Loan Exhibitions to venues in Great Britain were organized and these served to encourage the development of Country Friends. Also, September 1983 saw the first issue of *RA*, a magazine for the Friends of the Royal Academy, which then replaced the more humble and prosaic news-letter that had hitherto been circulated. It is an attractive publication and appears to be much appreciated by a growing clientèle of readers.

Following the appointment of Alan Bowness as Director of the Tate Gallery in 1981, the situation regarding the Chantrey collection has become considerably more satisfactory. He took over a number of acquisitions on behalf of the gallery which had previously been refused by them, reinstated a Tate recommending committee (matched by one from the Academy) and suggested that, in collaboration with the Tate, the Academy should try each year to find one major British work that the national collection really needs. The Chantrey Trustees, although concerned about the works still in store at Burlington House, were pleased with these developments but stressed that the President and Council of the Royal Academy must not abrogate the duty imposed upon them by Chantrey's will to use their discretion. Such purchases so far have included the oil paintings *L'Heure du Thé* by Anthony Green, *Max Wall and his Image* by Maggi Hambling, *Open Window, Spitalfields* by Anthony Eyton, *Gloucester Gate, Regent's Park, May 1982* by Adrian Berg and *Self-portrait with Decoy Duck* by Norman Blamey.

Meanwhile, there were yet more changes in personnel at the Academy. Bryan Kneale took over from Willi Soukop as Master of the Sculpture School in the autumn of 1982 and in 1983–84 Victor Pasmore was the first artist to be elected direct as a Senior Academician, Lord Clark died and was replaced by Francis Haskell as Professor of the History of Art and, it being known that Peter Greenham would shortly be retiring, Edward Middleditch was appointed to succeed him as Keeper from 1 October 1985. In addition, it had been decided to have an Education Officer (MaryAnne Stevens) to organize lectures, seminars and other related events. Also Robin Leigh-Pemberton gave up his chairmanship of the Appeal Committee on being appointed Governor of the Bank of England and was succeeded by John Raisman, Chairman of Shell (UK).

There was, however, an even greater change looming in that the President, Sir Hugh Casson, who was nearing the Academy's age limit, resolved not to seek re-election in December 1984. He had done so much in his nine years in the post to create the current outgoing atmosphere and to encourage a hive of activity, busy yet pleasantly informal. Typical of his enthusiasm was his immediate reaction to the proposal for a Venetian exhibition – 'Let's flood the courtyard and bring the visitors across in gondolas'. As a suggestion it was completely impractical, of course, but the spontaneity of such remarks fired the imagination. His little Mini no longer brings him quite so frequently to Burlington House and he has numerous other commitments, yet he still finds the time to make journeys to America on the Academy's behalf. He was made a Companion of Honour and Peter Greenham was commissioned to paint his portrait.

The painter, Roger de Grey (Plate 90), was elected President on 6 December 1984 by a considerable majority, polling thirty-six votes against an aggregate of twenty-one spread among ten other Academicians (five for Sir Philip Powell, three each for Frederick Gore and Eduardo Paolozzi, two each for Robert Buhler, Jeffery Camp and Leonard Rosoman, and one each for Anthony Green, Rodrigo Moynihan, Richard Rogers and David Tindle). It was a clear-cut victory and, bearing in mind his own professionalism and his long experience in teaching at King's College in the University of Newcastle, in the Painting School at the Royal College of Art and, latterly, as Principal of the City and Guilds of London Art School, it was not surprising that he quickly announced among his aspirations that of promoting more contemporary art at the Academy. His election to the Presidency left the Treasurership vacant and Sir Philip Powell was chosen to fill the post. Thus all four Officers of the Royal Academy (President, Keeper, Treasurer and Secretary) were replaced within a relatively short time.

The *Genius of Venice* exhibition (Plate 89), including a splendid array of Titians, had been on view from November 1983 to March 1984, and been seen by almost 453,000 visitors. It was followed by, among other shows, *The Orientalists: Delacroix to Matisse* that spring, *The Age of Vermeer and de Hooch*, *Modern Masters from the Thyssen-Bornemisza Collection*, *Chagall* and *Elisabeth Frink* (Plate 91) in the winter of 1984–85, then *Peter Greenham*, *Edward Lear* and *The Burlington House Fair*. The autumn of 1985 was taken up with *German Art in the Twentieth Century*, coupled with a truly comprehensive programme of related events (lectures, concerts, films etc.), and scheduled to be the first of a series on the arts of various countries during this period. By this time some seventy to eighty paintings by Sir Joshua Reynolds were placed on view at the Grand Palais in Paris, forming the nucleus of the much larger Reynolds exhibition held at the Academy early in 1986. Many of the successes at Burlington House in recent years have then been shown elsewhere, most frequently in America, and, although the order in this case was reversed, it was yet another example of close collaboration with comparable authorities abroad. Most of these exhibitions had been in the pipe-line before Roger de Grey became President and now, following the recent show of works by Sir Alfred Gilbert (best known to most people as the sculptor of *Eros* in Piccadilly Circus), one awaits those subsequently conceived.

The rate of inflation had mercifully diminished but its effects were still troublesome and charges had once again to be increased for the Summer Exhibition of 1984. The handling fee rose to £15 (£30 for Members) and the commission on sales to 25 per cent, unpalatable but still far less than in most dealers' galleries; the admission charge stayed at £2 but the prices of the catalogue and of *The Royal Academy Illustrated* became £1.50 and £3.90 respectively. Sales figures on the first Private View Day broke all previous records – 1,166 works for £262,049. This meant that, on average throughout the day, from 10 a.m. to 6 p.m., a work was purchased every 24.7 seconds. The Librarian, who for many years had undertaken the job on that day of affixing a red disc by the side of each work sold and wore a pedometer for the occasion, clocked up 9¼ miles in her perambulations around the galleries – not an easy assignment through masses of people. Indeed, since the growth of the Friends' organization, the Private View Days (formerly just one for each exhibition) have had to be increased gradually to three full days.

Yet more works, amounting to 1,337, were sold on the comparable day in 1985 but the rate was not so high since the hours were extended to 8 p.m. The grand total of sales, including duplicate prints, throughout the exhibition was 4,119 for £814,573 and the aggregate of attendances (143,706, including 40,884 visits by Friends and their guests but not the participants in evening events) was the best for twenty-five years. Most people seemed to prefer the hanging, with the abstract works mingled with the figurative instead of being hived off in cold seclusion. For the first time ever, the prices were printed in the catalogue and even those artists whose submissions had straightaway been passed by the committee for further consideration, but were not ultimately placed on show, were given a record of their having been 'Accepted but not hung'. Altogether some 15,400 works had been sent in, of which 4,840 from 'outsiders' (that is, not Members of the Royal Academy) had survived the preliminary selection, and the completed exhibition comprised 1,712 works by almost a thousand artists.

In 1986 the handling fee was changed to £7.50 per work submitted and again there had to be small increases in the charges for admission and in the prices of the publications. The sales figures on the first Private View Day exceeded even the 1984 record – 1,593 works were sold for £485,809, an amazing average of one every 22.6 seconds throughout ten hours. The Charles Wollaston Awards continued annually and, by now, were joined by no fewer than eleven other substantial prizes from various sources.

The E. A. Abbey Mural Fund commissioned two paintings by Graeme Willson, *Mother and Child* and *The Last Supper*, which were placed behind the altars of a Church of England and a Roman Catholic church in St Paul's Centre at Thamesmead, also *The Blackbird* by Mary Fedden for the Grahame Park Health Centre at Colindale and *Burlington House: Interior–Exterior* (frontispiece) by Leonard Rosoman for the Royal Academy Restaurant, while the E. Vincent Harris Mural Decoration Fund made contributions towards a huge external painting (*The Battle of Cable Street, 4 October 1936*, the joint effort of David Binnington, Paul Butler, Desmond Rochfort and Ray Walker) on the side of the old St George's Town Hall at Stepney in the East End of London, and towards tapestries designed by Ursula Benker-Schirmer for Chichester Cathedral and by Thelma Beswick for Derriford Hospital, Plymouth.

Since 1982 the new Associates have included the painters David Hockney, Ken Howard, R. B. Kitaj and Joe Tilson, and the architects Norman Foster and James Stirling. In 1985–86, Bryan Kneale was elected Professor of Sculpture and Norman Adams Professor of Painting (the first such appointments since 1911) and, on the retirement of Walter Woodington, Ian Tregarthen Jenkin became Curator in the Schools; the post of Registrar, instituted in 1862, was abolished and its holder, Laurie Bray, took over special responsibilities in regard to the trust funds and the membership. Meanwhile there had been a small amendment to the Laws under which each member reaching seventy-five years of age would become a Senior Member 'on the first day of October following his or her attainment of this age'. This was merely to conform with the Academy's year which now ends on 30 September. More trust funds had been acquired and a complete list of them to date is given in Appendix F. They can, of course, only operate within their means and, as a safeguard and on the advice of the Financial Advisory Committee, the investments in many of them have been changed, involving in some cases a reduction in their current spending power in order to obtain a reasonable prospect of growth in capital and income in the future.

The general financial situation, although by no means fully solved, is now not quite so restricting and just recently it has at long last been possible to make a start on much needed improvements within the Academy. In 1983–84 the boilerhouse installation was renewed, achieving savings in fuel costs and paving the way for better environmental controls throughout the building, while much work was involved in repairing the ravages of dry rot and in dealing with electrical wiring. Various studies of Burlington House, prepared by the Surveyor, were amalgamated into one document as a feasibility study for structural alterations which were to include the construction of a picture store in the basement, thus making the Gibson Gallery available for a new Library, whose previous premises on the ground floor could then be converted into a more commodious apartment for the Friends, to be followed by a scheme of rehabilitation in the remaining three Diploma Galleries. It was an ambitious programme which, obviously, could only be undertaken in stages and with minimal interruption to the institution's activities.

In 1984–85, the new picture store was brought into operation and work was started on the new Library, reached by the Diploma Gallery staircase and lift and made possible by a generous grant from the Wolfson Foundation. Some doubts were expressed on the adequacy of the space available, but the height of the apartment enabled bookshelving to be installed at two levels and, with the insertion of windows north and south, the result, designed by Professor H. T. Cadbury-Brown and achieved in the following year, is very attractive. By then parts of the ceiling of the old Library had collapsed and it was necessary to strengthen the floor of the Reynolds Room above it. Both apartments were out of action while the work was undertaken and all the books were removed from the building for temporary storage. Coinciding with their return, MaryAnne Stevens was appointed Librarian and Constance-Anne Parker, on retiring from the post, has been enabled to concentrate on lectures and exhibitions of works from the Academy's permanent collections.

The Friends, numbering 37,600 on 30 September 1985, certainly needed a larger rest-room, where lectures and other relevant events could be held, and this should be ready towards the end of 1986. This organization's activities, both within the Academy and on study tours, have increased tremendously and so has the number of exhibitions of the Academy's own possessions sent to provincial towns. Indeed, this outward-looking policy, never previously attempted systematically, has become an important feature of the institution's work in the past few years. The pity is that it could not have been started sooner.

The Diploma Galleries, newly arranged by Norman Foster, should be available for reoccupation at about the same time as the rest-room and, meanwhile, workshops for the Framing Department have been provided in the basement and the Restaurant has been enlivened both in its décor and its service. In 1985, the Academy was allocated two small rooms on the ground floor of the adjacent building on the east side of the courtyard and, by housing the Artists' General Benevolent Institution therein, regained comparable accommodation below the Keeper's Studio. Thus, with these various changes, the shortage of space has to some extent been mitigated and, within the limitations of the fabric, the environmental conditions have been greatly improved.

There is certainly no feeling of smug complacency at the Academy. So much more remains to be done but, at least, the battle for survival, against considerable odds, seems to have been won and it has been possible to bring this narrative up to date optimistically. But what of the future?

Undoubtedly the Royal Academy is a peculiar institution. Indeed it might almost be called 'a Royal peculiar' since the Sovereign is its only superior authority. There is no doubt of George III's close connections with the foundation and development of the Academy and each successive Sovereign has been graciously pleased to continue as 'patron, protector and supporter', to approve alterations in the Laws and the appointment of Officers, to sign the annual business of the institution and generally to take a personal interest in its welfare. The Instrument of Foundation, duly signed by George III, even committed the Privy Purse 'to pay all deficiencies'.[5] This, as has been seen, was done for each of the first twelve years of the Academy's existence but could hardly be expected these days. Furthermore, the King granted rooms for the Academy's use, and the present tenure of Burlington House, including of course the ground on which the Academy built its own galleries and Schools in the nineteenth century, is a direct outcome of this munificence.

The main result of the close connection with the Crown has been the Academy's freedom from bureaucratic control although, in recent years, this independence has been threatened by serious financial problems. Nowhere else in the world is there an institution of comparable standing which runs art schools with the possibility of free places and which holds such a variety of art exhibitions without regular, official grants. All others with similar activities are subsidized by taxes in some form. In Britain, the official museums and galleries, whether national or provincial, have had their permanent collections open to the public without direct payment on admission although, very recently, a few have introduced mandatory or voluntary charges, and all usually require an entrance fee for specially organized displays. The Academy has to charge for entry into its exhibitions as a prime source of revenue and cannot afford any great succession of losses. It is in a curious position in that it is regarded by the man in the street as a national institution and yet it has to be self-supporting.

The Schools and exhibitions are the Academy's paramount activities and, as far as one can see, this pattern is unlikely to change. The training, in what are the oldest established schools of art in England, was for over two centuries completely free and, even now, a limited number of free places are maintained. Until recent years the teaching was almost entirely undertaken by the Academicians and Associates, although notable exceptions included two Teachers of Perspective, H. A. Bowler and Walter Bayes, also F. Ernest Jackson, later made an Associate, who taught regularly in the Life School in the evenings between the two world wars. Men such as Turner and Millais worked in the Schools, first as students and then as mentors, from the time of their youth until their death. Others, trained elsewhere, have supported the Academy Schools to the full after being elected and there developed in succeeding generations a feeling of family ties between members and students. The tradition of Academicians and Associates attending as Visitors for a term at a time was dropped in the 1930s and there are now, in addition to the Keeper and a small permanent staff, about twenty or so visiting artists, drawn partly from the membership and partly from outside the Academy, who teach on a more regular basis. Candidates for entry into the Schools must normally be under thirty years of age and the competition for admission is keen. Currently there is a total of some ninety students and the courses are each of three years' duration.

The exhibitions fall into two categories – the annual Summer Exhibitions of the work of living artists, the first of which was held in 1769, and the Loan Exhibitions started in 1870. The present regulations for the Summer Exhibition allow members to submit six works and non-members three. Approximately twelve to fifteen thousand works are sent in each year and there is reasonable space for, say, fifteen to seventeen hundred. More have from time to time been included, particularly in the latter part of the nineteenth century, but such hanging is certainly not in accordance with present-day taste.

The works have to be delivered on specified days and those by non-members are considered by a committee consisting of the thirteen members of Council for that year and, if desirable for balance within the categories, other members specially appointed. All are professional artists with marked individual opinions and their first task, which takes several days, is to separate the works into three divisions. Those receiving unanimous votes in their favour are chalked on the back with an 'A' for 'Accepted' and must be placed in the exhibition. Those with only one vote or no vote at all are marked with an 'X' as 'Rejected' and the remainder are classed as 'D' for 'Doubtful'. Hardly any ever achieve an 'A', about three to five thousand are marked 'D' and the remainder 'X'. The members of the committee sit in an arc (Plates 51 and 60) as one by one the pictures are brought before them and the President is equipped with three letters in brass, mounted on wooden handles, so that he may raise the appropriate one according to the judgment.

The committee's next duty is to inspect the works by the Members and to arrange an exhibition of them together with any non-members' works marked 'A' and with a large selection of those marked 'D'. This takes the best part of two weeks and is not unlike a gigantic jigsaw puzzle with the added hazards of there being endless permutations and far too many pieces. The usual procedure is to decide which are to be placed in important positions, such as on the line in the centres of walls and the vistas from one gallery to another, and then to surround them so that, as far as possible, there is both harmony and variety in the arrangement. Rooms thereby attain a character all their own and every effort is made to show works to their best advantage. The submissions of the Academicians and Associates are not above jurisdiction although it is seldom that any are omitted and, as has been indicated, they are exempt from the preliminary selection. Roughly speaking, almost half the 'Doubtful' works are placed and the others have to be refused as 'D – Not Hung' or, in artists' vernacular, 'Crowded out'. The inevitable outcome is always sad and the committee, which usually starts its spate of hanging each year with a cry from the heart that there are not enough good works, ends up by trying frantically to find space for all those which are too good to cast aside. The President and Council take ultimate responsibility for the exhibition by approving it (Plate 81) and sometimes making changes.

There then follows a considerable amount of administrative work. The catalogue is compiled, notices are sent to all who submitted items, the prices of the pictures and sculpture for sale are recorded, members and non-members are given the opportunity to check their exhibits on the Varnishing Days and, at last, following the Annual Dinner and the

Private View Days, the exhibition is opened to the public. The event was for long regarded as marking the beginning of the London season and, when the flags are hoisted on the Piccadilly frontage, the Academy once again invites attention.

It is to be hoped that these exhibitions, which have now been held each year without a break for well over two centuries, may always continue but this need not preclude perhaps smaller and more specialized shows at other times. There are some artists who for good reasons do not wish their works to be on view in such large-scale displays and it might be possible in the future to develop a series which would attract their support. The galleries are adaptable and there are many would-be visitors who prefer their art in smaller helpings. They find the normal Summer Exhibition somewhat indigestible although, as a feast, it offers a rich choice for anyone with the appetite and time to enjoy it.

The Loan Exhibitions vary enormously in size and scope but have two things in common. Their organization requires the help of specialist advisers and their realization the generous co-operation of the owners of the works to be borrowed. It is exhilarating to be able to assemble the ingredients of a particular theme but many lenders, especially private persons, are thereby deprived of their choicest possessions for several months and usually left with disfiguring gaps in their homes. The art-loving public is therefore greatly indebted to them and, with so many such requests these days, the Royal Academy is fortunate in being able to mount such exhibitions so frequently. It can often be claimed, however, that the pictures and objects themselves are eventually returned with reputations enhanced.

The costs of packing and transporting these works, frequently borrowed from far afield, are of course very heavy and, with the expenses of installation and safe custody, have to be weighed carefully against the anticipated receipts from admissions. It may be necessary in the future to curtail these exhibitions in size but it is to be hoped that the standard of their content may always remain high. Public collections grow richer year by year but it is surely neither practical nor desirable that they should ever render unnecessary the uses, and indeed the delights, of temporary exhibitions.

Contrary to popular belief in the past, the Academy is not a rich institution financially. The days of its being able to carry on its work from profits on exhibitions are long since gone and, indeed, the majority of art exhibitions elsewhere in the world are run at a loss. Its main income in the general fund is now very much dependent on its trading activities, on the support of the Friends of the Royal Academy and on the outcome of the Appeal organized through the Royal Academy Trust.

The Academy's trust funds, of which there are now over sixty, are of course all self-supporting but their income may only be used for their specific purposes – the provision of scholarships, prizes and annuities, the purchase and commissioning of works of art and sundry relevant commitments. They are used to sponsor highly desirable activities which otherwise could not be afforded but they cannot in the main be used for the day-to-day conduct of the institution's affairs.

The Academy, however, has other assets besides money. It has the long lease, with almost nine hundred years still to run, of old Burlington House and the ground adjoining it to the north on which stand its own galleries and Schools. This site and building, in the centre of London's West End, is of almost inestimable value but the cost of upkeep is considerable. The walls of the original house are now over three hundred years old and the nineteenth-century additions are no longer new. The fabric of both requires constant attention and the building's services and decoration are relatively expensive to keep in good order. It is indeed a stately home and fitting for its purpose but its proper maintenance is an increasing liability.

Conversely, and happily, the institution's collection of works of art grows in number and, for the most part, in financial value. New Diploma Works are added as Academicians are elected and the purchases through certain trust funds have mounted up in recent years. Nothing comparable with the Michelangelo tondo or Constable's *The Leaping Horse* has been received this century but more modest gifts and bequests are made from time to time and are very welcome. Except for the sale of the Leonardo cartoon and, in 1967, of some engravings, there has never been any intention of disposing of any of these possessions but they are important assets.

The Academy's library, comprising a large resource of books and catalogues on the fine arts and allied subjects, together with prints, drawings and reproductions, is an information centre, indeed a treasure-house, of inestimable value. It includes a number of comparatively rare publications in their early editions and, understandably, is strong in its representation of British artists. In addition, the archives contain original material, such as the sitters' notebooks of Sir Joshua Reynolds and the correspondence of Sir Thomas Lawrence, and a selection of palettes and other relics of past members. All these mementoes provide a revealing insight into the lives of their one-time owners.

Lastly there is a collection of silver (Plate 76) since, besides depositing a Diploma Work, every Academician from the foundation has been expected to give a piece of plate, although the custom has lapsed in recent years. It has few outstanding items of great rarity but it does provide a creditable assortment of tableware which is frequently in use.

If the total value of all these assets were ever to be reckoned, the final figure would no doubt be substantial and surprising but their worth to the Academy far exceeds whatever sum they might realize by sale. The building, or a comparable substitute, is obviously essential for the institution's activities; the works of art, the library and various other treasures are a growing heritage which, provided the annual budget can be balanced, should not only be enjoyed today but held in trust for future generations.

The public can help in this by supporting the Academy and the institution in its turn has obligations to the nation – a duty to train young artists along broad lines, approving serious experiment but deploring gimmicks, and a duty to support the endeavours of artists of all ages without prejudice. Tradition and invention are far from being incompatible and, more often than not, are necessary to one another.

At first thought, more than two hundred years would seem to have been ample time in which to have settled all differences of opinion in the art world but art itself is never at a standstill. It reflects its environment but is not tied down by it. It is the outcome of independent vision but needs encouragement. The Royal Academy has done much to help its growth in the past and undoubtedly has the potential to play a prominent part in the future.

The Royal Academy of Arts

NOTES

The following abbreviations are used:
Coll: = in the collection of;
RA = Royal Academy of Arts, London

CHAPTER 1

1. Edmond Malone, *The Works of Sir Joshua Reynolds* (London, 1797), Vol. 1, p. 5.
2. Ibid., p. 6.
3. Ibid., p. 8.
4. Ibid., p. 7.
5. Ibid.
6. Ibid., p. 8.
7. The Walpole Society, Vol. XVIII (Oxford, 1930), p. 156.
8. J. Payne, *The Life of John Evelyn* (London, 1755), pp. viii–ix.

CHAPTER 2

1. The Walpole Society, Vol. XXX (Oxford, 1955), p. 169.
2. Ibid., Vol. XXII (Oxford, 1934), p. 92.
3. Ibid.
4. W. T. Whitley, *Artists and their Friends in England, 1700–1799*, Vol. 1, p. 13.
5. The Walpole Society, Vol. XX (Oxford, 1932), p. 125.
6. Edward Edwards, *Anecdotes of Painters* (London, 1808), p. xx.
7. W. T. Whitley, op. cit., p. 18.
8. Ibid., p. 27.
9. Horace Walpole, *Anecdotes of Painting in England* (London, 1871, reprint of 1786 edition), p. 363.
10. Ibid., p. 316.
11. R. H. Nichols and F. A. Wray, *The History of the Foundling Hospital* (London, 1935), p. 259.

12. The Walpole Society, XVIII (Oxford, 1930), p. 10.
13. Ibid., Vol. XX (Oxford, 1932), p. 150.
14. Ibid., p. 151.
15. Ibid., p. 155.
16. Ibid., Vol. XXX (Oxford, 1955), p. 150.
17. Lionel Cust and Sir Sidney Colvin, *The History of the Society of Dilettanti* (London, 1914), pp. 52–5.
18. Robert Strange, *An Inquiry into the Rise and Establishment of the Royal Academy of Arts* (London, 1775), p. 62.
19. Lionel Cust and Sir Sidney Colvin, op. cit., pp. 52–5.
20. J. Gwynn, *An Essay on Design including proposals for erecting a Public Academy . . .*, (London, 1749).
21. Ibid., p. 6.
22. Ibid., p. 44.
23. Anonymous (probably Alexander Nesbit), *An Essay . . . on the Necessity and Form of a Royal Academy . . .* (London, 1755), p. 5.
24. Ibid., p. 6.
25. Ibid.
26. Ibid., p. 17.
27. Ibid., p. 7.
28. Ibid., p. 20.
29. Ibid., pp. 24–5.
30. Ibid., p. 34.

CHAPTER 3

1. R. H. Nichols and F. A. Wray, *The History of the Foundling Hospital* (London, 1935), p. 251.

2. Ibid., p. 252.
3. Ibid.
4. Ibid.
5. W. T. Whitley, *Artists and their Friends in England, 1700–1799* (London, 1928), Vol. 1, p. 165.
6. Ibid.
7. Ibid.
8. Edward Edwards, *Anecdotes of Painters* (London, 1808), p. xxv.
9 Ibid.
10. Ibid., pp. xxv–xxvi.
11. W. T. Whitley, op. cit., p. 172.
12. Ibid., p. 174.
13. Ibid., p. 199.
14. *Coll*: Royal Academy of Arts, London.

CHAPTER 4

1. John Galt, *The Life, Studies and Works of Benjamin West* (London, 1820), Part II, p. 36.
2. Ibid., p. 37.
3. *Coll*: HM The Queen.
4. John Galt, op. cit., p. 40.
5. Ibid., p. 41.
6. See para. I of *The Instrument of Foundation* (Appendix A).
7. RA General Assembly Minutes, Vol. I, pp. 1–4.
8. John Galt, op. cit., p. 42.
9. Ibid., p. 43.
10. James Northcote, *The Life of Sir Joshua Reynolds* (London, 1819), p. 166.
11. RA General Assembly Minutes, Vol. I, pp. 1–4.
12. Ibid., p. 6.
13. RA Council Minutes, Vol. I, pp. 2–3.
14. Ibid., pp. 4–6.
15. Edward Malone, *The Works of Sir Joshua Reynolds* (London, 1797), Vol. I, p. 11.
16. Ibid., p. 12.
17. Ibid., p. 9.
18. Ibid.

CHAPTER 5

1. The exterior is shown in a drawing by John Coney, 1796. *Coll*: British Museum (Department of Prints and Drawings), London – Crace Portfolio XI, No. 55, Sheet 23.
2. W. T. Whitley, *Artists and their Friends in England, 1700–1799* (London, 1928), Vol. I, p. 256.
3. RA Council Minutes, Vol. I, p. 17.
4. Ibid., p. 26.
5. RA General Assembly Minutes, Vol. I, p. 19.
6. *Instrument of Foundation* (Appendix A), Clause III.
7. RA Council Minutes, Vol. I, pp. 34–5.
8. Ibid., p. 49.
9. Ibid., p. 4.
10. Ibid., p. 20.
11. Ibid., p. 8.
12. RA General Assembly Minutes, Vol. I, p. 17.
13. RA Council Minutes, Vol. I, p. 11.
14. A dictionary of all works shown in the Summer Exhibitions from 1769 to 1904 is given in an eight-volume work by Algernon Graves entitled *The Royal Academy of Arts* (London, 1905–6) and from 1905 to 1970 in six volumes of *Royal Academy Exhibitors 1905–1970* (Wakefield, 1973–82). They are in the alphabetical order of the artists and a typescript continuation to date is kept at the Royal Academy.
15. Edmond Malone, *The Works of Sir Joshua Reynolds* (London, 1797), Vol. I, p. 17.
16. Ibid.
17. A complete list of the students from 1769 to 1830, together with the medals won, is given by Sidney C. Hutchison in the Walpole Society, Vol. XXXVIII (London, 1962).
18. John Galt, *The Life, Studies and Works of Benjamin West* (London, 1820), Part II, pp. 49–50.
19. *Coll*: National Gallery of Ireland, Dublin.
20. *Coll*: HM The Queen.
21. *Coll*: National Gallery of Scotland, Edinburgh.
22. *Coll*: National Gallery, London.
23. W. T. Whitley, op. cit., p. 349; the

original picture appears to be lost but several versions exist, sometimes called *Lydia*.

24. *Coll*: Royal Academy of Arts, London.
25. RA Council Minutes, Vol. I, pp. 268–9.
26. James Northcote, *The Life of Sir Joshua Reynolds* (London, 1819), Vol. I, p. 171.
27. RA General Assembly Minutes, Vol. I, p. 98.
28. Joseph Farington's Diary, 10 December, 1804.
29. William Sandby, *The History of the Royal Academy of Arts* (London, 1862), Vol. I, pp. 94–5.
30. Ibid., p. 108.
31. W. G. Constable, *Richard Wilson* (London, 1953), p. 55.
32. RA General Assembly Minutes Vol. I, p. 102.
33. RA Council Minutes, Vol. I, p. 269.
34. Ibid., p. 247.
35. Ibid., p. 99.
36. Ibid., p. 95.

CHAPTER 6

1. Sir William Chambers, *Report to the House of Commons, 1 May, 1780*.
2. Sir William Chambers, *A Treatise on the Decorative Part of Civil Architecture* (Third edition, London, 1791), p. 10.
3. Thomas Malton, *A Picturesque Tour through the Cities of London and Westminster* (London, 1792), Vol. I, Plates XXVI–XLII (dated 1796).
4. *The Microcosm of London* (London, 1808), Vol. I, Plate 1.
5. J. Baretti, *A Guide through the Royal Academy* (London, c. 1781), p. 9.
6. *Coll*: Royal Academy of Arts, London.
7. Ibid.
8. Ibid.
9. Ibid.
10. Ibid.
11. Ibid.
12. Ibid.
13. *Coll*: British Museum (Department

of Prints and Drawings), London – Nos. 1936–9–18–1 and 1904–1–1–1, 2 and 3.

14. *The Microcosm of London* (London, 1808), Vol. I, Plate 2.
15. James Northcote, *The Life of Sir Joshua Reynolds* (London, 1819), Vol. II, p. 143.
16. *Coll*: Royal Academy of Arts, London.
17. Ibid.
18. RA Council Minutes, Vol. I, p. 358.
19. *Coll*: Royal Academy of Arts, London.
20. Edward Malone, *The Works of Sir Joshua Reynolds* (London, 1797), Vol. I, p. 294.
21. James Northcote, op. cit., p. 239.
22. C. R. Leslie and Tom Taylor, *Life and Times of Sir Joshua Reynolds* (London, 1865), Vol. II, p. 83.
23. RA Council Minutes, Vol. II, p. 96.
24. Ibid., Vol. I, p. 327.
25. Ibid., p. 133.
26. W. T. Whitley, *Artists and their Friends in England, 1700–1799* (London, 1928), Vol. 2, p. 129.
27. *Coll*: Royal Academy of Arts, London.
28. Edmond Malone, op. cit., p. 346.
29. RA Council Minutes, Vol. II, p. 151.

CHAPTER 7

1. W. T. Whitley, *Artists and their Friends in England, 1700–1799* (London, 1928), Vol. 2, p. 161.
2. John Galt, *The Life, Studies and Works of Benjamin West* (London, 1820), Part II, pp. 77–8.
3. Ibid., p. 81.
4. Ibid., p. 190.
5. Ibid.
6. Joseph Farington's Diary, 11 November 1796.
7. Ibid.
8. RA Council Minutes, Vol. II, p. 357.
9. *Coll*: Royal Academy of Arts, London.
10. Ibid.
11. Ibid.
12. Ibid.

13. Edmond Malone, *The Works of Sir Joshua Reynolds* (London, 1797), Vol. I, p. 122.
14. RA Council Minutes, Vol. II, p. 245.
15. Joseph Farington's Diary, 31 December 1795.
16. RA Council Minutes, Vol. III, pp. 25–6.
17. RA General Assembly Minutes, Vol. II, p. 83.
18. RA Council Minutes, Vol. III, pp. 44–5.
19. Ibid.
20. Ibid., pp. 15–17.
21. Tom Taylor, *Life of Benjamin Robert Haydon* (Second edition, London, 1853), Vol. I, p. 32.
22. Ibid., p. 33.
23. *Coll*: Metropolitan Museum of Art, New York.
24. Joseph Farington's Diary, 13 November 1803.
25. Ibid., 10 December 1804.

CHAPTER 8

1. *Coll*: Royal Academy of Arts, London.
2. RA Council Minutes, Vol. IV, p. 160.
3. RA General Assembly Minutes, Vol. II, pp. 361–2.
4. *Coll*: Royal Academy of Arts, London.
5. Ibid.
6. *Coll*: Earl of Mansfield.
7. W. T. Whitley, *Art in England, 1800–1820* (Cambridge, 1928), p. 210.
8. *Coll*: National Gallery, London.
9. *Coll*: Tate Gallery, London.
10. Mrs Uwins, *A Memoir of Thomas Uwins* (London, 1858), Vol. I, p. 39.
11. A. J. Finberg, *The Life of J. M. W. Turner* (Oxford, 1939), p. 241.
12. RA Summer Exhibition Catalogue, 1818, No. 165. *Coll*: Earl Bathurst.
13. John Pye, *Patronage of British Art* (London, 1845), p. 302.
14. *Coll*: Dulwich College Picture Gallery, London.
15. A. P. Oppé, *Thomas Rowlandson, his drawings and watercolours* (London, 1923), Plate 50.
16. Dennis Farr, *William Etty* (London, 1958), p. 32.
17. RA Council Minutes, Vol IV, p. 184.
18. RA General Assembly Minutes, Vol. III, p. 174.
19. RA Council Minutes, Vol. IV, p. 218.
20. Ibid., pp. 99–101.
21. Richard and Samuel Redgrave, *A Century of Painters of the English School* (London, 1866), Vol. II, p. 95.
22. Ibid.
23. It was exhibited at the Royal Academy in 1810 (No. 58). *Coll*: Museum of Fine Arts, Boston, Massachusetts.
24. It was not recorded in the Royal Academy Catalogue of that year.
25. *Coll*: HM The Queen but on loan to the Victoria and Albert Museum, London.
26. RA Council Minutes, Vol. XI, p. 148.
27. RA General Assembly Minutes, Vol. III, pp. 95–7.
28. Tom Taylor, *Life of Benjamin Robert Haydon* (Second edition, London, 1853), Vol. I, p. 177.
29. Walter Thornbury, *The Life of J. M. W. Turner* (London, 1862), Vol. II, p. 99.
30. RA General Assembly Minutes, Vol. III, p. 169.
31. RA Council Minutes, Vol. IV, p. 280.
32. Ibid., Vol. VI, p. 91.
33. *Coll*: Pennsylvania Academy of Fine Arts, Philadelphia.
34. W. T. Whitley, op. cit., p. 225.

CHAPTER 9

1. W. P. Frith, *My Autobiography and Reminiscences* (Second edition, London, 1887), Vol. I, p. 57.
2. C. R. Leslie, *Memoirs of the Life of John Constable* (London, 1843), p. 63.
3. *Coll*: National Gallery, London.
4. *Coll*: Musée du Louvre, Paris.

5. *Coll*: Wellington Museum, London.
6. *Coll*: Earl of Durham.
7. *Coll*: National Gallery of Scotland, Edinburgh.
8. *Coll*: Petworth House (National Trust).
9. W. T. Whitley, *Art in England, 1821–37* (Cambridge, 1930), p. 191.
10. Ibid., p. 131.
11. *Coll*: Tate Gallery, London.
12. *Coll*: Victoria and Albert Museum, London.
13. *Coll*: National Gallery, London.
14. *Coll*: Tate Gallery, London.
15. *Coll*: Victoria and Albert Museum, London.
16. W. T. Whitley, op. cit., p. 189.
17. C. R. Leslie, op. cit., pp. 71–2.
18. W. T. Whitley, op. cit., p. 236.
19. RA Council Minutes, Vol. VI, p. 291.
20. Ibid., p. 312.
21. *Coll*: Royal Academy of Arts, London.
22. Ibid.
23. *Coll*: Accademia, Florence.
24. *Coll*: Royal Academy of Arts, London.
25. Ibid.
26. Ibid., but certain items have been sold from 1967.
27. RA Council Minutes, Vol. VI, p. 207.
28. Ibid., p. 203.
29. Ibid., p. 249.
30. Ibid., p. 403.
31. Ibid., Vol. VII, p. 119.
32. W. T. Whitley, op. cit., p. 187.
33. Ibid.
34. Tom Taylor, *Life of Benjamin Robert Haydon* (Second edition, London, 1853), Vol. II, pp. 259–60.
35. C. R. Leslie, op. cit., p. 68.
36. M. A. Shee, *The Life of Sir Martin Archer Shee* (London, 1860), Vol. I, p. 418.
37. RA General Assembly Minutes, Vol. III, p. 439.
38. RA Council Minutes, Vol. VIII, pp. 74–81.
39. M. A. Shee, op. cit., Vol. II, p. 370.
40. RA Council Minutes, Vol. VII, pp. 524–5.
41. Ibid.

CHAPTER 10

1. W. P. Frith, *My Autobiography and Reminiscences* (Second edition, London, 1887), Vol. I, p. 56.
2. W. T. Whitley, *Art in England, 1821–1837* (Cambridge, 1930), p. 334.
3. *Coll*: Department of the Environment, London.
4. RA Exhibition Catalogue, 1837, p. 3.
5. *Coll*: Royal Academy of Arts, London.
6. Sir Martin Archer Shee, *A Letter to Lord John Russell . . .* (London, 1837), pp. 5–6.
7. Ibid.
8. RA Council Minutes, Vol. IX, pp. 13–14.
9. Ibid., pp. 50–1.
10. RA General Assembly Minutes, Vol. IV, p. 318.
11. Ibid., p. 337.
12. *Coll*: Tate Gallery, London.
13. Sir Francis Chantrey's Will, 31 December 1840.
14. Ibid.
15. Ibid.
16. *Coll*: National Gallery, London.
17. G. D. Leslie, *The Inner Life of the Royal Academy* (London, 1914), p. 75.
18. RA Council Minutes, Vol. IX, pp. 290 and 292.
19. Ibid., p. 220.
20. J. E. Millais, *The Life and Letters of Sir John Everett Millais* (London, 1899), Vol. I, p. 19.
21. Present whereabouts unknown. The descendants possess a pencil sketch for it.
22. *Coll*: Mrs E. M. Clarke.
23. W. Holman Hunt, *Pre-Raphaelitism and the Pre-Raphaelite Brotherhood* (London, 1905), Vol. I, p. 177.
24. Ibid., p. 183.
25. RA Council Minutes, Vol. IX, pp. 337–9.

26. Ibid., Vol. X, pp. 183–4.
27. Ibid., p. 193.
28. Ibid., p. 68.
29. RA General Assembly Minutes, Vol. V, pp. 61–3.

CHAPTER 11

1. RA General Assembly Minutes, Vol. V, p. 160.
2. Ibid., pp. 168–9.
3. Ibid., p. 160.
4. Ibid., p. 186.
5. Lady Eastlake, 'Memoir of Sir Charles Lock Eastlake' – printed in *Contributions to the Literature of the Fine Arts* by Sir C. L. Eastlake (London, 1870), p. 187.
6. RA Council Minutes, Vol. X, p. 335.
7. RA General Assembly Minutes, Vol. V, p. 212.
8. RA Council Minutes, Vol. X, p. 318.
9. RA General Assembly Minutes, Vol. V, p. 238.
10. Ibid., pp. 242–50.
11. Ibid., p. 238.
12. *Coll*: Tate Gallery, London.
13. *Coll*: John Dewar and Sons Ltd., London.
14. W. P. Frith, *My Autobiography and Reminiscences* (London, 1887), Vol. I, p. 289.
15. *Coll*: HM The Queen.
16. *Coll*: Tate Gallery, London.
17. W. P. Frith, op. cit., p. 289.
18. Ibid., p. 296.
19. RA Council Minutes, Vol. X, p. 373.
20. Ibid, Vol. XI, p. 21.
21. Walter Thornbury, *The Life of J. M. W. Turner* (London, 1862), Vol. II, p. 187.
22. Ibid.
23. RA Council Minutes, Vol. XI, pp. 103–4.
24. Ibid., Vol. XII, p. 84.
25. RA Laws, *Turner Fund*.
26. RA Council Minutes, Vol. XII, p. 218.
27. RA Exhibition Catalogue, 1865, p. 5.
28. RA Council Minutes, Vol. XXII, p. 35.
29. Ibid., p. 61.

30. Ibid., p. 88.
31. Ibid., Vol. XI, p. 371.
32. Ibid., p. 339.
33. Ibid., p. 371.
34. RA General Assembly Minutes, Vol. VI, p. 210.
35. RA Council Minutes, Vol. XII, p. 205.
36. Ibid., Vol. XI, p. 228.
37. Ibid., pp. 243–5.
38. *Report of the Commissioners appointed to inquire into the present position of the Royal Academy . . . with the Minutes of Evidence* (London, 1863), p. iii.
39. Ibid., p. v.
40. Ibid., p. ix.
41. Ibid., p. viii.
42. Ibid.
43. Ibid., p. xii.
44. RA Council Minutes, Vol. XII, pp. 410–1.
45. RA General Assembly Minutes, Vol. V, p. 404.
46. RA Council Minutes, Vol. XI, p. 280.
47. *Coll*: Earl of Cromer.
48. RA General Assembly Minutes, Vol. VI, p. 361.
49. RA Council Minutes, Vol. XIII, p. 1.

CHAPTER 12

1. See *The Survey of London*, Vol. XXXII (London, 1963), pp. 390–429, and Sidney C. Hutchison, *The Homes of the Royal Academy* (London, 1956), pp. 19–30.
2. Colen Campbell, *Vitruvius Britannicus* Vol. III (London, 1725), pp. 7–8 and Plates 22–5.
3. Horace Walpole, *Anecdotes of Painting in England* (London, 1871, reprint of the 1786 edition), p. 383.
4. Kent's letter, 19 January 1720, to Burrell Massingberd (*Coll*: Society of Genealogists, London – MSS of Captain P. C. D. Mundy).
5. Ibid.
6. The Walpole Society, Vol. XXII (Oxford, 1934), p. 74.
7. Horace Walpole, *Journals of Visits to*

Country Seats, etc. (Walpole Society, Vol. XVI, p. 39; Oxford, 1928).

8. London, 1727.
9. First published in *The Daily Courant*, 26 January 1716.
10. Colen Campbell, op. cit., Plate 25.
11. Horace Walpole, *Anecdotes of Painting in England*, op. cit., p. 382.
12. RA Annual Report, 1869, p. 10.
13. Ibid., p. 12.
14. Ibid., p. 4
15. *Coll*: Tate Gallery, London.
16. *Coll*: Walker Art Gallery, Liverpool.
17. *Coll*: Musée du Louvre, Paris.
18. E. R. and J. Pennell, *The Life of James McNeill Whistler* (London, 1909), Vol. I, p. 213.
19. G. M. Trevelyan, *English Social History* (Second edition, London, 1946), p. 525.
20. RA General Assembly Minutes, Vol. VII, 1 December 1873 and 15 January 1874.
21. RA Annual Report, 1876, p. 6.
22. Anonymous (probably John E. Soden), *A Rap at the R.A.* (London, 1875), p. 14.
23. Ibid., p. 21.
24. RA Annual Report, 1872, p. 7.
25. Ibid., 1873, pp. 17–18.
26. *Coll*: Tate Gallery, London.
27. Ibid.
28. Ibid.
29. RA Annual Report, 1878, p. 23.

CHAPTER 13

1. Mrs Russell Barrington, *The Life, Letters and Work of Frederic Leighton* (London, 1906), Vol. I, p. 39.
2. J. G. Millais, *The Life and Letters of Sir John Everett Millais* (London, 1899), Vol. I, p. 259.
3. *Coll*: HM The Queen.
4. Mrs Russell Barrington, op. cit., p. 6.
5. Appendix A, Clause I.
6. RA Annual Report, 1879, p. 20.
7. RA Annual Report, 1891, p. 13.
8. *The Graphic*, 7 May 1887.
9. *Coll*: All in Tate Gallery, London.
10. The statue is in Calcutta and there

is a smaller version on the Horse Guards Parade, London.

11. *Coll*: National Portrait Gallery, London.
12. RA Annual Report, 1882, p. 6.
13. Ibid., 1891, pp. 6–7.
14. Ibid., 1894, p. 5.
15. *Coll*: Royal Academy of Arts, London.
16. RA Annual Report, 1881, p. 25.
17. Ibid., 1894, p. 18.
18. Edmond Malone, *The Works of Sir Joshua Reynolds* (London, 1797), Vol. I, p. 13.
19. G. Burne-Jones, *Memorials of Edward Burne-Jones* (London, 1904), Vol. II, p. 150.
20. Ibid., p. 151.
21. Ibid., pp. 232–3.
22. Ibid., pp. 233–4.
23. Ibid., p. 234.
24. RA Annual Report, 1889, pp. 62–73.
25. Ibid., pp. 19–25.
26. *Coll*: Royal Academy of Arts, London.
27. RA Annual Report, 1896, p. 60.
28. Ibid., p. 12.
29. RA Laws, *Leighton Fund*.
30. J. G. Millais, op. cit., Vol. II, p. 330.
31. G. D. Leslie, *The Inner Life of the Royal Academy* (London, 1914), p. 36.

CHAPTER 14

1. RA Annual Report, 1908, p. 23.
2. Ibid., 1912, p. 11.
3. Ibid., 1914, p. 28.
4. *Coll*: Lady Lever Art Gallery, Port Sunlight.
5. *Coll*: Tate Gallery, London.
6. Cassell & Co. Ltd, *Royal Academy Pictures, 1908*, (London, 1908), p. 47.
7. Ibid., 1913 (London, 1913), p. 41.
8. *Coll*: All in Tate Gallery, London.
9. *Report of the Select Committee of the House of Lords on the Chantrey Trust* (London, 1904), para. 14; reprinted in RA Annual Report, 1904, pp. 58–65.

10. RA Annual Report, 1904, pp. 65–6.
11. Ibid., p. 69.
12. Ibid., p. 70.
13. Ibid., p. 66.
14. W. J. Laidlay, *The Royal Academy – its uses and abuses* (London, 1898).
15. RA Annual Report, 1899, p. 8.
16. Ibid., 1904, p. 5.
17. Ibid., 1905, p. 5.
18. Ibid., 1904, p. 12.
19. Ibid,, 1910, p. 27.
20. Ibid., 1905, p. 6.
21. Ibid., p. 62.
22. Ibid., 1907, p. 20.
23. Ibid., 1914, p. 28.
24. Ibid., 1908, p. 11.
25. Ibid., 1905, p. 8.
26. Ibid., 1930, p. 31.
27. Ibid., 1908, pp. 8–9.
28. In St. George's Chapel, Windsor Castle.
29. RA Annual Report, 1908, p. 9.
30. RA Annual Report, 1909, p. 10. This fund is administered by the President, Keeper and Secretary of the Royal Academy and not by the Council as a whole.
31. *Coll*: National Portrait Gallery, London.
32. *Coll*: Duke of Wellington.
33. Cassell & Co. Ltd, *Royal Academy Pictures, 1914* (London, 1914), p. 75.
34. *Coll*: National Gallery, London.
35. RA Annual Report, 1914, p. 15.

CHAPTER 15

1. RA Annual Report, 1915, pp. 13–4.
2. Ibid., 1916, p. 21.
3. *Royal Academy Illustrated 1916*, p. 5.
4. Ibid., p. 21.
5. Ibid., p. 76.
6. Ibid., p. 11.
7. Ibid., p. 61.
8. *Coll*: All in Tate Gallery, London.
9. RA Annual Report, 1917, p. 76.
10. Ibid., p. 10.
11. Ibid., 1918, p. 10.
12. Ibid., p. 23.
13. Ibid., 1919, p. 23.
14. Ibid., 1924, p. 11

15. *Coll*: Tate Gallery, London.
16. RA Annual Report, 1926, p. 5.
17. *Coll*: Royal Academy of Arts, London.
18. RA Annual Report, 1926, p. 42.
19. Ibid., p. 16.
20. Ibid., 1927, pp. 39–41.
21. Ibid., p. 15.
22. Ibid., p. 7.
23. Ibid., 1926, p. 82.
24. Ibid., 1928, pp. 8–9.
25. Ibid., p. 23.

CHAPTER 16

1. *Coll*: HM The Queen.
2. RA Annual Report, 1929, p. 18.
3. *Coll*: Tate Gallery, London.
4. *Coll*: Galleria degli Uffizi, Florence.
5. *Coll*: Pinacoteca de Brera, Milan.
6. *Coll*: Museo Capodimonte, Naples.
7. *Coll*: Palazzo Pitti, Florence.
8. *Coll*: Accademia, Venice.
9. *Coll*: Museo Capodimonte, Naples.
10. RA Annual Report, 1929, p. 79.
11. Ibid., 1932, p. 16.
12. *Coll*: British Museum, London.
13. *Royal Academy Illustrated*, 1930, p. 89.
14. Ibid., 1932, p. 111.
15. *Coll*: City Art Gallery and Museum, Bradford.
16. *Coll*: Lady Lever Art Gallery, Port Sunlight.
17. *Royal Academy Illustrated*, 1936.
18. Ibid., 1939, p. 6.
19. *Coll*: Glasgow Art Gallery.
20. *Coll*: All in Tate Gallery, London.
21. RA Annual Report, 1936, p. 16.
22. Ibid., 1932, p. 21.
23. Ibid., 1934, p. 51.
24. Ibid., 1931, p. 30.
25. *Coll*: Laing Art Gallery, Newcastle-upon-Tyne.
26. *Coll*: Tate Gallery, London (Chantrey Bequest Purchase, 1967).
27. *Coll*: Royal Academy of Arts, London.
28. Ibid.
29. Ibid.
30. *Coll*: National Portrait Gallery, London.

31. *Coll*: Royal Academy of Arts, London.
32. RA Annual Report, 1935, p. 13.
33. *Coll*: Royal Academy of Arts, London.
34. *Coll*: Durban Municipal Art Gallery.
35. *Coll*: Royal Academy of Arts, London.
36. Ibid.
37. RA Annual Report, 1938, p. 50.
38. W. Curtis Green: Notice in *Sunday Times*, 2 January 1944.

CHAPTER 17

1. *Coll*: Harris Art Gallery, Preston.
2. RA Annual Report, 1946, p. 23.
3. Ibid., 1941, p. 58.
4. *Coll*: Mrs Dermot Daly.
5. RA Annual Report, 1949, p. 25.
6. Ibid., p. 6.
7. *Daily Telegraph*, 29 April 1949, p. 1.
8. RA Laws, Section II, Clause 1.
9. Ibid., Clause 8.
10. RA Annual Report, 1951, p. 6.
11. *Royal Academy Illustrated*, 1950, p. 12.
12. Ibid., pp. 26–7.
13. Ibid., *1952*, p. 64.
14. *Coll*: Royal College of Music, London.
15. *Coll*: Tate Gallery, London (Chantrey Bequest Purchase).
16. *Coll*: Royal Academy of Arts, London.
17. Ibid.
18. *Coll*: All in Tate Gallery, London.

CHAPTER 18

1. Quoted from the author's personal recollections.
2. Ibid.
3. Ibid.
4. *Coll*: Museu de Arte Antiga, Lisbon.
5. Ibid.
6. *Coll*: Museu dos Côches, Lisbon.
7. *Coll*: Royal Academy of Arts, London.
8. *Coll*: National Gallery, London.
9. RA Annual Report, 1962, p. 60.
10. Ibid., p. 53.
11. Ibid., p. 63.

12. Ibid.
13. Ibid., p. 56.
14. *Coll*: Museo del Prado, Madrid.
15. Ibid.
16. Quoted from the author's personal recollections.
17. *Coll*: Royal Academy of Arts, London.
18. RA Annual Report, 1968, pp. 6–7.
19. Ibid., pp. 7, 13–4.
20. Ibid., p. 6.
21. Ibid., p. 7.
22. Ibid., p. 5.
23. Ibid., pp. 32–3.
24. Ibid., p. 9.
25. Ibid., pp. 8, 48.

CHAPTER 19

1. RA Annual Report, 1969, pp. 43–4.
2. Ibid., pp. 48–52.
3. Ibid., 1970, p. 6.
4. Ibid.
5. Ibid., 1967, p. 7.
6. Ibid., 1970, p. 16.
7. Ibid., 1971, p. 39.
8. Ibid., p. 24.
9. Ibid., 1973, p. 7.
10. Ibid., pp. 53–6.
11. Ibid., pp. 8, 36–7.
12. Ibid., 1974, pp. 22–3.
13. Ibid., pp. 23–4.
14. Ibid., p. 8.
15. Ibid.

CHAPTER 20

1. RA Annual Report, 1975–76, p. 7.
2. RA Magazine, No. 5, December 1984, p. 20.
3. RA Annual Report, 1976–77, pp. 8–9.
4. Ibid., 1980–81, p. 32.
5. EMI Music Publishing Ltd, London, 1977.
6. RA Annual Report, 1976–77, p. 11.
7. Ibid., 1977–78, p. 8.
8. Ibid., pp. 7–8.
9. Ibid., 1980–81, p. 8.
10. Minutes of Evidence (HMSO, ISBN 010 295481x), pp. 263–78, 296–301.

11. Eighth Report, Vol. I, p. lxxxiv (HMSO, ISBN 010 009312 4, 1982).
12. RA Annual Report, 1977–78, pp. 8–9.
13. Ibid., 1981–82, p. 7.
14. Ibid., 1977–78, pp. 19–20.
15. Ibid., 1980–81, p. 19.
16. Ibid., 1981–82, p. 27.
17. RA General Assembly Minutes, 8 December 1983.
18. RA Annual Report, 1979–80, p. 30.
19. Ibid., 1976–77, p. 32.
20. Ibid., 1979–80, p. 26.
21. Ibid., 1977–78, p. 7.
22. Ibid., 1981–82, pp. 10–1, 49–51.

CHAPTER 21

1. RA Annual Report, 1981–82, p. 8.
2. Ibid., p. 17.
3. Ibid., 1982–83, Finance Committee Report.
4. Ibid., 1981–82, p. 10.
5. See Appendix A, Clause VIII.

APPENDICES

THE INSTRUMENT OF FOUNDATION

[*The original scheme for the establishment and government of the Royal Academy signed by King George III on 10 December 1768*]

Whereas sundry persons, resident in this Metropolis, eminent Professors of Painting, Sculpture, and Architecture, have most humbly represented by Memorial unto the King, that they are desirous of establishing a Society for promoting the Arts of Design, and earnestly soliciting His Majesty's patronage and assistance in carrying this their plan into execution; and, Whereas, its great utility hath been fully and clearly demonstrated, His Majesty, therefore, desirous of encouraging every useful undertaking, doth hereby institute and establish the said Society, under the name and title of the Royal Academy of Arts in London, graciously declaring himself the patron, protector, and supporter thereof; and commanding that it be established under the forms and regulations hereinafter mentioned, which have been most humbly laid before His Majesty, and received his royal approbation and assent.

I. The said Society shall consist of forty Members only, who shall be called Academicians of the Royal Academy; they shall all of them be artists by profession at the time of their admission, that is to say, Painters, Sculptors, or Architects, men of fair moral characters, of high reputation in their several professions; at least five-and-twenty years of age; resident in Great Britain; and not members of any other society of artists established in London.

II. It is His Majesty's pleasure that the following forty* persons be the original Members of the said Society, viz.:

Joshua Reynolds	G. Michael Moser
Benjamin West	Samuel Wale
Thomas Sandby	Peter Toms
Francis Cotes	Angelica Kauffman
John Baker	Richard Yeo
Mason Chamberlain	Mary Moser
John Gwynn	Wm. Chambers
Thomas Gainsborough	Joseph Wilton
J. Baptist Cipriani	George Barret
Jeremiah Meyer	Edward Penny
Francis Milner Newton	Augustino Carlini
Paul Sandby	Francis Hayman
Francesco Bartolozzi	Domenic Serres

*Only thirty-six names are inserted.

Charles Catton	John Richards
Nathaniel Hone	Francis Zuccharelli
William Tyler	George Dance
Nathaniel Dance	William Hoare
Richard Wilson	Johan Zoffany

III. After the first institution, all vacancies of Academicians shall be filled by election from amongst the exhibitors in the Royal Academy; the names of the candidates for admission shall be put up in the Academy three months before the day of election, of which day timely notice shall be given in writing to all the Academicians; each candidate shall, on the day of election, have at least thirty suffrages in his favour, to be duly elected; and he shall not receive his Letter of Admission, till he hath deposited in the Royal Academy, to remain there, a Picture, Bas-relief, or other specimen of his abilities, approved of by the then sitting Council of the Academy.

IV. For the Government of the Society, there shall be annually elected a President and eight other persons, who shall form a Council, which shall have the entire direction and management of all the business of the Society; and all the officers and servants thereof shall be subservient to the said Council, which shall have power to reform all abuses, to censure such as are deficient in their duty, and (with the consent of the general body, and the King's permission first obtained for that purpose), to suspend or entirely remove from their employments such as shall be found guilty of any great offences. The Council shall meet as often as the business of the Society shall require it; every Member shall be punctual to the hour of appointment under the penalty of a fine, at the option of the Council; and at each meeting, the attending Members shall receive forty-five shillings to be equally divided amongst them, in which division, however, the Secretary shall not be comprehended.

V. The seats in the Council shall go by succession to all the Members of the Society, excepting the Secretary, who shall belong thereto. Four of the Council shall be voted out every year, and these shall not re-occupy their seats in the Council, till all the rest have served; neither the President nor Secretary shall have any vote, either in the Council or General Assembly, excepting the suffrages be equal, in which case the President shall have the casting vote.

VI. There shall be a Secretary of the Royal Academy, elected by ballot, from amongst the Academicians, and approved of by the King; his business shall be to keep the Minutes of the Council, to write letters and send summonses, &c.; he shall attend at the Exhibition, assist in disposing the performances, make out the Catalogues, &c.; he shall also, when the Keeper of the Academy is indisposed, take upon himself the care of the Academy, and the inspection of the Schools of Design, for which he shall be properly qualified; his sallary shall be sixty pounds a year, and he shall continue in office during His Majesty's pleasure.

VII. There shall be a Keeper of the Royal Academy, elected by ballot, from amongst the Academicians; he shall be an able painter of History, Sculptor, or other Artist, properly qualified. His business shall be to keep the Royal Academy, with the Models,

Casts, Books, and other moveables belonging thereto; to attend regularly the Schools of Design, during the sittings of the students, to preserve order among them, and to give them such advice and instruction as they shall require; he shall have the immediate direction of all the servants of the Academy, shall regulate all things relating to the Schools, and with the assistance of the Visitors, provide the living Models, &c. He shall attend at the Exhibition, assist in disposing the performances, and be constantly at hand to preserve order and decorum. His sallary shall be one hundred pounds a year; he shall have a convenient apartment allotted him in the Royal Academy, where he shall constantly reside; and he shall continue in office during the King's pleasure.

VIII. There shall be a Treasurer of the Royal Academy, who, as the King is graciously pleased to pay all deficiencies, shall be appointed by His Majesty from amongst the Academicians, that he may have a person in whom he places full confidence, in an office where his interest is concerned; and His Majesty doth hereby nominate and appoint William Chambers, Esquire, Architect of his Works, to be Treasurer of the Royal Academy of Arts, which office he shall hold, together with the emoluments thereof, from the date of these presents, and during His Majesty's pleasure. His business shall be to receive the rents and profits of the Academy, to pay its expences, to superintend repairs of the buildings and alterations, to examine all bills, and to conclude all bargains; he shall once in every quarter lay a fair state of his Accounts before the Council, and when they have passed examination and been approved there, he shall lay them before the Keeper of His Majesty's Privy Purse, to be by him finally audited, and the deficiencies paid; his salary shall be sixty pounds a year.

IX. That the Schools of Design may be under the direction of the ablest Artists, there shall be elected annually from amongst the Academicians nine persons, who shall be called Visitors; they shall be Painters of History, able Sculptors, or other persons properly qualified; their business shall be, to attend the Schools by rotation, each a month, to set the figures, to examine the performances of the Students, to advise and instruct them, to endeavour to form their taste, and turn their attention towards that branch of the Arts for which they shall seem to have the aptest disposition. These officers shall be approved of by the King; they shall be paid out of the Treasury ten shillings and sixpence for each time of attending, which shall be at least two hours, and shall be subject to a fine of ten shillings and sixpence whenever they neglect to attend, unless they appoint a proxy from amongst the Visitors for the time being, in which case he shall be entitled to the reward. At every election of Visitors, four of the old Visitors shall be declared non-eligible.

X. There shall be a Professor of Anatomy, who shall read annually six public Lectures in the Schools, adapted to the Arts of Design; his sallary shall be thirty pounds a year; and he shall continue in office during the King's pleasure.

XI. There shall be a Professor of Architecture, who shall read annually six public Lectures, calculated to form the taste of the Students, to instruct them in the laws and principles of composition, to point out to them the beauties or faults of celebrated productions, to fit them for an unprejudiced study of books, and for a critical examination of structures; his salary shall be thirty pounds a year; and he shall continue in office during the King's pleasure.

XII. There shall be a Professor of Painting, who shall read annually six Lectures, calculated to instruct the Students in the principles of composition, to form their taste of design and colouring, to strengthen their judgment, to point out to them the beauties and imperfections of celebrated works of Art, and the particular excellencies or defects of great masters, and, finally, to lead them into the readiest and most efficacious paths of study; his sallary shall be thirty pounds a year; and he shall continue in office during the King's pleasure.

XIII. There shall be a Professor of Perspective and Geometry, who shall read six public Lectures annually in the Schools, in which all the useful propositions of Geometry, together with the principle of Lineal and Aerial Perspective, and also the projection of shadows, reflections, and refractions shall be clearly and fully illustrated; he shall particularly confine himself to the quickest, easiest and most exact methods of operation. He shall continue in office during the King's pleasure; and his sallary shall be thirty pounds a year.

XIV. The Lectures of all the Professors shall be laid before the Council for its approbation, which shall be obtained in writing, before they can be read in the public Schools. All these Professors shall be elected by ballot, the three last from amongst the Academicians.

XV. There shall be a Porter of the Royal Academy, whose sallary shall be twenty-five pounds a year; he shall have a room in the Royal Academy, and receive his orders from the Keeper or Secretary.

XVI. There shall be a Sweeper of the Royal Academy, whose sallary shall be ten pounds a year.

XVII. There shall be an Annual Exhibition of Paintings, Sculptures and Designs, which shall be open to all Artists of distinguished merit; it shall continue for the public one month, and be under the regulations expressed in the bylaws of the Society, hereafter to be made. Of the profits arising therefrom, two hundred pounds shall be given to indigent artists, or their families, and the remainder shall be employed in the support of the Institution. All Academicians, till they have attained the age of sixty, shall be obliged to exhibit at least one performance, under a penalty of five pounds, to be paid into the treasury of the Academy, unless they can show sufficient cause for their omission; but, after that age, they shall be exempt from all duty.

XVIII. There shall be a Winter Academy of Living Models, men and women of different characters, under the regulations expressed in the bylaws of the Society, hereafter to be made, free to all students who shall be qualified to receive advantage from such studies.

XIX. There shall be a Summer Academy of Living Models, to paint after, also of Laymen with draperies, both Antient and Modern, Plaister Figures, Bas-reliefs, models and designs of Fruits, Flowers, Ornaments, &c., free to all artists qualified to receive advantage from such studies, and under the regulations expressed in the bylaws of the Society hereafter to be made.

XX. There shall be a Library of Books of Architecture, Sculpture, Painting, and all the Sciences relating thereto; also prints of bas-reliefs, vases, trophies, ornaments, dresses, ancient and modern customs and ceremonies, instruments of war and arts, utensils of sacrifice, and all other things useful to Students in the Arts; which Library shall be open one day in every week to all Students properly qualified. One of the Members of the Council shall attend in the room during the whole time it is open, to keep order, and to see that no damage be done to the books; and he shall be paid 10s. 6d. for his attendance. No books shall, under any pretence, be suffered to be taken out of the Library; but every Academician shall have free ingress at all seasonable times of the day to consult the books, and to make designs or sketches from them.

XXI. There shall be annually one General Meeting of the whole body, or more if requisite, to elect a Council and Visitors; to confirm new laws and regulations; to hear complaints and redress grievances, if there be any; and to do any other business relative to the Society.

XXII. The Council shall frame new laws and regulations; but they shall have no force, till ratified by the consent of the General Assembly, and the approbation of the King.

XXIII. Though it may not be for the benefit of the Institution absolutely to prohibit pluralities, yet they are as much as possible to be avoided, that His Majesty's gracious intention may be comply'd with, by dividing as nearly as possible the emoluments of the Institution amongst all its Members.

XXIV. If any Member of the Society shall, by any means, become obnoxious, it may be put to the ballot, in the General Assembly, whether he shall be expelled, and if there be found a majority for expulsion, he shall be expelled, provided His Majesty's permission be first obtained for that purpose.

XXV. No Student shall be admitted into the Schools, till he hath satisfied the Keeper of the Academy, the Visitor, and Council for the time being, of his abilities; which being done, he shall receive his Letter of Admission, signed by the Secretary of the Academy, certifying that he is admitted a Student of the Royal Schools.

XXVI. If any Student be guilty of improper behaviour in the Schools, or doth not quietly submit to the Rules and Orders established for their regulation, it shall be in the power of the Council, upon complaint being first made by the Keeper of the Academy, to expel, reprimand, or rusticate him for a certain time; but if he be once expelled, he shall never be re-admitted into the Royal Schools.

XXVII. All modes of elections shall be regulated by the bylaws of the Society, hereafter to be made for that purpose.

I approve of this Plan; let it be put in execution.

GEORGE, R.

ST JAMES'S, *December* 10, 1768

ALPHABETICAL LIST OF MEMBERS FROM THE FOUNDATION

RA = Royal Academician ARA = Associate
P = Painter, S = Sculptor, A = Architect, E = Engraver and/or Print-maker,
D = Draughtsman,
FM = Foundation Member (1768), NM = Nominated Member (1769)

		Born	ARA	RA	Died
Abbey, Edwin Austin	P	1852	1896	1898	1911
Adams, Norman	P	1927	1967	1972	
Aitchison, Craigie	P	1926	1978		
Aitchison, George	A	1825	1881	1898	1910
Aldridge, John	P	1905	1954	1963	1983
Allan, Sir William	P	1782	1825	1835	1850
Allston, Washington	P	1779	1818	—	1843
Alma-Tadema, Sir Lawrence, OM	P	1836	1876	1879	1912
Anderson, Stanley, CBE	E	1884	1934	1941	1966
Ansdell, Richard	P	1815	1861	1870	1885
Ardizzone, Edward, CBE	P	1900	1962	1970	1979
Armitage, Edward	P	1817	1867	1872	1896
			(Retired 1894)		
Armstead, Henry Hugh	S	1828	1875	1879	1905
Armstrong, John	P	1893	1966	—	1973
Arnald, George	P	1763	1810	—	1841
Austin, Robert	E	1895	1939	1949	1973
Ayres, Gillian, OBE	P	1930	1982		
Bacon, John	S	1740	1770	1778	1799
Bacon, John Henry Frederick, MVO	P	1866	1903	—	1914
Baily, Edward Hodges	S	1788	1817	1821	1867
			(Retired 1862)		
Baker, Sir Herbert, KCIE	A	1862	1922	1932	1946
Baker, John	P	1736	—	FM	1771
Banks, Thomas	S	1735	1784	1785	1805
Barlow, Thomas Oldham	E	1824	1873	1881	1889
Barret, George	P	1732	—	FM	1784
Barry, Sir Charles	A	1795	1840	1842	1860
Barry, Edward Middleton	A	1830	1861	1869	1880

		Born	ARA	RA	Died
Barry, James	P	1741	1772	1773	1806
			(Expelled 1799)		
Bartolozzi, Francesco	P	1727	—	FM	1815
Bateman, James	P	1893	1935	1942	1959
Bates, Harry	S	1850	1892	—	1899
Bawden, Edward, CBE	D	1903	1947	1956	
Beechey, Sir William	P	1753	1793	1798	1839
Beeton, Alan	P	1880	1938	—	1942
Belcher, George	P	1875	1931	1945	1947
Belcher, John	A	1841	1900	1909	1913
Bell, Robert Anning	P	1863	1914	1922	1933
Bigg, William Redmore	P	1755	1787	1814	1828
Birch, Charles Bell	S	1832	1880	—	1893
Birch, Samuel John Lamorna	P	1869	1926	1934	1955
Bird, Edward	P	1772	1812	1815	1819
Bishop, Henry	P	1868	1932	1939	1939
Blackadder, Elizabeth, OBE	P	1931	1971	1976	
Blake, Peter, CBE	P	1932	1974	1981	
Blamey, Norman C.	P	1914	1970	1975	
Blomfield, Sir Arthur William	A	1829	1888	—	1899
Blomfield, Sir Reginald Theodore	A	1856	1905	1914	1942
Blow, Sandra	P	1925	1971	1978	
Bodley, George Frederick	A	1827	1882	1902	1907
Boehm, Sir Joseph Edgar, Bt.	S	1834	1878	1882	1890
Bone, Henry	P	1755	1801	1811	1834
Bonomi, Joseph	A	1739	1789	—	1808
Boughton, George Henry	P	1833	1879	1896	1905
Bourgeois, Sir Peter Francis	P	1756	1787	1793	1811
Bowey, Olwyn	P	1936	1970	1975	
Bowyer, William	P	1926	1974	1981	
Boxall, Sir William	P	1800	1851	1863	1879
			(Retired 1877)		
Bramley, Frank	P	1857	1894	1911	1915
Brangwyn, Sir Frank	P	1867	1904	1919	1956
Bratby, John	P	1928	1959	1971	
Brett, John	P	1832	1881	—	1902
			(Retired 1901)		
Briggs, Henry Perronet	P	1791	1825	1832	1844
Brock, Sir Thomas, KCB	S	1847	1883	1891	1922
Brockhurst, Gerald Leslie	P	1890	1928	1937	1978
			(Retired 1957)		
Bromley, William	E	1769	1819	—	1842
Brooker, William	P	1918	1980	—	1983
Brown, Sir John Arnesby	P	1866	1903	1915	1955
Brown, Ralph	S	1928	1968	1972	
Browne, John	E	1741	1770	—	1801
Brundrit, Reginald Grange	P	1883	1931	1938	1960
Buhler, Robert	P	1916	1947	1956	
Bundy, Edgar	P	1862	1915	—	1922

251

Alphabetical List of Members from the Foundation—continued

		Born	ARA	RA	Died
Burch, Edward	S	1730	1770	1771	1814
Burges, William	A	1827	1881	—	1881
Burgess, John Bagnold	P	1830	1877	1888	1897
Burn, Rodney Joseph	P	1899	1954	1962	1984
Burne-Jones, Sir Edward, Bt.	P	1833	1885	—	1898
			(Resigned 1893)		
Burnet, Sir John James	A	1857	1921	1925	1938
Butler, James Walter	S	1931	1964	1972	
Cadbury-Brown, H. T., OBE	A	1913	1971	1975	
Calderon, Philip Hermogenes	P	1833	1864	1867	1898
Callcott, Sir Augustus Wall	P	1779	1806	1810	1844
Cameron, Sir David Young	P	1865	1911	1920	1945
Camp, Jeffrey, B.	P	1923	1974	1984	
Canot, Peter Charles	E	1710	1770	—	1777
Carlini, Agostino	S	?	—	FM	1790
Carr, Henry Marvel	P	1894	1957	1966	1970
Casson, Sir Hugh Maxwell, CH, KCVO	A	1910	1962	1970	
			(President, 1976–84)		
Catton, Charles	P	1728	—	FM	1798
Chalon, Alfred Edward	P	1781	1812	1816	1860
Chalon, John James	P	1778	1827	1841	1854
Chamberlin, Mason	P	?	—	FM	1787
Chamberlin, Peter, CBE	A	1919	1975	1978	1978
Chambers, Thomas	E	1724	1770	—	1789
Chambers, Sir William	A	1723	—	FM	1796
Chantrey, Sir Francis Leggatt	S	1781	1816	1818	1841
Charoux, Siegfried Joseph	S	1896	1949	1956	1967
Christopher, Ann	S	1947	1980		
Cipriani, John Baptist	P	1727	—	FM	1785
Clark, John Cosmo, CBE, MC	P	1897	1949	1958	1967
Clarke, Geoffrey	S	1924	1970	1975	
Clarke, Theophilus	P	1776	1803	—	1831
Clatworthy, Robert	S	1928	1968	1973	
Clausen, Sir George	P	1852	1895	1908	1944
Clint, George	P	1770	1821	—	1854
			(Resigned 1836)		
Cockerell, Charles Robert	A	1788	1829	1836	1863
			(Retired 1862)		
Coker, Peter	P	1926	1965	1972	
Cole, Vicat	P	1833	1870	1880	1893
Collins, William	P	1788	1814	1820	1847
Collyer, Joseph	E	1748	1786	—	1827
Colton, William Robert	S	1867	1903	1919	1921
Connard, Philip, CVO	P	1875	1918	1925	1958
Constable, John	P	1776	1819	1829	1837
Cook, Richard	P	1784	1816	1822	1857
Cooke, Edward William	P	1811	1851	1863	1880

		Born	ARA	RA	Died
Cooke, Jean	P	1927	1965	1972	
Cooper, Abraham	P	1787	1817	1820	1868
			(Retired 1866)		
Cooper, Sir Edwin	A	1872	1930	1937	1942
Cooper, Thomas Sidney, CVO	P	1803	1845	1867	1902
Cope, Sir Arthur Stockdale, KCVO	P	1857	1899	1910	1940
Cope, Charles West	P	1811	1843	1848	1890
			(Retired 1883)		
Copley, John Singleton	P	1737	1776	1779	1815
Corbet, Matthew Ridley	P	1850	1902	—	1902
Cosway, Richard	P	1740	1770	1771	1821
Cotes, Francis	P	1725	—	FM	1770
Cousins, Samuel	E	1801	1835	1855	1887
			(Retired 1879)		
Cowern, Raymond Teague	D	1913	1957	1968	1986
Cowper, Frank Cadogan	P	1877	1907	1934	1958
Creswick, Thomas	P	1811	1842	1851	1869
Crofts, Ernest	P	1847	1878	1896	1911
Crosby, Theo	A	1925	1982		
Crowe, Eyre	P	1824	1876	—	1910
			(Retired 1910)		
Cuming, Frederick	P	1930	1969	1974	
Cundall, Charles	P	1890	1937	1944	1971
Dall, Nicholas Thomas	P	?	1771	—	1776
Dalwood, Hubert	S	1924	1976	—	1976
Danby, Francis	P	1793	1825	—	1861
Dance, George	A	1740	—	FM	1825
Dance, Nathaniel (later Sir Nathaniel Dance-Holland, Bt.)	P	1734	—	FM	1811
			(Resigned 1790)		
Daniell, Thomas	P	1749	1796	1799	1840
Daniell, William	P	1769	1807	1822	1837
Dannatt, Trevor	A	1920	1977	1983	
Darwin, Sir Robin, CBE	P	1910	1966	1972	1974
Davis, Arthur Joseph	A	1878	1933	1942	1951
Davis, Henry William Banks	P	1833	1873	1877	1914
Dawber, Sir Edward Guy	A	1861	1927	1935	1938
Dawe, George	P	1781	1809	1814	1829
Deering, John Peter (formerly Gandy)	A	1787	1826	1838	1850
De Glehn, Wilfrid Gabriel (formerly Von Glehn)	P	1870	1923	1932	1951
De Grey, Roger	P	1918	1962	1969	
			(President, 1984–)		
De Loutherbourg, Philip Jacob	P	1740	1780	1781	1812
De Sausmarez, Maurice	P	1915	1964	—	1969
De Soissons, Louis, CVO, OBE	A	1890	1942	1953	1962
Devas, Anthony	P	1911	1953	—	1958
Dick, Sir William Reid, KCVO	S	1878	1921	1928	1961

253

Alphabetical List of Members from the Foundation—continued

		Born	ARA	RA	Died
Dicksee, Sir Frank, KCVO	P	1853	1881	1891	1928
			(President, 1924–8)		
Dickson, Jennifer	E	1936	1970	1976	
Dobson, Frank, CBE	S	1888	1942	1953	1963
Dobson, William Charles Thomas	P	1817	1860	1871	1898
			(Retired 1895)		
Dodd, Francis	P	1874	1927	1935	1949
Doo, George Thomas	E	1800	1856	1857	1886
			(Retired 1866)		
Downman, John	P	1750	1795	–	1824
Dowson, Sir Philip, CBE	A	1924	1979	1985	
Dring, William	P	1904	1944	1955	
Drummond, Samuel	P	1770	1808	—	1844
Drury, Alfred	S	1857	1900	1913	1944
Dugdale, Thomas Cantrell	P	1880	1936	1943	1952
Duncan, Thomas	P	1807	1843	—	1845
Dunlop, Ronald Ossory	P	1894	1939	1950	1973
Dunstan, Bernard	P	1920	1959	1968	
Durham, Joseph	S	1814	1866	—	1877
Durst, Alan Lydiat	S	1883	1953	—	1970
Dyce, William	P	1806	1844	1848	1864
East, Sir Alfred	P	1849	1899	1913	1913
Eastlake, Sir Charles Lock	P	1793	1827	1830	1865
			(President, 1850–65)		
Edridge, Henry	P	1768	1820	—	1821
Edwards, Edward	P	1738	1773	—	1806
Egg, Augustus Leopold	P	1816	1848	1860	1863
Ehrlich, Georg	S	1897	1962	—	1966
Elmer, Stephen	P	?	1772	—	1796
Elmore, Alfred	P	1815	1845	1857	1881
Elwell, Frederick William	P	1870	1931	1938	1958
Elwes, Simon	P	1902	1956	1967	1975
Erith, Raymond	A	1904	1959	1964	1973
Etty, William	P	1787	1824	1828	1849
Eurich, Richard, OBE	P	1903	1942	1953	
Eves, Reginald Grenville	P	1876	1933	1939	1941
Eyton, Anthony	P	1923	1976		
Faed, Thomas	P	1826	1861	1864	1900
			(Retired 1892)		
Farington, Joseph	P	1747	1783	1785	1821
Farquharson, David	P	1839	1905	—	1907
Farquharson, Joseph	P	1846	1900	1915	1935
Fell, Sheila Mary	P	1931	1969	1974	1979
Fildes, Sir Luke, KCVO	P	1843	1879	1887	1927
Fisher, Mark	P	1841	1911	1919	1923

		Born	ARA	RA	Died
Fisher, Samuel Melton	P	1859	1917	1924	1939
Fittler, James	E	1758	1800	—	1835
Fitton, James	P	1899	1944	1954	1982
Flaxman, John	S	1755	1797	1800	1826
Fleetwood-Walker, Bernard	P	1893	1946	1956	1965
Flint, Sir William Russell	P	1880	1924	1933	1969
Foley, John Henry	S	1818	1849	1858	1874
Forbes, Stanhope Alexander	P	1857	1892	1910	1947
Ford, Edward Onslow	S	1852	1888	1895	1901
Foster, Norman	A	1935	1983		
Frampton, Sir George	S	1860	1894	1902	1928
Frampton, Meredith	P	1894	1934	1942	1984
			(Retired 1953)		
Fraser, Donald Hamilton	P	1929	1975	1985	
Freeth, Hubert Andrew	E	1912	1955	1965	1986
Frink, Dame Elisabeth, DBE	S	1930	1971	1977	
Frith, William Powell, CVO	P	1819	1845	1853	1909
			(Retired 1890)		
Frost, William Edward	P	1810	1846	1870	1877
			(Retired 1876)		
Fry, Edwin Maxwell, CBE	A	1899	1966	1972	
Fullard, George Mathias	S	1923	1973	—	1973
Furse, Charles Wellington	P	1868	1904	—	1904
Fuseli, Henry	P	1741	1788	1790	1825
Gainsborough, Thomas	P	1727	—	FM	1788
Gandy, Joseph	A	1771	1803	—	1843
Garbe, Louis Richard	S	1876	1929	1936	1957
Garrard, George	P	1760	1800	—	1826
Garvey, Edmund	P	?	1770	1783	1813
Geddes, Andrew	P	1783	1832	—	1844
George, Sir Ernest	A	1839	1910	1917	1922
Gere, Charles March	P	1869	1934	1939	1957
Gibberd, Sir Frederick, CBE	A	1908	1961	1969	1984
Gibson, John	S	1790	1833	1836	1866
Gilbert, Sir Alfred, MVO	S	1854	1887	1892	1934
		(Resigned 1908, resumed membership 1932)			
Gilbert, Sir John	P	1817	1872	1876	1897
Gill, Eric	S	1882	1937	—	1940
Gillick, Ernest George	S	1874	1935	—	1951
Gillies, Sir William George, CBE	P	1898	1964	1971	1973
Gilpin, Sawrey	P	1733	1795	1797	1807
Ginner, Charles, CBE	P	1878	1942	–	1952
Goldfinger, Ernö	A	1902	1971	1975	
Goodall, Frederick	P	1822	1852	1863	1904
			(Retired 1902)		
Gooden, Stephen Frederick, CBE	E	1892	1937	1946	1955
Gordon, Sir John Watson	P	1790	1841	1851	1864
Gore, Frederick	P	1913	1964	1972	

Alphabetical List of Members from the Foundation—continued

		Born	ARA	RA	Died
Gow, Andrew Garrick	P	1848	1881	1891	1920
Gowing, Sir Lawrence, CBE	P	1918	1978		
Graham, Peter	P	1836	1877	1881	1921
Grant, Sir Francis	P	1803	1842	1851	1878
			(President, 1866–78)		
Graves, Robert	E	1798	1836	—	1873
Green, Anthony	P	1939	1971	1977	
Green, Valentine	E	1739	1775	—	1813
Green, William Curtis	A	1875	1923	1933	1960
Greenham, Peter George, CBE	P	1909	1951	1960	
Gregory, Edward John	P	1850	1883	1898	1909
Greiffenhagen, Maurice	P	1862	1916	1922	1931
Griggs, Frederick Landseer Maur	E	1876	1922	1931	1938
Gross, Anthony, CBE	P	1905	1979	1980	1984
Gunn, Sir James	P	1893	1953	1961	1964
Gwynn, John	A	?	—	FM	1786
Gwynne-Jones, Allan, CBE, DSO	P	1892	1955	1965	1982
Hacker, Arthur	P	1858	1894	1910	1919
Hall, Oliver	P	1869	1920	1927	1957
Hamilton, William	P	1751	1784	1789	1801
Harcourt, George	P	1868	1919	1926	1947
Hardiman, Alfred Frank	S	1891	1936	1944	1949
Hardwick, Philip	A	1792	1839	1841	1870
			(Retired 1869)		
Harpley, Sydney	S	1927	1974	1981	
Harris, Emanuel Vincent, OBE	A	1876	1936	1942	1971
Hart, Solomon Alexander	P	1806	1835	1840	1881
Hartwell, Charles Leonard	S	1873	1915	1924	1951
Haward, Francis	E	1759	1783	—	1797
Hayes, Colin	P	1919	1963	1970	
Hayman, Francis	P	1708	—	FM	1776
Heath, James	E	1757	1791	—	1834
Hemy, Charles Napier	P	1841	1898	1910	1917
Henry, George	P	1858	1907	1920	1943
Hepple, Norman	P	1908	1954	1961	
Herbert, John Rogers	P	1810	1841	1846	1890
			(Retired 1886)		
Herkomer, Sir Hubert von, CVO	P	1849	1879	1890	1914
Hermes, Gertrude, OBE	E	1901	1963	1971	1983
Hillier, Tristram	P	1905	1957	1967	1983
Hilton, William	P	1786	1813	1819	1839
Hoare, William	P	1706	—	NM	1792
Hockney, David	P	1937	1985		
Hodges, William	P	1744	1786	1787	1797
Hodgson, John Evan	P	1831	1873	1879	1895
Hogarth, Paul	D	1917	1974	1984	
Holford, Lord (William)	A	1907	1961	1968	1975

		Born	ARA	RA	Died
Holl, Francis	E	1815	1883	—	1884
Holl, Frank	P	1845	1878	1883	1888
Hollins, John	P	1798	1842	—	1855
Hone, Horace	P	1755	1779	—	1825
Hone, Nathaniel	P	1718	—	FM	1874
Hook, James Clarke	P	1819	1850	1860	1907
			(Retired 1907)		
Hoppner, John	P	1758	1793	1795	1810
Horsley, John Callcott	P	1817	1855	1864	1903
			(Retired 1897)		
Howard, Henry	P	1769	1800	1808	1847
Howard, Ken	P	1932	1983		
Howell, William, DFC	A	1922	1974	—	1974
Hoyland, John	P	1934	1983		
Hughes-Stanton, Sir Herbert	P	1870	1913	1920	1937
Humphry, Ozias	P	1742	1779	1791	1810
Hunter, Colin	P	1841	1884	—	1904
Jack, Richard	P	1866	1914	1920	1952
Jackson, Francis Ernest	P	1873	1944	—	1945
Jackson, John	P	1778	1815	1817	1831
Jackson, Sir Thomas Graham, Bt.	A	1835	1892	1896	1924
Jagger, Charles Sargeant	S	1885	1926	—	1934
James, Charles Holloway	A	1893	1937	1946	1953
James, George	P	?	1770	—	1794
John, Augustus Edwin, OM	P	1878	1921	1928	1961
		(Resigned 1938, re-elected 1940)			
John, Sir William Goscombe	S	1860	1899	1909	1952
Jones, Allen	E	1937	1981		
Jones, George	P	1786	1822	1824	1869
Joseph, George Francis	P	1764	1813	—	1846
Kauffmann, Angelica	P	1741	—	FM	1807
Kelly, Sir Gerald Festus, KCVO	P	1879	1922	1930	1972
			(President 1949–54)		
Kennington, Eric Henri	P	1888	1951	1959	1960
Kenny, Michael	S	1941	1976		
King, Phillip, CBE	S	1934	1977		
Kitaj, R. B. (Ronald Brooks)	P	1932	1984		
Kneale, Bryan	S	1930	1970	1974	
Knight, Harold	P	1874	1928	1937	1961
Knight, John Prescott	P	1803	1836	1844	1881
Knight, Dame Laura, DBE	P	1877	1927	1936	1970
Koralek, Paul	A	1933	1986		
La Dell, Edwin	E	1914	1969	—	1970
Lamb, Henry, MC	P	1883	1940	1949	1960
Lambert, George Washington	P	1873	1922	—	1930
Lambert, Maurice	S	1901	1941	1952	1964
Landseer, Charles	P	1799	1837	1845	1879

Alphabetical List of Members from the Foundation—continued

		Born	ARA	RA	Died
Landseer, Sir Edwin Henry	P	1802	1826	1831	1873
Landseer, John	E	1769	1806	—	1852
Landseer, Thomas	E	1795	1868	—	1880
Lane, Richard	E	1800	1827	—	1872
La Thangue, Henry Herbert	P	1859	1898	1912	1929
Lavery, Sir John	P	1856	1911	1921	1941
Lawrence, Alfred Kingsley	P	1893	1930	1938	1975
Lawrence, Sir Thomas	P	1769	1791	1794	1830
			(President, 1820–30)		
Lawson, Sonia	P	1934	1982		
Leader, Benjamin Williams	P	1831	1883	1898	1923
Le Bas, Edward, CBE	P	1904	1943	1954	1966
Ledward, Gilbert, OBE	S	1888	1932	1937	1960
Lee, Frederick Richard	P	1798	1834	1838	1879
			(Retired 1871)		
Lee, Sydney	P	1866	1922	1930	1949
Leighton, Lord (Frederic)	P	1830	1864	1868	1896
			(President, 1878–96)		
Le Jeune, Henry	P	1819	1863	—	1904
			(Retired 1886)		
Leslie, Charles Robert	P	1794	1821	1826	1859
Leslie, George Dunlop	P	1835	1868	1876	1921
Levene, Ben	P	1938	1975		
Lewis, John Frederick	P	1805	1859	1865	1876
			(Retired 1876)		
Llewellyn, Sir (Samuel Henry) William,	P	1858	1912	1920	1941
GCVO *(President, 1928–38; date of birth was recorded as 1863 until after his death)*					
Long, Edwin	P	1829	1876	1881	1891
Lorimer, Sir Robert Stodart, KBE	A	1864	1920	—	1929
Lowry, Laurence Stephen	P	1887	1955	1962	1976
Lucas, John Seymour	P	1849	1886	1898	1923
Lutyens, Sir Edwin Landseer, OM, KCIE	A	1869	1913	1920	1944
			(President, 1938–44)		
Macbeth, Robert Walker	P	1848	1883	1903	1910
			(Retired 1908)		
Macbeth-Raeburn, Henry Raeburn	E	1860	1922	1933	1947
Macdowell, Patrick	S	1799	1841	1846	1870
			(Retired 1870)		
McEvoy, Ambrose	P	1878	1924	—	1927
McFall, David	S	1919	1955	1963	
Machin, Arnold, OBE	S	1911	1947	1956	
Mackennal, Sir Bertram, KCVO	S	1863	1909	1922	1931
Maclise, Daniel	P	1811	1835	1840	1870
McMillan, William, CVO	S	1887	1925	1933	1977
McMorran, Donald Hanks	A	1904	1955	1962	1965
MacTaggart, Sir William	P	1903	1968	1973	1981
MacWhirter, John	P	1839	1879	1893	1911

		Born	ARA	RA	Died
McWilliam, Frederick Edward, CBE	S	1909	1959	—	
			(Resigned 1963)		
Mahoney, Charles	P	1903	1961	1968	1968
Major, Thomas	E	1720	1770	—	1799
Manasseh, Leonard, OBE	A	1916	1976	1979	
Marchant, Nathaniel	S	1739	1791	1809	1816
Marks, Henry Stacy	P	1829	1871	1878	1898
			(Retired 1896)		
Marochetti, Baron Carlo	S	1805	1861	1866	1867
Marshall, William Calder	S	1813	1844	1852	1894
			(Retired 1890)		
Martin, Elias	P	1740	1770	—	1804
Martin, Sir Leslie	A	1908	—	1985	
Mason, Arnold Henry	P	1885	1940	1951	1963
Mason, George Hemming	P	1818	1869	—	1872
Maufe, Sir Edward Brantwood	A	1883	1938	1947	1974
Medley, Robert, CBE	P	1905	—	1985	
Methuen, Lord (Paul Ayshford)	P	1886	1951	1959	1974
Meyer, Jeremiah	P	1735	—	FM	1789
Middleditch, Edward, MC	P	1923	1968	1973	
Millais, Sir John Everett, Bt.	P	1829	1853	1863	1896
			(President, 1896)		
Monnington, Sir (Walter) Thomas	P	1902	1931	1938	1976
			(President, 1966–76)		
Moore, Henry	P	1831	1885	1893	1895
Morley, Harry	P	1881	1936	—	1943
Morris, Philip Richard	P	1838	1877	—	1902
			(Retired 1900)		
Mortimer, John Hamilton	P	1741	1778	—	1779
Moser, George Michael	P	1704	—	FM	1783
Moser, Mary (Mrs Hugh Lloyd)	P	1744	—	FM	1819
Moynihan, Rodrigo, CBE	P	1910	1944	1954	
			(Resigned 1957, reinstated 1979)		
Muirhead, David Thomson	P	1867	1928	—	1930
Mulready, William	P	1786	1815	1816	1863
Munnings, Sir Alfred James, KCVO	P	1878	1919	1925	1959
			(President, 1944–49)		
Murray, Sir David	P	1849	1891	1905	1933
Nash, John Northcote, CBE	P	1893	1940	1951	1977
Nevinson, Christopher Richard Wynne	P	1889	1939	—	1946
Newton, Algernon	P	1880	1936	1943	1968
Newton, Ernest, CBE	A	1856	1911	1919	1922
Newton, Francis Milner	P	1720	—	FM	1794
Newton, Gilbert Stuart	P	1794	1828	1832	1835
Nicol, Erskine	P	1825	1866	—	1904
			(Retired 1885)		
Nimptsch, Uli	S	1897	1958	1967	1977

Alphabetical List of Members from the Foundation—continued

		Born	ARA	RA	Died
Nixon, James	P	1741	1778	—	1812
Nollekens, Joseph	S	1737	1771	1772	1823
North, John William	P	1842	1893	—	1924
		(Retired 1914)			
Northcote, James	P	1746	1786	1787	1831
Oakes, John Wright	P	1820	1876	—	1887
Oliver, Archer James	P	1774	1807	—	1842
Olsson, Julius	P	1864	1914	1920	1942
O'Neil, Henry Nelson	P	1817	1860	—	1880
Opie, John	P	1761	1786	1787	1807
Orchardson, Sir William Quiller	P	1835	1868	1877	1910
O'Rorke, Brian	A	1901	1947	1956	1974
Orpen, Sir William, KBE	P	1878	1910	1919	1931
Osborne, Malcolm, CBE	E	1880	1918	1926	1963
Ouless, Walter William	P	1848	1877	1881	1933
Owen, William	P	1769	1804	1806	1825
Paolozzi, Eduardo, CBE	S	1924	1972	1979	
Parry, William	P	1742	1776	—	1791
Pars, William	P	1742	1770	—	1782
Parsons, Alfred	P	1847	1897	1911	1920
Partridge, John, CBE	A	1924	1980		
Pasmore, Victor, CH, CBE	P	1908	—	1983	
Patten, George	P	1801	1837	—	1865
Pearson, John Loughborough	A	1817	1874	1880	1897
Pegram, Henry Alfred	S	1863	1904	1922	1937
		(Retired 1936)			
Penny, Edward	P	1714	—	FM	1791
Peters, Revd Matthew William	P	1742	1771	1777	1814
		(Resigned 1790)			
Pettie, John	P	1839	1866	1873	1893
Philipson, Sir Robin	P	1916	1973	1981	
Phillip, John	P	1817	1857	1859	1867
Phillips, Thomas	P	1770	1804	1808	1845
Phillips, Tom	E	1937	1984		
Philpot, Glyn Warren	P	1884	1915	1923	1937
Pickersgill, Frederick Richard	P	1820	1847	1857	1900
		(Retired 1888)			
Pickersgill, Henry William	P	1782	1822	1826	1875
		(Retired 1872)			
Pitchforth, Roland Vivian	P	1895	1942	1953	1982
Pomeroy, Frederick William	S	1856	1906	1917	1924
Poole, Henry	S	1873	1920	1927	1928
Poole, Paul Falconer	P	1807	1846	1861	1879
		(Retired 1879)			
Powell, Sir Philip, CH, OBE	A	1921	1972	1977	

		Born	ARA	RA	Died
Poynter, Sir Edward John, Bt, GCVO	P	1836	1869	1876	1919
		(President, 1896–1918)			
Priestman, Bertram	P	1868	1916	1923	1951
Prinsep, Valentine Cameron	P	1838	1879	1894	1904
Prior, Edward Schroder	A	1852	1914	—	1932
Procter, Dod	P	1891	1934	1942	1972
Procter, Ernest	P	1886	1932	—	1935
Prout, Margaret Fisher	P	1875	1948	—	1963
Raeburn, Sir Henry	P	1756	1812	1815	1823
Ravenet, Simon François	E	1706	1770	—	1774
Rebecca, Biagio	P	1735	1771	—	1808
Redgrave, Richard, CB	P	1804	1840	1851	1888
		(Retired 1881)			
Redpath, Anne	P	1895	1960	—	1965
Reinagle, Philip	P	1749	1787	1812	1833
Reinagle, Ramsay Richard	P	1775	1814	1823	1862
		(Resigned 1848)			
Reynolds, Sir Joshua	P	1723	—	FM	1792
		(President, 1768–92)			
Richards, John Inigo	P	?	—	FM	1810
Richardson, Sir Albert Edward, KCVO	A	1880	1936	1944	1964
		(President, 1954–6)			
Richmond, George	P	1809	1857	1866	1896
		(Retired 1887)			
Richmond, Sir William Blake, KCB	P	1842	1888	1895	1921
Ricketts, Charles	P	1866	1922	1928	1931
Rigaud, John Francis	P	1742	1772	1784	1810
Riviere, Briton	P	1840	1878	1881	1920
Roberts, David	P	1796	1838	1841	1864
Roberts, William	P	1895	1958	1966	1980
Roberts-Jones, Ivor, CBE	S	1913	1969	1973	
Robertson, Sir Howard	A	1888	1949	1958	1963
Robinson, Frederick Cayley	P	1862	1921	—	1927
Robinson, John Henry	E	1796	1856	1867	1871
Rogers, Richard	A	1933	1978	1984	
Rooker, Michael Angelo	P	1743	1770	—	1801
Rosoman, Leonard, OBE	P	1913	1960	1969	
Ross, Sir William Charles	P	1794	1838	1843	1860
Rossi, John Charles Felix	S	1762	1798	1802	1839
Rothenstein, Michael	E	1908	1977	1983	
Rushbury, Sir Henry George, KCVO, CBE	E	1889	1927	1936	1968
Russell, John	P	1744	1772	1788	1806
Russell, Sir Walter Westley, CVO	P	1867	1920	1926	1949
Sandby, Paul	P	1725	—	FM	1809
Sandby, Thomas	A	1721	—	FM	1798
Sanders, Christopher Cavania	P	1905	1953	1961	
Sandle, Michael	S	1936	1982		

Alphabetical List of Members from the Foundation—continued

		Born	ARA	RA	Died
Sant, James, CVO	P	1820	1861	1869	1916
			(Retired 1914)		
Sargent, John Singer	P	1856	1894	1897	1925
Schilsky, Eric	S	1898	1957	1968	1974
Scott, Sir George Gilbert	A	1811	1855	1860	1878
Scott, Sir Giles Gilbert, OM	A	1880	1918	1922	1960
Scott, William, CBE	P	1913	1977	1984	
Serres, Dominic	P	1722	—	FM	1793
Shannon, Charles Haslewood	P	1863	1911	1920	1937
Shannon, Sir James Jebusa	P	1862	1897	1909	1923
Shaw, Richard Norman	A	1831	1872	1877	1912
			(Retired 1909)		
Shee, Sir Martin Archer	P	1769	1798	1800	1850
			(President, 1830–50)		
Sheppard, Sir Richard, CBE	A	1910	1966	1972	1982
Shepperson, Claude	E	1867	1919	—	1921
Short, Sir Frank	E	1857	1906	1911	1945
Sickert, Walter Richard	P	1860	1924	1934	1942
			(Resigned 1935)		
Sims, Charles	P	1873	1908	1915	1928
Sisson, Marshall Arnott, CVO, CBE	A	1897	1956	1963	1978
Skeaping, John Rattenbury	S	1901	1950	1959	1980
Smirke, Robert	P	1752	1791	1793	1845
Smirke, Sir Robert	A	1780	1808	1811	1867
			(Resigned 1859)		
Smirke, Sydney	A	1798	1847	1859	1877
			(Retired 1877)		
Smith, Anker	E	1759	1797	—	1819
Smythe, Lionel Percy	P	1839	1898	1911	1918
			(Retired 1914)		
Soane, Sir John	A	1753	1795	1802	1837
Solomon, Solomon Joseph	P	1860	1896	1906	1927
Soukop, Wilhelm Josef	S	1907	1963	1969	
Spear, Ruskin, CBE	P	1911	1944	1954	
Spence, Sir Basil, OM, OBE	A	1907	1953	1960	1976
Spencer, Gilbert	P	1892	1950	1959	1979
			(Resigned 1968, reinstated 1971)		
Spencer, Sir Stanley, CBE	P	1891	1932	1950	1959
			(Resigned 1935, re-elected 1950)		
Spurrier, Steven	P	1878	1943	1952	1961
Stacpoole, Frederic	E	1813	1880	—	1907
			(Retired 1891)		
Stanfield, William Clarkson	P	1793	1832	1835	1867
Stephens, Edward Bowring	S	1815	1864	—	1882
Stephenson, Ian	P	1934	1975	1986	
Stevens, Edward	A	?	1770	—	1775
Stevens, Norman	E	1937	1983		

		Born	ARA	RA	Died
Stirling, James	A	1926	1985		
Stocks, Lumb	E	1812	1853	1871	1892
Stokes, Adrian	P	1854	1910	1919	1935
Stone, Frank	P	1800	1851	—	1859
Stone, Marcus	P	1840	1877	1887	1921
Storey, George Adolphus	P	1834	1876	1914	1919
Stothard, Thomas	P	1755	1791	1794	1834
Stott, Edward	P	1855	1906	—	1918
Strang, William	E	1859	1906	1921	1921
Street, George Edmund	A	1824	1866	1871	1881
Stubbs, George	P	1724	1780	—	1806
Sutton, Philip	P	1928	1977		
Swan, John MacAllan	P	1847	1894	1905	1910
Swanwick, Betty	D	1915	1972	1979	
Swynnerton, Annie Louisa	P	1844	1922	—	1933
Symons, Patrick	P	1925	1983		
Talmage, Algernon Mayow	P	1871	1922	1929	1939
Tapper, Sir Walter John, KCVO	A	1861	1926	1935	1935
Taylor, Leonard Campbell	P	1874	1923	1931	1969
Theed, William	S	1764	1811	1813	1817
Thomson, Alfred Reginald	P	1894	1938	1945	1979
Thomson, Henry	P	1773	1801	1804	1843
Thorburn, Robert	P	1818	1848	—	1885
			(Retired 1885)		
Thornycroft, Sir Hamo	S	1850	1881	1888	1925
Tilson, Joe	E	1928	1985		
Tindle, David	P	1932	1973	1979	
Titchell, John	P	1926	1986		
Todd, Arthur Ralph Middleton	P	1891	1939	1949	1966
Tomkins, William	P	1730	1771	—	1792
Toms, Peter	P	?	—	FM	1776
Tresham, Henry	P	1756	1791	1799	1814
Trevelyan, Julian	P	1910	—	1986	
Tuke, Henry Scott	P	1858	1900	1914	1929
Tunnard, John	P	1900	1967	—	1971
Tunnicliffe, Charles Frederick, OBE	E	1901	1944	1954	1979
Turner, Alfred	S	1874	1922	1931	1940
Turner, Charles	E	1773	1828	—	1857
Turner, Joseph Mallord William	P	1775	1799	1802	1851
Tyler, William	A	?	—	FM	1801
Uwins, Thomas	P	1782	1833	1838	1857
Wadsworth, Edward	P	1889	1943	—	1949
Wakeford, Edward	P	1914	1968	—	1973
Wale, Samuel	P	?	—	FM	1786
Walker, Arthur George	S	1861	1925	1936	1939

Alphabetical List of Members from the Foundation—continued

		Born	ARA	RA	Died
Walker, Dame Ethel, DBE	P	1861	1940	—	1951
(Date of birth was recorded as 1867 until after her death)					
Walker, Frederick	P	1840	1871	—	1875
Ward, Edward Matthew	P	1816	1846	1855	1879
Ward, James	P	1769	1807	1811	1859
Ward, John Stanton, CBE	P	1917	1956	1965	
Ward, William	E	1766	1814	—	1826
Waterhouse, Alfred	A	1830	1878	1885	1905
			(Retired 1903)		
Waterhouse, John William	P	1849	1885	1895	1917
Waterlow, Sir Ernest Albert	P	1850	1890	1903	1919
Watson, George Spencer	P	1869	1923	1932	1934
Watts, George Frederick, OM	P	1817	1867	1867	1904
			(Retired 1896)		
Webb, Sir Aston, GCVO, CB	A	1849	1899	1903	1930
			(President, 1919–24)		
Webber, John	P	1752	1785	1791	1793
Webster, Thomas	P	1800	1840	1846	1886
			(Retired 1876)		
Weekes, Henry	S	1807	1851	1863	1877
			(Retired 1877)		
Weight, Carel, CBE	P	1908	1955	1965	
Wells, Henry Tanworth	P	1828	1866	1870	1903
West, Benjamin	P	1738	—	FM	1820
		(President, 1792–1805 and 1806–1820)			
Westall, Richard	P	1765	1792	1794	1836
Westall, William	P	1781	1812	—	1850
Westmacott, Sir Richard	S	1775	1805	1811	1856
Westmacott, Richard	S	1799	1838	1849	1872
			(Retired 1871)		
Wheatley, Francis	P	1747	1790	1791	1801
Wheatley, John Laviers	P	1892	1945	—	1955
Wheeler, Sir Charles, KCVO, CBE	S	1892	1934	1940	1974
			(President, 1956–66)		
Whishaw, Anthony	P	1930	1980		
Wilkie, Sir David	P	1785	1809	1811	1841
Wilkins, William	A	1778	1823	1826	1839
Williams, Kyffin, OBE	P	1918	1970	1974	
Williams, Terrick	P	1860	1924	1933	1936
Willmore, James Tibbetts	E	1800	1843	—	1863
Wilson, Richard	P	1714	—	FM	1782
Wilton, Joseph	S	1722	—	FM	1803
Witherington, William Frederick	P	1785	1830	1840	1865
			(Retired 1863)		
Wolfe, Edward	P	1897	1967	1972	1982
Wood, Francis Derwent	S	1871	1910	1920	1926
Woodford, James, OBE	S	1893	1937	1945	1976
Woodforde, Samuel	P	1763	1800	1807	1817

		Born	ARA	RA	Died
Woodington, William Frederick	S	1806	1876	—	1893
			(Retired 1885)		
Woods, Henry	P	1846	1882	1893	1921
Woolner, Thomas	S	1825	1871	1874	1892
Worthington, Sir Hubert, OBE	A	1886	1945	1955	1963
Wragg, John	S	1937	1983		
Wright, Joseph	P	1734	1781	—	1797
Wyatt, James	A	1748	1770	1785	1813
			(President, 1805–6)		
Wyatville, Sir Jeffrey (formerly Wyatt)	A	1766	1822	1824	1840
Wyllie, William Lionel	P	1851	1889	1907	1931
Wyon, William	S	1795	1831	1838	1851
Yeames, William Frederick	P	1835	1866	1878	1918
			(Retired 1913)		
Yenn, John	A	1750	1774	1791	1821
Yeo, Richard	S	?	—	FM	1779
Zoffany, Johann	P	1735	—	NM	1810
Zuccarelli, Francesco	P	1702	—	FM	1789
Zucchi, Antonio	P	1726	1770	—	1795

CHRONOLOGICAL LISTS OF OFFICERS AND PROFESSORS

PRESIDENTS

The election of the President takes place annually, normally in December. Each holder of the office so far has been re-elected whilst still eligible and willing to serve.

Sir Joshua Reynolds (*1723–92*)	1768–1792
Benjamin West (*1738–1820*)	1792–1805
James Wyatt (*1748–1813*)	1805–1806
Benjamin West (*1738–1820*)	1806–1820
Sir Thomas Lawrence (*1769–1830*)	1820–1830
Sir Martin Archer Shee (*1769–1850*)	1830–1850
Sir Charles Lock Eastlake (*1793–1865*)	1850–1865
Sir Francis Grant (*1803–78*)	1866–1878
Lord Leighton of Stretton (*1830–96*)	1878–1896
Sir John Everett Millais, Bt. (*1829–96*)	1896
Sir Edward John Poynter, Bt., GCVO (*1836–1919*)	1896–1918
Sir Aston Webb, GCVO, CB (*1849–1930*)	1919–1924
Sir Frank Dicksee, KCVO (*1853–1928*)	1924–1928
Sir William Llewellyn, GCVO (*1858–1941*)	1928–1938
Sir Edwin Landseer Lutyens, OM, KCIE (*1869–1944*)	1938–1944
Sir Alfred James Munnings, KCVO (*1878–1959*)	1944–1949
Sir Gerald Kelly, KCVO (*1879–1972*)	1949–1954
Sir Albert Edward Richardson, KCVO (*1880–1964*)	1954–1956
Sir Charles Wheeler, KCVO, CBE (*1892–1974*)	1956–1966
Sir (Walter) Thomas Monnington (*1902–76*)	1966–1976
Sir Hugh Casson, CH, KCVO (*1910– *)	1976–1984
Roger de Grey (*1918– *)	1984–

KEEPERS

Only Academicians were eligible for the Keepership until 1945, since when Associates also have been eligible though none so far has been elected. In 1873 the term of office was limited to five years and, in 1927, to three years. Re-election is permitted and usual whilst the holder is still eligible and willing to serve.

George Michael Moser (*1704–83*)	1768–1783
Agostino Carlini (*?–1790*)	1783–1790

Joseph Wilton (*1722–1803*)	1790–1803
Henry Fuseli (*1741–1825*)	1804–1825
Henry Thomson (*1773–1843*)	1825–1827
William Hilton (*1786–1839*)	1827–1839
George Jones (*1786–1869*)	1840–1850
Charles Landseer (*1799–1879*)	1851–1873
Frederick Richard Pickersgill (*1820–1900*)	1873–1887
Philip Hermogenes Calderon (*1833–98*)	1887–1898
Ernest Crofts (*1847–1911*)	1898–1911
Andrew Carrick Gow (*1848–1920*)	1911–1920
Charles Sims(*1873–1928*)	1920–1926

Charles Sims having resigned the Keepership in November 1926, Sir George Clausen was appointed temporary Director of the Schools for the Lent Term and George Harcourt for the Summer Term, 1927

Sir Walter Westley Russell, CVO (*1867–1949*)	1927–1942
Sir Gerald Kelly, KCVO (*1879–1972*)	1943–1945
Philip Connard, CVO (*1875–1958*)	1945–1949
Sir Henry Rushbury, KCVO, CBE (*1889–1968*)	1949–1964
Peter Greenham, CBE (*1909– *)	1964–1985
Edward Middleditch, MC (*1923– *)	1985–

TREASURERS

Only Academicians have ever been eligible for the Treasurership. The appointment was entirely in the hands of the Sovereign until 1874, since when it has been by election. In 1880 the term of office was limited to five years but re-election is permitted and usual whilst the holder is still eligible and willing to serve.

Sir William Chambers (*1723–96*)	1768–1796
John Yenn (*1750–1821*)	1796–1820
Sir Robert Smirke (*1780–1867*)	1820–1850
Philip Hardwick (*1792–1870*)	1850–1861
Sydney Smirke (*1798–1877*)	1861–1874
Edward Middleton Barry (*1830–80*)	1874–1880
George Edmund Street (*1824–81*)	1880–1881

Richard Norman Shaw was elected in succession to G. E. Street but resigned the appointment within three weeks.

John Callcott Horsley (*1817–1903*)	1882–1897
Alfred Waterhouse (*1830–1905*)	1897–1901
Sir Thomas Graham Jackson, Bt. (*1835–1924*)	1901–1912
Sir Aston Webb, GCVO, CB (*1849–1930*)	1912–1919
Sir Frank Short (*1857–1945*)	1919–1932
Sydney Lee (*1866–1949*)	1932–1940
Sir Edwin Cooper (*1872–1942*)	1940–1942
Emanuel Vincent Harris, OBE (*1876–1971*)	1942–1954
Sir Edward Maufe (*1883–1974*)	1954–1958
Louis de Soissons, CVO, OBE (*1890–1962*)	1958–1962
Sir Basil Spence, OM, OBE (*1907–76*)	1962–1964

Sir James Gunn was elected in succession to Sir Basil Spence but died within a few weeks.

Chronological Lists of Officers and Professors—continued

Donald McMorran (*1904–65*)	1965
Marshall Sisson, CVO, CBE (*1897–1978*)	1965–1970
Lord (William) Holford (*1907–75*)	1970–1975
Sir Hugh Casson was elected in succession to Lord Holford but became President a few weeks later.	
Roger de Grey (*1918–*)	1976–1984
Sir Philip Powell, CH, OBE (*1921–*)	1985–

SECRETARIES

Only Academicians were eligible for election as Secretary until 1873, since when laymen have been appointed. There has never been a time limit for the office.

Francis Milner Newton (*1720–94*)	1768–1788
John Inigo Richards (*?–1810*)	1788–1810
Henry Howard (*1769–1847*)	1811–1847
John Prescott Knight (*1803–81*)	1847–1873
Sir Frederick A. Eaton (*1838–1913*)	1873–1913
Sir Walter R. M. Lamb, KCVO (*1882–1961*)	1913–1951
Humphrey Brooke, CVO (*1914–*)	1952–1968
Sidney C. Hutchison, CVO (*1912–*)	1968–1982
Piers Rodgers (*1944–*)	1982–

LIBRARIANS

The first Librarian was elected in 1770. Only Academicians were eligible until 1920 and, in 1873, the term of office was limited to five years but re-election was permitted. Laymen have been appointed since 1920 without limitation of tenure.

Francis Hayman (*1708–76*)	1770–1776
Richard Wilson (*1714–82*)	1776–1782
Samuel Wale (*?–1786*)	1782–1786
Joseph Wilton (*1722–1803*)	1786–1790
Dominic Serres (*1722–93*)	1792–1793
Edward Burch (*1730–1814*)	1794–1812
Thomas Stothard (*1755–1834*)	1814–1834
George Jones (*1786–1869*)	1834–1840
William Collins (*1788–1847*)	1840–1842
Sir Charles Lock Eastlake (*1793–1865*)	1842–1844
Thomas Uwins (*1782–1857*)	1844–1855
Henry William Pickersgill (*1782–1875*)	1856–1864
Solomon Alexander Hart (*1806–81*)	1864–1881
John Evan Hodgson (*1831–95*)	1882–1895
William Frederick Yeames (*1835–1918*)	1896–1911
Andrew Carrick Gow (*1848–1920*)	1911–1920
Ernest E. V. Wright (*1878–1955*)	1920–1948
Sidney C. Hutchison, CVO (*1912–*)	1949–1968

Philip James, CBE (1901–74)   1969–1974
Constance-Anne Parker (1921–   )   1974–1986
MaryAnne Stevens (1947–   )   1986–

PROFESSORS OF PAINTING

Only Academicians were eligible for this Professorship until 1886 when it was opened also to Associates. It was in abeyance from 1911 to 1986.

Edward Penny (*1714–91*)	1768–1782
James Barry (*1741–1806*)	1782–1799
Henry Fuseli (*1741–1825*)	1799–1805
John Opie (*1761–1807*)	1805–1807
Henry Tresham (*1756–1814*)	1807–1809
Henry Fuseli (*1741–1825*)	1810–1825
Thomas Phillips (*1770–1845*)	1825–1832
Henry Howard (*1769–1847*)	1833–1847
Charles Robert Leslie (*1794–1859*)	1847–1852
Solomon Alexander Hart (*1806–81*)	1854–1863
Charles West Cope (*1811–90*)	1866–1875
Edward Armitage (*1817–96*)	1875–1882
John Evan Hodgson (*1831–95*)	1882–1895
Sir William Blake Richmond, KCB (*1842–1921*)	1895–1899
Sir Hubert von Herkomer, CVO (*1849–1914*)	1899–1900
Valentine Cameron Prinsep (*1838–1904*)	1900–1903
Sir George Clausen (*1852–1944*)	1903–1906
Sir Hubert von Herkomer, CVO (*1849–1914*)	1906–1909
Sir William Blake Richmond, KCB (*1842–1921*)	1909–1911
Norman Adams (*1927– *)	1986–

PROFESSORS OF SCULPTURE

Only Academicians were eligible for this Professorship from its commencement in 1810 until 1886 when it was opened also to Associates. It was vacant from 1878 to 1900 and in abeyance from 1911 to 1985; there were Masters of the Sculpture School during most of the latter period.

John Flaxman (*1755–1826*)	1810–1826
Sir Richard Westmacott (*1775–1856*)	1827–1856
Richard Westmacott (*1799–1872*)	1857–1868
Henry Weekes (*1807–77*)	1868–1876
Thomas Woolner (*1825–92*)	1877–1878
Sir Alfred Gilbert, MVO (*1854–1934*)	1900–1904
William Robert Colton (*1867–1921*)	1907–1911
Henry Poole (Master) (*1873–1928*)	1921–1927
William McMillan, CVO (Master) (*1887–1977*)	1929–1941
Maurice Lambert (Master) (*1901–64*)	1950–1958
Arnold Machin, OBE (Master) (*1911– *)	1959–1966
Uli Nimptsch (Master) (*1897–1977*)	1967–1969
Willi Soukop (Master) (*1907– *)	1969–1982
Bryan Kneale (Master; Professor from 1985) (*1930– *)	1982–

Chronological Lists of Officers and Professors—continued

PROFESSORS OF ARCHITECTURE

Only Academicians were eligible for this Professorship until 1886 when it was opened also to Associates. It was in abeyance from 1911 to 1946.

Thomas Sandby (*1721–98*)	1768–1798
George Dance (*1740–1825*)	1798–1805
Sir John Soane (*1753–1837*)	1806–1837
William Wilkins (*1778–1839*)	1837–1839
Charles Robert Cockerell (*1788–1863*)	1839–1859
Sydney Smirke (*1798–1877*)	1860–1865
Sir George Gilbert Scott (*1811–78*)	1866–1873
Edward Middleton Barry (*1830–80*)	1873–1880
George Edmund Street (*1824–81*)	1880–1881
George Aitchison (*1825–1910*)	1887–1905
Sir Reginald Blomfield (*1856–1942*)	1907–1911
Sir Albert Edward Richardson, KCVO (*1880–1964*)	1946–1961
Sir Basil Spence, OM, OBE (*1907–76*)	1961–1967
E. Maxwell Fry, CBE (*1899– *)	1967–1975
H. T. Cadbury-Brown, OBE (*1913– *)	1975–

PROFESSORS OF PERSPECTIVE

Academicians holding this post have been entitled Professors. Others were called Teachers, until 1975 when, after a lapse of thirty-six years, the appointment was renewed but without such restriction.

Samuel Wale (*?–1786*)	1768–1786
Edward Edwards (Teacher) (*1738–1806*)	1788–1806
J. M. W. Turner (*1775–1851*)	1807–1837
J. P. Knight (*1803–81*)	1839–1860
Henry Alexander Bowler (Teacher) (*1824–1903*)	1861–1899
George Adolphus Storey (Teacher; Professor from 1914) (*1834–1919*)	1900–1919
Walter Bayes (Teacher) (*1869–1956*)	1927–1939
B. A. R. Carter (*1909– *)	1975–1983
Frederick Dubery (*1926– *)	1983–

PROFESSORS OF ANATOMY

William Hunter (*1718–83*)	1768–1783
John Sheldon (*1752–1808*)	1783–1808
Sir Anthony Carlisle (*1768–1840*)	1808–1824
Joseph H. Green (*1791–1863*)	1825–1851
Richard Partridge (*1805–73*)	1852–1873
John Marshall (*1818–91*)	1873–1890
William Anderson (*1842–1900*)	1891–1900
Arthur Thomson (*1858–1935*)	1900–1934

Alexander Macphail (*1872–1938*)	1934–1938
Arthur Beeny Appleton (*1888–1950*)	1938–1950
James Dixon Boyd (*1907–68*)	1950–1956
William James Hamilton (*1903–75*)	1956–1975
Gerald Libby (*1944– *)	1975–

PROFESSORS OF CHEMISTRY

Frederick S. Barff (*1823–86*)	1871–1879
Sir Arthur Herbert Church, KCVO (*1834–1915*)	1879–1911
Arthur Pillans Laurie (*1861–1949*)	1912–1936
Harold James Plenderleith, CBE, MC (*1898– *)	1936–1958
Louis Arnold Jordan, CBE (*1892–1964*)	1958–1962
A. E. Anthony Werner (*1911– *)	1962–1975
Stephen Rees Jones (*1909– *)	1975–

APPENDIX D
CHRONOLOGICAL LISTS OF HONORARY MEMBERS

The first honorary office created was that of Secretary for Foreign Correspondence, in 1769. In the following year a Professor of Ancient Literature, a Professor of Ancient History and an Antiquary were appointed. The Chaplaincy was instituted in 1784 and the Professorships of Law in 1928 and History of Art in 1968. Honorary Academicians have been elected since 1869 and Honorary Corresponding Members since 1909; the word 'Foreign' was included in the titles until 1933. Presidents of the Royal Scottish Academy and the Royal Hibernian Academy have been Honorary Members *ex officio* since 1911. Sir Winston Churchill was appointed Honorary Academician Extraordinary in 1948. A class of Honorary Fellows was instituted in 1978.

CHAPLAINS

Revd Matthew William Peters, RA (*1742–1814*)	1784–1788
Rt. Revd Thomas Barnard, Bishop of Killaloe, later Bishop of Limerick (*1728–1806*)	1791–1806
Rt. Revd John Fisher, Bishop of Exeter, later Bishop of Salisbury (*1748–1825*)	1807–1825
Rt. Revd The Hon. Edward Legge, Bishop of Oxford (*1767–1827*)	1826–1827
Rt. Revd C. J. Blomfield, Bishop of Chester, later Bishop of London (*1786–1857*)	1827–1857
Rt. Revd Samuel Wilberforce, Bishop of Oxford, later Bishop of Winchester (*1805–73*)	1857–1873
Most Revd William Thomson, Archbishop of York (*1819–90*)	1873–1890
Most Revd William Connor Magee, Bishop of Peterborough, Archbishop Elect of York (*1821–91*)	1891
Most Revd William Dalrymple Maclagan, Archbishop of York (*1826–1910*)	1892–1910
Rt. Revd The Hon. Edward Carr Glyn, Bishop of Peterborough (*1843–1928*)	1911–1919
Rt. Revd Herbert Edward Ryle, KCVO, Dean of Westminster (*1856–1925*)	1919–1925
Very Revd William Foxley Norris, KCVO, Dean of Westminster (*1859–1937*)	1926–1937
Most Revd Archbishop Lord (Geoffrey Francis) Fisher of Lambeth, GCVO, Bishop of London, later Archbishop of Canterbury (*1887–1972*)	1939–1968

Very Revd W. P. Baddeley, Rector of St. James's Church, Piccadilly (*1914–*)	1968–1980
Revd Donald Reeves, Rector of St. James's Church, Piccadilly (*1934–*)	1980–

PROFESSORS OF ANCIENT HISTORY

Oliver Goldsmith (*1728–74*)	1770–1774
Revd Dr T. Francklin (*1721–84*)	1774–1784
Edward Gibbon (*1737–94*)	1787–1794
William Mitford (*1744–1827*)	1818–1827
Henry Hallam (*1777–1849*)	1836–1859
George Grote (*1794–1871*)	1859–1871
Rt. Revd Connop Thirlwall, Bishop of St David's (*1797–1875*)	1871–1875
Rt. Hon. W. E. Gladstone (*1809–98*)	1876–1898
Sir Richard C. Jebb, OM (*1841–1905*)	1898–1905
Very Revd H. D. M. Spence-Jones, Dean of Gloucester (*1836–1917*)	1906–1917
Sir Frederic George Kenyon, GBE, KCB (*1863–1952*)	1918–1952
Earl of Crawford and Balcarres, KT, GBE (*1900–75*)	1952–1965
Sir Mortimer Wheeler, CH, CIE, MC (*1890–1976*)	1965–1976
Sir Ronald Syme, OM (*1903–*)	1976–

PROFESSORS OF ANCIENT LITERATURE

Samuel Johnson (*1709–84*)	1770–1784
Bennet Langton (*1737–1801*)	1787–1801
Charles Burney (*1757–1817*)	1803–1817
Rt. Revd William Howley, Bishop of London, later Archbishop of Canterbury (*1766–1848*)	1818–1830
Rt. Revd Edward Coplestone, Bishop of Llandaff (*1776–1849*)	1831–1849
Lord Macaulay (*1800–59*)	1850–1859
Very Revd Henry Hart Milman, Dean of St Paul's (*1791–1868*)	1860–1868
Very Revd Arthur Penrhyn Stanley, Dean of Westminster (*1815–81*)	1868–1881
Very Revd Henry George Liddell, Dean of Christ Church (*1811–98*)	1882–1898
Rt. Revd Mandell Creighton, Bishop of London (*1843–1901*)	1898–1901
Viscount Morley of Blackburn, OM (*1838–1923*)	1903–1923
John William Mackail, OM (*1859–1945*)	1924–1945
Revd Henry John Chaytor (*1871–1954*)	1946–1954
Thomas Bertram Lonsdale Webster (*1905–74*)	1955–1968
Sir Maurice Bowra (*1898–1971*)	1968–1971
Colin Hardie (*1906–*)	1971–

PROFESSORS OF LAW

Sir Francis George Newbolt, KC (*1863–1940*)	1928–1940
Lord (Hugh Pattison) Macmillan, PC, GCVO (*1873–1952*)	1941–1952

Chronological Lists of Honorary Members—continued

Viscount (Gavin Turnbull) Simonds, PC (*1881–1971*)   1952–1971
Lord (Edward Holroyd) Pearce, PC (*1901–*   )   1971–

ANTIQUARIES

Richard Dalton (c. *1715–91*)	1770–1784
Samuel Lysons (*1763–1819*)	1818–1819
Sir Henry Englefield, Bt. (*1752–1822*)	1821–1822
Sir Walter Scott, Bt. (*1771–1832*)	1827–1832
Sir Robert H. Inglis, Bt. (*1786–1855*)	1850–1855
Earl Stanhope (*1805–75*)	1855–1875
Sir Philip de M. Grey Egerton, Bt. (*1806–81*)	1876–1881
Sir Charles T. Newton, KCB (*1816–94*)	1881–1894
Sir Augustus Wollaston Franks, KCB (*1826–97*)	1895–1897
Francis Cranmer Penrose (*1817–1903*)	1898–1903
Viscount (Harold Arthur) Dillon, CH (*1844–1932*)	1903–1932
Sir Charles Reed Peers, CBE (*1868–1952*)	1933–1952
Sir James Gow Mann, KCVO (*1897–1962*)	1954–1962
Sir Karl T. Parker, CBE (*1895–*)	1962–

PROFESSORS OF THE HISTORY OF ART

Lord (Kenneth) Clark, OM, CH, KCB (*1903–83*)   1974–83
Francis Haskell (*1928–*   )   1983–

SECRETARIES FOR FOREIGN CORRESPONDENCE

Joseph Baretti (*1719–89*)	1769–1789
James Boswell (*1740–95*)	1791–1795
Prince Hoare (*1755–1834*)	1799–1834
Sir George Staunton, Bt. (*1781–1859*)	1839–1859
Sir Henry Holland, Bt. (*1788–1873*)	1860–1873
Sir William Stirling Maxwell, Bt. (*1818–78*)	1874–1878
Lord Houghton (*1809–85*)	1878–1885
Robert Browning (*1812–89*)	1886–1889
Rt. Hon. Sir Austen Henry Layard (*1817–94*)	1890–1894
Rt. Hon. William E. H. Lecky (*1838–1903*)	1895–1903
Lord Avebury (*1834–1913*)	1904–1913
Earl of Crawford and Balcarres, KT (*1871–1940*)	1914–1940
Earl of Halifax, KG, OM, GCSI, GCIE (*1881–1959*)	1941–1959
Marquess of Salisbury, KG, PC (*1893–1972*)	1960–1972
Lord Butler of Saffron Walden, KG, CH (*1902–82*)	1972–1982
Lord (Peter) Carrington, KG, PC, CH, KCMG, MC (*1919–*)	1982–

HONORARY CORRESPONDING MEMBERS

Giacomo Boni (? –1925)	1909–1925
Osman Hamdy Bey (1842–1910)	1909–1910
Roberto Paribeni (? – ?))	1930–1941
Homer Saint-Gaudens (1880–1958)	1942–1958
Ernst Buschbeck (1889–1963)	1959–1963
Xavier de Salas, Hon. CBE (1907–82)	1965–1982
Jean Renoir (1894–1979)	1970–1979
Armand Hammer (1898–)	1974–
Paul Mellon, Hon. KBE (1907–)	1977–
Emmanuel Jacquin de Margerie (1924–)	1984–

HONORARY MEMBERS EX-OFFICIO

Sir James Guthrie (1859–1930)	1912–1930
Dermod O'Brien (1865–1945)	1912–1945
Sir James Lawton Wingate (1846–1924)	1919–1924
Sir George Washington Browne (1853–1939)	1924–1939
Sir George Pirie (1866–1946)	1933–1946
Sir Frank C. Mears (1880–1953)	1944–1953
James Sleator (1889–1950)	1946–1950
Sir William O. Hutchison (1889–1970)	1950–1970
John Keating (1889–1977)	1950–1977
Sir William MacTaggart, RA (1903–81)	1959–1981
Maurice MacGonigal (1900–79)	1963–1979
Sir William H. Kininmonth (1904–)	1969–
Sir Robin Philipson, RA (1916–)	1973–
Raymond McGrath (1903–77)	1977
David Hone (1928–)	1978–1983
H. Anthony Wheeler, OBE (1919–)	1983–
Thomas Ryan (1929–)	1983–

HONORARY ACADEMICIANS

Louis Gallait (1810–87)	1869–1887
Claude Guillaume (1822–1905)	1869–1905
Eugene E. Viollet-le-Duc (1814–79)	1869–1879
Louis P. Henriquel-Dupont (1797–1892)	1869–1892
Jean Louis Meissonier (1815–91)	1869–1891
Jean Léon Gérôme (1824–1904)	1869–1904
Ludwig Knaus (1829–1910)	1882–1910
Paul Dubois (1829–1905)	1896–1905
Adolf Menzel (1815–1905)	1896–1905
Jules Breton (1827–1906)	1899–1906
Léon Bonnat (1834–1922)	1904–1922
Emmanuel Frémiet (1824–1910)	1904–1910
Josef Israels (1824–1911)	1906–1911
Augustus Saint-Gaudens (1848–1907)	1906–1907

Chronological Lists of Honorary Members—continued

Antonin Mercié (*1845–1916*)	1908–1916
Pascal Adolphe Jean Dagnan-Bouveret (*1852–1929*)	1908–1929
Jean Paul Laurens (*1838–1921*)	1909–1921
Jean Baptiste Edouard Détaille (*1848–1912*)	1910–1912
Paul Albert Besnard (*1849–1934*)	1921–1934
Albert Bartholomé (*1848–1928*)	1921–1928
Jean Louis Forain (*1852–1931*)	1930–1931
Ragnar Ostberg (*1866–1945*)	1930–1945
Lucien Simon (*1861–1945*)	1930–1945
Cass Gilbert (*1859–1934*)	1930–1934
Carl Milles (*1875–1955*)	1940–1955
Pierre Bonnard (*1867–1947*)	1940–1947
Ivar Justus Tengbom (*1878–1968*)	1947–1968
André Dunoyer de Segonzac (*1884–1974*)	1947–1974
Walter Gropius (*1883–1969*)	1967–1969
Pier Luigi Nervi (*1891–1979*)	1967–1979
Oskar Kokoschka (*1886–1980*)	1970–1980
Giacomo Manzù (*1908– *)	1970–
Marc Chagall (*1889–1985*)	1979–1985
Joan Miró (*1893–1983*)	1980–1983
Josep-Lluis Sert (*1902–83*)	1980–1983
Balthus (Count Balthazar Klossowski de Rola) (*1908– *)	1981–
Stanley William Hayter, CBE (*1901– *)	1981–
Willem de Kooning (*1904– *)	1983–
Eduardo Chillida (*1924– *)	1983–
Jean Dubuffet (*1901–85*)	1985
Ralph Erskine (*1914– *)	1985–
Rufino Tamayo (*1899– *)	1985–
Jorn Utzon (*1918– *)	1985–

HONORARY ACADEMICIAN EXTRAORDINARY

Rt. Hon. Sir Winston Spencer Churchill, KG, OM, CH (*1874–1965*)	1948–1965

HONORARY FELLOWS

Lord (Martin) Charteris of Amisfield, GCB, GCVO, OBE (*1913– *)	1981–
Sir Trenchard Cox, CBE (*1905– *)	1981–
Sir Brinsley Ford, CBE (*1908– *)	1981–
Baroness (Jennie) Lee of Asheridge (*1904– *)	1981–
Lord (Harold) Lever of Manchester (*1914– *)	1981–
Sir Isaiah Berlin, OM, CBE (*1909– *)	1982–
Sir Ernst Gombrich, CBE (*1909– *)	1982–
Sir David Piper, CBE (*1918– *)	1983–
Dame (Mary) Jennifer Jenkins, DBE (*1921– *)	1984–
Lady (Margaret) Casson (*1913– *)	1985–

SUBJECT-INDEX OF EXHIBITIONS

The Summer Exhibition of the work of living artists has taken place annually without a break in the sequence from 1769. It was held at Lambe's Auction Rooms in Pall Mall from 1769 to 1779, at Somerset House in the Strand from 1780 to 1836, in the eastern half of the building in Trafalgar Square which was shared with the National Gallery from 1837 to 1868 and, since 1869, has been held at Burlington House in Piccadilly.

The Loan Exhibitions commenced in the 1870s within a few months of the Academy's move to the Burlington House site and, in addition, the galleries have been lent from time to time since 1915 for special exhibitions organized by outside bodies. The following index gives the subject-matters and dates of the main such exhibitions.

Aalto, Alvar, 1978
Abbey, Edwin Austin, 1912
Afghan Art, 1967
Alma-Tadema, Sir Lawrence, 1913
American Contemporary Art (*Art: USA: Now*), 1963
American Naive Painting, 1968
Armstrong, John, 1975
Arts and Crafts Exhibition Society, 1916, 1923, 1926, 1928, 1931, 1938, 1946
Assheton-Bennett Collection, 1965
Australian Art, 1923

Bauhaus, 1968
Big Paintings for Public Places, 1969
Blackadder, Elizabeth, 1982
Blake, William, 1893, 1894
Blow, Sandra, 1979
Bonnard, Pierre, 1966
Brangwyn, Sir Frank, 1952
Brazilian Painters, 1944
British Architecture, 1937
British Art, 1934
British Art – Kings and Queens, 1953
British Art in Industry, 1935
British Art Now, 1980
British Colour Council (*Colour in Everyday Life*), 1944

British Drama League (*The British Playhouse*), 1945
British Painting, 1977
British Portraits, 1956/7
British Primitive Paintings, 1923
British School, Deceased Masters of the, 1871–3, 1875–96, 1901, 1903, 1904, 1906–8, 1910, 1912
British Sculptors, 1972
British Watercolours, 1891, 1892, 1949
Brock, Sir Thomas, 1905
Burlington Fine Art Fair, 1977, 1979
Burlington House Fair, 1980, 1982, 1983, 1985

Callcott, Sir Augustus Wall, 1875
Calvert, Edward, 1893
Camoufleur Artists, 1919
Canadian War Memorials, 1919
Chagall, 1985
Chantrey Collection, 1949, 1981
Charles II, The Age of, 1960/1
Chatsworth, 1969, 1980/1
Children's Art, 1970
Chinese Art, 1935/6, 1973/4, 1982
Churchill, Sir Winston S., 1959
Cimabue, 1983
Cityscapes, 1978

APPENDIX F

TRUST AND SPECIAL FUNDS ADMINISTERED BY THE ROYAL ACADEMY

EDWIN AUSTIN ABBEY MEMORIAL TRUST FUND FOR MURAL PAINTING IN GREAT BRITAIN
Received from the widow of E. A. Abbey, RA (died 1911) under a trust deed dated
28 April 1931, for commissioning mural paintings in public buildings or charitable
institutions in Great Britain; it is administered by a specially appointed committee.

AITCHISON
Bequeathed by George Aitchison, RA (died 1910) to augment the Sandby Gift (*q.v.*)
in respect of architects or their families. (See also the Norman Shaw Fund.)

ALMA-TADEMA
Bequeathed by Sir Lawrence Alma-Tadema, OM, RA (died 1912, although not
received until 1944–5) to found an Alma-Tadema Scholarship.

ARMITAGE
Received from Edward Armitage, RA, in 1877, to found Armitage Prizes for a figure
picture in monochrome; they are offered to students of the Royal Academy.

HERBERT BAKER
Bequeathed by Sir Herbert Baker, KCIE, RA (died 1946) to found scholarships for
fostering inter-collaboration between the arts of architecture, sculpture, painting
and poetic literature.

MARGARET LOUISE BAND
Received from Miss Margaret Louise Band in 1973 for an annual prize to a student
in the Royal Academy Schools for an anatomical drawing.

BENEFACTORS'
Comprises contributions for the relief of distress among artists of reputation or their
widows.

BIZO
Bequeathed by John Bizo, in 1884, for scientific investigation into the nature of
pigments, varnishes, etc.

281

Trust and Special Funds administered by the Royal Academy—continued

BOWLER

Bequeathed by Henry Archer Bowler (died 1926) for providing help for accomplished and deserving artists or artists in reduced circumstances.

CHANTREY

Received annually under the will of Sir Francis Chantrey, RA (died 1841) for the purchase of works of art of the highest merit in painting and sculpture, executed entirely within the shores of Great Britain, to form a public national collection of British Fine Art.

ERNEST COOK

Received from the Ernest Cook Trust in 1981–2 for bursaries to students in the Royal Academy Schools who are in need of financial assistance.

E. W. COOKE

Bequeathed by Edward William Cooke, RA (died 1880) for the benefit or relief of painters in oil or water-colour, of 60 years or more and not Members of the Royal Academy.

S. I. V. COOKE

Bequeathed by Miss Sybil Irene Verdun Cooke (died 1973) to purchase pictures exhibited in the Royal Academy Summer Exhibition (preference being given to those of exhibitors resident in Cheshire, Lancashire or Hampshire and the pictures to be given to galleries in these counties which are open free to the public).

COUSINS

Received from Samuel Cousins, RA, in 1883, to provide annuities to deserving artists, not being Members of the Royal Academy.

CRESWICK

Received from Miss Maryanne Creswick, in 1879, to found an annual Creswick Prize for an oil painting of landscape from nature; it is offered to students of the Royal Academy.

JOHN CROMPTON

Received from Miss Dorothea Crompton, in 1962–4, to found a prize (or prizes), in memory of her father, for the encouragement of good craftsmanship in the Royal Academy Schools.

DOOLEY

Received from Dr Denis Dooley, in 1980 and 1984, for an annual prize to a student in the Royal Academy Schools who has produced the best work related to anatomy.

EDWARDS

Received from William Joseph Edwards, in 1891, for the benefit of poor artists or artistic engravers and for the encouragement of art.

ELLERMAN

Bequeathed by Sir John Reeves Ellerman, Bt., CH (died 1933 but not received until 1984–6), as to one-fifth for the purchase of British and colonial pictures and statuary, and, as to the residue, for the purchase of contemporary foreign pictures.

FRED ELWELL

Bequeathed by F. W. Elwell, RA (died 1958) to provide an annual prize (or prizes) for still-life painting in the Royal Academy Schools, to be known as the Fred Elwell Prize.

RICHARD FORD AWARD

Received from (Sir) Brinsley Ford in 1976, in memory of his great-grandfather, Richard Ford, for awards to enable British figurative painters to visit Spain for the purpose of studying paintings, particularly in the Museo del Prado, Madrid.

FLORENCE FOX

Bequeathed by Miss Florence Fox, in 1964, for contributions towards the general expenses of the Royal Academy Schools.

GEORGE FRAMPTON

Bequeathed by Sir George Frampton, RA (died 1928 but not received until 1986) for executing in permanent material works by British sculptors currently existing only in material of a non-permanent nature, to be presented to the nation or placed in any park, open space, museum or art gallery in the United Kingdom or in its Dominions, Colonies or Dependencies.

GLAZEBROOK

Bequeathed by Hugh de T. Glazebrook (died 1937) to provide lectures, in memory of the testator and his wife, on the vital interests and problems of art or other pertinent subjects.

A. F. GRACE

Bequeathed by L. V. Grace, in 1959, to establish, in memory of his father, a fund for the relief of distress among artists of reputation or their widows.

DUFF GREET

Received from Mrs Duff Greet, in 1923, for an annual prize for the best pencil study of a landscape foreground by a student in the Royal Academy Schools.

ARTHUR HACKER

Received from Miss Hacker, in 1920, in memory of her brother, Arthur Hacker, RA (died 1919), to provide two annual prizes for painting in the Royal Academy Schools, viz. for a head and shoulders from the life and for two paintings of a head from the life.

HAITE

Bequeathed by Miss E. B. E. F. Haité (died 1971), in memory of her father, George Charles Haité, for a scholarship in connection with landscape painting.

E. VINCENT HARRIS

Its capital derives from the sale, in 1969, of the London studio and office of Emanuel Vincent Harris, OBE, RA (died 1971 but see p. 194); under an agreement with him, half the annual income forms the E. Vincent Harris Fund for Mural Decoration (q.v.) and the other half is allocated towards the general purposes of the Royal Academy Schools.

Trust and Special Funds administered by the Royal Academy—continued

E. VINCENT HARRIS MURAL DECORATION

Administered by the same committee as for the E. A. Abbey Memorial Trust Fund for Mural Painting in Great Britain (*q.v.*), it is available to commission or contribute towards mural decorations (see E. Vincent Harris Fund).

VINCENT HARRIS PRIZE

Its capital derives from the sale of a house and land at Dunham Massey which was donated, in 1953, by Emanuel Vincent Harris, OBE, RA, for its income to be devoted to a Vincent Harris Prize in Mural Decoration, competed for annually in the Royal Academy Schools.

HERITAGE-PETERS

Bequeathed by John Heritage-Peters (died 1965 but not received until 1986) for scholarships and/or awards to students of the Royal Academy Schools for drawing, painting and sculpture, and, if the income permits, for the purchase of paintings, drawings or sculpture, by Members of the Royal Academy (Academicians and Associates), which have been exhibited at the annual exhibitions of the Royal Academy.

WILLIAM HILTON

Received in 1922 from the Executors of Miss H. H. Tatlock, in memory of William Hilton, RA (died 1839), for providing or supplementing the relief of distress amongst members of the Royal Academy.

ANNIE HUGILL

Bequeathed by Miss Annie Hugill, in 1939, for the purchase from time to time of water-colour or other drawings exhibited at the Royal Academy, to be given to public art galleries in England.

RICHARD JACK

Received from Mrs G. V. Whitehead, in 1953, for the endowment of annual prizes in the Royal Academy Schools in memory of her father, Richard Jack, RA (died 1952).

ERIC KENNINGTON

Received from W. O. Kennington, in 1960, in memory of his brother, Eric Kennington, RA (died 1960), for the encouragement of good representational draughtsmanship in the Royal Academy Schools, to provide a prize (or prizes) for drawings in any medium, including pastel or chalk, without a set subject.

LANDSEER

Bequeathed by Charles Landseer, RA (died 1879), to found Landseer Scholarships for the encouragement of art students; they are awarded to students in the Royal Academy Schools.

GILBERT LEDWARD

Bequeathed by Gilbert Ledward, OBE, RA (died 1960), for the benefit of the Sculpture School of the Royal Academy.

SYDNEY LEE

Bequeathed in 1953 by the widow of Sydney Lee, RA (died 1949), free of any conditions, and allotted to the Royal Academy Library.

LEIGHTON FUND

Received in 1896 from Mrs Orr and Mrs Matthews, in memory of their brother, Lord Leighton, PRA (died 1896), for acquiring or commissioning works of decorative painting, sculpture and architecture . . . for the adornment of public places.

VICTORIA LEVIN

Bequeathed by Mrs Gertrude Priestley, in 1938, to found a Victoria Levin Scholarship for a female student who shows promise in her studies and is in need of pecuniary assistance; it is awarded to such a student in the Royal Academy Schools.

J. H. LORIMER

Bequeathed by John H. Lorimer in 1937, without conditions, and allocated for the purchase of books for the Royal Academy Library.

AGNES ETHEL MACKAY

Received in 1981 from the estate of the late Miss Agnes Ethel Mackay, in memory of André Dunoyer de Segonzac, Hon. RA (died 1974), and used to award travelling scholarships for students in the Royal Academy Schools.

DOROTHY M. MORGAN

Bequeathed in 1974 by Mrs J. C. Loftus (née Dorothy M. Morgan) for an annual prize to a student of the Royal Academy Schools for the best work in a set subject.

DAVID MURRAY STUDENTSHIPS

Its capital derives from the will of Sir David Murray, RA (died 1933) and a scheme relating thereto approved by the Chancery Division of the High Court of Justice, on 20 February 1939, and administered by a special committee, for the encouragement of the study of landscape painting by making grants or allowances to elected David Murray Students.

NEWTON

Bequeathed by H. C. Newton, in 1882, for an annual donation (Newton's Bequest) to a widow, in indigent circumstances, of a deceased artist who has been a painter in oil or water-colour; the widow must be resident in, and the painter a native of, Great Britain or Ireland.

AILEEN O'DONNELL PEET

Bequeathed by Mrs Aileen O'Donnell Peet (died 1977) for an annual prize for painting to an artist over thirty years of age, preferably not a student.

POYNTER

Bequeathed by Miss Henrietta May Poynter, in 1933, for the purchase of books for a promising student in architecture, in memory of her father, Ambrose Poynter, Architect.

Trust and Special Funds administered by the Royal Academy—continued

REDGRAVE

Received in 1908 from Gilbert, Frances and Evelyn Redgrave, in memory of their father, Richard Redgrave, CB, RA (died 1888), for an annuity to a painter in oil or water-colour who shall have been an Exhibitor at the Royal Academy and be in want from age or sickness.

SANDBY

Bequeathed by William Arnold Sandby, in 1904, to provide an annual Sandby Gift, in memory of Thomas and Paul Sandby, Foundation Members of the Royal Academy, to be awarded alternately to an architect or landscape painter, or to the families of such artists needing assistance. (See also the Aitchison and Norman Shaw Funds.)

NORMAN SHAW

Its capital is the surplus, made over in 1915, of a fund collected for a public memorial to Richard Norman Shaw, RA (died 1912) and its income is for augmenting the Sandby Gift (*q.v.*) when architects or their families are the recipients. (See also the Aitchison Fund.)

SIR FRANK AND LADY SHORT

Bequeathed by their daughter, Miss Dorothea Mary Short (died 1972) to provide an annual Sir Frank Short prize for engraving and for the teaching of engraving and the maintenance and equipment of the Engraving School at the Royal Academy.

S. J. SOLOMON

The capital derives from gifts from the Maccabeans since 1929 for the annual award of a medal in memory of S. J. Solomon, RA (died 1927) for compositions in colour by a student of the Royal Academy.

CATHERINE ADELINE SPARKES

Bequeathed by John Charles Lewis Sparkes (died 1907, although not received until 1926) for the benefit of female students in the Royal Academy.

INA SPERRY

Received in 1980 from August W. Sperry for the benefit of one or more sculpture students of the Royal Academy.

G. A. STOREY

Its capital derives from settlements in 1917 and 1923, under which its income was paid to the widow and daughter of George Adolphus Storey, RA (died 1919) during their lifetimes and made available subsequently for pensions to Royal Academicians of sixty-five years and upwards.

EDWARD STOTT

Bequeathed by Edward Stott, ARA (died 1918) for the purchase of modern pictures or to form scholarships for art students.

TURNER

Its capital derives from the portion of the estate of Joseph Mallord William Turner, RA (died 1851) which was allotted to the Royal Academy by the Court of Chancery in 1856, without conditions. The income is used for grants to artists of reputation (but not Members of the Royal Academy) who are in need, for a biennial medal and scholarship to a student of the Royal Academy for a landscape painting and for annual contributions towards the support of the Royal Academy Schools.

VANDELEUR

Bequeathed by Mrs Adela Grace Vandeleur (died 1968) for Vandeleur scholarships to painting and sculpture students of the Royal Academy.

HARRISON WEIR

Bequeathed by Harrison William Weir, in 1950, for the purchase, for the benefit of the nation, of pictures of high merit (excluding pictures of flowers, fruit and still-life) to be placed in the collection of the Royal Academy.

CHARLES WOLLASTON AWARD

Its capital, derived from donations by Charles Wollaston from 1977, provides annual awards for the most distinguished exhibit in each year's Royal Academy Summer Exhibition, on the recommendation of a specially appointed panel.

BIBLIOGRAPHY

ANONYMOUS (probably Alexander Nesbit): An Essay in two parts, on the Necessity and Form of a Royal Academy for Painting, Sculpture and Architecture (London, 1755).

ANONYMOUS (probably John E. Soden): A Rap at the R.A. (London, 1875).

BARETTI, Joseph: A Guide through the Royal Academy (London, c. 1781).

BARRINGTON, Mrs Russell: The Life, Letters and Work of Frederic Leighton (2 Vols., London, 1906).

BARRY, James: The Works of James Barry, Esq. (London, 1809).

BROOKE, John: King George III (London, 1972).

BURY, Adrian: Shadow of Eros (London, 1954).

CAREY, William: Desultory Exposition of an Anti-British System of Incendiary Publication, etc., intended to sacrifice the Honor and Interests of the British Institution, the Royal Academy, and the whole Body of the British Artists and their Patrons (London, 1819). Some Memoirs of the Patronage and Progress of the Fine Arts, in England and Ireland, during the reigns of George the Second, George the Third, and his present Majesty . . . (London, 1826).

CASSON, Sir Hugh: Hugh Casson Diary (London, 1981).

CHARTERIS, Hon. Evan: Life of J. S. Sargent, R. A. (London, 1927).

CONSTABLE, W. G.: Richard Wilson (London, 1953).

CUNNINGHAM, Allan: The lives of the most eminent British Painters (London, 1829). The Life of Sir David Wilkie (3 Vols., London, 1843).

CUST, Lionel, and COLVIN, Sir Sidney: The History of the Society of Dilettanti (London, 1914).

EASTLAKE, Lady: Memoir of Sir Charles Lock Eastlake (published in 'Contributions to the Literature of the Fine Arts' by Sir Charles Lock Eastlake, London, 1870).

EDWARDS, Edward: Anecdotes of Painters (London, 1808).

ENGLEFIELD, W. A. D.: The History of the Painter-Stainers Company (London, 1923).

FARINGTON, Joseph: The Farington Diary (8 Vols. edited by James Greig, London, 1922). *There are typescripts of the complete Diary in the Libraries of Windsor Castle and the British Museum.*

FINBERG, A. J.: The Life of J. M. W. Turner, R. A. (Oxford, 1939).

FRITH, W. P.: My Autobiography and Reminiscences (2 Vols., London, 1887). Further Reminiscences (London, 1888).

GALT, John: The Life, Studies and Works of Benjamin West, Esq. (London, 1820).

GARLICK, Kenneth: Sir Thomas Lawrence (London, 1954).

GILCHRIST, Alexander: Life of William Etty, R. A. (2 Vols., London, 1855).

GORDON, Esmé: The Royal Scottish Academy, 1826–1976 (Edinburgh, 1976).

GRAVES, Algernon: The Royal Academy of Arts – A complete Dictionary of Contributors and their work from its foundation in 1769 to 1904 (8 Vols., London, 1905–6). *There is a continuation series*, Royal Academy Exhibitors 1905–1970 (6 vols., Wakefield, 1973–82).

GWYN, J.: An Essay on Design including proposals for erecting a Public Academy to be supported by Voluntary Subscription (Till a Royal Foundation can be obtained) for Educating the British Youth in Drawing and the several Arts depending thereon (London, 1749).

HARCOURT-SMITH, Sir Cecil: The Society of Dilettanti, its Regalia and Pictures (London, 1932).

HARRIS, John: Sir William Chambers (London, 1970).

HILLES, Frederick Whiley: Letters of Sir Joshua Reynolds (Cambridge, 1929). The Literary Career of Sir Joshua Reynolds (Cambridge, 1936).

HOBSON, Anthony: The Art and Life of J. W. Waterhouse, R. A., 1849–1917 (London, 1980).

HODGSON, J. E., and EATON, Fred. A.: The Royal Academy and its Members, 1768–1830 (London, 1905).

HOUFE, Simon: Sir Albert Richardson – The Professor (Luton, 1980).

HUDSON, Derek: Sir Joshua Reynolds (London, 1958). For Love of Painting – The Life of Sir Gerald Kelly, KCVO, PRA (London, 1975).

HUNT, W. Holman: Pre-Raphaelitism and the Pre-Raphaelite Brotherhood (2 Vols., London, 1905).

HUTCHISON, Sidney C.: The Homes of the Royal Academy (London, 1956). The Royal Academy Schools, 1768–1830 (Walpole Society, London, Vol. XXXVIII, 1962). The History of the Royal Academy, 1768–1968 (London, 1968).

LAIDLAY, W. J.: The Royal Academy, its Uses and Abuses (London, 1898).

LAMB, Sir Walter R. M.: The Royal Academy (London, 1935 and 1951).

LAYARD, G. S.: Sir Thomas Lawrence's Letter Bag (London, 1906).

LESLIE, C. R.: Memoirs of the Life of John Constable, R. A. . . . (London, 1843).

LESLIE, C. R., and TAYLOR, Tom: Life and Times of Sir Joshua Reynolds (2 Vols., London, 1865).

LESLIE, G. D.: The Inner Life of the Royal Academy (London, 1914).

MALONE, Edmond: The Works of Sir Joshua Reynolds, Knt . . . (2 Vols., London, 1797).

MILLAIS, J. G.: The Life and Letters of Sir John Everett Millais (2 Vols., London, 1899).

MORGAN, H. C.: The Lost Opportunity of the Royal Academy: an assessment of its position in the nineteenth century (Warburg and Courtauld Institutes' Journal, London, Vol. XXXII, 1969).

MUNNINGS, Sir Alfred: An Artist's Life (London, 1950). The Second Burst (London, 1951). The Finish (London, 1952).

NICHOLLS, R. H., and WRAY, F. A.: The History of the Foundling Hospital (Oxford, 1935).

NICHOLS, John: Biographical Anecdotes of William Hogarth (London, 1785).

NORTHCOTE, James: The Life of Sir Joshua Reynolds (London, 1819).

PARKER, Constance-Anne: Mr. Stubbs – The Horse Painter (London, 1971).

PEVSNER, Nikolaus: Academies of Art Past and Present (Cambridge, 1940).

REDGRAVE, Richard and Samuel: A Century of Painters of the English School (London, 1866).

ROBERTSON, David: Sir Charles Eastlake and the Victorian Art World (Princeton, 1978).

ROYAL COMMISSION: Report of the Commissioners appointed to inquire into the Present Position of the Royal Academy in relation to the Fine Arts together with the Minutes of Evidence (2 Vols., London, 1863).

SANDBY, William: The History of the Royal Academy of Arts (2 Vols., London, 1862).

SHANES, Eric: The Genius of the Royal Academy (London, 1981).

SHEE, Sir Martin Archer: A Letter to Lord John Russell on the Alleged Claim of the

Public to be admitted *gratis* to the Exhibition of the Royal Academy (London, 1837).

SKAIFE, Thos.: Exposé of the Royal Academy of Arts (London, 1854).

SMITH, J. T.: Nollekens and his times (2 Vols., London, 1828; reprinted, London, 1949).

STRANGE, Sir Robert: An Inquiry into the Rise and Establishment of the Royal Academy of Arts ... (London, 1775). The Conduct of the Royal Academicians (London, 1771).

SURVEY OF LONDON: Vol. XX. The Parish of St Martin-in-the-Fields, Part 3 – Trafalgar Square and Neighbourhood (London, 1940). Vols. XXIX and XXX. The Parish of St James', Westminster, Part 1 – South of Piccadilly (London, 1960). Vols. XXXI and XXXII. The Parish of St James', Westminster, Part 2 – North of Piccadilly (London, 1963).

TAYLOR, Tom: Life of Benjamin Robert Haydon (3 Vols., London, 1853).

THICKNESSE, Philip: A Sketch of the Life and Paintings of Thomas Gainsborough, Esq. (London, 1788).

THORNBURY, Walter: The Life of J. M. W. Turner, R. A. (2 Vols., London, 1862).

VERTUE, George: Notebooks (Walpole Society, London, Vols. XVIII, XX, XXII, XXIV, XXVI, XXIX and XXX, 1929–50).

WALPOLE, Horace: Anecdotes of Painting in England (5 Vols., Strawberry Hill, 1762–71).

WATERHOUSE, Sir Ellis: Painting in Britain, 1530 to 1790 (London, 1953). Reynolds (London, 1941). Gainsborough (London, 1958).

WHEELER, Sir Charles: High Relief – The Autobiography of a Sculptor (London, 1968).

WHINNEY, Margaret, and MILLAR, Sir Oliver: English Art, 1625–1714 (Oxford, 1957).

WHITLEY, William T.: Artists and their Friends in England, 1700–1799 (2 Vols., London, 1928). Art in England, 1800–1820 (Cambridge, 1928). Art in England, 1821–1837 (Cambridge, 1930). Thomas Gainsborough (London, 1915).

WILLIAMS, D. E.: The Life and Correspondence of Sir Thomas Lawrence, Kt. (2 Vols., London, 1831).

WOODALL, Mary: The Letters of Thomas Gainsborough (Ipswich, 1963).

INDEX

The titles of works of art, exhibitions and publications are in italics and plate numbers are in bold type. Unless otherwise indicated, the institutions and societies named are or were in London.

The detailed contents of Appendix B (Members from the Foundation (pp. 250–65)), Appendix E (Exhibitions (pp. 277–80)) and Appendix F (Trust and Special Funds (pp. 281–7)), which are in alphabetical order, are not repeated in this index. References to the other Appendices are given in brackets.

Abbreviations: *Coll.* = Collection; *Exh.* = Exhibition